GW01228219

THE ANNOTATED
JULES VERNE

From the Earth to the Moon

I do not believe I go too far when I say that in the future we shall have trains of projectiles in which people will be able to travel comfortably from the Earth to the Moon. Engraving from the first illustrated edition (1872).

THE ANNOTATED
JULES VERNE

From the Earth to the Moon

Direct in Ninety-seven Hours and Twenty Minutes

The Only Completely Rendered and Annotated Edition

WALTER JAMES MILLER

THOMAS Y. CROWELL, PUBLISHERS
New York   Established 1834

THE ANNOTATED JULES VERNE: FROM THE EARTH TO THE MOON. Copyright © 1978 by Walter James Miller. All rights reserved. Printed in the United States of America. No part of this book may be used or reproduced in any manner whatsoever without written permission except in the case of brief quotations embodied in critical articles and reviews. For information address Thomas Y. Crowell, Publishers, 10 East 53rd Street, New York, N.Y. 10022. Published simultaneously in Canada by Fitzhenry & Whiteside Limited, Toronto.

FIRST EDITION

Designed by Abigail Moseley

Library of Congress Cataloging in Publication Data

Miller, Walter James, date
  The annotated Jules Verne, From the earth to the moon, direct in ninety-seven hours and twenty minutes.

    "The only completely rendered and annotated edition."
    1. Verne, Jules, 1828–1905. De la terre à la lune.
I. Verne, Jules, 1828–1905. De la terre à la lune.
II. Title.
PQ2469.D33M5   843'.8   78-3327
ISBN 0-690-01701-4

78 79 80 81 82 10 9 8 7 6 5 4 3 2 1

FOR
KURT VONNEGUT, JR.
because he defies annotation

ACKNOWLEDGMENTS

Bonnie E. Nelson has supervised the complicated logistics. Dr. David Woodruff of Bristol Community College has served as chief technical consultant. The Library of Congress supplied photostats of the original French text. The Smithsonian Institution and the Maryland Historical Society provided illustrations for Chapter III, the Harvard College Observatory for Chapter IV, and the Florida Department of Transportation for Chapter XIII. Individual specialists who helped with research and illustrations include R. W. Chalfant and Katy Thomsen of the Museum and Library of Maryland History; Kathryn B. Lindeman of the Smithsonian; Jon S. Beazley, Florida State Topographic Engineer; Joseph F. Dracus of the National Geodetic Survey; Professor Irwin Unger of New York University; and Eunice McAuley, who did valuable research at the Bibliothèque Nationale. Richard Chalfin has helped locate many nineteenth-century texts. The basic idea of an *Annotated Jules Verne* is the brainchild of the editorial staff of Thomas Y. Crowell. My editor there, Hugh Rawson, presides fondly but permissively over its development.

WJM

CONTENTS

FOREWORD	The Many Worlds of Jules Verne	ix
CHAPTER I	The Gun Club	1
CHAPTER II	President Barbicane's Message	8
CHAPTER III	The Effect of Barbicane's Speech	14
CHAPTER IV	Reply from the Cambridge Observatory	19
CHAPTER V	The Romance of the Moon	24
CHAPTER VI	What it is Impossible not to Know and what it is no longer Permissible to Believe in the United States	31
CHAPTER VII	The Hymn to the Cannonball	35
CHAPTER VIII	The Story of the Cannon	43
CHAPTER IX	The Powder Question	48
CHAPTER X	One Enemy out of Twenty-Five Million Friends	54
CHAPTER XI	Florida and Texas	60
CHAPTER XII	*Urbi et Orbi*	66
CHAPTER XIII	Stony Hill	72
CHAPTER XIV	Pickaxe and Trowel	77
CHAPTER XV	The Festival of the Casting	83
CHAPTER XVI	The Columbiad	88
CHAPTER XVII	A Telegram	94
CHAPTER XVIII	The Passenger on the *Atlanta*	96
CHAPTER XIX	A Mass Meeting	103
CHAPTER XX	Attack and Riposte	110
CHAPTER XXI	How a Frenchman Settles a Quarrel	117
CHAPTER XXII	The New Citizen of the United States	125
CHAPTER XXIII	The Vehicle-Projectile	129
CHAPTER XXIV	The Telescope in the Rocky Mountains	135
CHAPTER XXV	Final Preparations	141
CHAPTER XXVI	Fire!	148
CHAPTER XXVII	Cloudy Weather	153
CHAPTER XXVIII	A New Heavenly Body	158
AFTERWORD	Revaluation of *From the Earth to the Moon*	161
APPENDIX A	How Barbicane Calculated His Initial Velocity	164
APPENDIX B	Some Notes for Purists on Verne's Translators	166
BIBLIOGRAPHY		168

A slender, idealized version of Jules Verne as the narrator of the novel *A Floating City* (1871). He reclines on the deck of the *Great Eastern,* "watching the storm rise."

FOREWORD
The Many Worlds of Jules Verne

Verne as Political Writer

Jules Verne was pushing thirty-seven. The American Civil War was dragging on into its fourth year. With two recent best-sellers behind him, he must have felt manic, for now he sought answers to questions that so numbed most minds of his day they didn't even know the questions were there.

As he read the dispatches from the New World battlegrounds, he was appalled at the very dimensions, the enormity of recent developments. Three million men in uniform, and one out of every three wounded or dead. Whole armies moving unheard-of distances in a few hours as railroads became juggernauts. A cannon twenty-five feet long, cast from 160,000 pounds of molten iron that took fifteen days to cool, a cannon now flinging half-ton shells at targets six miles away. And the savagery unleashed by the times! Northern troops, for example, slaughtering men, women, and children—and then slicing away the private parts of dead warriors—in an Indian encampment at Sand Creek! And Sherman inventing a new process: total war.

How—the red-haired, burly but dreamy-eyed, manic Frenchman wondered—how could all this wartime technology be reconverted to peacetime industry? All these destructive energies and talents be rechanneled into creative projects? He tried to imagine some new gigantic enterprise that would swiftly, miraculously reunite the North and the South—even make the whites join hands with the blacks—in one overwhelming common cause.

Chafing at political conditions in his own beloved France, he knew from the start that some of the energy he would tap for this enterprise would come from his anger at his own government. "His" emperor was using the American Civil War as a screen for a scandalous venture into Mexico, so that France in effect now had a vested interest in a permanently divided America, in a victory for slavery. Of course, any Vernean attacks on his own dictatorial government would have to be made slyly, covertly. But that intensified the literary challenge. Indeed, everything that could disturb Verne—the evils of imperialism, war, official hypocrisy, misuse of technology, and everything that could inspire him, like the nature of the future *if* science could be steered in the right direction—in short, everything that could fire him to dash off thousands of words a day could, it seemed, be found in North America in 1864–1865.

Risky, though, this new book he had in mind. His best-sellers—*Five Weeks in a Balloon, Journey to the Center of the Earth*—had catapulted him into sudden fame because of something *he* had invented: a new kind of futuristic fiction that emphasized, indeed systematically exploited, the big questions in science and exploration. Here he was now pondering something essentially social and political. But in his musical comedies, those farces that had seduced him away from science these many years, he had had some mild success in social satire. Could he bring his comedy of manners up to the level required by such stupendous questions as the Civil War posed? Up to the level, indeed, of his science fiction?

The Civil War ended in April 1865. By September all France was reading Verne's *From the Earth to the Moon* in an adult periodical called *Journal des Débats,* for here was a swift novel that combined immediate history with bold hunches about the future. Not the least of its many charms was the fact that under cover of its enthusiastic appreciation of American know-how and its bitter attack on American power-madness, the novel also delivered many a telling blow against Emperor Napoleon III.

In Europe, *From the Earth to the Moon,* like most of Verne's books, has enjoyed continuous popularity. Millions of copies are sold every year in adult editions alone. Critics and cultural historians of all persuasions—psychoanalytic, structuralist, Marxist, "pop," religious—find that Verne has the self-renewing power to challenge every generation anew.

But in the English-speaking world, *From the Earth to the Moon,* like most of Verne's books, has suffered a long downgrading and metamorphosis. Two so-called translations of this novel appeared in the 1870s. First an English clergyman, Lewis Page Mercier, working in this case under the name of Louis Mercier, and his assistant, Eleanor E. King, dashed off an abridged version. Their wholesale cuts weakened Verne's science, his characterization, his humor, his social and political message. Their translation was issued on both sides of the Atlantic.

Meanwhile, a Philadelphia schoolteacher put out a version in which, he boasted, he had "improved" Verne. He padded every chapter, adding not only miscellaneous details *ad nauseam* but also his own opinions, changing Verne as he saw fit.

These frauds—the clergyman's jerky, thin tale, and the schoolteacher's turgid travesty—became the standard English translations!

The mangled Mercier-King is the version usually found in our libraries, the one favored by paperback publishers, most often used in our schools, most responsible for shaping American critical opinion of this novel.

Early mistranslations of other Verne works—especially the clergyman's tendentious hatchet-job on *Twenty Thousand Leagues under the Sea*—further diminished any chance Americans might have had to enjoy and judge the real Verne. By mid-twentieth century his allegedly "thin" stories were considered fit only for children. In 1961 *Galaxy* magazine administered an easy *coup de grâce,* claiming that Verne's work is replete with errors in science and mathematics, that he lazily omits essential information, that *Twenty Thousand Leagues* contains "not [one] valid speculation . . . none of its predictions has come true. . . . It is non-science." The author of *that* torpedo job and his editors were apparently unaware that almost every error, fault, and omission they had found in "Verne" was the translator's.

Ironically, the early twentieth-century pioneers who were paving the way for the real Space Age—Konstantin Tsiolkovsky, Hermann Oberth, for example—were actually *learning* from Verne, as we shall see in this book. And by the time the Apollo 8 crew was orbiting the moon, and the Apollo 11 crew was walking on it, there was an affectionate, nostalgic revival of interest in Verne's space effort. There were even one or two new translations which (for reasons we'll consider later) failed to capture the market dominated by the standard versions. Anyhow, this revival of interest in Verne did not lead so often to a rereading of Verne himself as it did to an enjoyment of newspaper, magazine, and TV commentaries on his remarkable scientific predictions. In other words, Verne's moon story became a *myth,* disembodied from his books, a myth detached from his social and political message.

I like to believe the tide began to turn in 1965 when my essay "Jules Verne in America" demonstrated that Verne was innocent, and his translators guilty, of most of the charges leveled against him. All I had to do to discover this, of course, was compare the "standard" translations with the original French, and the American criticism with the European. Still, fifteen publishers continued to issue (often expensive gift editions of) the "standard" texts! But at least the British science-fiction writer Brian W. Aldiss agreed with me. In his popular *Billion Year Spree* (1973), our first mature history of s-f, he reached a larger audience than I had with his opinions: "The poverty of English translations" has dimmed Verne's chances of a fair critical appraisal. A properly rich translation "might effect a revaluation of his vast *oeuvre.*"

Meanwhile, fortunately, the public had welcomed Martin Gardner's *Annotated Alice* and similar efforts to put other classics in a true perspective. Here was a new format in which we could dramatize our case for Verne's rehabilitation. My *Annotated Jules Verne: Twenty Thousand Leagues under the Sea* has, I feel, proved once and for all that the "English" Verne, "fit merely for boys," was a cynical creation of his early translators, that the "real" Verne is a challenging writer for adults.

In that edition, we also made it clear, largely by restoring cut passages, that Verne refuses to consider science except in its social and political context. That becomes one of the main themes of this second volume.

Today we, the fifth generation of Verne readers, are far better qualified than our fathers and grandfathers were to judge *From the Earth to the Moon*. We are able to compare Verne's brilliant speculations about the chance of travel into Outer Space with the actual accomplishments of the Space Age. And we may go beyond appreciation of him as a *science* prophet. Since he conceived of his novel as an ideal answer to monstrous social problems created by modern, mechanized, total war, we should consider now how he rates as a *social* prophet. Some European critics say that Jules Verne is, like H. G. Wells, basically a political writer. Americans have yet to appreciate *that* Verne. And our consideration here of that side of his talents should serve once again to increase Verne's stature in American eyes.

We shall follow the procedure we used in the first *Annotated Jules Verne* but with some major differences. In our review of Verne's life, we shall take into account the most recent revelations and discoveries by French writers and we shall emphasize how Verne drew on his personal experience in shaping and peopling his moon novels.

Then we shall examine the novel itself. This time we shall use our own, totally new translation. In our edition of *Twenty Thousand Leagues,* we used the standard translation, restored the cut passages, and in the annotations showed how the clergyman's sins of omission and commission had weakened an artist's work and his reputation. But we no longer need to prove that point passage by passage. This time we shall simply summarize the early translators' damage in a compact essay at the back of the book (Appendix B).

Thus we can save all our annotations for appreciation of Verne's science, his social and political views, his sources and literary maneuvers. Many annotations will supply background information on matters well known in Verne's day but perhaps obscure today.

To help put Verne's work in proper context, we offer 115 illustrations, all but one from his period. There are 33 engravings from the first illustrated edition of *From the Earth to the Moon* (1872), plus twelve from other Verne novels. Most of the remainder are engravings from nineteenth-century works on science and a popular 1873 encyclopedia, all such as Verne's original readers might themselves have consulted. Reproductions of several period portraits, photographs, and drawings help us visualize the cast and the setting. Only once shall we depart from our policy of using illustrations exclusively from Verne's day: it seems valuable to include a 1973 aerial photograph of Verne's launching site. At the time that that picture was made, the immediate terrain was still similar to the one Verne describes.

After we have enjoyed this in-depth study of the novel and Verne's world, I shall offer, in the Afterword, the first critical analysis in English of *From the Earth to the Moon* to be based on the complete text.

Verne as Private, Public, and Literary Selves

Jules Verne was a late bloomer. When *From the Earth to the Moon* appeared, success was still new to him. He had finally found himself, his *métier,* his direction, only two years before, at the age of thirty-five. And now, in the mid-1860s, he was on the brink of the most fruitful decades of his life. But behind the scenes, behind the glamour, his personal life was shaping up as a series of self-renewing failures. He kept these troubles from the world, burning his private papers, telling reporters they should be interested only in his writings, not the man behind them. For decades after his death in 1905, his family cooperated to keep his secrets. Only in recent years have some of them been revealed or discovered.

Everything that would impel him finally to invent a new literary genre can be seen in his early life. His mother and father, their two families, provided the kind of vivid contrasts that help make an artist *if* he can balance these forces inside himself. In 1825, Pierre Verne, son of a judge, grandson of a magistrate, bought a legal practice in Nantes, a port on the Loire, forty miles from the sea. In 1827 he married Sophie Allotte de la Fuÿe. Jules was born on February 8, 1828, his brother Paul a year later, then his sisters Anna, Mathilde, Marie.

Flourishing as a maritime lawyer, Pierre soon could afford a comfortable apartment in town and a lovely country house in nearby Chantenay. And it's at Chantenay that we view the tableau that best symbolizes Pierre and his effect on Jules, for at Chantenay Pierre kept a marine telescope focused on a distant monastery clock. He regulated his—and his family's—life thereby. His servitude to mechanical time figures mightily in Jules Verne's *oeuvre,* especially in the moon novels. And Pierre's keeping the *monastery* in view is equally symbolic: he was extremely pious, he practiced (we now know) self-flagellation. Within these severe limits he loved literature, read wholesome novelists—Scott and Cooper—to his children, and composed verses for family gatherings. Pierre's portrait pictures him against a background of shelves of uniformly bound books. Jules' life, it was understood, would replicate Pierre's: he would study law and inherit Pierre's practice.

Sophie came from a long line of soldiers and sailors. Her relatives, in-laws, and other connections included painters, explorers, a ne'er-do-well father so given to wandering that his wife obtained a legal separation. Sophie enjoyed a lively, sometimes tumultuous imagination. In her portrait she sits next to a pianoforte.

School and town tended to strengthen the maternal, romantic elements in Jules' early years. One of his first teachers, "Widow" Sambain, taught her pupils the mysteries of life by telling and retelling the story of her marriage to a sea-captain. After their honeymoon he sailed away to the antipodes, never to return: Was he stranded on a desert isle? Would he ever be rescued? The questions she planted in Jules' mind disturbed him for almost half a century until he resolved them in *Mistress Branican* (1881). After school hours the town of Nantes became, for Jules and Paul at least, the real schoolroom, the hub of an expanding universe. The horizon was a forest of masts, the quays teemed with swarthy sailors back from distant seas, sometimes home from lands so recently discovered their names could not be found on the maps. And weaving among all those sailing vessels, a new steamboat plied the Loire, a harbinger of technical change. Typical of the old salts who taught Jules his most unforgettable lessons was Jean-Marie Cabidoulin, who haunted Jules' imagination until, himself an old man, he resurrected Cabidoulin in *The Sea Serpent* (1901).

Wandering with his brother over the meadows and through the copses of Chantenay, sailing rented boats on the glinting river, young Jules surely resented the fate that said Paul was free someday to go to sea but Jules was not. The eleven-year-old laid his plans well. He bribed a cabin boy to give up his berth. Then, one summer dawn, he stole out of the Chantenay cottage and was rowed out to the three-masted *Coralie,* bound, after a stop at Paimboeuf, for the West Indies. But maritime lawyer Pierre consulted the tide tables and timetables, boarded the steamboat, intercepted the three-master at Paimboeuf, trotted his son home, caned him, sentenced him to bread and water. His mother made him promise: "From now on, I'll travel only in my imagination."

Today French psychoanalysts see this event as traumatic. They say that the broad-shouldered boy, he of the beautiful teeth, flaming red-gold hair, and penetrating gaze, now became withdrawn, ambivalent, an unconscious rebel against authority. And we, in our first *Annotated,* have wondered whether it was this event that taught Verne to wear the mask of gay irony behind which he forever hid his real feelings.

In any event, his penchant for a double life was now deeply ingrained. Told to prepare for law, he clerked politely in his father's office, studied the codes civil and criminal, earning the right to go to Paris—to associate with the great legal brains of his capital. Told to wander only in his mind, he passionately devoured Hugo and Dumas, composed verse-dramas, read them aloud to the Nantes literary circle, and prepared to go to Paris—to hobnob with writers.

Ironically, he was helped on his way to the capital by early setbacks in love. Until recently, it was believed he had suffered only one such frustration. Now the evidence is clear he was rejected twice before he was twenty. It has always been known that he loved a beautiful tease, his cousin Caroline Tronson. When they were both eighteen, he proposed. She took it as a joke. Later she announced her engagement to someone else. Jules fell into such bitter gloom his parents arranged to have him miss the next big family reunion, planned for Caroline's wedding. They packed him off to stay first with a great-aunt in Paris, where he passed his preliminary law examination and haunted the theater, and then to visit his paternal grandmother in Provins. On his return to Chantenay, we now know, he fell in love, maybe on the rebound, maybe as his first genuine passion, with Herminie Arnault-Grossetière. Soon she announced her engagement to someone else.

Now Jules tumbled into such deep despair his family decided he should enjoy a second trip to Paris. He arrived there soon after the republicans had overthrown the king, and he became a devoted, lifelong adherent to the principles of the 1848 Revolution. Answering a letter from his mother, he described how he had had a "fateful dream" about a wedding presided over by the angel of death. After the married couple retired to the bridal chamber, "all that dark long night a man in rags sharpened his teeth on the door knocker. . . . And now your letter informs me my dream was true!'' Herminie had been married. And Jules became a misogynist, forever comparing the marriage rites to a funeral, always alone outside that door. Meanwhile Paul, launched on the career of his own choice, shipped out to the West Indies as a naval apprentice. Back home, Jules acted so cynical the neighbors talked. By fall he had no trouble convincing his family he should continue his law studies not in Nantes but in Paris.

Now his talents for irony and suspense flourished in a game of cat-and-mouse. A typical letter would assure his father, oh yes he would return to take over the office in Nantes; then it would describe the gay life he was leading among composers and authors; then reassure; then hail the life of art as the only life worth living. Pierre would reply that mingling with dissolute artists would dim one's chances of salvation. Jules would soberly agree, and then proudly describe an evening spent with Alexandre Dumas and company. Indeed, Jules did submit his thesis, did pass his final examinations, but also produced a play, *Broken Straws,* under the aegis of Dumas himself, and then went right on writing songs, revues, operettas, short stories, articles. Not until Pierre tried to call a halt, summoning him home to keep his pledge, did Jules finally put it plain: He was going to stay in Paris to become a writer. Still Pierre did not give up.

For years Verne thought his destiny lay with the theater. An occasional mild success with one of his comedies or operettas (he was writing libretti for the composer Aristide Hignard) helped blind him to his real career. How could he yet see that he was made for a medium that did not yet exist? All this time he was ignoring the real implications of his three other activities. He enjoyed studying mathematics with his older cousin, Henri Garcet, professor at the École Polytechnique and the *lycée* Henri IV. He enjoyed discussing the latest theories in astronomy, geology, and physiognomy with scientists he met at the home of Jacques Arago, world traveler. And in spite of himself, he was developing a talent for romantic fiction, as a series of sales to the magazine *Musée des Familles* should have made clear. One of his most significant successes was a story in which for the first time he emphasized science: *Master Zacharius* (1854) is about a clockmaker who sees the escape mechanism as akin to the human soul. Incredibly, Pierre liked this story, at least on the conscious level, although it could be one of the deep-down reasons that he, only fifty-four, now sold his law practice outside the family.

Incredibly, too, Jules still plugged away in the theater, taking time out only for a trip to Nantes to enjoy a visit with Paul—home on leave after six years at sea—and to seek a wife. He wrote and starred in a skit produced at a costume ball, where he imagined his attentions were being seriously returned by a certain dark-eyed slender Laurence Janmar. When the mademoiselle allowed him to overhear her remark to a friend that her whalebone corset was "killing her," Jules—forgetting he was in the provinces—sighed a loud stage sigh: "If only I could fish for whales on that coast." (In French, *côte* means not only coast but rib.) The next day, Jules sent Pierre to Janmar's father formally to ask her hand in marriage. He was rejected; it developed later she was already, secretly, engaged to another. Since she had nevertheless flirted with Jules, he became convinced that women—bourgeois women at least—were wily and unworthy.

In 1856 he traveled to Amiens to serve as best man at the wedding of Auguste Lelarge, Garcet's brother-in-law, to Mlle. Aimée du Fraysne de Viane. And there the misogynist fell in love with the bride's sister, Honorine Anne Hebé Morel. She was twenty-six, witty and pretty, a good soprano, a dainty-footed dancer, an excellent cook, and a recent widow, mother of two girls, totally uninterested in the bohemian life. Her brother offered to help Jules buy a seat on the stock exchange: it would cost 50,000 francs, about $60,000 in today's money. Verne had been living hand-to-mouth, supplementing a small allowance from home with an occasional sale to editor or producer. In a rapid series of letters to Nantes, he suspensefully unveiled his need for a big loan. His clinching arguments ran like this: "I am at the age when the urge for . . . cohabitation is stronger than anything else, and legitimacy in such matters is better than the alternative." True, Pierre was shocked at the thought of Jules' earning a living through speculation. But he was even more horrified by the threat of that "alternative." On January 10, 1857, a month before Jules' twenty-ninth birthday, he and Honorine started married life in a Paris flat conveniently close to the Bourse (Stock Exchange).

At last, he had solved the problem of loneliness, or so he thought. But he still had to find himself as a writer, and under difficult circumstances: he now had a regular time-consuming job with Eggly & Co., stockbrokers; he had four mouths to feed and a big loan to pay off. And soon he was suffering from an unexpected complication. Honorine, a gay partner in social repartee, proved indifferent to his needs as a writer and intellectual. She never learned not to interrupt him when he was composing, and she could not follow his speculations over new scientific and political trends. Both parts of his long day proved unsatisfactory to her. He arose at five A.M. to get in several hours at his writing-desk and then went reluctantly off to the Bourse where he proved to be only a mediocre broker. Within two years Jules was again spending most of his time with male companions. In 1859 he traveled to Scotland with Hignard. Again in mid-June 1861, when Honorine was seven months' pregnant, he embarked with Hignard on a six-week trip to Norway. Until recently, the official family story has always been that he returned just in the nick of time. Now, with publication of *Jules Verne* by grandson Jean Jules-Verne, the full truth is out. Jules Verne missed the birth of his son Michel on August 3, 1861.

And back home, Jules hung out at the *Cercle de la Presse Scientifique,* usually with one of the most remarkable men of the day, Gaspard-Felix Tournachon, a bluff red-haired, blue-eyed giant who, in his many callings, used the name Nadar. He was an author, a cartoonist, one of the truly great photographers, and now a pioneer balloonist. In all his endeavors, Nadar combined technical inventiveness with romantic imagination. He was founding a society for development of heavier-than-air flying machines, with Verne as secretary. But to raise the funds to build his helicopters, Nadar was now designing a gigantic balloon, *Le Géant,* in which he planned to go barnstorming, taking people aloft for a fee of 1,000 francs per head. Meanwhile Verne, who had published a balloon story in 1851, was planning a full-length novel called *Five Weeks in a Balloon.* The way these two friends coordinated their two enterprises—the real with the fictional—must surely qualify as one of the greatest publicity stunts of all time.

First, with Nadar's help, Verne sold his novel to Pierre Hetzel, a hero of the 1848 Revolution recently back from exile and back in business as a publisher. Hetzel put Verne under a twenty-year contract for three books a year starting at 1,925 francs each (about $2,300 today). The significance of this fee becomes clear when we learn that Balzac and George Sand, name-authors on Hetzel's list, received not much more at that time—2,000 francs per book.

Published in 1863 directly in book form, *Five Weeks in a Balloon* became an instant best-seller in both the adult and juvenile markets. It established Verne, it established a new genre, it provided him with an ideal formula he could now use for scores of books. That is, his novel combined the kind of scientific invention and the area of exploration most in the news at the time of its appearance: in this case, aerial travel and Africa. Verne and Nadar had indeed invented a new and plausible kind of balloon control. And one of Verne's prophecies was fulfilled in a matter of months, when John Hanning Speke returned from Africa to announce he had discovered the source of the Nile. But Verne's hero, Doctor Ferguson, sailing over Africa in his giant balloon *Victoria,* had already made exactly the same discovery. That was how Verne established his audience and their expectations. He predicted developments they themselves would live to see. Thus he gained their confidence even when he extrapolated far into the future.

Sales for *Five Weeks* zoomed again when Nadar exhibited *Le Géant* in the center of the Champ-de-Mars. Taller than Notre Dame, it consisted of a huge silvery pear from which hung a two-story wicker basket. Posters plastered all over Paris announced that on October 4, 1863, Nadar and a crew of twelve would embark on a trial flight. Of course, Verne's book, the talk of the town, helped focus attention on Nadar's venture. Thousands of Parisians crowded the field to watch the Princess de la Tour d'Auvergne, the astronauts Louis and Jules Godard, Nadar, and other notables rise over Paris and drift to the east. That night, after dining and wining aloft, they descended in Meaux, twenty-five miles away. On a subsequent flight Nadar and his wife traveled 400 miles before crashing in Hanover. In the popular imagination, Doctor Ferguson's *Victoria* and Nadar's *Le Géant* became one. And such happy symbiosis continued: Verne depended on scientists and explorers to identify the new areas of investigation, while the Spekes and Nadars found themselves glorified in the new science fiction . . .

. . . which Verne began turning out fast, even though he could not immediately quit Eggly (as we once believed). He set his lifelong pace by publishing, in 1864, *The English at the North Pole* in Hetzel's new *Magasin d'Education et de Recreation,* an essay on Poe's science fiction in the *Musée des Familles,* and *Journey to the Center of the Earth* in book form. In 1865 he issued the first of a series of novels based on the American Civil War: *The Blockade Runners* in *Musée* and, as we have seen, *From the Earth to the Moon* in *Journal des Débats.*

Nadar's *Le Géant* ready to take off from the Champ-de-Mars, October 4, 1863, as depicted in the *Musée des Familles*.

As we learn in greater detail later in this book, in writing his first space novel Verne drew heavily on his associations with Arago, Pierre Verne, and Nadar. And so, we naturally might wonder, in the light of his romantic failures, including the failure of his marriage, how did the women in his life figure in his fiction?

In his recent excellent book about his grandfather, Jean Jules-Verne suggests that Gräuben in *Journey to the Center of the Earth* represents what Jules wished Honorine had been: Gräuben supports her man at the difficult start of his destined task. And Jules-Verne leads us to realize that Jenny Halliburt, heroine of *The Blockade Runners* who converts Captain Playfair to her political views, could represent the intellectual interests that Honorine lacked and Verne so needed in a woman. But as Verne turned out a steady stream of books for the next forty years, as he predicted virtually every major technical development of our own time, as he explored every area of the globe for its exotic geography and its political tensions, he found many heroes and few heroines.

After *From the Earth to the Moon* appeared, Verne acquired a summer cottage in Le Crotoy, a fishing village on the Somme only five miles from the open sea. There he also bought a large weather-beaten fishing smack which he redesigned as his "floating study" and male refuge. He created a tiny forecastle for a crew of two, and a small cabin in the stern with two bench-bunks and a table for writing. He called it the *Saint Michel* after his son. He now spent a great deal of time on the water, sometimes taking a turn at the tiller or helping trim the sails, crisscrossing the English Channel, following the coast down to Bordeaux, sailing back to Amiens. Often he wrote lying out on the deck. On one of her few ventures on board, Honorine remarked, "How do you manage to write such beautiful things, poor boy, when you look at the sky only with your bottom?" Most of her witty comments about his boating were less congenial: she complained bitterly

Verne's own rapid sketch of *Le Saint Michel,* made for his friend Adrien Marx who used it as the frontispiece for an 1873 American version of *The Tour of the World in Eighty Days.*

that he was hardly home but planning to leave on the next tide. Letters have been found in which he asks Hetzel to call him to Paris so that he can sail there on the Seine.

And it was not Honorine but Paul who accompanied him on his eventful 1867 voyage on the *Great Eastern.* After all his years on the seven seas, Paul admitted he had never seen such an angry ocean. On board Jules met and interviewed Cyrus Field, flushed with his recent success in finally laying the Atlantic Cable. In New York, the brothers spent a hectic week at all the usual tourist attractions, from a play at Barnum's Theatre to the trip up the Hudson and the visit to Niagara Falls, all while the Great Eastern was loading for the turnaround. The journey provided Verne with much of the technical information he needed for *Twenty Thousand Leagues* (1870)—his *Nautilus* is a luxurious submarine equivalent of the *Great Eastern*—as well as the actual setting and some of the circumstances for *A Floating City* (1871), his fictionalized account of the trip. In this last work, a woman named Ella is forced to marry the wrong man but is rescued by the man she really loves. Was this the way Verne saw Herminie's marriage of twenty years before? Did he still nourish such hopes?

Those last two works—Verne's masterpiece followed by one of his typical "entertainments"—appeared in one of the most hectic periods of his life. In August 1870 he arrived home from a jaunt on his smack to find he had been awarded the Legion of Honor. Although Ferdinand de Lesseps, builder of the Suez Canal had nominated him, Verne bristled at the thought of accepting it from the imperial regime he despised. "You deserved it," Hetzel wrote, "no matter what the political circumstances in which you received it." Meanwhile Honorine discovered, or suspected, Jules was having an affair. "My husband is slipping away from me," she wrote frantically to Hetzel in a letter only recently published; "help me to hold on to him." And only recently has the family fully admitted there was another woman in Verne's life. Jean Jules-Verne identifies her as a certain Mme. Duchesne and thinks she might have been Herminie. He insists it must have been a platonic friendship. But at least one relative has been heard to remark, "He has no proof of that."

In any event, Jules and Honorine were separated when Emperor Napoleon III declared war on Germany. Verne was commissioned as commander of the *Saint Michel* and patrolled the Bay of the Somme with rotating crews totaling twelve men. He sent Honorine to Amiens (for safety!) before it was captured by the Prussions: they quartered four infantrymen in her house. Jules wrote to Pierre: "Honorine gives them a lot of rice to keep them as constipated as possible. It's less messy. As usual, she has everything under control." Since there was no action on the Somme, he finished drafts of four novels while on duty, including *Measuring a Meridian* (1872), which satirizes war and even nationalism.

After peace was declared in May 1871, Verne discovered that during the siege of Paris, Nadar had served heroically as a balloonist and Garcet had died. Then Pierre suffered a stroke and succumbed soon after Jules reached his bedside. Verne decided to move his family to Amiens, midway between Paris and Le Crotoy, where he set up a huge household with his own separate apartment on the top floor. As a resident of Amiens he would earn his greatest honors, achieve his greatest material prosperity, suffer his worst personal defeats.

In 1872 he was elected to the Académie d'Amiens and won a literary prize from the Académie Française. In 1888 he startled his conservative relatives by running for the Amiens Town Council on a slightly-left-of-center ticket. He won and was reelected in 1892, 1896, 1900. He served on committees that regulated and encouraged the arts and recreation. On the one hand, as a councillor he praised the police for quelling an anarchist demonstration and advised female graduates to steer clear of feminism. On the other hand, he defended the rights of traveling performers—carnival companies, for example, whose very arrival always upset the middle class. The novelist was still living out the schizophrenic pattern of his teens. He stood for propriety and dutiful conformity in civic and public life, but passionately explored the alternatives in the arts and in his secret life. The books he produced during this same period—*The Steam House* (1880), *Family without a Name* (1889), *The Survivors of the "Jonathan"* (1909), to name just a few—simply throng with rebels, outcasts, dissidents.

The grand saloon of the *Great Eastern* as pictured in Verne's *A Floating City*, his novel based on his April 1867 voyage to America.

Meanwhile he himself flowered in a "rain of gold"—the actual phrase used by his first family biographer, Marguerite Allotte de la Fuÿe. His novel *Around the World in Eighty Days* (1873) made a fortune first for *Le Temps,* the newspaper in which it ran, then for Verne after it was adapted for the stage in 1874. Then he scored a similar success with his novel *Michael Strogoff, Courier of the Czar* (1876). The stage production was so splendid that for a while Parisians praised anything successful as *beau comme Strogoff*. After a tour of the theater capitals, these two plays ran alternately, without a break, for fifty years at the Chatelet in Paris! Revenues "rained" from other sources: Hetzel raised Verne's fee to 6,000 francs per book and then started paying royalties; publishers in many foreign countries were buying translation rights. Recent studies suggest Verne's writing brought him one million francs (but Hetzel five million!).

Symbolic of his material success is his sensational role as yachtsman and grand host. He abandoned his simple fishing smack for a larger vessel in 1876, and soon after bought a magnificent steam yacht from the Marquis de Préaulx. The *Saint Michel III* required a crew of ten, including the cook and mess boy. Verne and his distinguished guests sailed to all the ports of Europe and North Africa. Everywhere he was honored: by diplomats, heads of state, garrison commanders, royalty, the Pope. In Amiens he presided over costume balls with elaborate entertainment for up to 800 guests. At one of these affairs Nadar arrived dressed as Ardan, the hero of *From the Earth to the Moon* (1865) and *Round the Moon* (1870)—in other words, Nadar played a fictional character modeled on himself. Verne explained these high-society extravaganzas to the shocked democrat Hetzel (who refused to attend) as necessary to maintain Honorine's status in society.

Again, the double life: concerned with Honorine's dignity *in society,* avoiding her *at home.* "The part of Amiens you know best," she said to Verne in the presence of their grandson, "is the train station." For he made weekly trips to Paris, ostensibly to see Hetzel, actually to visit Mme. Duchesne at whose home in Asnieres he often worked on manuscripts, galleys, page proofs. Was she at last his Gräuben, his Jenny, his Ella? When she died, around 1885, she left him all her property, one material reward he did not accept. Psychoanalytic critics are yet to trace all the clues to this affair to be found in Verne's work. But it seems safe to assume that *The Carpathian Castle* (1892), in which Verne predicts such miracles as the combination of moving pictures with sound track, explores in a surrealist mode the author's grief over the loss of his "unique siren."

In turning away from his marriage, in seeking refuge at his desk, at the Town Hall, in the house in Asnieres, Verne was neglecting his son and the rest of his family. This neglect apparently fostered rebellion in the next generation, the full extent of which has only recently been revealed by Jean Jules-Verne.

We had long known that one evening in 1876 the novelist had had a tragic encounter with Paul's son Gaston. Returning from the Amiens library to the house where he had composed twenty novels in fourteen years, Jules was about to open the garden door when Gaston, waving a revolver, rushed up to him shouting "They're after me!" Verne insisted he could see no one in pursuit of Gaston, upon which the nephew cried, "So even you will not defend me!" He fired twice, one bullet lodging in the stone lintel, the other in the bone of Verne's left leg. Before he collapsed, the novelist helped the servants subdue Gaston, who spent the rest of his life in mental institutions. The diagnosis then was persecution mania. More recent speculation includes the possibility that Gaston, a talented civil servant, was reacting to a sensation of being smothered by his uncle's fame. Surely he was appealing for his uncle's help and felt he wasn't going to get it.

What we have learned only recently is that Verne's own son fought not just a brief, symbolic scuffle with the novelist but a series of all-out feuds starting in his teens and running into his early manhood. When young Michel, neglected by his father, hung around with "undesirables," ran up debts, "defied" parental authority, the novelist failed to see this behavior as an appeal for a closer relationship. Instead of trying to reach Michel man to man, Verne vacillated between severe repressive measures on the one hand and bribes—more spending money—on the other. All of these impersonal methods of course embittered Michel and made things worse. Yes, Verne confined his boy to a home for juvenile delinquents, let him out on trial without doing anything to improve the personal bond between them, panicked when Michel ran up new debts, got a court order committing his son to jail until he could be sent to sea as an apprentice pilot! The boy's correspondence reveals how he enjoyed all this importance he finally was gaining, but resented the impersonality, the distance. On Michel's return home eighteen months later, the cycle started all over, Verne calling in the mayor and the police, unable to negotiate with his son, apparently, except under their auspices—in the police station. Then Michel ran away with an actress, married her, and left her for a pianist. The actress became a dependent in Verne's own home until she resolved the situation by granting a divorce so that Michel could marry his new love. Verne's acceptance of the divorce and second marriage permanently alienated many religious members of his own family, including some in Michel's generation.

Ironically, in those final years when he walked with a limp and suffered all these family resentments, Verne found his main solace, his one close relationship, with Michel. When in 1889 they worked together on the clever tale *In the Year 2889*—which predicts TV news, call-in programs, and the power of opinion polls—the novelist discoverd, belatedly, that his son had talents and interests similar to his own. Jules Verne—who had probably never helped his son with his homework—now explored every new idea for his fiction with Michel. And when Verne, pleading on his death bed for family unity, finally succumbed to diabetes in 1905 at the age of 77, Michel became his literary executor in every sense of the word. He piloted most of Verne's still unpublished works through the press, nine books in all. Since Verne had always counted on doing final revisions just before publication, we may assume these posthumous works gained that final polish from Michel. The son also directed and produced film versions of Verne's works and supervised the perennial productions at the Chatelet.

But the great romanticist explosion in the Verne line was over. One of Michel's sons, Jean Jules-Verne, returned to the older family tradition. After a lifetime devoted to law, he became chief justice of Toulon. Retiring in 1961, he has devoted his time to writing critical and biographical works about Jules Verne.

WALTER JAMES MILLER

New York University

. . . wooden legs, hinged arms, hooks for hands. . . . Gun Clubbers as represented in the first illustrated edition of *From the Earth to the Moon* (1872).

CHAPTER I

The Gun Club

During the Civil War in the United States, a highly influential club was founded in the city of Baltimore, in the middle of Maryland.[1] Everyone will remember the vigor with which that nation of shipowners, shopkeepers, and mechanics discovered their instinct for warfare. Simple businessmen leaped over their counters to become captains, colonels, generals, without ever having studied at West Point. In no time at all, they mastered "the art of war" and, like their colleagues in the Old World, they won battles through lavish expenditure of bullets, millions, and men.

Indeed, in one branch of military science—ballistics—the Americans even surpassed the Europeans.[2] It was not that American weapons attained a higher degree of perfection, but rather that they were built bigger and so could shoot further. In such matters as grazing, plunging, or direct fire; oblique, raking, or flank fire, the English, French, and Prussians have nothing to learn; but their guns, their howitzers, their mortars are mere pocket pistols compared to the awesome mechanisms of the American artillery.

This should not surprise us. The Yankees, the world's greatest mechanics, are engineers the way Italians are musicians and Germans are metaphysicians—by birth. It was only natural for Americans to take their bold ingenuity with them when they ventured into the realm of ballistics. And so they developed their gigantic cannon, far less useful than their sewing machines, but equally amazing and much more admired. Witness the marvels of Parrott, Dahlgren, and Rodman.[3] The Armstrongs, the Pallisers, and the Treuilles de Beaulieu[4] could only bow to their rivals across the sea.

So, in the terrible struggle between Northerners and Southerners, the artillerymen lorded it over the rest. Union newspapers celebrated their inventions with enthusiasm. There was no storekeeper so obscure, no "booby" so naive, that he wasn't racking his brain day and night calculating mad trajectories.

Now when an American has an idea, he looks for a second American to share it. When they become three, they elect a president and two secretaries. Four, they appoint an archivist, and now they're in business. Five, they call a general meeting, and the club is officially

1. *War . . . United States . . . Maryland* Verne packs his first sentence with plenty of bait. Every phrase here is calculated to take full advantage of his readers' current interests—and his own. When this novel appears in 1865, all Europe is watching the outcome of the American *Civil War*. Verne, his publisher Jules Hetzel, and the iconoclasts they hang out with have supported the North simply because of their hatred of slavery. Verne has made his own position clear in *The Blockade Runners* (1865): he will play on his readers' concern over the North-South conflict in five other novels.

But long before *the Civil War,* Verne and his audience have been excited about *the United States* as a vast testing-ground for new ideas. Imagine a country where private citizens have the freedom to band themselves into *a highly influential club!* And so Verne commandeers that country as the perfect setting for his own experiments. A great believer in national "types," he wants to know: what new kind of person will this new kind of society turn out? Although he takes his readers to every corner of the earth, he will always favor the U.S.A. Twenty-three of his sixty-four novels are set in America, or feature Americans, or both.

Even that innocent-looking place-name *Baltimore* is guaranteed to catch the eye. Such a strange place it must be, to have earned two contradictory nicknames: "Monumental City" and "Mobtown"! World-renowned for her warm architecture and splendid civic planning and her international character—in 1865 one of every four Baltimoreans is foreign-born—she is also infamous for her frequent riots, her armed gangs that decide her elections. And how often she has figured in the war news: clamped under martial law by Lincoln, put to work banging out iron plate for the *Monitor,* shifting vast numbers of troops on the B & O. If Verne's story begins here, then his readers look for new understanding of cosmopolitan America, futuristic America, violent America.

2. *Americans . . . surpassed . . . Europeans* Still, after the Civil War an American encyclopedia launches its article on "Ballistics" with this lament: "The properties connected with the flight of projectiles are not all fully understood, despite the intelligent study devoted to the subject." In this novel, Verne becomes the first person to apply this study to the peaceful task of shooting man himself into Outer Space.

3. *Parrott, Dahlgren, . . . Rodman* In 1865 these three rate so high in world news that Verne need only mention their names to gain his desired effect. Robert P. *Parrott* (1804–1877) supplies an early example of ties between business and war that Eisenhower later characterizes as "the military-industrial complex." In 1836 the Army assigned Parrott as ordnance inspector at the West Point Foundry, Cold Spring, New York (another place whose fame Verne will exploit in this book). But the foundry owners induced Parrott to resign his commission and become manager of the company! Now like most foundries, West Point was boring gun-barrels smooth. A projectile emerging from a smooth bore *tumbles* over and over as it flies through the air. Of course, gunsmiths knew they could double the range and accuracy of their arms by cutting spiral grooves into the bore: rifling makes a projectile *spin:* this keeps it steady, pointed in one direction. But until 1849, rifling had worked only with small arms. Then Parrott heard that Krupp in Germany had mastered a secret technique for rifling cannon; he decided America would too. In 1861 he patented his famous rifled guns and shells. The Parrott rifle can accommodate a greater explosive charge because he strengthens the breech (the part to the rear of the bore) by encasing it in wrought-iron hoops applied hot and shrunk into position as they cool. More than 1,700 Parrotts have been cast in time for the Civil War. They have earned a reputation as the world's best ordnance—not wholly deserved, as we soon see.

One of the guns that suggested the Civil War joke that the "parrott" should replace the eagle as the national bird. From *The American Cyclopaedia* (1873).

Admiral John *Dahlgren* (1809–1870) is a Navy scientific officer who worked out a revolutionary principle: a gun-barrel wall need be no thicker at any point than is required to contain the pressures at that point. He casts his guns thickest at the breech, where the explosion occurs, and curves them inward toward the

Baltimore as seen from Federal Hill. Engraving from *The American Cyclopaedia* (1873).

constituted. And so it went in Baltimore. The man who had invented a new cannon associated with the man who first cast it and the man who first bored it. This proved to be the nucleus of the Gun Club.[5] Just one month after it was founded, the Club already numbered 1,833 active members and 30,575 corresponding members.[6]

There was one *sine qua non* requirement for membership: the applicant must have invented, or at least improved, a cannon; if not a cannon, at least some sort of firearms. But to tell the truth, inventors of fifteen-chambered revolvers, pivoting carbines, or sabre-pistols were not held in very high esteem. Artillerymen consistently took precedence.

"The respect they enjoy," said one of the more scientific orators of the Gun Club, "is proportional to the mass of their cannon, and in direct ratio to the square of the distances attained by their projectiles!"

This was Newton's law of universal gravitation translated into moral philosophy.

Once the Gun Club was organized, it was easy to see its effect on the inventive genius of the Americans. Engines of war took on colossal proportions, and projectiles, going way beyond the expected range, cut innocent pedestrians in half. These inventions left far behind the timid instruments of European artillery. One may judge by the following figures.

"In the good old days," a 36-pound cannonball, fired into the enemy's flank from a distance of 300 feet, could cut through 36 horses[7] and 68 men. But the art was only in its infancy. Since then artillery has made great progress. The Rodman cannon, which flung a shell weighing half a ton for a distance of seven miles, could easily have bowled over 150 horses and 300 men. At the Gun Club they talked of conducting official tests to prove the validity of these claims. Perhaps the horses were willing to take part, but the men required for the experiment could not be found.

In any case, these cannons were murderous. With every shot, combatants fell like wheat before the scythe. Compared with these American projectiles, what was that famous cannonball that put 25 men *hors de combat* at Coutras in 1587? Or the one that killed 40 footsoldiers at Zorndorf in 1758? Or that Austrian gun that made 70 men bite the dust whenever it spoke at Kesselsdorf in 1742? What was so amazing about the gunfire at Jena and Austerlitz, which was credited with deciding the outcome of the battle? That was nothing compared to the American War between the States! In the Battle of Gettysburg, a conical projectile fired by a rifled cannon hit 173 Confederates. During the crossing of the Potomac, a Rodman ball dispatched 215 Southerners into an obviously far better world.[8] We must mention too the formidable mortar invented by J. T. Maston, distinguished member and permanent secretary of the Gun Club, which was murderous in quite an unexpected way. At its first public trial, it killed 337 people—by bursting,[9] we must admit.

What could we add to these figures, so eloquent in themselves? Nothing. Therefore it will be easy to accept in silence the following calculation, worked out by Pitcairn the statistician. By dividing the number of deaths due to Gun Club weapons by the number of members in the Club, he concluded that each member had, on the average, killed 2,375 men and a fraction.[10]

Such a figure makes it clear that the sole preoccupation of this learned society was the destruction of humanity for philanthropic reasons and the perfection of weapons as instruments of civilization. It was a gathering of Exterminating Angels who were nevertheless the best fellows in the world.

It is only fair to add that these Yankees were gallant in every ordeal: they did not confine themselves to theories, they paid for every advance with their own persons. Among their members they counted officers of every rank, from lieutenant to general, soldiers of every age, some making their début in the profession of arms, others growing old over their gun-carriages. Many whose names figured in the Honor Roll of the Gun Club were now sleeping on the field of battle, and of those who had come back alive, most bore the marks of their unassailable valor. Crutches, wooden legs, hinged arms, hooks for hands, rubber jaws, silver craniums, platinum noses, no proof of combat experience was missing from their collection. Pitcairn had further calculated that the Gun Club could muster slightly less than one arm for every four persons, and only two legs for every six.[11]

But these valiant artillerymen were not bothered by such details. They felt justifiably proud when the day's dispatches showed that the number of casualties was ten times greater than the number of projectiles fired.

One day, however—sad, lamentable day—the survivors made peace. Detonations were heard no more; the mortars were mute; the howitzers were muzzled and the guns, heads bent low, returned to the arsenals, and the cannonballs were piled up in pyramids in the parks; the bloody memories faded; cotton plants flourished in the well-fertilized fields; mourning clothes wore thin along with the grief itself; and the Gun Club was plunged into tedious unemployment.

Admittedly, a few rabid workhorses still labored away at their ballistical calculations, dreaming always of gigantic bombs and incomparable shells. But with no chance to put their ideas into practice, what

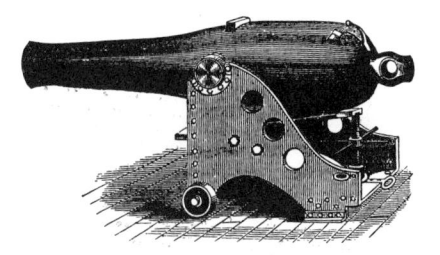

One of Admiral Dahlgren's "soda-water bottles." From *The American Cyclopaedia* (1873).

muzzle. His smooth curve strengthens the metal since it regularizes crystallization as the barrel cools. Because of their distinctive shape, 9-, 10-, 11-inch Dahlgrens are called "soda-water bottles."

General Thomas J. *Rodman* (1815–1871) earns repeated mention here because he casts bigger guns that shoot bigger bullets. Usually cannon had been cast as solid iron cylinders and cooled from the outside in before they were bored. But Rodman tried casting his cannon hollow around a removable core-tube (a technique Verne adopts in this story). Through the core Rodman pours water, cooling the cannon from the inside out. This makes tougher barrels that contain bigger explosions which mean greater ranges. Result: Rodman Columbiads, giants of 15-inch, even 20-inch caliber. But gigantic cannon need bigger projectiles which need more powerful gunpowder. Traditional propellants burn fast, hitting the projectile a sudden, brief blow. In the 1850s Parrott developed his "mammoth" powder, a slow burner that gives his projectiles a prolonged steady push up the barrel.

4. *Armstrongs . . . de Beaulieu* Sir William *Armstrong* (1810–1900) has addressed himself to the melancholy fact that cannon fired in the Crimea often burst without warning. Following Parrott, Armstrong developed "built-up" guns with hoops or helixes to encase the barrel. Armstrongs do not burst suddenly: they give ample warning by slow deformation. Sir William *Palliser* (1830–1882) is famous for his own version of a "built-up" cannon, adopted by the British Army, and for his projectiles, favored by the Royal Navy for piercing armor plate. French General Treuille *de Beaulieu* (1809–1886) has developed a rifled cannon that doesn't jam, as Engish rifles were wont to do at Sebastopol in 1854. Treuille's four-pounders performed brilliantly in Italy in 1859.

In Edward Roth's 1874 translation of this novel, he adds the Krupps to Verne's list of Europeans who could *only bow to their rivals across the sea*. Head of the Krupp works in Prussia, Alfred Krupp (1812–1887) has pioneered in steel guns of great size and ruggedness. We might wonder why Verne himself does not include the Prussians. Maybe he does not think the Krupps *are being surpassed* by the Americans. Maybe he can't joke about Prussian militarism: in the 1860s he feels dire forebodings about the Germans. After the Franco-Prussian War, when he bases *The Begum's Fortune* (1877) on a contrast between alleged French and German talents, he will wax savage in his satire on Germanic love of ordnance. That contrast will also be staged in the U.S.A.

5. *Gun Club* This description of the Gun Club suggests another reason why Verne bases his fictitious Club in Baltimore: that's where the Army's ballistics experts meet, where the Light Artillery Board has updated its *Instruction for Field Artillery* (1859).

6. *30,575 . . . members* In stressing how Americans pool their ideas, Verne intends a moral for Europeans. "In Verne's day," says French critic Jean Chesneaux, "American society was one in which scientific and technical problems were dealt with publicly and discussed by all shades of opinion, rather than being hidden away, as in Old Europe, in dusty offices of learned societies. . . ."

7. *cut through . . . horses* A familiar sight in combat. At the Battle of Gettysburg, Colonel Thomas Osborn was surprised by Confederate guns on his right flank: "I saw one shell go through six horses standing broadside."

8. *far better world* Verne evokes his readers' schoolboy memories of classic battles and recent memories of Civil War news. At *Coutras*, French Protestants, because of their strong artillery, defeated a Catholic force twice their size. At *Zorndorf*, the Prussians inflicted 50% casualties on the Russians: the *40 footsoldiers* were Russian grenadiers mowed down by a single cannonball fired 1,200 yards away. At *Kesselsdorf*, the Austrians' murderous gun did not save them from defeat by the Prussians. At *Jena*, October 14, 1806, Napoleon destroyed half the Prussian Army. But Verne's readers know *Austerlitz*, December 2, 1805, as Napoleon's "masterpiece": he lured the Russians and Austrians into a mass trap. Closing around them from all sides with incessant artillery fire plunging from surrounding heights, he forced them to retreat over frozen lakes: then he broke the ice with a storm of shot. Nearly 20,000 died, most by drowning. For every man Napoleon lost, he destroyed four of his foe. But the most intense of all artillery engagements up to Verne's time occurs at *Gettysburg,* July 1–3, 1863. 362 Federal cannon faced 272 Confederate guns along a two-mile stretch: they fired 50,000 rounds. General John Gibbon described the fierce cannonading as "the most infernal pandemonium it has ever been my fortune to look upon." These massed batteries accounted for a large portion of 23,000 casualties in the Union ranks, maybe 27,000 among the rebels. General Robert E. Lee's forces withdrew, recrossing the *Potamac* the night of July 13–14.

9. *by bursting* Such disasters are all too familiar to Verne's readers. When a crowd gathered in Charleston to watch Confederate gun-

was the point of theorizing? The club rooms were often deserted now, servants were sleeping in the antechambers, newspapers piled up unread on the library tables, dark corners rang with gloomy snores. Members of the Gun Club, once so boisterous but now silenced by this disastrous peace, dropped off into reveries of platonic artillery!

"This is so demoralizing," said brave Tom Hunter one evening. His wooden legs, resting on the fender of the fireplace in the smoking room, were slowly charring. "Nothing to do! Nothing to live for! What a bore! Where are the days when we were awakened every morning by the joyous sounds of war?"

"Those days seem gone forever," replied the spirited Bilsby. He tried to stretch the arms he no longer had. "Yes, those were the days. You designed your howitzer and as soon as it was cast, you could rush off and try it out on the enemy. And then you would return to camp to get an encouraging word from Sherman or a handshake from McClellan! But now the generals have gone back behind their counters. Instead of projectiles, they dispatch bales of cotton. Oh, Saint Barbara![12] There is no future for artillery in America!"

"Right, Bilsby," cried Colonel Blomsberry, "life can be so deceptive! One day you give up the pleasures of civilian life, you learn the manual of arms, you leave Baltimore for the battlefield, you conduct yourself like a hero, but two or three years later, you lose all the benefit of your sacrifice. You're forced to stand by, useless, with hands stuffed into your pockets."

Despite his choice of words, the valiant colonel would have found it difficult to make such a gesture of idleness, though it was not pockets he lacked.

"And no war in sight!" said the famous J. T. Maston, scratching his gutta-percha[13] skull with his iron hook. "Nary a cloud in the sky, and just when there's so much to be done in the science of artillery! Why believe me, just as sure as I'm talking to you now, this very morning I completed the design—with plan, section, and elevation—of a mortar that would change the laws of war!"

"Really?" replied Tom Hunter, involuntarily harking back to the last experiment by the Honorable J. T. Maston.

"Really," Maston assured him. "But what's the point of so much research, so many discoveries? I've been working for nothing. The peoples of the New World seem determined to live in peace. Have you noticed, even our bellicose *Tribune* has been reduced to making scary predictions about the consequences of the scandalous increase in population!"

"But Maston," resumed Colonel Blomsberry, "over in Europe, they're always fighting to uphold the principle of nationalities!"[14]

"So?"

"Well, maybe we could conduct some experiments over there, if they would accept our services—"

"What are you thinking of!" cried Bilsby. "Conducting ballistic tests for the benefit of foreigners?"

"That surely would be better than conducting no tests at all," the colonel retorted.

"Of course that would be better," said J. T. Maston, "but it's foolish to get up your hopes."

A combat correspondent in the midst of the American Civil War, as pictured in the 1875 illustrated edition of Verne's novel *The Mysterious Island*.

"And why do you say that?" demanded the colonel.

"Because in the Old World they have crazy notions about advancement. They're contrary to all our American customs. Those people believe you can't become a general unless you started as a second lieutenant. That's like saying you can't aim a gun unless you cast it yourself! Why, it's simply . . . simply . . ."

"Absurd." Tom Hunter, hacking the arm of his chair with his Bowie knife,[15] found the right word for Maston. "And since that's the way it is, there's nothing left for us to do, except maybe plant tobacco, or distill whale oil."[16]

"You don't mean to say," cried J. T. Maston in a booming voice, "that we can't devote the rest of our days to perfecting our firearms? That we shall never have another chance to test the range of our projectiles? That the atmosphere will never again be lighted up with the flash of our cannon? That we shall never again be provoked into declaring war? Can't we count on the French to sink one of our

ners try out a new cannon on Federal ships in the harbor, the gun burst, killing 40 spectators. When a Federal fleet attacked Fort Fisher, nearly all their Parrotts burst, causing 45 casualties, while the enemy guns caused only 11 casualties! A civilian gun-maker, Norman Wiard, claimed "four of our gunners have been killed by the bursting of our heavy guns, for one by the projectiles of the enemy." Wiard said Rodman himself would never stand near a big Columbiad when it was rapid-firing! Nevertheless, gun-makers were such popular heroes that one wag suggested the "parrott" ought to replace the eagle as the national bird. Unhappily, Dahlgren's name did not lend itself to such word-play. Not one Dahlgren gun burst in the entire war.

10. *2,375 . . . and a fraction* The real statistics that inspired this satire are grim enough. The Union, with 2,000,000 men under arms, suffered 640,000 casualties, including 110,000 dead. The South, with 750,000 in uniform, suffered 450,000 casualties, 94,000 killed. "The butcher's bill," says Shelby Foote, "thus came to about 1,090,000 men for more than 10,000 military actions. . . ." Nearly 8,000 cannon fired about 6,500,000 projectiles.

After Verne's sustained satire, you will not be surprised to hear that his grandson calls him "a congenital pacifist." In writing to his father in the late 1860s, the novelist says about France's new military preparations: "When will men learn to reason without rifles? . . . Will they never listen to any arguments other than those of the professional military caste?"

11. *two legs for every six* In the first year after the war the state of Mississippi spends one fifth of its revenue for artificial arms and legs.

12. *Saint Barbara!* Bilsby invokes the aid of the patron saint of artillerymen. As Gun Club members doubtless know, her image is often placed on arsenals, guns, and powder-magazines. As Verne well knows from his brother's talk, the powder-room in a French warship is called the *Sainte Barbe*. She is variously reported as martyred in Egypt (306) or Bithynia (235) or in Tuscany. Her pagan father, fearful he would lose her because of her great beauty, confined her to a tower. Somehow she managed to entertain a Christian leader (Origen?) who baptized her. Her father haled her before the prefect who, impressed by her beauty and intelligence, tried to argue her back to paganism. She remained faithful to Christianity; the prefect tortured her; her father struck off her head. Some say he was instantly hit by lightning; others, that it happened on his way home. Gunners, presumably aspiring to hit their mark so summarily, adopted her as their patron. A medieval French play about her devoted three of the five days of action to the tortures. And apparently artillerymen are still fond of her. Brigadier O. F. G. Hogg dedicated his *Artillery: Its Origin, Heyday and Decline* (1970) to "St. Barbara, who until her expulsion from the Calendar of Saints, had been the Patron Saint of Artillery since its birth." Perhaps he sees her "expulsion" as symbolizing the "decline" of great guns, their military task taken over by bombers and rockets.

13. *gutta-percha* In Verne's day, this rubbery substance is a good new example of man's triumphant exploitation of Nature. Engineers use it for insulating telegraph cables, dentists for taking impressions of teeth, prosthetic surgeons for making artificial parts of the body. The Chinese and Malays have known for centuries that *gutta-percha,* put in boiling water, becomes soft and plastic: when they mold it into any shape, it retains that form after it cools. They use it for making basins, axe-handles, even shoes. But Europeans did not begin large-scale tapping of gutta-percha trees until the 1840s.

. . . get an encouraging word from Sherman . . . General William Tecumseh Sherman as seen in the *World-Wide Encyclopedia and Gazetteer* (1899).

A sprig of gutta-percha leaves, with flower and berry, as represented in *The American Cyclopaedia* (1873).

14. *principle of nationalities* Verne himself champions the principle that every nationality should be free of control by other nationalities. His fiction highlights the struggles of various peoples to free themselves from foreign masters: for example, Russian Baltic peasants from German overlords; Greeks, Cretans, Bulgarians from the Turks; the Irish, French Canadians, and Indians from the English. Verne does not overlook his own country's guilt in violating this principle: *The Invasion of the Sea* (1905) deals sympathetically with Tuareg resistance to French conquest.

15. *Bowie knife* "A dagger with a broad blade," Verne tells his French audience in a footnote. Ten to fifteen inches long, more than an inch wide, it's single-edged except for its double-edged point. It's named after either Rezin Bowie, its putative inventor, or his brother, Texas Army Colonel James Bowie, who popularized it by using it in a duel "with terrible effect," says a nineteenth-century encyclopedia. Bowie fell at Fort Alamo in the Texan War (1836).

steamers, or the English to hang three or four Americans in defiance of the rights of mankind!" [17]

"No, Maston," Colonel Blomsberry prophesied, "we shall have no such luck! No such joyous incidents will occur. Or if they do, we won't make anything out of them. Every day Americans are becoming less warlike and more effeminate."

"Yes, we are humiliating ourselves," said Bilsby.

"And we are being humiliated," added Tom Hunter.

"Exactly!" said J. T. Maston with new vehemence. "There are a thousand reasons in the air for fighting, yet we're not fighting. We're being economical with the arms and legs of people who don't even know how to put them to good use! Now we don't have to look very far for reasons for going to war—didn't North America once belong to the English?"

"Without a doubt." Tom Hunter fiercely poked the fire with his crutch.

"Well," Maston concluded, "now it should be England's turn to belong to America!"

"That sounds fair," said Colonel Blomsberry.

"But take this proposal to the President of the United States," sneered J. T. Maston. "Just see how far you'll get."

"He wouldn't even entertain the idea," Bilsby murmured through the four teeth he had salvaged from combat.

"I swear," J. T. Maston cried out, "in the next election he won't get my vote."

"He won't get mine either!" the bellicose invalids shouted in chorus.

"Meanwhile," continued J. T. Maston, "and in conclusion, if I don't get a chance to try out my new mortar in actual combat, I shall tender my resignation from the Gun Club and go and bury myself in the swamps of Arkansas!" [18]

"And we'll go with you," the chorus assured the audacious J. T. Maston.

Tempers were mounting higher and higher. The Club faced the threat of dissolution. But an unexpected development prevented such a deplorable catastrophe.

The very next day after this conversation, each member of the Club received a notice worded as follows:

Baltimore, October 3

The President of the Gun Club has the honor to inform his colleagues that at the meeting called for October 5 he will deliver a message of the utmost importance. Consequently he urges them to put aside all other business and to give this meeting the highest priority.

Very cordially yours,
Impey Barbicane [19]
President
The Gun Club

The Washington Monument, one of many reasons why Baltimore is known as "Monumental City." The 15-foot statue of the first president stands 195 feet above the ground. From *The American Cyclopaedia* (1873).

16. *whale oil* Still widely used in Hunter's day for illumination and lubrication, but whales are becoming scarcer and whale oil has a new competitor: underground oil, discovered in Pennsylvania in 1858.

17. *rights of mankind* Verne exploits the fact that France and England are recently guilty of hostile acts toward Washington. Some Americans, like Maston, believe the U.S. may soon be at war with one or both of these nations. The French, taking advantage of Washington's preoccupation with a civil war, have invaded Mexico and put the Austrian Archduke Maximilian in power as Emperor. As Verne writes, Washington is preparing to invoke the Monroe Doctrine. We hear more about poor Maximilian in Chapter XII. The British have allowed Confederate ships to be armed in British ports, an overt violation of their neutrality. For this Washington will prosecute Britain before an international tribunal, winning the famous "*Alabama* Claims" case in 1871.

18. *swamps of Arkansas* In Maston's day, the low, flat eastern part of Arkansas, washed by the Mississippi, is covered with dense forests, swamps, lakes, and ponds, frequently with stagnant, unhealthful water.

19. *Impey Barbicane* Verne loves to make fun with names. Impey sounds like a diminutive for English *imp,* or little devil; in French it also connotes *impie,* an impious person. And a *barbican* is a tower that protects the gatehouse of a castle. The European term probably derives from the Arabic *bab-al-bagara,* a gate with loop-holes. Such a bristling sobriquet, coming in the signature of a letter, creates suspense about the man who has written it.

CHAPTER II

President Barbicane's Message

By eight P.M. on October 5, thick crowds were pressing into the Gun Club at 21 Union Square. All the active members living in Baltimore had responded to their president's call. As for the corresponding members, express trains were bringing them in by the hundreds. Although the meeting hall was enormous, it could not accommodate all these savants. They overflowed into adjoining rooms, down to the ends of the hallways, right out into the courtyards.

There they encountered the ordinary citizens who were pushing against the gates, trying to get closer, all eager to find out what Barbicane had to say, elbowing their way forward, jostling, crushing each other with that freedom of action peculiar to people nurtured on the idea of "self-government."

No stranger, no matter how much he might be willing to pay, could hope to gain admission to the auditorium; seats were reserved exclusively for active and corresponding members. Baltimore's leading citizens, even members of the city council, were forced to wait outside in the crowd if they wanted to hear whatever news might filter out.

And the meeting hall itself presented a marvelous spectacle. This immense room was wonderfully suited to its purpose.[1] Its lofty columns—made of cannon fitted end-to-end, with thick mortars at the base—supported the delicate arches, perfect specimens of cast-iron lacework. Trophies—blunderbusses, arquebuses, muskets, carbines, all types of weapons old and new[2]—were interlaced in picturesque patterns on the walls. Gaslight blazed from chandeliers made of a thousand revolvers, from girandoles[3] of pistols, and from candelabra formed of clusters of rifles. Models of cannon, specimens of bronze castings, muzzle sights dented by bullets, iron plates crushed by the cannonballs of the Gun Club, collections of rammers and sponges, sticks of bombs, necklaces of projectiles, garlands of shells—in a word, all the artilleryman's paraphernalia dazzled the eye in arrangements that made one think their true function was more decorative than deadly.

In the place of honor, preserved in a beautiful glass case, rested a fragment of a breech, broken and twisted by the effects of gunpowder, a holy remnant of J. T. Maston's giant mortar.

1. *suited to its purpose* With Verne, such fanfare usually means: stand by for a tour de force!

2. *weapons old and new* In his choice of weapons, Verne does a good job of reviewing the history of small arms. The *blunderbuss* is an early short gun, with a wide bore and a bell muzzle, that could scatter shot at close range without exact aim. In medieval Dutch it was called a *donderbus*, or "thunder-gun." The English name may be a pun, a joke about the gun's "blind" firing. The *arquebus*, developed in the 1400s, was a heavy portable weapon that could be fired from a tripod, or a forked rest, to which it was attached by a hook. The *arquebus*, and its immediate successor, the *musket*, were smooth-bore guns. But by the mid-1800s, most soldiers are carrying rifled-bore weapons. Verne's French word *carbines* covers two types known in English as the *rifle* proper, the full-length weapon, and the *carbine*, a short-barreled light rifle.

3. *girandoles* Lights arranged around mirrors.

4. *trunnions* Cylinders that project from opposite sides of a cannon, near its center of gravity; they support the cannon on its carriage and form the axis on which the gun pivots.

5. *carronades* A short, thick cannon, the carronade enjoyed a vogue for half a century after the first model was cast in *Carron*, Scotland, in 1779. The carronade was easier to handle, could fire heavier projectiles, deliver more damage than any other gun.

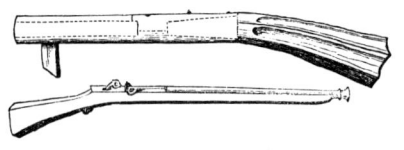

An arquebus with a serpentine lock to hold the match. From *The American Cyclopaedia* (1875).

At the far end of the hall, the president, attended by four secretaries, sat on a broad dais. His chair, resting on a carved gun-carriage, was shaped like a mighty 32-inch mortar. It was aimed at a 90° angle and suspended on trunnions,[4] so he could seesaw gently as though sitting in a rocking chair, a real pleasure on hot days especially. On his desk, a huge iron plate supported on six carronades,[5] stood an ink-pot, made from a Biscayen[6] engraved with exquisite taste, and a detonating bell which, at the appointed time, would go off like a revolver. Still, during heated discussions, this unusual bell would hardly be heard over the voices of this legion of overexcited artillerymen.

In front of the president's desk, benches arranged in a zigzag pattern—like the circumvallations of an entrenchment—formed a series of bastions and curtains[7] where the members of the Gun Club took their seats. On that night one could truly say, "All the world was on the ramparts." And all the members knew their president well enough to be sure he would never have inconvenienced them without a strong motive.

Impey Barbicane was a man of forty, calm, cold, austere, eminently serious and self-contained; punctual as a chronometer;[8] in temperament, ready for any ordeal, in character unshakeable; adventurous but not romantic, always bringing practical ideas to bear on the boldest ventures; the ultimate New Englander, the colonizing Northerner; the descendant of the Roundheads, who were so deadly for the Stuarts; indeed the implacable foe of all Cavaliers, whether royalists in the Old Country or Southern gentlemen in the new. In short a Yankee through and through.[9]

Barbicane had made a fortune in timber. Appointed Chief of Artillery[10] during the Civil War, he proved to be fertile in inventions. Daring in his thinking, he contributed mightily to the development of weaponry and constantly inspired new research.

He was a man of medium height, and—a rare exception in the Gun Club—he still had all four limbs intact. His features, strongly accentuated, could have been marked out with a T-square and a drawing pen.

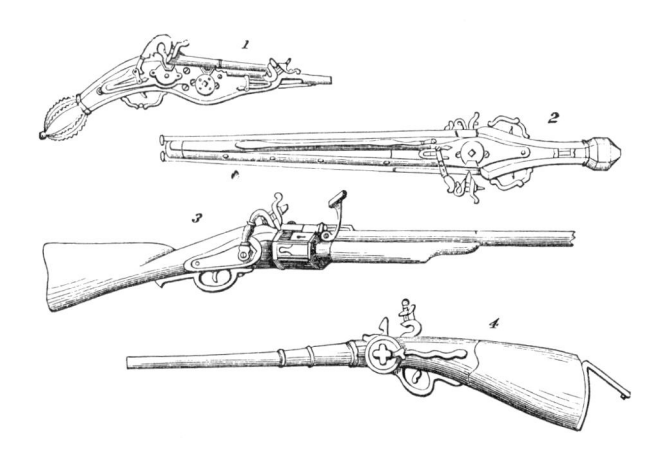

. . . weapons old and new probably included these seventeenth-century types: (1) a double-barreled pistol with two wheel locks made around 1612, (2) a later model, (3) a revolver carbine with flint lock from the days of Charles I, and (4) a repeating carbine used in Cromwell's time. From *The American Cyclopaedia* (1875).

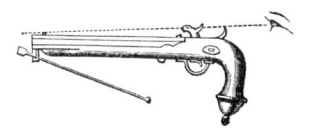

An early nineteenth-century pistol designed by Henri Gustave Delvigne. "At 200 yards and more it made a better target than the French musket of that day," says *The American Cyclopaedia* (1875).

6. *Biscayen* A large iron bullet designed to be fired from a long musket first made in Biscay.

7. *bastions and curtains* See how all this military terminology ties in with the name *Barbicane*. A *circumvallation* is a system of ramparts around a place under siege; a *bastion* is a projecting rampart; a *curtain* is a wall or rampart that connects two towers or bastions. And *Barbicane* is a cross between French *barbacane* and English *barbican*, which mean a *military tower*.

8. *punctual . . . chronometer* Characters obsessed with time have strong personal associations for Verne and figure frequently in his novels. His model for the human being *punctual as a chronometer* is his own father, Pierre. When the Vernes spent summers at Chantenay, Jules was accustomed to seeing his father train a marine telescope on a distant monastery clock. People would say lawyer Pierre knew exactly how many steps he had to take from home to office. For Jules, his father stood for mathematical objectivity and patriarchal logic. And in Verne's novels, father-figures like Barbicane symbolize that part of modern man that yearns to be an automaton.

9. *Yankee through and through* Verne strikes a telling parallel between the peoples who fought the English Civil War (1642–1648) and those who fought the American Civil War (1861–1865). English Puritans, who supported Parliament in its struggle against the king, were derisively dubbed *Roundheads* because of their short, bowl-like haircuts. This tag contrasted them with supporters of the *Stuart* King Charles I, aristocrats who wore wigs and were called *Cavaliers*. When the *Roundheads* overthrew the *royalists* and established a republic, they abolished theater and other frivolities like Maypole dancing. Meanwhile other Puritans were settling in New England: Verne sees the American "work ethic" as Northern in origin. He contrasts this grim Yankee ideology with the more easygoing attitude of *Southern gentlemen* who lived well on the labor of slaves.

10. *Chief of Artillery* Barbicane's counterpart in real life would be General Henry Hunt (1819–1889), *Chief of Artillery* in the Army of the Potomac, a member of the Artillery Board headquartered in Baltimore. But Hunt is a West

Pointer and a career soldier, while Verne makes Barbicane one of those merchants who earned stars overnight.

11. *character from . . . profile* In Verne's day, artists and scientists take a lively interest in physiognomy, the "science" of judging character by the face. As we shall see, Verne makes good artistic use of the current theories of Louis-Pierre Gratiolet (1815–1865). But here he probably has in mind the classic studies of Johann Kaspar Lavater (1741–1801) who could deduce detailed descriptions of a man's temperament from his *profile* alone.

12. *American skulls* Barbicane sports a "stovepipe," so-called because its tall cylinder resembles the large-diameter pipe used for stove chimneys. Like everyone else at the meeting, he wears his indoors and out.

13. *thirty-six other states* The thirty-sixth state, Nevada, has been admitted in 1864.

14. *selenographic* "From σελήνη, or Selene, the Greek word for moon," Verne reminds us in a footnote. Selenography is the science of the physical geography of the moon. Hesiod, poet who wrote shortly after Homer, says Selene is the sister of the Sun, daughter of the Titan Hyperion and the Titaness Theia.

15. *pictures of our satellite* Verne footnotes this with a reference to a man much in the news at this time: "See the magnificent plates of the moon obtained by Warren De La Rue." In 1857 De La Rue gave the Royal Astronomical Society positive copies from a negative picture of the moon he had made with his new collodion process. His July 16, 1860 plates have proved conclusively that the "prominences" seen during solar eclipses belong not to the moon but to the sun.

16. *Fabricius* German clergyman and astronomer (1564–1617) who pioneered in the scientific use of the telescope.

17. *Spanish Adventurer* Like Edgar Allan Poe and many other nineteenth-century readers, Verne believes Baudoin was actually the author of this popular and influential work. But Baudoin's book was simply a translation of *The Man in the Moone: or a Discourse of a Voyage thither. By Domingo Gonsales The speedy Messenger* (1638), written by the English Bishop Francis Godwin. Using a narrative technique that Poe and Verne both adopt, Godwin opens with ordinary travels so as to soften his readers' disbelief of extraordinary ones to follow. With his black servant (forerunner of Defoe's "man Friday"), Gonsales visits an island where he trains wild geese to carry a chair into the air. He sends a lamb aloft, "whose happiness I much envied, that he should be the first living creature to take flight" in such an "engine." This is Godwin's first prophecy: the Brothers Montgolfier would use sheep and fowl in a trial balloon-flight (1783), the Russians would use a

If it is true that we can read a man's character from his profile,[11] then we should say that Barbicane's proclaimed a man of energy, audacity, and *sang-froid*.

At the moment, he was sitting motionless in his armchair, silent, lost in his own thoughts, sheltered under his tall hat, one of those cylinders of black silk which seem screwed on to American skulls.[12]

His colleagues were chatting all around him without distracting him. They queried each other trying to guess what was on Barbicane's mind, to find the value of x, the unknown factor, in his imperturbable physiognomy.

But when the detonating clock in the meeting hall sounded eight, he stood up suddenly, like a spring in recoil. Silence fell over the hall as the president began to speak in a slightly pompous tone:

"Esteemed colleagues, for too long now a sterile peace has plunged the members of the Gun Club into lamentable idleness. After several productive years, so rich with opportunity, we have had to abandon our work and stop short on the road to progress. I do not hesitate to say that any incident that would put us back on a war footing would be most welcome—"

"Yes, war!" cried the impetuous J. T. Maston.

"Quiet! Shhh!" came from all sides.

"But war," said Barbicane, "war is unlikely under present circumstances. No matter how much my honorable interrupter yearns for war, many years will pass before we once again hear our guns thundering on the battlefield. We must make the most of a bad situation and look for a new outlet for our restless creativity!"

The assembly, sensing the president was coming to the point, listened intently.

"For several months, my gallant colleagues, I have been wondering whether, without going outside our field, we could not conduct some great experiment worthy of the nineteenth century; one in which our progress in ballistics would guarantee our success. I have searched, labored, calculated, and I am sure now that we can succeed in an enterprise which in any other country would be regarded as folly. This project, thought out at great length, will be the subject of my message tonight. It is worthy of you, worthy of our great past, and I assure you it will make a great noise all over the world."

"A great noise?" cried a passionate gunner.

"A great noise in every sense of the word," replied Barbicane.

"No interruptions! No interruptions!" several voices pleaded.

"Gentlemen, please," Barbicane continued, "may I have your full attention."

A rustle ran through the assembly. Having steadied his stovepipe hat with a swift efficient movement, he went on calmly:

"My colleagues, there is no one here who has not seen the moon or at least heard of it. Do not be surprised if at this point I talk about that celebrity of the night. Perhaps it has been reserved to us to be the Columbuses of that unknown world. Listen intently, support me with all your strength, and I will lead you to conquer that world, its name will be added to those of the thirty-six other states[13] that already belong to the Union!"

"Hurray for the moon!" cried the Gun Club with one voice.

The assembly . . . listened intently. Engraving from the 1872 edition.

"The moon has been carefully studied," Barbicane resumed. "We know its mass, density, weight, volume, composition, movements, distance, and its role in the solar system. Cartographers have made selenographic[14] maps with a precision equaling if not surpassing that of terrestrial maps. Photographers have given us incomparably beautiful pictures of our satellite.[15] In a word, then, we know all that the mathematical sciences, astronomy, geology, optics can tell us about the moon. But no one has ever established direct communication with her."

These words were greeted with involuntary expressions of surprise.

"May I remind you how some ardent spirits have embarked on imaginary voyages and claimed to have discovered the secrets of our satellite. In the seventeenth century a certain David Fabricius[16] boasted that with his own eyes he had seen the inhabitants of the moon. In 1649 a Frenchman, Jean Baudoin, published *Journey to the Moon by Domingo Gonsales, Spanish Adventurer.*[17] In the same period, Cyrano de Bergerac published his account of his celebrated expedition[18] which became so popular in France. Later, another

dog in a space probe (1957). And Verne, as we shall see, follows Godwin in this kind of experiment. On his first "manned flight," Gonsales flies over water to take advantage of what we call "splashdown," should anything go wrong. But his 25 "gansas" carry him to the moon: that's where they go on their annual migrations! There he studies lunar gravity: "if a man doe but spring upward, . . . he shall be able to mount 50 or 60 foote high. . . . ." In passages that influence Swift's *Gulliver*, Gonsales describes some moon-men as "twice the height of ours." Thus Godwin helped create the literary genre of the "space voyage" which dramatizes scientific theories about other worlds.

18. *celebrated . . . expedition* Cyrano de Bergerac's *The Comic History of the States and Empires of the Moon* (1657) is a satire on the very idea of space travel. Cyrano's first effort to reach the moon is based on the fact that the sun sucks up moisture. He ties about him "a great many glasses full of Dew." As the sun rises, "the Heat, which attracted them, carried me up. . . ." Fearing he will by-pass the moon, he tries to control his flight by breaking some of his glasses, but breaks too many and falls back to Earth. Then he builds a winged machine powered by a "spring." He crashes and, while he anoints his wounds with beef-marrow, soldiers drape his machine with firecrackers. Thus he unwittingly becomes, as Professor Marjorie Nicolson says, "the first flyer in literary history to reach the moon by means of a rocket ship." When the "combustible matter" is spent, he is still drawn moonward: Cyrano counts on the popular belief that as the moon wanes she sucks up the marrow of animals, with which he is anointed! Alternating between ingenuity and reliance on the supernatural, Cyrano gets back to Earth and mounts another expedition in *The Comic History of the States and Empires of the Sun* (1662).

19. *masterpiece in its time* In Bernard de Fontenelle's *Dialogues on the Plurality of Worlds* (1686), a philosopher takes a noblewoman on moonlight walks to teach her astronomy. They consider whether earthlings and moon-men might exchange visits. He warns that if she tries to fly moonward, she might find "the upper air not fit for respiration," and moon-men might "be able to swim on the exterior surface of our air, and through curiosity to see us, fish for us." Reflecting the popular excitement over new worlds that science is opening up, the lady replies: "I would throw myself into their nets to have the pleasure of seeing those who fished for me."

20. *astronomical observations* Herschel spent 1833–1838 surveying the southern skies, discovering 1,200 double and multiple stars and 1,300 new nebulae. In 1864 he has presented the Royal Society with a catalogue of 5,079 nebulae and clusters. Then in 1865 this novel has run serially in *Journal des Débats*. Readers and critics, laymen and scientists have been so impressed with Verne's graceful handling of the mathematics involved that the rumor is running through Paris that Herschel himself has supplied Verne with his calculations. One person who surely has mixed feelings about this is Henri Garcet, Verne's cousin, a mathematics professor, author of *Leçons Nouvelles de Cosmographie* (1853) and *Éléments de Mécanique* (1856), for it's Garcet who guarantees the mathematical accuracy of Verne's work.

21. *recognized as a hoax* The original story was published anonymously as a series in *The New York Sun* (*not* the *American*) in August–September 1835. The graphic account gained instant credibility: everyone knew Herschel and his telescope were at the Cape, everyone was expecting great discoveries, and the story was purportedly based on "advanced sheets" of an article Herschel supposedly had submitted to the *Edinburgh Journal of Science*. Perhaps not even Richard Adams Locke, *Sun* editor and author of the series, knew this *Journal* was defunct. Locke's "scoop" raised the circulation of the "Penny" *Sun* by 500% and put that paper on a firm financial basis. As soon as the series ended, the *Sun* reissued the story in *pamphlet* form: it sold 60,000 copies in one month and was widely translated. Herschel received copies at the Cape and finally accepted it as a joke.

22. *I mean Poe* His *Unparalleled Adventures of One Hans Pfaall* appeared in *The Southern Literary Messenger* just three weeks before the *Sun* perpetrated its hoax. Poe's story was frankly fictitious and humorous, but still much more scientific in its pretensions than Locke's. Pfaall (a pun on The Fall), a former Rotterdam bellows-maker, sends a message back home from, so he says, his new quarters on the moon. He has survived his trip through Outer Space because he had invented an apparatus for condensing the rarefied atmosphere. He landed on the satellite amidst a vast crowd of "ugly little people" without ears, one of whom he now sends to Earth as his emissary. At first impressed, the Rotterdammers soon suspect a trick. The earless, two-foot-high "messenger" may not be a moon-man after all: he resembles a certain dwarf reported missing from a nearby town.

When Locke's story followed fast on Poe's, Poe at once denounced it as a hoax: he felt it had been inspired by *Pfaall*. Other New York newspapers also sensed some connection. They reprinted the "Herschel" story and *Pfaall* side by side: had the *Sun* stolen Poe's ideas or had Poe written the *Sun* serial anonymously? In 1846 Poe assumed a more forgiving attitude when he recalled the situation in his article, "The Literati of New York," published in *Godey's Lady's Book*. He claimed that he had originally planned a second part of *Pfaall* which would have indulged his own "day dreams about the scenery of the moon." But after reading Locke's description of the lunar landscape, he left his own story "unfinished" because he felt Pfaall could add little to "the minute and authentic account of Sir John Herschel." Poe

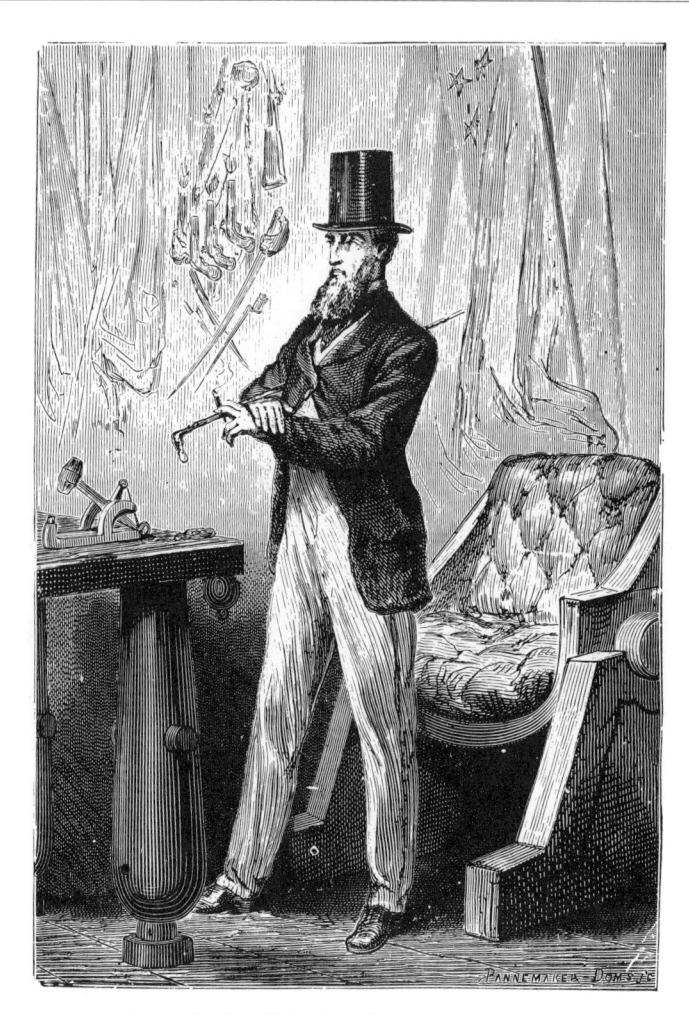

. . . a rare exception in the Gun Club—he still had all four limbs intact. President Barbicane as pictured in the first illustrated edition (1872).

Frenchman—Frenchmen are greatly preoccupied with the moon—one Fontenelle by name, wrote *Plurality of Worlds,* a masterpiece in its time.[19] But the march of science surpasses even masterpieces! In about 1835, a pamphlet, reprinted from an article in *The New York American,* recounted how Sir John Herschel, sent to the Cape of Good Hope to conduct some astronomical observations,[20] used a telescope, improved through internal lighting, that brought the moon to an apparent distance of 80 yards. He was supposed to have seen caves inhabited by hippopotami, green mountains fringed with golden lace, sheep with horns of ivory, white roe deer, and moon people with membranous wings like a bat's. This pamphlet, the work of an American named Locke, enjoyed a tremendous circulation. But it was soon recognized as a hoax,[21] and the French were the first to laugh.''

"Laugh at an American!" cried J. T. Maston. "That's it! That's our grounds for war!"

"Relax, my worthy friend. Before they laughed at him, the French had been completely duped by our compatriot. To bring this rapid sketch to an end, let me add that a certain Hans Pfaall of Rotterdam, ascending in a balloon inflated with a gas derived from nitrogen, a gas thirty-seven times lighter than hydrogen, reached the moon in nineteen days. Like all the earlier efforts, this voyage was purely imaginary, but it was the work of a popular American writer, a strange, moody genius. I mean Poe.''[22]

"Hurray for Edgar Poe!" cried the assembly, electrified by their president's speech.

"So much for those expeditions," he continued, "which I consider purely literary, since they provide no serious means for establishing relations with the luminary of the night. But I should add that some practical minds have tried to enter into serious communication with the moon. Several years ago, for example, a German geometrician suggested that a team of scientists be sent to the steppes of Siberia. There, on the vast plains, they would set up enormous geometric figures, outlined in luminous materials, among others the square of the hypotenuse (vulgarly called 'the ass's bridge' by the French). Every intelligent being, this geometrician maintained, would comprehend the scientific meaning of that figure. The Selenites,[23] if there are any, will indicate they have understood by responding with a similar figure. Once communication is established, it should be easy to create an alphabet that will make it possible to converse with the inhabitants of the moon. This is what the German geometrician[24] suggested, but his plans have never been carried out, and until now there has been no direct link between Earth and her satellite. Such an accomplishment has been reserved for the practical genius of the Americans: they can establish contact with the sidereal world. The method I shall propose is simple, easy, certain, infallible: and this is the main point of my speech."

A brouhaha, a tempest of exclamations greeted these words. There was not one listener who was not entranced by this orator.

"Quiet! Shhh!" came from every corner of the room.

When the storm had subsided, Barbicane resumed his discourse in a somewhat graver voice:

"You know what great progress we have made in ballistics, how we could have greatly improved our weapons if only the war had lasted. You know too that, generally speaking, the strength of cannon and the expansive force of gunpowder are unlimited. So, starting from this principle, I wonder whether, with a cannon large and strong enough to contain the explosion required, we could not send a projectile to the moon!"

A huge "Oh!" of stupefaction escaped from a thousand mouths. Then there was a moment of silence, like the profound stillness that precedes a thunderstorm. Indeed, the storm did come: a thunder of applause, of cries, of shouts, which made the auditorium tremble. The president tried to speak; he was unable to. It was fully ten minutes before he could make himself heard.

"Let me finish," he said calmly. "I have attacked this problem from every possible angle. I have verified my calculations. I find that any projectile aimed at the moon with an initial velocity of 12,000 yards per second[25] will arrive there out of scientific necessity. And so, my esteemed colleagues, it gives me great honor to propose to you that we go ahead with this little experiment!"[26]

admired the impetus the moon hoax had given to the "penny" press: "We are indebted to the Genius of Mr. Locke for one of the most important steps ever yet taken in the pathway of human progress."

23. *Selenites* "Inhabitants of the moon," Verne adds in a footnote.

24. *the German geometrician* Karl F. Gauss (1777–1855), also distinguished for his work in astronomy, proposed marking the Earth with the geometric figure used to demonstrate the Pythagorean theorem: a right-angled triangle with a square on each of its three sides. The lines could be formed by wide strips of dark forest, while the spaces enclosed could be planted with some bright-colored crop like wheat. But it was another German astronomer, Joseph J. von Littrow (1781–1840), who suggested such figures be illuminated. He proposed digging ditches in the Sahara Desert in the form of, say, equilateral triangles: they could be filled with water, topped with kerosene, and lighted at night.

In our time, astronomers assume civilizations would try to communicate by radio.

25. *12,000 yards per second* This is nearly seven miles per second, or more than 24,000 miles per hour. Barbicane has arrived at this figure by using a form of the "energy balance" equation:

$$\frac{GmM}{r_1} - \frac{GmM}{r_2} = \frac{1}{2}mv^2$$

where G is the universal gravitational constant, M the Earth's mass, m the projectile's mass, r_1 is Earth's radius, r_2 the moon's radius or distance from Earth in its perigee position (closest to Earth), and v is the projectile's speed. For a popular explanation of the "energy balance" equation, and a demonstration of how it can be used to calculate the velocity the projectile must attain, see Appendix A.

26. *this little experiment* Verne has launched his book with a brilliant satire on war and the military mind. And he has tackled a serious social question: How can we make good use of military talent when peace comes? How can we reconvert militarized industries to peacetime pursuits? Verne's 1865 solution precisely anticipates world-wide developments a century later. Then it will be the military-industrial complex, in both the U.S.S.R. and the U.S.A., who will channel some of their excess energies into launching the Space Age.

So it's about time to consider what it means that Verne is called a science-fiction writer who excels in scientific predictions, for here we have seen him in action as a superb social satirist and humorist, equally good at social prophecy. If he keeps that up, we must ask, why do the arbiters of public taste insist on their one-sided description of a many-sided talent?

CHAPTER III

The Effect of Barbicane's Speech

It is impossible to recapture the effect produced by the president's concluding words. What yelling! What screaming! Wave on wave of rumblings, hurrays, "hip! hip! hip!" and all the other onomatopoeias that thrive in American speech! The tumult, the brouhaha were indescribable. Mouths were shouting, hands were clapping, feet were stomping on the floor. If all the weapons in this artillery museum had been fired simultaneously, they could not have agitated the sound waves more violently. That should not surprise us. There are cannoneers who roar almost as loudly as their cannon.

Barbicane remained calm amid the enthusiastic clamor. Perhaps he was hoping to say a few more words to his colleagues, for his gestures called for silence, and he wore out his detonating bell. No one could hear it. Soon he was lifted out of his chair, carried out in triumph, and from the shoulders of his loyal comrades he was passed into the arms of the equally excited crowd waiting outside.

Nothing stops an American. The French often say that the word "impossible" is not in their language. But clearly there's been a mix-up in dictionaries. For it's in America that everything is easy, everything is simple, and as for mechanical difficulties, they die there before birth. No true Yankee could admit that any real obstacle stood in the way of Barbicane's project. "No sooner said than done."

The president's triumphal march lasted far into the night—a regular torchlight parade. Irishmen, Germans, Frenchmen, Scots, all the mixed nationalities[1] that make up the population of Maryland, were shouting in their native languages, and the vivas, the hurrahs, the bravos merged into indescribable élan.

As if it sensed it was the focus of attention, the moon shone that night with serene magnificence, its intense radiance eclipsing the surrounding stars. All Yankees directed their gaze at its glowing disk. Some waved their hands at it, others called it by the most tender names; some sized it up, others shook their fists at it. Before midnight an optician on Jones Falls Street[2] made his fortune selling telescopes. Some observers studied the luminary of the night through their opera glasses, as though she were a lady of high society. Others treated the moon with the familiarity of owners. It seemed as though pale Phoe-

---

1. *mixed nationalities* Verne is always excited by the heterogeneous character of the American people. French Acadians and Irishmen were among the first Catholics to settle in Baltimore. German immigrants provided the city's first butcher, brewers, and many of her first craftsmen.

2. *Jones Falls Street* Jones Falls is a stream that enters Baltimore from the north and flows into the North West Branch of the Patapsco River. Since 1788, there has been a road running the length of Jones Falls Valley, crisscrossing the stream on quaint stone bridges.

be[3] now belonged to these bold conquerors and was already a state in the Union. And yet, they were only planning to send a projectile to the moon, a rather brutal way of opening negotiations, even with a satellite, but one much in favor among civilized nations.

Midnight struck, and still enthusiasm ran high in all classes of the population: the politician, the scientist, the banker, the storekeeper, the stevedore, educated people as well as "greenhorns,"[4] all felt stirred to the very depths of their being. This was a national enterprise. The "Old Town," the "New Town,"[5] the wharves washed by the waters of the Patapsco,[6] the ships confined to their docks, all spilled forth their crowds drunk with joy—and even with gin or whiskey. Everyone was chattering, speechifying, arguing, holding forth, nodding approval, applauding, from the nonchalant gentleman stretched out on a banquette in the barroom with his mug of sherry-cobbler[7] to the boatman getting tipsy on his "thorough knock-me-down"[8] in the dark tavern of Fells Point.[9]

But by two A.M., things began to quiet down. President Barbicane

The president's triumphal march lasted far into the night—a regular torchlight parade. Engraving from the first illustrated edition (1872).

3. *pale Phoebe* A Romanticist's pet name for the moon: the word *Phoebe* means "the bright one" in Greek. Hesiod says Phoebe was one of the twelve Titans, or children of the primeval couple, Uranus and Ge. She was grandmother of Artemis, virgin goddess of the moon and the hunt.

4. *"greenhorns"* A "completely American expression that designates naive people," Verne explains in a footnote. But this simple definition overlooks the fact that in Barbicane's day the term is used to express contempt for recent immigrants, unassimilated and inexperienced in American ways. And it's not *completely* American: the *Oxford English Dictionary* traces it back to 1460. Originally it denoted a young animal with immature horns.

5. *"Old . . . New Town"* "Old Town," also known as Jones Town, lies to the east of Jones Falls, "New Town" to the west. In the French, Verne calls them *uptown* and *downtown*.

6. *the Patapsco* Baltimore is situated on an arm of the Patapsco River, a deepwater estuary of Chesapeake Bay.

7. *sherry-cobbler* "A mixture of rum, orange juice, sugar, cinnamon, and nutmeg," Verne adds in a footnote. "This brownish liquid is sucked up from mugs through a glass straw."

8. *"thorough knock-me-down"* In his text, Verne calls it *casse-poitrine,* raw liquor, and in a footnote he supplies the name we have used, describing it as "an appalling drink of the lower classes." In his 1874 version, Roth translates it as "bug juice," or inferior whiskey, a name taken from the tobacco-colored secretion of grasshoppers!

9. *Fells Point* A peninsula jutting into the North West Branch of the Patapsco, Fells Point is Baltimore's maritime section. Hundreds of ships launched here include the *Virginia,* the Continental Navy's first frigate, and the *Ann McKim,* the first true clipper ship, built for the China trade in 1832. And here are the saloons and flophouses that cater to sailors ashore, and the "cribs" where they can buy time with a woman.

10. *four railroads . . . four corners* "For Verne, the United States was above all others the country of railways," says Chesneaux. And Verne's audience knows of Baltimore as a pioneer in the use of track to link far-flung places. When other cities still thought of railways for local traffic, Baltimore started in 1830 to send a line all the way to the Ohio River. That year the B & O became the first U.S. railroad to operate as a common carrier; by 1852 it finally did reach the Ohio; in 1863 it established another first when it shifted 20,000 Union troops from the Potomac to Chattanooga: one of the earliest great military uses of rail transport.

11. *"Crescent City"* New Orleans derives this nickname from its location: the city is built along a bend in the Mississippi. For Verne's French readers, *"Crescent City"* has special associations. Founded in 1718 by the French governor of Louisiana, it was named after the *duc d'Orléans*. In Verne's day, as in ours, the city is world-renowned for its "Creole" character, the word designating descendants of the original Latin settlers. One of the city's six newspapers is published in French. The very phrase for which New Orleans is best known, *Mardi Gras,* means in French "fat Tuesday," last day before Lent.

12. *248,447 miles per second* "The speed of electricity," Verne says smugly in a footnote. The error is not his fault: there's still widespread confusion on this question in his day. Charles Wheatstone reported (1834) that the speed of electricity in copper wire was about one-and-a-half times the speed of light, or about 279,000 miles per second. Later investigators arrived at similar results. But H. L. Fizeau and E. Gounelle measured velocities (1850) ranging from one-third that of light in iron wire to nearly two-thirds in copper wire. Finally Gustav Kirchoff determined mathematically (1857) that the speed of electricity in a perfectly conducting aerial telegraph wire would be exactly the speed of light (186,335 miles per second). That means of course—since all conductors are *imperfect*—that the speed of electricity in a wire will always be below the speed of light.

Since we now believe nothing can travel faster than light, we might well wonder, how did Wheatstone and his followers manage to clock such fantastic speeds as the one Verne reports? It seems that to save space in measuring velocities over great distances, they would lay out a given length of wire in a close zigzag fashion or in coils or spirals. They assumed the electric impulse would travel *inside* the full length of the wire. They were unaware it could jump the gaps, taking the shortest route possible. Hence they gave the current credit for traveling many more thousands of miles per second than it actually did. Fizeau and Gounelle, however, conducted their tests on telegraph wire strung out in straight lines between distant cities. Since the current could take no short cuts, they were reckoning its speed from the true distance involved, and their results varied only with the type of wire used. Unfortunately, Verne has put his faith in a Wheatstone-type experiment.

13. *ten times . . . France* Verne is comparing only the States proper with France; their total area at the time is almost 2,000,000 square miles compared with France's 204,091. If Verne were to include the Territories—from Arizona to Montana—the area would total 3,000,000 square miles, almost fifteen times that of France.

. . . the Smithsonian Institution [made] *offers of financial and professional assistance.* Photograph of the main facade of the Smithsonian Building, in Washington, taken just after the Civil War. Courtesy of the Smithsonian Institution.

was able at last to get home, bruised, sore, and exhausted. Not even Hercules could have withstood such enthusiasm. Little by little the crowds thinned out of the squares and avenues. The four railroads that converge on Baltimore—from the Ohio, the Susquehanna, Philadelphia, and Washington—scattered the heterogeneous masses back to the four corners [10] of the United States. The town settled down to comparative quiet.

It would be a mistake though to think that Baltimore was the only city to enjoy such high spirits on that memorable night. All the big cities in the country—New York, Boston, Albany, Washington, Richmond, the "Crescent City," [11] Charleston, Mobile—from Texas to Massachusetts, from Michigan to Florida—they all took part in the general delirium. All the 30,000 corresponding members of the Gun Club had received copies of their president's letter, and those unable to make the trip to Baltimore were waiting with equal impatience for the celebrated announcement of October 5. And so, as fast as the words left the mouth of Barbicane, they were telegraphed to all the states of the Union at a speed of 248,447 miles per second. [12] Hence one can say with certainty that all America—ten times as large as France [13]—gave out with one single hurrah, and that 25,000,000 hearts, bursting with pride, beat as one.

The following day, 1,500 dailies, weeklies, twice-monthlies, and monthlies [14] began to study the project: they examined it from the physical, meteorological, economic, and moral points of view, they delved into the political consequences and the long-range implications for civilization. They wondered whether the moon was a completely developed world or if it was still undergoing any transformation. Was it like the Earth before the Earth had an atmosphere? [15] What does the other side of the moon look like, the side invisible to terrestrial man? True, the project called only for sending a projectile to the moon, but everyone saw that as just the first of a whole series of experiments.

Everyone hoped for the day when America would penetrate the last secrets of that mysterious disk. Some writers even wondered whether the impending conquest of the moon would disturb the balance of power in Europe.

Not one periodical doubted that the Barbicane plan would succeed. Journals, bulletins, newsletters, magazines published by the learned, literary, and religious societies all stressed the advantages of the project. The Society of Natural History in Boston, the American Society of Sciences and Arts in Albany, the Geographical and Statistical Society of New York, The American Philosophical Society[16] in Philadelphia, the Smithsonian Institution[17] in Washington sent the Gun Club a thousand letters of congratulations backed up with offers of financial and professional assistance.

Surely no project ever attracted such widespread support. No one expressed any serious doubts, hesitation, or fears. In Europe, and especially in France, the idea of sending a projectile to the moon would have been greeted with jokes, caricatures, and derisive songs. But in America, no one would think of satirizing such a project: and if he did, all the "life-preservers"[18] in the world would not have saved him from the general indignation. There are certain things one does not laugh at in the New World. From this day on, Impey Barbicane became one of the leading citizens of the United States, a kind of Washington of Science. One typical incident will demonstrate how an entire populace can suddenly become devoted to one man.

Several days after the famous meeting of the Gun Club, the director of an English theatrical company, on tour in the states, announced that

The largest room in the Smithsonian Building, the Great Hall, with its Victorian display cases, as photographed just after the Civil War. Courtesy of the Smithsonian Institution.

14. *1,500 . . . monthlies* With this big number, Verne reminds his reader that the nineteenth century, thanks to telegraphy and advances in printing technology, has seen a phenomenal increase in periodical literature. But overall totals depend on the types of periodicals one wants to count. The 1860 U.S. census gives a grand total of 4,501 "newspapers," including weeklies of many types Verne might not have in mind: sewing and gardening magazines, for example.

15. *before . . . Earth had . . . atmosphere* That is, after its crust had solidified but before enough gases had escaped from its interior to form the "air." Some cosmogonists believe this "air" is the Earth's second atmosphere. In its protoplanetary stage, they say, Earth was covered with an envelope of hydrogen, helium, methane, and other gases. This was blown off into Outer Space, leaving Earth as a solid rocky body ready to produce a new atmosphere.

16. *American Philosophical Society* This is the oldest organization on Verne's list. In 1734 Benjamin Franklin called for "constant correspondence" among "virtuosos," as men of science were then called, and as a result the Society was soon functioning in Philadelphia. In Barbicane's day it is well known for its museum and library.

17. *Smithsonian Institution* Verne likes the Smithsonian because its Secretary (director), the renowned physicist Joseph Henry, sends out to every scientific organization in Europe copies of *Contributions to Knowledge*. These are Smithsonian essays based on fresh and original research hitherto unreported in the literature of science. When he assumed the Secretaryship in 1846, Henry established a policy of supporting work not being carried on elsewhere. One of his first projects was publication of a valuable, expensive memoir on the archaeology of the Indians of the Mississippi Valley. He has also equipped astronomical expeditions, set up a network of 500 weather observers, and extended aid to linguists studying the grammar of the Yoruba (African) language.

Congress chartered the Smithsonian as a private institution to carry out the will of the English scientist James Smithson (1765–1829), who had bequeathed $515,169 to the United States for "the increase and diffusion of knowledge." The principal is on deposit in the Treasury; the SI draws the interest. In Verne's day, the spacious nine-tower Smithsonian Building, completed in 1858, houses a library, a museum, an art gallery, rooms for exhibits and experiments, bedrooms for scientists, and an east-wing apartment for Henry, his wife, and four children.

18. *"life-preservers"* "A pocket weapon made of flexible whalebone and a metal ball," Verne adds in a footnote. Sometimes cane is used for the handle, which is made flexible to increase the force of impact. At least the striking end, the ball, usually made of lead, is enclosed in leather. As the name *life-preserver* suggests, it is considered a weapon for self-defense. But if a member of the lower classes is caught with one, it might be seen as evidence he is a robber.

Today this weapon is better known as a blackjack: black for the color of the leather cover, jack as a colloquial term for an instrument.

19. *popular demand* Verne taps his 1865 readers' memories of what *popular demand* means in Baltimore. For example: In 1812, two riots over Congress' declaration of war on Britain; one of many casualties was Colonel Henry Lee of Revolutionary War fame, father of a five-year-old named Robert E. In 1838, a week of riots triggered by the failure of the Bank of Maryland; it took a force of 3,000 to restore order. In 1839, the anti-Catholic "Nunnery Riot." In the 1840s, rival fire companies frequently slugging it out at the scene of a fire. In the 1850s, major political parties spawning armed street gangs in every ward: the Eighth Ward Democrats, for example, being "represented" by the "Bloody Eights," and the Know Nothings sending out the "Plug Uglies" to beat up recent immigrants. In 1856, 10 dead, 140 hurt in the Election Day riot in Belair Market. In April 1861, armed civilians assaulting a Massachusetts regiment changing trains in Baltimore: four Blues, thirteen Baltimoreans dead, and Lincoln declaring martial law. So Verne adds one more riot to a list that runs into the hundreds.

20. *As You Like It* Verne has enjoyed a lifelong fondness for Shakespeare. In Paris in 1849, barely able to make ends meet on an allowance of 100 francs a month, he splurged 16 francs on a complete Shakespeare he found in an off-boulevard bookstall. "Cutting" his law class, he sat down on a boulevard bench, and lost himself in a play. Because of this extravagance, he had to live on dried prunes for three days. When he could afford a restaurant again, he read Shakespeare over dinner. On his 1859 trip to Britain with the composer Aristide Hignard, he had only two nights in London and spent one of them seeing *Macbeth*. In 1861, when the two friends, who had collaborated on five operettas, traveled to Scandinavia, they discussed Shakespeare continually: Hignard was working on his opera *Hamlet*. In the 1870s, Verne will mount two busts in his library: Moliere and Shakespeare. Verne's British biographer, Kenneth Allott, in his wise-guy style, will see these as "insignia of his position like the stone griffins at a gentleman's park gates." But Allott prefers line-by-line witticism to long-range understanding. Verne's upper-floor apartment in his home in Amiens is not furnished to create a public image. It is his absolutely private retreat, reflecting his personal needs and values. Shakespeare is part of both.

An 1858 wood engraving of Broadway, Fells Point. Courtesy of the Maryland Historical Society.

Much Ado about Nothing would open at a theater in Baltimore. But the people of the town saw in this title a snide allusion to Barbicane's project. They invaded the theater, ripped up the seats, and demanded that the unlucky director change his playbill. A man of wit, he yielded to popular demand.[19] He replaced the ill-chosen comedy with *As You Like It*.[20] For weeks afterward, he packed them in: Standing Room Only.

. . . a theatre in Baltimore was probably the Holliday Street Theatre. Detail from *View of Baltimore,* lithographed and published by E. Weber & Co. about 1848. Courtesy of the Maryland Historical Society.

CHAPTER IV

Reply from the Cambridge Observatory

Barbicane did not allow all this acclaim to distract him for a moment. Without delay, he conferred with his colleagues in the boardroom of the Gun Club. After some discussion, they agreed on the next step: they needed the advice of professional astronomers. Then, once they had comprehended the astronomical part of their enterprise, they could tackle the mechanical problems involved. They were determined to check every last detail to ensure the success of this grand experiment.

They drew up a letter posing a series of highly technical questions and addressed it to the observatory in Cambridge, Massachusetts. This town, where the first university in the United States had been founded, is justly famous for its observatory. It boasts scientists of the highest caliber, and it houses the powerful telescope that enabled Bond to resolve the nebula of Andromeda,[1] and Clark to discover a satellite revolving around Sirius.[2] No wonder then that the Gun Club turned to that celebrated institution with complete confidence.

President Barbicane waited impatiently for two days until he received the astronomers' reply. It was couched in these terms:

From the Director of the Cambridge Observatory to the President of the Gun Club in Baltimore.

Cambridge, October 7

Upon receipt of your esteemed favor of the 6th instant, addressed to the Cambridge Observatory in the name of the members of the Gun Club, our staff convened at once and judged it expedient[3] to reply as follows:

The questions you have posed for our consideration are these:

1. Is it possible to send a projectile to the moon?
2. What is the exact distance that separates the Earth from its satellite?
3. Once the projectile has been given the initial velocity required, how long will it take to travel that distance? Consequently, at what moment should it be fired in order to hit the moon at a predetermined point?
4. Exactly when will the moon be in the best position to receive the projectile?
5. At what point in the sky should the cannon that fires the projectile be aimed?

1. *Bond . . . Andromeda* The comet of 1843 so excited the citizens of Boston that they decided to buy the best telescope available for the "Observatory at Cambridge," as the Harvard Observatory was usually called. They ordered a 15-inch lens from Merz and Mahler of Munich, successors to the famous Fraunhofer firm. Cambridge's new telescope, one of the two largest refractors made up until that time, was installed in 1847. The public's investment paid off immediately. The observatory's director, William Cranch *Bond* (1789–1859), became the first to "partially resolve" *Andromeda,* that is, to be able to see some of its stars as separate entities (1847). He and his son, George P. Bond, went on to discover Hyperion, a new satellite of Saturn (1848), and then a third (comparatively dark) ring lying inside Saturn's two bright rings (1849). The elder Bond was elected to the Royal Astronomical Society, the first American so honored.

2. *Clark . . . Sirius* Bostonian Alvan Clark

Alvan Clark, who discovered *a satellite revolving around Sirius*. This portrait hangs in the Cambridge Observatory. Courtesy of the Harvard College Observatory.

is a successful portrait-painter who in his forties became interested in making telescopes, founded Clark and Sons, and, by a lucky accident, has become a famous astronomer. In 1862 the Clarks, ready to test their first large lens, 18½ inches wide, turned it on the bright star Sirius. They thus became the first actually to see the "Dog Star's" tiny white companion-star whose existence had been detected mathematically in 1844. That is, Sirius was known to follow a wavy instead of a straight path, and this had indicated that her motion must be influenced by a fellow-traveler, what Verne calls *a satellite revolving around* her. For this long-awaited visible proof that Sirius actually is a binary star *Clark* has won the French Academy of Science's Lalande Prize in 1863.

3. *expedient* Continuing his satire on the American way of life, Verne adds a footnote here: "The English text reads 'expedient,' which is absolutely untranslatable into French." And so he renders it *à propos*. The word expedient has added to its original meanings—*appropriate; serving to expedite, facilitate*—such connotations *as serving one's own interest*.

4. *perigee . . . apogee* With their Greek and Latin education, Verne's original readers are more apt to make these connections instantly. The classical roots mean, literally, *peri:* near; *apo:* away from; *ge:* earth. And since geometry is still required in school they know that an ellipse is an oval figure whose curve is determined by two foci (in contrast to a circle whose curve is measured from one focus, the center). Since Earth is at one of the foci of its satellite's elliptical orbit, it is "off-center," and this eccentricity creates the different *peri-* and *apo-*gee distances.

5. *247,552 . . . 218,657 miles* Today's astronomers say: apogee 252,000, perigee 226,000. Throughout Verne's life, as they are refining their techniques of measurement, different astronomers give different figures, ranging, for apogee, up to 253,000, for perigee, up to 222,000. In all such matters here, Verne is faced with a much slighter version of his earlier dilemma in choosing a suitable figure for the speed of electricity. His accuracy, then, must be judged solely in terms of the internal consistency among the figures he does choose. Those choices, as we soon see, are naturally influenced by artistic considerations.

6. *point you are aiming at* This is Verne's first major scientific prediction in this book. In 1969, one hundred and five years after he writes this passage, Apollo 11 will also take four days to reach the moon. Of course, time of flight depends on initial speed; unmanned Lunik II, for example, will make the trip in only 35 hours. But Verne is correct not only for his own fiction but for future fact. His projectile, launched at his initial velocity of 12,000 yards per second, properly aimed, will reach the moon four or five days later. And this does

An 1851 drawing of the Cambridge Observatory. Courtesy of the Harvard College Observatory.

6. What will be the position of the moon at the moment the projectile leaves the Earth?'

In answer to the first question: Is it possible to send a projectile to the moon?

Yes, so long as you give the projectile an initial velocity of 12,000 yards per second. Our calculations indicate that this velocity will suffice. As we move away from the Earth, the force of gravity diminishes in inverse ratio to the square of the distance. That is to say, at three times a given distance, the force of gravity is nine times as small. Consequently, the weight of the projectile will decrease rapidly, and it will drop to zero when the projectile reaches the point where the attraction of the moon equals that of the earth. And that is exactly what will happen when the projectile has traveled forty-seven fifty-seconds of the distance. At that point the projectile will have no weight at all, and if it passes that point, it will fall toward the moon in response to lunar gravity alone. Thus the theoretical possibility of your experiment has been fully demonstrated; but of course practical results will depend on the power and efficacy of the equipment you devise.

In regard to the second question: What is the exact distance that separates the Earth from its satellite?

In its trip around the Earth, the moon describes not a circle but an ellipse, and our globe occupies one of the foci. Hence the moon is sometimes nearer to the Earth, sometimes further away, or, in astronomical terms, sometimes in perigee, sometimes in apogee.[4] Now the variations in its distance are too great to be overlooked. In fact, at its apogee, the moon is 247,552 miles (99,640 four-kilometer leagues) away, but at its perigee only 218,657 miles[5] (88,010 leagues). This gives you a difference of 28,895 miles (11,630 leagues), or about one-ninth the greatest distance. Hence it is the perigeal distance which should serve as the basis for your calculations.

Now for your third question: Once the projectile is given the initial velocity required, how long will it take to reach the moon? At what moment should it be fired in order to hit the moon at a predetermined point?

If the projectile could maintain its initial velocity of 12,000 yards per second, it could reach its destination in about nine hours. But actually its velocity will be continuously decreasing. Our calculations show that the projectile will take 300,000 seconds, or eighty-three hours and twenty minutes, to reach the point where the moon's gravitational force equals that of the Earth. From that point the projectile will fall onto the moon in 50,000 seconds, or thirteen hours, fifty-three minutes, and twenty seconds. It is necessary then to fire the projectile ninety-seven hours, thirteen minutes, and twenty seconds before the moon arrives at the point you are aiming at.[6]

Concerning your fourth question: When will the moon be in the best position to receive the projectile?

From what we have said above, it is clear you should choose a time when the moon is at its perigee. But it should also be a time when the moon is crossing the zenith,[7] because that would further shorten the trip by a distance equal to the Earth's radius, or 3,919 miles. The final trajectory then need be only 214,976 miles[8] (86,410 leagues). However, although the moon reaches its perigee every month, it is not always at the zenith at that moment. Only at long intervals are both conditions met at the same time. And you should wait for this coincidence.[9] Fortunately, at midnight, December 4 of next year,[10] the moon will meet both requirements: then it will be at its perigee, that is, at its shortest distance from the Earth, and at the same time it will also pass through the zenith.

In reply to your fifth question: At what point in the sky should you aim the cannon that fires your projectile?

It follows naturally from our discussion above that you must aim the cannon at the zenith: thus the trajectory will be perpendicular to the plane of the horizon and the projectile will be able to escape from gravity much more rapidly. But to be able to aim at the moon at the zenith, your gunsite must be situated in a latitude no greater than the moon's declination: that is, the site must be between 0° and 28° of latitude, north or south.[11] At any other latitude, you would have to fire at an angle and that could dim your chances of success.

William Cranch Bond, first director of the Cambridge Observatory, from the 1849 portrait by Cephas G. Thompson. Courtesy of the Harvard College Observatory.

become a fairly typical initial speed for manned flights to our satellite.

7. *crossing the zenith* ". . . that point in the sky," Verne says in a footnote, "situated perpendicularly above the head of an observer."

8. *214,976 miles* But if 3,919 miles are subtracted from Verne's earlier value for the perigeal distance (218,657), then the "final trajectory" should be 214,738. It's easy to see that such slips—here a discrepancy of 238 miles—develop as Verne vacillates between one observatory's figures and another's. For example, some nineteenth-century authorities give not 3,919 miles for the Earth's radius but 3,960, which also proves to be today's value.

9. *wait for this coincidence* According to Professor David Woodruff, our technical adviser, this coincidence isn't absolutely necessary. The Gun Club does not need the moon at perigee, he says: the minor difference in velocity required to hit the moon at apogee or perigee is not that significant. Incidentally, to check out such technical details in this book, Dr. Woodruff worked in the library at the *Observatory in Cambridge, Massachusetts*.

10. *next year* Note that Verne does not specify which year that will be. First of all, as he writes this chapter (probably in 1864) he cannot be sure when the Civil War will end, and he wants to set his action *after* the war. Then, the exact years of such actual coincidence (e.g., 1876) would not suit his post-war needs at all. Finally, of course, he is establishing that limbo-in-timelessness that will become characteristic of the genre he has invented.

11. *0° and 28° . . . north or south* Verne footnotes this: "In fact, only in those global regions between the equator and the twenty-eighth parallel does the moon at its highest point reach the zenith; beyond the twenty-eighth degree, the moon is further from the zenith the closer one gets to the poles."

The dome of "The Great Refractor" at the Cambridge Observatory. Photograph courtesy of the Harvard College Observatory.

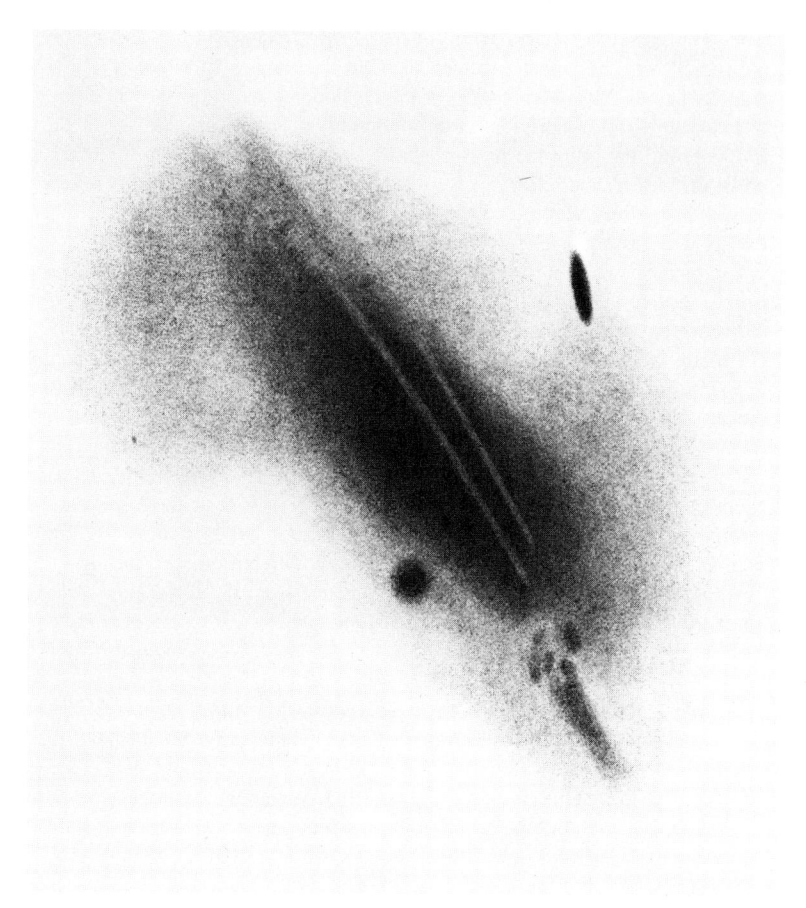

. . . the nebula of Andromeda as pictured in an 1848 paper by George P. Bond, assistant at the Cambridge Observatory. Courtesy of the Harvard College Observatory.

12. *another eleven degrees* But Dr. David Woodruff finds that only six degrees should be added to adjust for the rotation of the Earth.

13. *in round figures* Now that Verne himself uses this phrase, we may note this is the fourth time he has "rounded off" his figures: *12,000 yards* per second for *initial velocity, 300,000* plus *50,000 seconds* for the two stages of the trip to the moon, and now *64 degrees,* all convenient round sums. Those for the *350,000 seconds* in transit especially illustrate the literary or dramatic value of such rounding off, not to mention the mnemonic and didactic value: Verne is, after all, interested mainly in painless teaching of a general method, not of exhaustive details. In Appendix A, we suggest one way such rounding-off might have been accomplished. We cannot doubt for a moment that Verne has chosen his figures—from the various ones offered by different experts—with this literary, educational simplification in mind. And since there is no precedent, and no chance of competition for a long time to come, he faces only a tiny risk of criticism, a worthwhile risk for his dramatic purposes. Note finally that Garcet goes along with these minor simplifications, and the general results (as we reviewed them in our note on Herschel) prove Verne and Garcet to be justified.

In regard to your sixth and last question: Exactly where will the moon be at the moment the projectile leaves the Earth?

The moon advances thirteen degrees, ten minutes, and thirty-five seconds per day. Thus the projectile should be launched into space when the moon is four times this distance from the zenith: that is to say, fifty-two degrees, forty-two minutes, and twenty seconds, or the distance the moon will travel while the projectile is in flight. But you must also consider the fact that the rotation of the Earth would deflect the projectile from its course. By the time your projectile reached the moon, this deviation would be equal to sixteen times the Earth's radius, which, reckoned on the moon's orbit, would give you another eleven degrees [12] that you must add to the number already obtained, making a total—in round figures [13]—of sixty-four degrees. In other words, you must fire your projectile directly overhead when the moon is still sixty-four degrees from the perpendicular.

Thus we have answered the questions posed by the members of the Gun Club.

In summary:

1. You must place your cannon somewhere between 0° and 28° latitude, north or south.

2. You must aim it at the zenith.

3. You must give the projectile an initial velocity of 12,000 yards per second.

4. You must fire the projectile on December 1 one hour, thirteen minutes, and twenty seconds before midnight.

5. It should reach the moon four days later, at midnight of December 4,[14] at the moment the moon passes through the zenith.

The members of the Gun Club must get down to their work without delay, because if they miss their chance on December 4 of next year, they will have to wait eighteen years and eleven days before they will again find the moon in the same coincidence of perigee and zenith.

The staff of the Cambridge Observatory place themselves entirely at your disposal in all matters of theoretical astronomy, and with this letter[15] they add their good wishes to those extended by all America.

For the staff:

J. M. Belfast[16]

Director
Cambridge Observatory

... *the powerful telescope of the observatory in Cambridge,* a twin of the instrument used at the Russian Imperial Observatory at Pulkovo. Courtesy of the Harvard College Observatory.

14. *midnight of December 4* But if they *must fire the projectile on December 1, one hour, thirteen minutes, and twenty seconds before midnight,* and if the trip will take ninety-seven hours, thirteen minutes, and twenty seconds, then they would arrive *at midnight of December 5.* Or, if it is absolutely necessary to make their rendezvous with the moon at *midnight of December 4,* they would have to leave on the night of November 30–December 1, which is probably what Verne actually has in mind. The novel is published first in a magazine and then as a book before anyone catches the error, which speaks well at least for the way Verne's narrative sweeps the reader along.

Tongue in cheek, Verne will correct the error in the "Preliminary Chapter" of his sequel, *Round the Moon* (1870). "They could not arrive on the lunar disk," he will say, "until midnight of December 5, when the moon would be full, and not on December 4, as a few misinformed newspapers had announced."

15. *with this letter* Verne is fond of the letter as a novelistic device. It gives his readers a chance to *imagine* the circumstances of both the writing and reading of the letter, and it then provides some conflict as the characters discuss, interpret, or work out the message. So far, we have such effects (1) from Barbicane's notice about the meeting of October 5 and now (2) from the Observatory's memorandum; Verne will reap even more dramatic results (3) from a telegram in Chapter XVII. In *Twenty Thousand Leagues* he has three men thrown into comic confusion by a simple letter of invitation.

16. *J. M. Belfast* The actual Director of the Harvard Observatory at the time Verne is writing is George P. Bond, junior member of the father-son team that made the Observatory world-famous. He had succeeded his father in that post in 1859.

CHAPTER V

The Romance of the Moon

1. *depths of the skies* In 1865 all Verne can say about the original materials of the universe is that they were scattered through space. Today science knows more about where these *myriads of atoms* came from. In the 1920s astronomers discovered that all the galaxies are flying apart from each other. They concluded that the universe is expanding, that all its materials had burst forth from a highly condensed "egg" some ten or twenty billion years ago. According to this notion, called the "Big Bang" theory, the galaxies would gradually fade away, the universe become devoid of matter, energy, and life.

Later several scientists suggested that this expansion might regularly be offset by creation of fresh matter which fills up the spaces left by the spreading galaxies. Their theory of a "Steady State Universe" proved to be untenable.

A third group of scientists offered a reinterpretation of the "Big Bang" which is now a serious rival of the original theory. Suppose gravity slows down the expansion? In that case, the scattering matter would fall back upon itself, condensing once more into that primordial egg. Finally it would compress to the point where it would explode anew, expand, and then contract again. In other words, this would be an "Oscillating Universe." In our time, then, the big questions are: Was there only one "Big Bang," one unique "creation"? Or was the explosion that produced our world, our history, just one in an infinite series of explosions?

To find the answer astronomers must determine how much matter there is in the universe. They now estimate it contains approximately one atom for every 88 gallons of space. But they need to know the exact figure. For if there's less matter than this, then the total gravitational effect would be too weak to hold the galaxies together: they would indeed be dispersing forever into an "open" universe. And if there's more than one atom per 88 gallons, then the mutual attraction of all matter combined would suffice to check the expansion. This would trigger the contraction phase of a cyclical, "closed" universe.

When all matter was still in chaos, an observer blessed with infinite vision and standing at the unknown center around which the universe gravitates, would have seen all space filling with myriads of atoms. Gradually, over the centuries, he would have witnessed a change as these vagrant atoms came to obey a law of attraction. Combining chemically according to their affinities, they grouped themselves into molecules and formed those nebulous masses sprinkled throughout the depths of the skies.[1]

These masses were quickly pulled into a rotary motion around their central point. This center, composed of molecules loosely arranged, began to rotate and condense. Obeying the immutable laws of mechanics, the rotation increased in speed as the volume decreased through condensation. These two actions continued, and as a result there came into being a principal star, center of the nebulous mass.

Watching carefully, the observer would have seen the other molecules in the mass behaving like the central star, growing denser through gradually accelerating rotation, gravitating around the center in the form of countless stars. A nebula had formed. Astronomers now count almost five thousand such nebulae.[2]

One of these—known to men as the Milky Way—contains eighteen million stars, each one the center of a solar system.

Now if the observer had focused on one of the most modest and least brilliant of the eighteen million stars—a star of the fourth magnitude, known to arrogant mankind[3] as the sun—he would have witnessed in succession all the phenomena that have produced the universe.

He would have seen the sun, still in a gaseous state and composed of moving molecules, turning on its axis to complete its work of concentration. This motion, faithful to the laws of mechanics, accelerated with the diminution in volume. At a certain point in time, centripetal force—which tends to pull molecules toward the center—would have been overpowered by centrifugal force.

Then another phenomenon would have unfolded before the observer's eyes. Molecules situated at the sun's equator, escaping like the stone from a slingshot when the strap is snapped, formed concentric rings around the sun, resembling those around Saturn. In their turn, these rings of cosmic matter, whirling around the central mass, broke up and decomposed into secondary nebulosities, that is to say, into planets.

If our observer had concentrated all his attention on these planets, he would have seen them behaving exactly as the sun had behaved: giving birth to one or more cosmic rings, sources of those bodies we now call satellites.

Going then from atom to molecule, from molecule to nebulous mass, from nebulous mass to nebula, from nebula to principal star, from principal star to sun, from sun to planet, and from planet to satellite, we have the whole series of transformations that celestial bodies have undergone since the earliest days of the universe.[4]

Our sun seems lost in the boundless spaces of the starry universe, but, according to present-day scientific theories, it is definitely fixed in the nebula known as the Milky Way. It is the center of a solar system, and however small it seems to be up there in the ethereal regions, it is nevertheless enormous, for it is 1,400,000 times larger[5] than the Earth. Around it gravitate eight planets which issued from its entrails

Saturn as seen by Verne's space travelers in *Hector Servadac* (1878).

With their giant earth-based radio telescopes and their orbiting observatories tuned in to radiations from the *depths of the skies,* today's astronomers expect to come up with the right answer in short order. Not only cosmologists but theologians and philosophers are waiting. For if the universe is expanding eternally from a single "Big Bang," this would correspond to the Divine Creation, the Genesis that Western religions postulate. But if history comprises a succession of "Bangs"—what Malcolm Browne of *The New York Times* calls "an infinitely repeating series of accidental bounces"—that model could, as he points out, "be cited in argument against the Biblical version of the creation."

2. *five thousand such nebulae* And today they reckon them in the hundreds of millions. And they call them galaxies. We shall update enough of Verne's figures to emphasize a very Vernean message: scientists, thanks to improvements in their instruments and techniques, are constantly refining their measurements and expanding their scope.

3. *arrogant mankind* Verne's point—that astronomical discoveries make us increasingly aware of Earth's modest position in space—is even more valid today: astronomers now reckon that *the Milky Way* alone contains one hundred billion stars.

4. *transformations . . . universe* Verne has given his readers a neat nine-paragraph summary of the cosmogonic theory of his day known as the Kant-Laplace Nebular Hypothesis. After this novel appears (1865), this theory will go into a long eclipse, only to reemerge brighter than ever in our time.

The philosopher Immanuel Kant suggested (1755) that the solar system had originated in a whirling mass of cold gas and dust which had condensed and then split up into sun, planets, and moons. Later, working independently, Pierre Simon, Marquis de Laplace, advanced a similar concept in his popular *Exposition du Système du Monde* (1796). Laplace differed in some details: his system began with a hot gaseous cloud that developed the planets before the sun. But since the two savants agreed on the essential idea—that the solar system arose out of condensation of a gaseous nebula—their followers blended their notions into "the" Kant-Laplace Hypothesis.

Later this Nebular Hypothesis was challenged by the English physicist James Clerk Maxwell and finally superseded by Sir James Jeans' theory—which prevailed for the first third of the twentieth century—that the planets had been ripped out of the sun by a close-passing star. Now this had serious implications for the position of life in the universe. The Nebular Hypothesis, as Verne makes clear, suggests that planets, and hence life, can develop routinely wherever there are nebulae. Protoplasm and human intelligence are not necessarily alone in an otherwise lifeless vastness. The Jeans theory, on the other hand, makes life

Portrait of Marquis de Laplace, whose *Système du Monde* (1796) advanced the Nebular Hypothesis.

in the early days of creation. These bodies, in the order of their nearness to the sun, are Mercury, Venus, Earth, Mars, Jupiter, Saturn, Uranus, Neptune.[6] In addition, there are numerous smaller bodies that orbit between Mars and Jupiter, perhaps the debris of a planet shattered into thousands of pieces, ninety-seven of which have so far been sighted by telescope.[7]

Several of these attendants, which the sun keeps in their elliptic orbits by the great law of gravitation, have satellites of their own. Uranus has eight, Saturn eight, Jupiter four, Neptune perhaps has three, Earth has one;[8] this last, one of the least important in the solar system, we call the moon: and this was what the daring American genius now proposed to conquer.

From the beginning, because she is nearer and presents a spectacle of rapidly recurrent changes, the moon vied with the sun for man's attention. But watching the sun is hard on the eyes. Its dazzling splendor soon forces its admirers to look away.

Pale Phoebe is more humane, allowing us to observe her modest grace at our leisure; she is gentle on the eye, unostentatious, although she sometimes eclipses her brother, the splendid Apollo,[9] while never being eclipsed by him. The Mohammedans, feeling the debt of gratitude they owed to this friend of Earth, based the length of their month on the moon's revolution.[10]

In ancient times, there were special cults devoted to this chaste goddess. The Egyptians called her Isis; the Phoenicians named her Astarte; the Greeks worshiped her under the name of Phoebe, daughter of Latona and Jupiter, and they attributed her eclipses to her mysterious visits to the handsome Endymion. As mythology tells us, the Nemean lion roamed the lunar countryside before he appeared on Earth.[11] And as Plutarch tells us, the poet Agesianax celebrated the soft eyes, charming nose, and lovely mouth formed by the luminous parts of the adorable Selene.

rare if not unique, since near-collisions of stars are themselves very rare. Man, it seemed after all, was alone. But by World War Two the Jeans theory was abandoned and the Nebular Hypothesis regained favor. "Its essential premise . . . has withstood the test of time," say I. S. Shklovskii and Carl Sagan in *Intelligent Life in the Universe* (1966), "and we can find their basic idea in all contemporary theories of planetary origin."

But followers of the modern Nebular Hypothesis no longer believe the planets condensed from vapor: they see this as impossible. They do believe that solid materials stick together in the nebula to form the planets. And while astronomers are still not sure which came first, suns or planets, they have been able to extend "the" theory in several ways. For example, they now believe that solar systems can be recycled. Old stars can explode, spray their matter into space, and this old material can be reassimilated into new solar systems. Earth itself was probably formed out of such recycled matter maybe five billion years ago.

5. *1,400,000 times larger* That is, larger by volume. Today astronomers say the sun's volume is 1,300,000 times greater than Earth's.

6. *eight planets . . . Neptune* A ninth planet, Pluto, will not be discovered for sixty-five years after Verne is writing. The last two planets on his list have been discovered recently enough to help make astronomy a sensational subject in his day. Frederick William Herschel (1738–1822), father of the John Herschel we've already discussed, found Uranus in 1781, and Johann Gottfried Galle (1812–1910) discovered Neptune in 1846.

7. *ninety-seven . . . by telescope* Existence of the ninety-seventh asteroid, or minor planet called Klotho, will not be officially verified for

"Jupiter, Giant of the Solar System," as pictured by astronomer Richard A. Proctor in his best-selling *Other Worlds Than Ours* (1870).

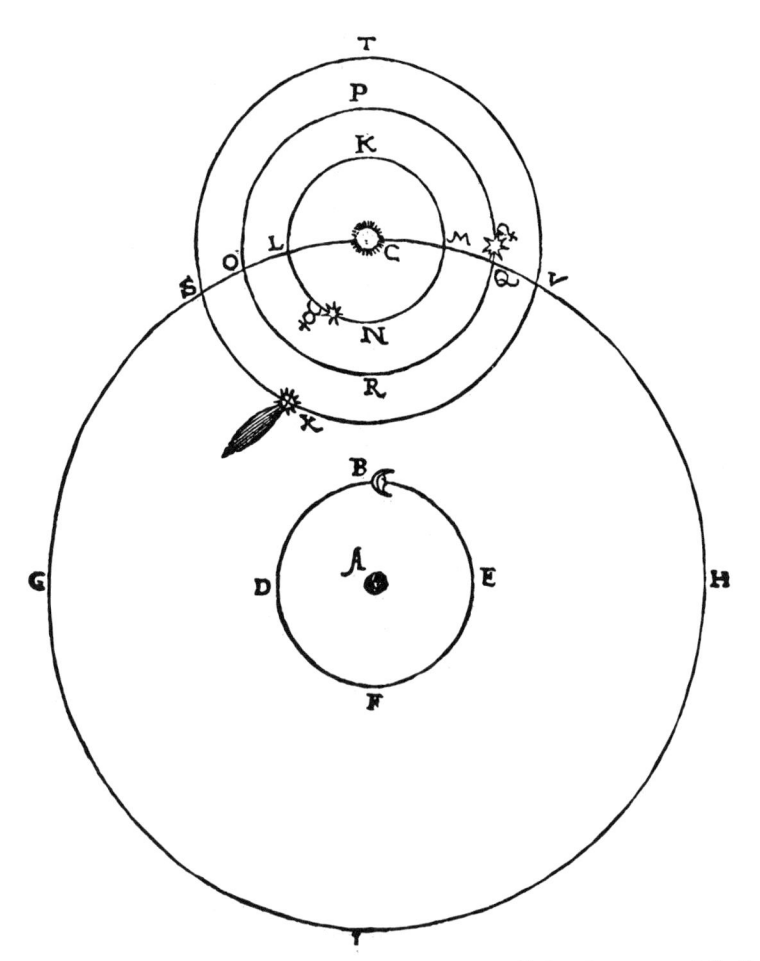

Tycho Brahe's conception of the solar system: He saw all the planets except Earth orbiting the sun which in turn orbited Earth. From his book on the comet of 1577, *De Mundi aetherei recentioribus Phaenomenis Liber secundus* (*Second Book About Recent Phenomena in the Celestial World,* 1603).

Granted, then, the ancients were well acquainted with the character, the temperament—in a word, the spiritual traits—of the moon, from the mythological point of view. But even the most learned among them were quite ignorant of selenography.

Nevertheless, some ancient astronomers did make certain discoveries that have been confirmed by modern science. While the Arcadians claimed to have lived on Earth before the moon was created; while Simplicius thought the moon was immobile and fastened to a crystal sphere; while Tatius saw her as a fragment detached from the solar disk; while Clearchus, a disciple of Aristotle, thought the moon was a polished mirror reflecting images of the ocean; while others saw her as a mass of vapors exhaled by Earth, or as a globe half fire, half ice, revolving on itself—still, a few scientists did make shrewd observations, even though they had no telescopes, and did surmise most of the laws that actually do govern the luminary of the night.

Thus Thales of Miletus, in 460 B.C., expressed the opinion that the moon is illuminated by the sun.[12] Aristarchus of Samos gave the cor-

three years after Verne writes this: but his knowing that it has been sighted gives us good evidence of how he is right on top of his subject. And as *we* write *this,* more than 1,800 such *smaller bodies* have so far been classified; A. P. Norton, in his *Norton's Star Atlas,* says there must be at least 40,000 altogether. Verne would chuckle over one recent updating of his remark that these bodies are *perhaps the debris of a planet shattered into . . . pieces.* Some thinkers wonder whether the inhabitants of that planet developed an "advanced" technology and blew themselves up. But most astronomers now believe that the asteroid belt is simply a collection of planetary materials that never condensed into a planet.

8. *Uranus . . . one* Space sciences advance so rapidly that all of Verne's figures have been superseded. Today his list would read: *Uranus five, Saturn nine, Jupiter fourteen, Neptune two,* with *Earth* adding *many artificial satellites.* Just twelve years after Verne composes this list, Asaph Hall will discover that *Mars has two moons.* This will especially delight Verne because his predecessor in space-voyage satire, Jonathan Swift, had anticipated this discovery: in *Gulliver's Travels* (1727) he gave details about these "two lesser stars" that came amazingly close to those actually determined by Hall (1877). Swift had used a technique that Verne perfects and extends: extrapolating from contemporary knowledge into the future.

9. *Pale Phoebe . . . Apollo* Here Verne identifies *Phoebe* with Artemis, a moon-goddess in ancient Greek mythology, and sister of *Apollo,* who is identified with the sun.

10. *moon's revolution* "About twenty-nine and a half days," Verne adds in a footnote.

11. *Nemean lion . . . on Earth* where he was strangled by Hercules in the first of his twelve labors.

12. *Thales . . . sun* Thales is called the Father of Philosophy because he was the first to search for a single imperishable substance basic to all reality: he took it to be water. He correctly predicted an eclipse of the sun by the moon. Today scholars date him in the seventh century B.C.

13. *Aristarchus . . . moon* A Greek astronomer of the third century B.C., *Aristarchus* wrote a treatise in which he gave an estimate of the moon's diameter that was close to the modern figure, and proposed an ingenious method for measuring the distances of the sun and moon.

14. *Hipparchus . . . moon's motions* Hipparchus is now rated with the great astronomers of all time. Among his numerous systematic accomplishments, he calculated with surprising accuracy the length of the solar year and the lunar month, and made a catalogue of 1,080 stars, giving not only their celestial longitude and latitude but relative brightness on a scale of six magnitudes.

15. *Ptolemy* An Alexandrian Greek, he wrote *Almagest* (*The Great Work*), which summed up the astronomical knowledge of the classical age. His system reigned supreme, in both theoretical astronomy and practical navigation, until the discoveries of Copernicus, Galileo, and Kepler.

16. *Abul-Wefa* "The last of the Baghdad astronomers," he also produced a treatise called *Almagest*. Often supposed to be a translation of Ptolemy, Abul-Wefa's book actually contains some new ideas and is organized on a different plan from Ptolemy's *Almagest*.

17. *Copernicus . . . celestial bodies* Polish astronomer Nicolaus Copernicus (1473–1543) promulgated the modern theory that the earth and the other planets move around the sun (the heliocentric or Copernican System). This superseded the theory that all heavenly bodies revolved around the earth (geocentric or Ptolemaic System). Verne oddly includes *Brahe* (1546–1601) and omits Johannes Kepler (1571–1630) whose work was far more important. *Brahe* preferred a system that was actually a step backward from the Copernican: he saw all the planets except Earth orbiting the sun which in turn orbited Earth! It was Kepler who discovered that the planets orbit in ellipses rather than in circles, as both *Copernicus* and *Brahe* had thought.

18. *Galileo . . . Riccioli* Galileo Galilei (1564–1642) became in 1609 the first person to study the moon through a telescope. Johannes Hevelius (1611–1687) published the first detailed map of the moon in his *Selenographia* (1647). Giovanni *Riccioli* (1598–1671), in his *Almagestum Novum* (1651), proposed names for lunar features most of which are still in use. More about the problem of lunar names in Chapter XXV.

This picture of Nicolaus Copernicus is believed to be a self-portrait.

Portrait of Galileo Galilei who *assigned an average height of 27,000 feet* to the lunar mountains.

rect explanation of the phases of the moon.[13] Cleomenes taught that it shines with reflected light. Berosus the Chaldean discovered that the duration of its rotation equals that of its revolution, and so he explained how it is that the moon always presents the same face to us. Finally Hipparchus, two centuries before the Christian era, detected some irregularities in the moon's motions.[14]

These various observations were later confirmed and proved useful to astronomers. Ptolemy,[15] in the second century, and the Arab Abul-Wefa[16] in the tenth, completed Hipparchus' observations on the moon's irregularities as it follows the wavy line of its orbit under the influence of the sun. Then Copernicus in the fifteenth century and Tycho Brahe in the sixteenth completely explained the system of the universe and the role played by the moon in the ensemble of celestial bodies.[17]

By this time, man had comprehended the movements of the moon but still knew very little about its physical constitution. Then Galileo explained that the light phenomena observed in certain lunar phases are caused by mountains. To these he assigned an average height of 27,000 feet.

Later Hevelius, a Danzig astronomer, reduced the maximum height to 15,600 feet, but his colleague Riccioli[18] raised it again to 42,000 feet.

At the end of the eighteenth century, Herschel, armed with a powerful telescope, considerably lowered these measurements. He estimated the highest mountains as 11,400 feet tall and the average height as only 2,400 feet. But not even Herschel was right. Only after the observations of Schroeter, Louville, Halley, Nasmyth, Bianchini, Pastorf,

Lohrmann, and Gruithuysen,[19] and especially the patient studies of Messieurs Beer and Mädler, was the question finally resolved. Thanks to these savants, the height of the lunar mountains is now perfectly established. Beer and Mädler have measured 1,905 elevations,[20] six of them over 15,600 feet and twenty-two of them over 14,400 feet. The highest peak towers 22,806 feet above the surface of the moon.[21]

Meanwhile, other studies of the moon were being completed. It appears to be riddled with craters,[22] and every new observation confirms its volcanic character.[23] From the absence of refraction in the light from planets occulted by the moon, we conclude that it has little if any atmosphere.[24] Absence of air suggests absence of water. It became obvious that to survive under such conditions, the Selenites must possess a special constitution and differ markedly from Earthmen.

Finally, thanks to new methods and improved instruments, astronomers could scan the moon without intermission, leaving not a single point of its face unexplored. Even though its diameter is 2,150 miles, about a quarter of the Earth's, its surface area one thirteenth that of the earth, its volume one forty-ninth, none of the moon's secrets could escape the scrutiny of astronomers, who continued to carry out their prodigious observations.[25]

For example, they noticed that certain areas of the lunar disk seem to be scored with white lines during the full moon, and with black lines during its phases. After making detailed studies, they were able to report on the nature of these lines. They are long, narrow furrows, with parallel sides, ending usually in the neighborhood of craters; they are between ten and a hundred miles long and about 4,800 feet wide. Astronomers called them "grooves," but they could do little more than name them. They could not resolve the question of whether these grooves are the dry beds of ancient rivers. Now the Americans hoped to solve this geological mystery.[26] They hoped too to be able to explain the true nature of that series of "parallel ramparts" discovered

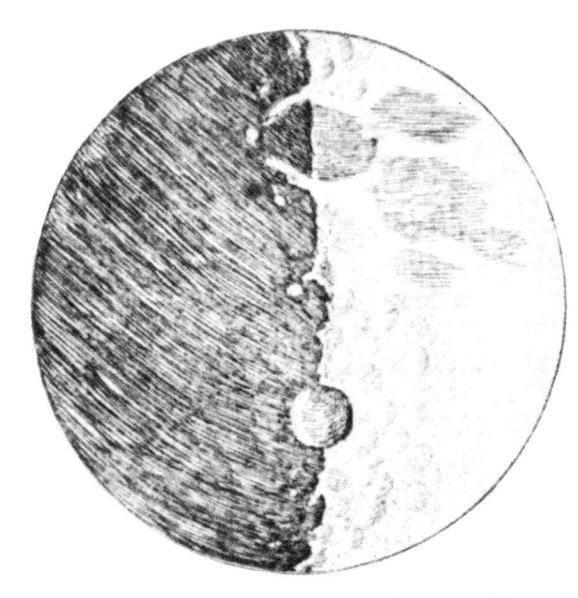

One of Galileo's drawings of the moon. From his 1610 book, *Sidereus Nuncius* (*The Sidereal Messenger*).

19. *Herschel . . . Gruithuysen* In Verne's day, readers of popular articles on astronomy are familiar with these names: Sir William *Herschel*, famous for his 1781 discovery of Uranus; Johann Hieronymus *Schroeter* (1745–1816), whose books on the moon have stimulated later investigators; the Chevalier de *Louville* (1671–1732), an early defender of Newtonian principles; Edmund *Halley* (1656–1742), famous discoverer of the fact that comets travel in ellipses and hence can return to our view at regular intervals; James *Nasmyth* (1808–1890), much in the news as inventor of the steam hammer and pile-driver, manufacturer of powerful telescopes; Francesco *Bianchini*, who published (1728) important studies of Venus; Johann Wilhelm *Pastorf* (1767–1838), who studied the sun-spots: after his death his four-and-a-half-foot refracting telescope became the property of the famous Beer and Mädler team whom Verne will mention soon and often; Wilhelm Gotthelf *Lohrmann*, mathematician and author of an 1824 work on the moon's topography; Franz von Paula *Gruithuysen*, Munich professor whose imaginative speculations about vegetation on Venus and engineering works on the moon at least excite public interest in worlds other than ours.

20. *measured 1,905 elevations* Wilhelm *Beer*, banker, and Johann H. von *Mädler*, professional astronomer, spent six hundred nights studying the moon's surface from their private observatory in the Berlin Tiergarten. In 1834 they published a chart about three feet in diameter, their famous *Mappa Selenographica*, which will figure inevitably in Verne's tale. Their book *Der Mond* (1837) became the standard reference work for decades: in 1875 *The American Cyclopaedia* will say it "must be consulted for a full account of the physical condition of our satellite." They discussed the moon's effects on Earth's weather, a question reopened in the 1960s, and the value of setting up an observatory on the far side of the moon where astronomers could work undisturbed by earthlight.

21. *highest peak . . . moon* Not even *Herschel*? Not even *Beer* and *Mädler* were right! As measured today, the highest peak approaches 30,000 feet.

22. *riddled with craters* On the night of June 18, 1178, English monks may have witnessed the creation of a crater. According to the chronicles kept by Gervase of Canterbury, six monks saw a "flaming torch" spring up from the crescent moon, "spewing out, over a considerable distance, fire, hot coals, and sparks." Dr. Jack B. Hartnung, of the State University of New York, suggests it was on that night that a colossal meteorite hit the moon and produced Giordano Bruno, a twelve-mile-wide crater. It appears to be one of the youngest such scars on the satellite.

23. *craters . . . volcanic character* Whether the moon has live volcanoes, whether its craters are volcanic in origin, are popular questions in Verne's time. Today's evidence suggests that most of the moon's craters have been caused by collision with meteorites and asteroids. But the moon did experience volcanism and lava flooding over a 700-million-year period ending three billion years ago. The molten rock apparently erupted out of the interior mainly through long fissures in the crust and flowed out over wide areas, occasionally accumulating into a mound. But it rarely if ever built up volcanic cones and craters at the point of eruption. Some authorities, like Robert Jastrow and Malcolm Thompson, seem to work by a rule of thumb: if the craters are scattered in a random pattern over an area, they are the sites of meteorite collisions. But if the craters appear in a row along the inside of a fissure, they "must be volcanic." Data from seismometers placed on the moon during the Apollo program suggest there is no intense volcanic activity or lava flooding anywhere on the moon today.

24. *little if any atmosphere* Verne often makes a teasingly brief reference to a phenomenon he intends to return to later. This one will be talked out, and annotated, in Chapter XX.

25. *prodigious observations* The diameter of the moon is now taken to be 2,160 miles. All of Verne's comparisons between moon and Earth still hold.

26. *geological mystery* What Verne calls *white* and *black lines* are now known as rays and rills. When a meteorite slams into the moon and creates a crater, the ejecta—the material thrown out of the crater—scours clean the ground around the crater, creating a system of light-colored rays. What Verne calls *grooves* were discovered by Johann Schroeter (1745–1816), who dubbed them *Rillen* or rills, with the implication that the walls of these dark crevasses are perpendicular. *Now the Americans* HAVE *partly solved this geological mystery.* The Apollo 15 astronauts' pictures of the Hadley Rille, a winding valley somewhat like the Grand Canyon, show the walls of the Rille to be composed of layers of rock that resemble successive flows of solidified lava. The Rille seems about 1,000 feet deep. Jastrow and Thompson say it was "formed by an unknown process which cut through the moon's crust like a scalpel." Some of these cracks may have been caused by meteor impact, some by early movements of the moon's crust.

27. *Selenite engineers* Franz von Paula Gruithuysen, the first person to theorize that moon craters are caused by meteorites, also suggested (1828) that some lunar features are actually ruins of old Selenite buildings.

28. *"earth-shine"* ". . . the new moone, wi the auld moone in hir arme," as the medieval balladeer so beautifully described it.

by the Munich professor Gruithuysen, who thought they might be fortifications built by Selenite engineers.[27] Obviously these two questions, like many others, could be answered only after direct contact had been established with the moon.

But there was nothing further to be discovered about the intensity of lunar light. Scientists knew it to be 300,000 times weaker than solar light and to have no appreciable effect on thermometers. As for the phenomenon called "ashy light," it is known to be the reflection of sunlight from the Earth's surface onto the moon's; this "earth-shine"[28] appears to complete the lunar disk when it is seen as a crescent in its first and last phases.

Such was the state of knowledge about Earth's satellite, which the Gun Club now proposed to complete from every point of view: cosmographic, geological, political, and spiritual.

The Moon's Disk. Engraving from the first illustrated edition of *From the Earth to the Moon* (1872).

CHAPTER VI

What it is Impossible not to Know and what it is no longer Permissible to Believe in the United States

As a consequence of Barbicane's proposal, astronomical facts about the moon became the order of the day. Everyone was now studying lunar data. It was as if the moon had appeared in the sky for the first time, as if no one had ever seen her before. She became fashionable, the darling of the hour, without losing any of her modesty. She took her place among the great celebrities without letting it go to her head. Newspapers revived all the old tales in which the "wolves' sun"[1] plays a part. They recalled the mysterious powers that the ignorance of olden times had attributed to her. They sang her praises in every key. They all but quoted her witty remarks. All America had moon on the brain.

Scientific journals, for their part, dealt more specifically with the technical questions involved in the Gun Club project. They printed the letter from the Cambridge Observatory, discussed it, and endorsed it without reservation.

In short, it was no longer permissible for even the least learned of Yankees to be ignorant of even one known fact about his satellite, or for even the most superstitious housekeeper to entertain any old wives' tales about it. Science reached them in every form, penetrating their eyes and ears. It was impossible for an American to be a dunce—in astronomy.

Until then, most people simply did not know how the distance between the Earth and the moon is calculated. But now they were informed that this distance is obtained by measuring the parallax of the moon. If the word parallax seemed to stupefy them, they were told it is the angle formed by two straight lines extended from opposite ends of the Earth's radius to the moon. If they questioned the accuracy of this method, it was immediately demonstrated to them not only that the mean distance is 234,347 miles[2] (94,330 leagues), but also that astronomers could not err by more than seventy miles (30 leagues) either way.

For those not familiar with the movements of the moon, the newspapers explained that it has two distinct motions, the first called rotation on its axis, the second known as revolution around the Earth,

1. *old tales . . . "wolves' sun"* Wolves come forth at night: the moon is their sun. In Verne's day, especially in the south of France, the superstition is still widespread that certain men are transformed into wolves at full moon. Such beliefs have flourished throughout history in any area where wolves howl and prowl. The ancient Greeks believed that King Lycaon had served human flesh to Zeus in order to test the god's omniscience; of course Zeus knew at once and punished Lycaon by changing him into a wolf. Herodotus, Pliny, Ovid, the Norse sagas all tell of people who, as the moon dictates, exchange skin for fur, walk on all fours, and attack and eat human beings. Belief in werewolves (the word means *man*-wolves in Anglo-Saxon) blended into Christian legendry: Saint Patrick, for example, was said to have changed King Vereticus into a wolf. But nowhere has lycanthropy—the affliction of Lycaon—thrived as in Verne's own country.

In the Middle Ages, the *old tales* included graphic accounts of werewolves breaking into convents to eat the nuns, or pouncing on plump abbots who waddled outside their monasteries. Trials of lycanthropes were common: many defendants freely acknowledged that they in fact were part-time wolves. Some of course in turn accused certain "hags" of having bewitched

The European wolf of Verne's day. Engraving from *The American Cyclopaedia* (1876).

them. The case of the fourteen-year-old Jean Garnier, tried at Bordeaux in 1603, is perhaps the most famous. When he felt his metamorphosis coming on, he would repair to the woods and wait near a pool for his victims. He confessed to having eaten fifty children; he complained that one old woman "proved to be as tough as leather." The name Garnier became so closely identified with lycanthropy that whole families with that name came under suspicion. The last authenticated case in France was tried when Verne was nineteen. An army sergeant confessed to having dug up bodies with his bare hands in order to eat them. "There can . . . be little doubt, from what he himself said, that he was in reality a wer[e]wolf," writes Elliott O'Donnell in his book *Werwolves* (1965).

2. *234,347 miles* Today the mean distance is given as 238,851 miles.

3. *twenty-seven and one-third days* "This," Verne explains in a footnote, "is the duration of the sidereal revolution, that is to say, the time the moon takes to return to a given star."

4. *falleth from the stars* Verne here echoes a line from *Le Cid* by the French dramatist Pierre Corneille (1606–1684).

5. *all other satellites* Giovanni Cassini (1625–1712), first of four generations of Cassinis to direct the Paris Observatory, discovered the rotation of Jupiter and drew up tables of the motions of Jupiter's moons. In 1792 William Herschel explained some of these motions by assuming that, like Earth's moon, Jupiter's satellites turn on their axes exactly once in every revolution about the parent planet.

6. *"libration" . . . one-hundredths* The modern value is fifty-nine one-hundredths. Galileo was first to notice that the moon does not keep exactly the same face to us at all times: certain features along her edge seem sometimes to disappear "around the corner." One reason for this apparent oscillation is that the moon's axis is tilted toward her orbit as she revolves. Thus we see sometimes 7° past her north pole, sometimes 7° past her south pole. This is known as *libration in latitude*. Another reason is that, while the moon rotates at a fairly constant rate, the length of arc of orbit that she moves through varies from day to day: she moves faster in perigee, slower in apogee. And so we can see nearly 8° past her eastern edge at one point in the month, 8° past her west "limb" two weeks later. This is *libration in longitude*. These motions are known as *librations* because they resemble the up-and-down movement of a balance scale, called *Libra* in Latin.

7. *lunation* The length of time from one new moon to the next, approximately twenty-nine and a half days, or a lunar month.

8. *Elliptical . . . otherwise* It was Kepler, as we have noted, who discovered that the planets

which both take the same length of time, twenty-seven and one-third days.[3]

Rotation is the motion that creates day and night on the moon's surface; but there is only one day and one night per lunar month, and each lasts three hundred and fifty-four and one-third hours. Happily for the moon, though, the side facing the Earth is lighted by it with an intensity equal to the light of fourteen moons. As for the other side, always invisible, it of course has three hundred and fifty-four and one-third hours of absolute night, tempered only by that "pale gleam that falleth from the stars."[4] This phenomenon is due to the fact that the moon's rotation and revolution are accomplished in exactly the same period of time, a phenomenon shared by Jupiter's satellites, according to Cassini and Herschel, and probably by all other satellites.[5]

Some well-meaning but slow-witted people had trouble grasping the reason why the moon always shows the same face to the Earth: namely that in the course of her revolution, she also turns once upon herself. They were advised: "Go into your dining room. Walk around the table always facing its center. By the time you have made one complete circle, you will also have completed one turn round yourself, since your eye will have ranged over every point in the room. Now, think of the dining room as the heavens, the table as the Earth, and yourself as the moon!" And they would go away enchanted with this comparison.

But, having demonstrated why the moon always shows the same side to the Earth, one should add that the moon also rocks from north to south and west to east in a motion known as "libration." And so she lets us see more than half of her disk, about fifty-seven one-hundredths.[6]

Once the ignoramuses had learned as much as the Cambridge director himself knew about the moon's rotation, they began to worry about the moon's revolution around the Earth, and some twenty scientific journals undertook to teach them. They learned that the firmament, with its infinitude of stars, may be thought of as a vast dial on which the moon moves to indicate the true time for people on Earth; that it is during this movement that the moon exhibits her different phases; that the moon is full when she is in opposition to the sun, which is to say, when these three heavenly bodies are in a straight line with the Earth in the middle; that the moon is new when she is in conjunction with the sun, that is, between the Earth and the sun; finally, that the moon is in either her first or her last quarter when she forms a right angle with sun and Earth with herself at the apex.

From these facts some perspicacious Yankees concluded that eclipses can occur only during conjunction or opposition. They reasoned well. In conjunction, the moon can eclipse the sun, whereas in opposition, it is the Earth's turn to eclipse the moon. If these eclipses do not occur twice every lunation,[7] that's because the plane of the moon's motion is inclined toward the ecliptic, in other words, toward the plane of the Earth's motion.

As for the height above the horizon that the celebrity of the night can attain, the Cambridge Observatory letter had reviewed all the facts. Everyone now knew that this height will vary according to the latitude of the observer. But the only regions of the globe in which the moon passes through the zenith—that is, passes directly over the ob-

William Herschel's forty-foot telescope, with which he observed the motions of Jupiter's satellites. From Arthur Berry's *A Short History of Astronomy* (1898).

server's head—are of necessity those located between the twenty-eighth parallels and the equator. Hence the important recommendation that the experiment be made from some point in that area, so that the projectile could be launched perpendicularly and thus escape the force of gravity more quickly. This was an essential condition for success, and public opinion insisted that it be met.

As for the path the moon takes in its revolution around the Earth, the Cambridge Observatory had made it clear, even to the dunces in every country, that this line is a re-entrant curve: not a circle but rather an ellipse, with the Earth situated at one of its foci. Elliptical orbits are common to all planets as well as to all satellites, and theoretical mechanics offers rigorous proof that it could not be otherwise.[8] And by now everyone understood that the moon is in its apogee when it is furthest from the Earth, and in its perigee when it is closest.

This, then, was what every American knew willy-nilly, what no person could decently be ignorant of. But if these true principles had quickly become public knowledge, there were still many errors, certain illusory fears, that were not easy to stamp out.

Some worthy souls, for instance, believed that the moon was an ancient comet which, following its elongated orbit about the sun, happened to pass close to the Earth and was caught in its circle of attraction. These armchair astronomers said this explained the scorched look of the moon, an irreparable calamity which they blamed on the heat of the sun. But if they were told that comets have an atmosphere and the moon has little or none, they were at a loss for a reply.[9]

Others, tremblers by nature, were actually afraid of the moon. They

move in elliptical orbits. But it was Newton who proved that any object moving under his "Inverse-square Law of Attraction" *must* follow an ellipse.

9. *ancient comet . . . a reply* Theories that our satellite originated elsewhere seemed doomed in 1969 when Apollo 11 astronauts Neil Armstrong and Edwin Aldrin collected moon samples: analysis of these rocks and soil showed that our satellite must have been formed in orbit about the same time Earth itself was formed. But two University of Texas scientists have since demonstrated (1977) that it is mathematically possible that our moon did originate as a planet and was later captured by the Earth. In any event, Professors V. Szebehely and R. McKenzie say that because of the eccentricity of Earth's orbit, the moon's orbit is so unstable it could escape and (once again?) become a planet. And theories about heavenly bodies shifting from one orbit into another are not confined to our moon. Some astronomers think the planet Pluto was once a satellite of Neptune. Others believe some of Jupiter's satellites might once have been asteroids that were captured by the combined attractions of the sun and Jupiter. These moons are now held in unstable orbits in which Jupiter's gravity is almost balanced off by the sun's. Hence, under certain conditions, one of these could escape from Jupiter and move into a new orbit—as a new planet?

10. *observations . . . Caliphs* Medieval Arab astronomers were famous for their regular, systematic, almost continuous observations of the heavens. The Caliphs, successors to Mohammed as rulers of the Moslem world, built observatories for this purpose in Baghdad and Damascus. Their scientists even noted the positions of the known stars before and after an eclipse as a way of making sure they had a precise record of the time and context of the event. Their most important observations were described in formal affidavits which they signed and which were notarized by lawyers. As a result of these detailed records, Arab astronomers were able to correct, revise, and extend the Greek astronomical tables. Aside from their intellectual curiosity—which made their universities superior in many respects to the schools of medieval Europe—the Arabs were motivated by religious considerations. Timing of Moslem feasts and fasts depends on reliable knowledge of the moon's movements: as Verne observed in Chapter V, the Mohammedans use a lunar calendar. And Mohammedan ceremonies are based on the worshipers' position in regard to Mecca: a knowledge of astronomy helps them determine the proper direction.

11. *foreseeable future* Actually, Laplace and the *tremblers* were both wrong. He did prove mathematically that variations and "aberrations" in the movements of heavenly bodies were self-correcting in the long run. But he had not taken into account the effect of tidal forces. These are slowing down the Earth's rotation, making each day one-hundred-millionth of a second longer, and pushing the moon further away. In billions of years, if the Earth-moon system still exists, Earth's day will finally become a month long. Then the tidal forces will change. Gradually the moon will orbit back closer and closer to our planet. But she will never *fall into the earth*. Instead, when she's orbiting about 10,000 miles away, Earth's tidal forces exerted on the moon will exceed the gravitational forces that hold the satellite together. She will disintegrate, scattering her remains in a ring about the Earth.

12. *Doctor Mead* Richard Mead (1673–1754) became the recognized head of his profession in 1714. He attended Queen Anne on her deathbed and was the personal physician of George II. He wrote voluminously. His principal work was *Medicina Sacra* (1748) in which he maintained that so-called demoniacal possessions were a form of insanity. His *Medical Works* (1762) make important contributions to preventive medicine.

13. *the truth alone* Not all assumptions of a connection between *the moon, the life system,* and *human destiny* are *vulgar errors*. For example, a study conducted in New York hospitals has suggested that hemorrhages after surgery are significantly related to the phase of the full moon.

14. *America* For two chapters now, Verne has lost sight of his characters. He has done a good job of popularizing the Nebular Hypothesis and reviewing the state of man's knowledge of the moon. But he has told us all this as "the author omniscient," referring just occasionally to Barbicane and the Gun Club, never dramatizing his material from their point of view or in their terms. In this respect, he is no more guilty of writing "essays" than any other nineteenth-century novelist. Still, he's at his best when he manages to popularize and dramatize at the same time, as he did in Chapters II and IV, and as he gets back to doing in the next chapter.

had heard that, since the observations recorded in the time of the Caliphs,[10] the moon's revolution around the Earth was accelerating at a definite rate. Quite logically, they deduced that an acceleration in movement must involve a corresponding diminution in distance between the two bodies and that, if this double effect were to continue, the moon would someday fall into the Earth. However, they calmed themselves, they stopped worrying about future generations, when they heard that, according to the calculations of Laplace, a famous French mathematician, this acceleration has its limits, and that a compensating decrease in speed is sure to follow. The equilibrium of the solar system cannot be disturbed in the foreseeable future.[11]

Finally, there was the class of superstitious people; they are not content simply to ignore what is true, they also believe what is not true, and about the moon there is a great deal of that. Some regarded its disk as a polished mirror by means of which people in different parts of the Earth could see each other and even communicate their thoughts. Others claimed that out of one thousand new moons that had been observed, nine hundred and fifty had caused remarkable changes like cataclysms, revolutions, earthquakes, floods, and so on. They believed that the celebrity of the night exercises a mysterious influence on human destinies; they saw her as the "veritable counterweight" of existence; they thought each Selenite was linked to some inhabitant of the earth by a bond of sympathy. Along with Doctor Mead,[12] they maintained that the life system was entirely dependent on the moon, clinging to their conviction that boys are mostly born during the new moon, girls during the last quarter, and so on and on. But finally they had to renounce these vulgar errors and return to the truth alone.[13] And if some of the moon's followers were now disillusioned and turned their backs on her, the vast majority of the people came out in her favor. As for the Yankees, their sole ambition now was to take possession of that new continent in the sky, to plant on its highest peak the starry flag of the United States of America.[14]

CHAPTER VII

The Hymn to the Cannonball

The Cambridge Observatory, in its memorable letter of October 7, had treated the question from the astronomical point of view. But now the mechanical problems had to be solved. In any other country, such practical difficulties would seem insurmountable. But Americans regard such things as child's play.

With no waste of time, President Barbicane named an executive committee from the inner circle of the Gun Club. Instructed to devote three meetings to the three major questions of cannon, projectile, and powder, the committee comprised four members who were experts in such matters: Barbicane, with the deciding vote in case of a tie; General Morgan; Major Elphiston, and finally the inevitable J. T. Maston, to whom were entrusted the duties of recording secretary.

On October 8 the committee convened in President Barbicane's house at 3 Republican Street. Since serious discussion should not be interrupted by the cries of the stomach, the four sat around a table covered with sandwiches and teapots. J. T. Maston screwed his pen into his iron hook and the meeting was under way.

Barbicane spoke first:

"My dear colleagues," he said, "we must solve one of the most important problems in ballistics, that supreme science,[1] which treats of the movement of projectiles, that is to say, bodies launched into space by some propellant force, and then left to themselves."[2]

"Oh! ballistics! ballistics!" cried J. T. Maston with emotion.

"Perhaps it would seem more logical," Barbicane resumed, "to devote this first session to a discussion of the cannon—"

"Quite so," said General Morgan.

"But," Barbicane went on, "after much reflection, it seems to me that the question of the projectile is prior to that of the cannon, since the dimensions of the latter must depend on those of the former."

"I demand the floor," cried J. T. Maston.

And he got it with swift deference to his magnificent past.

"My worthy friends," he spoke in inspired tones, "our president is right to give priority to the question of the projectile! This cannonball that we are sending to the moon is our messenger, our ambassador,

1. *ballistics, that supreme science* In continuing his satire on the military mind, Verne is adding several names to a long list of memorable characters, in both literature and history, who consider war the highest state of civilization. In literature the list begins with Homer's Achilles, who prefers early death in battle to a long life of domestic peace. In history, the Achilles-Barbicane-Maston syndrome is summed up in a letter in which General George Patton (1885–1945) wrote: "War is the only place a man realy [sic] lives." Spelling, being a peaceful means of communication, was not the general's concern.

2. *then left to themselves* This anti-climactic phrase, trailing off so poignantly, betrays Barbicane's complex state of mind. It's a proud, ironic phrase: thanks to the ballistician's talents, projectiles aren't really *left to themselves:* their course is largely predetermined. But it's also an anxious, ambivalent phrase: some slight miscalculation, some hidden defect in the manufacturing, some last-minute shift in wind, and projectiles *are* out of control. And it's a phrase that, by its very distractedness, suggests Barbicane has something else in mind, something he does not want to mention just yet. At Verne's best, he is sensitive to tone of voice and semi-slips of the tongue.

3. *heavenly bodies . . . are . . . projectiles* The point that heavenly bodies and projectiles are essentially similar was originally made in a brilliant imaginary experiment described by Sir Isaac Newton. But it's possible that Verne develops this idea on his own. According to his grandson, "Verne had not read Newton." Verne's use of the idea not only prepares us for the end of his novel but also prophesies the development of artificial satellites in the twentieth century.

In the third book of his *Principles of Natural Philosophy* (1687), Newton explains the orbital motion of the moon. He asks his reader to imagine a cannon placed on a mountaintop and aimed horizontally. When the cannoneer fires a cannonball, it moves forward under the pressures exerted by the propellant forces. But it is also pulled downward by the force of gravity. The resultant of these forward and downward forces is a curved line: the projectile falls to the Earth. If the cannoneer increases his charge, the forward velocity will be greater, the projectile moves further before it is pulled to the ground. Newton's diagram of this experiment shows four such shots, the last reaching halfway round the globe. But now imagine, he asks, a cannon so powerful it can fire a projectile all around the planet without its hitting the Earth. The resultant of the forward motion produced by the propellant force and the downward deflection caused by gravity would make the projectile follow a circular trajectory: an orbit. The projectile would now be a satellite. And of course, Newton was in effect describing what would happen from 1957 on when first the U.S.S.R. and then the U.S.A. would put unmanned "projectiles" into orbit around the Earth. Seeing this analogy between ballistics and astronomy made for good science writing in Newton's case, good science fiction in Verne's.

Barbicane spoke first . . . Engraving from the first illustrated edition (1872).

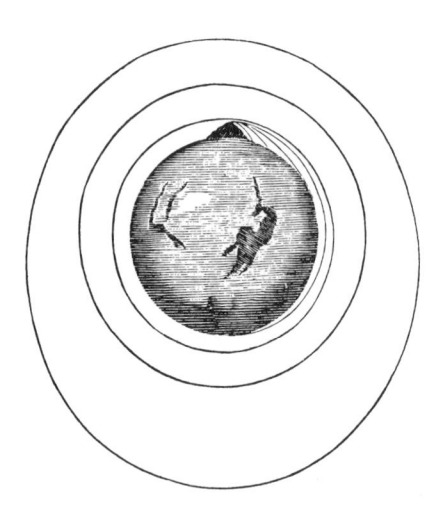

Newton's diagram of his brilliant imaginary experiment to illustrate the motion of the moon. From the third volume of his *Principles of Natural Philosophy* (1687).

and I ask your permission to consider it from a strictly moral, intellectual point of view."

This new way of looking at a cannonball piqued the curiosity of the committeemen; they gave their full attention to Maston's words.

"My dear colleagues," he resumed, "I shall be brief; I shall pass over the physical cannonball, the cannonball that kills, in order to ponder the mathematical cannonball, the moral cannonball, the philosophical cannonball. For me the cannonball is the most brilliant example of human power, which it epitomizes. When he created the cannonball, man came closest to his own Creator!"

"Well said!" exclaimed Major Elphiston.

"Indeed," cried the orator, "if God made the stars and the planets, man made the cannonball, that criterion of speed on Earth, that miniature of heavenly bodies moving in space which are, in the last analysis, nothing but projectiles![3] God has the speed of electricity, the speed of light, the speed of the stars, the speed of the comets, the speed of the planets, the speed of the satellites, the speed of sound, the speed of the wind! But we have the speed of the cannonball, a hundred times greater than the speed of the fastest trains and horses!"

J. T. Maston was transported; his voice took on a lyrical quality as he sang his sacred hymn to the cannonball.

"Do you want some figures?" he continued. "Here are some eloquent ones! Simply take the modest twenty-four-pounder. While it travels 800,000 times more slowly than electricity, seventy-six times more slowly than the Earth in its orbiting of the sun, nevertheless when it leaves the cannon, it travels faster than sound,[4] going 200 fathoms a second; 2,000 fathoms in ten seconds; fourteen miles a minute (six leagues); 840 miles an hour (360 leagues); 20,100 miles per day (8,640 leagues), which is to say, almost the speed reached by a point on the equator during the Earth's rotation; 7,336,500 miles a year (3,155,760 leagues). It would take eleven days to reach the moon, twelve years to reach the sun, 360 years to reach Neptune at the outer edge of the solar system.[5] That is what this modest cannonball, the work of our hands, could do! What will happen then when we multiply its speed twenty times and we launch it at seven miles per second! Ah! superb cannonball! splendid projectile! I like to think you will be welcomed up there with all the honors due an Ambassador of Earth!"

Hurrahs greeted his sonorous peroration. Deeply affected, J. T. Maston sat down amidst the congratulations of his colleagues.

"And now that we have given poetry its due," said Barbicane, "let's get directly to the question."

"We're all set," the committeemen replied, as each consumed half a dozen sandwiches.

"You know," the president went on, "the problem to be solved: how to give a projectile a speed of 12,000 yards per second. I have good reason to believe we can do it. But first let's consider the speeds obtained so far. General Morgan can enlighten us on that subject."

"Easily, since I was on the Experimental Committee during the war," the general reminded them. "I should point out that Dahlgren's hundred-pounders, which had a range of 2,500 fathoms, gave their projectile a muzzle velocity of 500 yards per second."

"Good. And Rodman's Columbiad?"[6] the president asked.

"In its initial trials at Fort Hamilton, New York, the Rodman Columbiad shot a projectile weighing half a ton a distance of six miles, with a muzzle velocity of 800 yards per second. Such results were never obtained by Armstrong and Palliser in England."

"Oh! the English!" exclaimed J. T. Maston, shaking his formidable hook at the eastern horizon.

"So," said Barbicane, "800 yards must be the greatest velocity reached so far?"

"Yes," Morgan replied.

"I should add, however," J. T. Maston broke in, "that if my mortar had not burst—"

"Yes, but it did burst," Barbicane said with a kind gesture. "So let us take this muzzle velocity of 800 yards per second as our starting point. We must multiply it twentyfold. Putting off for another session the question of how to produce this velocity, I shall ask you, my dear colleagues, to consider the proper dimensions of our cannonball. You

Portrait of Sir Isaac Newton, whose point that *heavenly bodies . . . are . . . nothing but projectiles* gives J. T. Maston some of his best ammunition.

4. *faster than sound* "Therefore, once you have heard the gun fired, you can no longer be struck by the cannonball," Verne adds in a footnote.

5. *outer edge of the solar system* Today, of course, Maston would have to calculate the time to get to Pluto, whose orbit now marks the known outer boundary of the planetary system. Neptune is 2,790,000,000 miles from the sun, Pluto is 3,670,000,000. Maston's projectile would take about 480 years to get there. He is ignoring the comets, unaware that in the future, astronomers will regard the cometary orbits as the real *outer edge of the solar system*. More of that when comets enter the story in Chapter XIX.

6. *Rodman's Columbiad* "The Americans gave the name of Columbiad to these enormous engines of destruction," Verne says in a footnote. Actually, Americans had been fondly calling cannons "Columbiads" ever since the War of 1812. "Columbia" was a feminine personification of the U.S.A. (after Columbus) much favored by early patriotic writers. In 1807, for example, Joel Barlow published *The Columbiad,* an enlargement of his *Vision of Columbus* (1787), a poetic paean to the New World in nine books.

realize it is no longer a matter of projectiles weighing at most half a ton!''

"Why not?" asked the major.

"Because this cannonball," J. T. Maston quickly pointed out, "must be big enough to attract the attention of the inhabitants of the moon—if there are any."

"And for another reason even more important," Barbicane added.

"What do you have in mind, Barbicane?" the major inquired.

"I mean it's not enough to launch a projectile and give it no further thought.[7] We must follow it throughout its course, until the moment it hits its target."

"Well!" exclaimed the general and the major, a bit taken aback by this idea.

"Absolutely," Barbicane spoke with self-assurance. "Absolutely. Otherwise our experiment would be pointless."

"But then you must be thinking of an enormous projectile?" the major asked.

"No. Listen carefully. You know that we have greatly perfected our optical instruments. With certain telescopes, we are able to enlarge ob-

7. *no further thought* Now we know what else Barbicane had in mind earlier when he half-ruefully talked of projectiles as launched into space *and then left to themselves.*

The Rodman Columbiad as pictured in the first illustrated edition (1872).

Thomas Nast's cartoon "Peace Secure" (1875) showing the popular identification of the Columbiad cannon with Columbia, a feminine personification of the U.S.A. (after Columbus).

jects 6,000 times and to bring the moon, so to speak, within forty miles of us (sixteen leagues). Now at that distance objects sixty feet square are perfectly visible. The reason we have not further improved the power of our telescopes is simply this: as the image becomes larger, it also becomes increasingly blurred. And the moon, which is only a reflecting mirror, does not give off an intense enough light to permit enlargements beyond this point."

"So then! What can you do?" asked the general. "Give your projectile a diameter of sixty feet?"

"Not at all!"

"Take it upon yourself to increase the luminosity of the moon?"

"Exactly."

"Oh come on now!" cried J. T. Maston.

"But it's quite simple," Barbicane said. "If I could reduce the density of the atmosphere that the moon's light must travel through, wouldn't I, in effect, be increasing the moon's luminosity?"

"True."

"Well, to do all that, I need only put my telescope on some very high mountain. Which is what we'll do."

"I give up, I give up," answered the major. "You have a way of

8. *Bastille . . . wise* The bomb, then, traveled almost four miles. In this clever remark, which includes a veiled attack on the Emperor Louis Napoleon, Verne condenses much history into one tight antithesis. In the time of King *Louis XI* (1423–1483), *the Bastille* was only a minor fortification. But later, when it was expanded to comprise eight 100-foot towers connected by 100-foot walls behind a moat 80 feet wide, the Bastille dominated all Paris. In the eighteenth century, it was used for detention of "dangerous" thinkers, like the great Voltaire, and for "safe" deposit of confiscated books, like the *Encyclopédie*. It had long served as a symbol of despotism when it was stormed by revolutionaries on July 14, 1789.

But Verne's remark about the *mad* locking up the *wise* also has its immediate connotations for Verne's audience. In 1852 Louis Napoleon overthrew the republic, shipped many of his political opponents abroad to penal colonies, and set up a new government with virtually all authority vested in himself as Emperor Napoleon III. He curtailed the freedoms of press, speech, and assembly, and even the right of the legislature to legislate. As Verne, then twenty-four, wrote to his parents: "One dare not say a word for risk of hanging." Many French intellectuals, like Verne's publisher Hetzel and the leading writer Victor Hugo, have spent years of their lives in exile, enforced or voluntary. And so Verne is here reminding his reader: once again, the *mad* lock up the *wise*.

Later in this novel (Chapters X, XII) and again in *Twenty Thousand Leagues,* Verne will keep up his indirect attacks on the Emperor, in the latter work simply by paying attention to writers like George Sand, Jules Michelet, and Hugo, all out of favor with the regime. "Opposition," one historian says, "could be expressed only indirectly. . . ."

The village of *Charenton,* as *The American Cyclopaedia* (1873) puts it, "contains an excellent lunatic asylum . . . capable of accommodating 500 patients." Charenton also has its political ironies for Verne's original readers. The seminal French author, Marquis de Sade (1740–1814), one of the prisoners liberated by the storming of the Bastille in 1789, disagreed with Napoleon I, Louis Napoleon's uncle, and in 1801 was committed to Charenton for the rest of his life. Today's readers know Charenton as the setting of Peter Weiss' play *Marat/Sade* which won the Drama Critics Circle Award for 1966 and later was made into a movie by United Artists.

making things easy. And how great a magnification do you expect to get this way?"

"A magnification of 48,000. That will bring the moon to within five miles of us, so to speak. Then objects need be only nine feet wide to be perfectly visible."

"Perfect!" cried J. T. Maston. "So our projectile will be nine feet in diameter?"

"Precisely."

"But then I must warn you," said Major Elphiston, "we'll have such a great weight—"

"Oh! major," answered Barbicane, "before we talk about the weight, let me tell you about the miracles our forefathers accomplished in that department. I'm not denying that modern ballistics has made great progress. But you must keep in mind that even in the Middle Ages, they obtained results more surprising than ours."

"Is that so?" Morgan replied.

"Can you prove that?" J. T. Maston cried out heatedly.

"Certainly, I have all the evidence I need," Barbicane said. "When Mohammed II laid siege to Constantinople in 1453, his men discharged stone cannonballs that weighed 1,900 pounds, and they must have been huge."

"Oh! oh," exclaimed the major. "Nineteen hundred pounds! What an enormous figure!"

"At Malta, in the days of the crusaders, a certain cannon of the Fortress Saint Elmo launched projectiles weighing 2,500 pounds."

"Impossible!"

"And according to a French historian, in the time of Louis XI a mortar launched a bomb of only 500 pounds, but that bomb, fired from the Bastille, where the mad lock up the wise,[8] went as far as Charenton, where the wise lock up the mad."

"Very good!" said J. T. Maston.

"And what have we ourselves seen, since then? The Armstrong cannons launch a 500-pound ball; the Rodman Columbiads, a half-ton projectile! It seems that what projectiles have gained in range, they have lost in weight. Still, if we put our minds to it, and take advantage of scientific progress, we should be able to make cannonballs ten times heavier than those of Mohammed II and the Knights of Malta."

"Obviously," answered the major. "But what metal do you plan to use in our projectile?"

"Regular cast iron," said General Morgan.

"Pooh! Cast iron!" cried J. T. Maston with deep disdain. "That's so ordinary for a cannonball destined to reach the moon."

"Let's not go overboard, my honorable friend," Morgan answered. "Cast iron will do."

"All right then!" said Major Elphiston. "Since the weight is proportional to the volume, an iron cannonball nine feet in diameter will be unbelievably heavy!"

"Yes, if it is solid. No, if it's hollow," said Barbicane.

"Hollow! So it's going to be a shell?"

"In which we could send messages and documents," J. T. Maston added, "and samples of terrestrial artifacts!"

"Yes, a shell," Barbicane replied. "That's absolutely necessary. A

"At Malta, in the days of the crusaders, a certain cannon . . . launched projectiles weighing 2,500 pounds." Engraving from the 1872 edition.

solid 108-inch cannonball would weigh over 200,000 pounds, obviously too great a weight. Still, our projectile must maintain a certain stability, so I propose we give it a weight of 20,000 pounds." [9]

"How thick would the casing have to be?" asked the major.

"If we follow the usual rule of thumb," Morgan replied, "a diameter of 108 inches would mean a casing at least two feet thick."

"Far too much," said Barbicane. "Don't forget, this cannonball doesn't have to pierce armor plate. It just has to have a strong enough casing to withstand the pressure of the gases in the powder. Then here's the problem: how thick should the walls of a cast-iron shell be if it must weigh only 20,000 pounds? Our lightning calculator, the worthy Maston, can tell us right off."

"Nothing could be easier," replied the honorable secretary of the committee.

So saying, he put some algebra to paper. Under his pen appeared some π's and x's raised to the second power. In a detached manner, but apparently without any effort, he extracted a cube root, and said:

9. *weight of 20,000 pounds* In 1968, Colonel Frank Borman will command the Apollo 8 mission, the first manned flight to the moon: he and two other astronauts will orbit the satellite ten times before splashing down in the Pacific. Later Colonel Borman will write to Jean Jules-Verne, the novelist's grandson and biographer, expressing astonishment over the many similarities between Borman's space vehicle and Barbicane's. For example, they "had the same weight." We'll come back to Borman's letter as Verne's other prophecies develop in later chapters.

10. *manufacture aluminum?* Here Verne is using a technique that has proved eminently successful in his earlier novels. He is extrapolating from the daily news into the not-so-distant future. Thus he predicts developments that his readers will live to see in a matter of years. And so he more easily gains their credence when he extrapolates into the more distant future.

Aluminum is the third most abundant element on the Earth's surface. Found in combination with other elements in 195 species of minerals, it makes up about eight percent of the Earth's crust. Still, until Verne's day, it has been difficult to extract except at great expense, as many early investigators had discovered. For example, in 1845, the German chemist Friedrich Wöhler was able to derive aluminum only with the aid of expensive metallic potassium.

Then in 1853 *Deville,* Sorbonne chemistry professor who had just discovered a new method of mineral analysis, turned his attention to the aluminum problem. He devised a method by which he could prepare aluminum on a large scale by using a cheap metallic sodium of his own invention. Bringing it out of the laboratory stage in 1854, he exhibited his new product at the 1855 Paris Exposition. Using capital provided by Emperor Louis Napoleon, he built the first commercial aluminum factory at Glacière, a Paris suburb.

Even so, as Verne writes this scene, aluminum is not yet fulfilling its potential; it's widely regarded as a great disappointment. The order that Barbicane will write for aluminum will be the biggest ever. But in 1886, a still cheaper (electrolytic) process for obtaining the new metal will be developed in both France and the United States, and Verne's predictions for its use in bulk will come true at last. Orders like Barbicane's will become routine for Aluminum Company of America, which will dominate the world market.

11. *67,440 . . . 19,250 pounds* Today's metallurgist would come up with higher weights for both the iron and the aluminum shells, but the ratio of about three-to-one would still be in favor of aluminum.

12. *idea of Earth's inhabitants* Verne hits here on a crucial theme in the psychology of space probes: the need to put one's best foot forward when contacting extraterrestrials! And how will humankind measure up when we finally meet with creatures from Outer Space? Just anticipating these encounters provides a new check on ourselves, a way of being self-conscious with constructive results. It's an idea Verne will use later as a serious yardstick of Maston's real values.

Just as Maston is proud to show off our aluminum to the Selenites, so twentieth-century space-scientists will seek appropriate messages to attach to spacecraft. In the early 1970s astronomer Carl Sagan and his wife, artist Linda Sagan, will design a plaque for Pioneer 10 and 11 vehicles to carry out into the galaxy. Their problem: How do you show who we are and what we know? Their cosmic greeting card will diagram our planets in relation to our sun, give astronomical clues to help extraterrestrials find us, picture the male and female figures, and top it all with a representation of two hydrogen atoms. Later in the 1970s, Dr. Frank Drake, director of the National Astronomy and Ionosphere Center; artist Jon Lomberg; novelist Anne Druyan; and the Sagans will put together a 120-minute recording which, together with equipment and instructions for playing it, will be attached to Voyager for its reconnoitering of Jupiter and Saturn. The record will include greetings from people and whales, samples of our music, and a series of blips that extraterrestrials may decode into the component dots of photographs. One of the illustrations they may thus reconstruct will be Isaac Newton's diagram showing how to put a projectile into orbit (see page 36). Will we have made it clear how advanced we are? Or how backward? What will Outer Space think of us?

"The casing could be no more than two inches thick."

"Would that suffice?" the major asked doubtfully.

"No," President Barbicane replied, "obviously not."

"Well, what do we do now?" Elphiston wondered with a puzzled air.

"Use some other metal."

"Copper?" said Morgan.

"No, that's still too heavy, and I can suggest something better."

"What?" said the major.

"Aluminum," Barbicane replied.

"Aluminum!" his three colleagues exclaimed in unison.

"Of course, my friends. As you know, in 1854 a famous French chemist, Henri Sainte-Claire Deville, succeeded in producing aluminum in a compact mass. Now, this precious metal has the whiteness of silver, the indestructibility of gold, the toughness of iron, the fusibility of copper, the light weight of glass. It's easily worked, it's plentiful in nature—since alumina constitutes the base of most rocks—it's three times lighter than iron, and it seems to have been created for one ultimate purpose: to give us the material for our projectile!"

"Hurrah for aluminum!" cried the secretary, always boisterous in his enthusiastic moments.

"But my dear president," said the major, "isn't it expensive to manufacture aluminum?" [10]

"It was, when it was first discovered," replied Barbicane. "Originally it cost $260 to $280 (about 1,500 francs) a pound. Then it fell to about twenty-seven dollars (150 francs), and now it costs only nine dollars (48 francs, 75 centimes)."

"But nine dollars a pound," persisted the major, who would not surrender so easily, "that's still an enormous sum!"

"No doubt, my dear major, but not beyond our reach."

"What will the projectile weigh?" asked Morgan.

"Here are my figures," said Barbicane. "A shell 108 inches in diameter with a twelve-inch casing would weigh 67,440 pounds if made of cast iron; if cast in aluminum, its weight would be reduced to—19,250 pounds." [11]

"Perfect!" cried Maston. "That suits our needs perfectly."

"Yes, perfect," granted the major, "but don't you realize that at nine dollars a pound, that projectile will cost—"

"Exactly $173,250 (928,437 francs, 50 centimes). I know that. But don't worry, my friends, our project will not have to beg for money, I assure you."

"Money will pour into our treasury," J. T. Maston added.

"Well! What do you think of aluminum?" the president asked.

"Motion adopted," answered the three committeemen.

"As for the shape of the projectile," Barbicane continued, "it doesn't much matter. Once it has passed through the atmosphere, the shell will be in a vacuum. Therefore I suggest a round projectile which can rotate if it likes, or behave as it pleases."

So ended the first session of the committee. The question of the projectile had been settled decisively. J. T. Maston rejoiced over the thought of sending an aluminum shell to the Selenites: "It will give them a very bold idea of Earth's inhabitants!" [12]

CHAPTER VIII

The Story of the Cannon

The resolutions passed at this meeting had a profound effect on the outside world. Timorous folk were made a bit nervous at the thought of a 20,000-pound shell being launched into the air. Many people wondered just what kind of cannon would be needed to give enough muzzle velocity to such a mass. The minutes of the second meeting of the committee would settle these questions triumphantly.

The very next evening, the four committeemen sat down before new mountains of sandwiches and beside a veritable ocean of tea. The discussion resumed its course at once, this time without poetic preamble.

"My dear colleagues," said Barbicane, "today we must consider the cannon itself, its length, its shape, its composition, and its weight. It will probably have to be enormous, but no matter how great the difficulties, our industrial genius will easily find a way. Listen carefully, but do not hesitate to fire your objections at me, point blank! I can handle them!"

A grunt of approval greeted this proposal.

"May I remind you how far we got yesterday. Our problem has shaped up like this: we must give an initial velocity of 12,000 yards per second to a 108-inch shell weighing 20,000 pounds."

"That's our problem all right," said Major Elphiston.

"I'll take it from there," said Barbicane. "When a projectile is launched into space, what happens? Three independent forces act upon it: the resistance of the air, the pull of Earth's gravity, and the propellant force that is applied to it. Let us consider these three forces. Resistance of the air will be of little importance. Indeed, the Earth's atmosphere is only forty miles (about sixteen leagues) thick.[1] Now at a velocity of 12,000 yards per second, the projectile will pass through the atmosphere in five seconds, and that is such a short time that we can regard the air resistance as negligible.[2] Let's move on to the pull of gravity, that is to say, the weight of the shell. We know this weight will diminish in inverse ratio to the square of the distance. This is what physics teaches us: when a body left to itself falls toward the surface of the Earth, it drops fifteen feet in the first second,[3] and if that same body were transported 257,542 miles away, in other words, the distance of the moon,[4] its fall would be reduced to about one twenty-

1. *only forty miles . . . thick* Barbicane is using a convenient, arbitrary figure; as he well knows, there is no clearly defined line where atmosphere ends and Outer Space begins. Ever since Evangelista Torricelli's invention of the barometer in 1643, man has known that air pressure is lower at the top of mountains. This was taken to mean that the atmosphere thins out gradually the higher one goes. It was Blaise Pascal (1623–1662) who demonstrated mathematically the exact way in which it happens. At an altitude of 14,282 feet, air weighs only half as much as it does at sea level; at twice that height, one-quarter as much. In other words, as a standard reference book puts it in Barbicane's day, "the law is that while the height increases in arithmetical ratio, 1,2,3,4,5, the weight, and consequently the pressure, decreases in a geometrical ratio, $1/2, 1/4, 1/8, 1/16$, etc." At *forty miles*, then, air pressure is about one ten-thousandth that at sea level. Still getting rarer and rarer, air extends all the way out to a height of 6,000 miles! But since 97 percent of the Earth's atmosphere stands within eighteen miles of the surface, Barbicane is fully justified, for his purposes, in setting its effective limit at *forty miles*.

2. *air resistance as negligible* Verne rushes over this problem because he has no real answer to it. The friction of the atmosphere would certainly overheat and destroy the Gun Club projectile. Most meteors burn up in the Earth's atmosphere at speeds near that of Barbicane's shell. In Verne's day, metallurgists have not yet developed metals that could survive those *five seconds* that Barbicane must regard as inconsequential.

3. *first second* Barbicane is using round figures again. A body falls 16 feet in the first second, 48 in the second second, with a constant acceleration of 32 feet per second per second.

4. *distance of the moon.* In Belfast's letter from the Cambridge Observatory, he gave the distance of the moon in apogee as 247,552 miles. Here Barbicane recalls it as 257,542, which seems to be somebody's (Verne's? printer's? Barbicane's?) reversal of a five and a four.

5. *twenty-fourth of an inch* In the French, Verne says *une demi-ligne* or "half a line," a *ligne* being an ancient French measure equal to about one-twelfth of an inch. Doctor Woodruff calculates the fall in this first second as being closer to one-twentieth of an inch.

6. *not . . . to be maneuvered* Since they will never have to move their cannon, they can make it as big, thick, heavy, and strong as is necessary to do the job.

7. *long chase* The chase is the part of the gun extending from the trunnions (or the place where the trunnions would be if the gun had them) to the muzzle.

8. *20,000 . . . 4,800,000 pounds* In the original French edition, Barbicane, without explanation, speaks here of a shell of 30,000 pounds and hence a cannon of 7,200,000 pounds. In some recent French editions, the first figure is corrected to 20,000, but, oddly, the second is not reduced to 4,800,000. Such slips—like the one above on the moon's distance—illustrate the heavy strain that the mathematical requirements of Verne's story put on himself and his editors. On himself, for example: maybe in an early draft of the story, he *had* used a weight of 30,000 pounds, and later, settling on the lighter weight, he failed to correct all the references to it.

9. *some objections* One fatal objection to such a long tube would be the tall column of air it would imprison. This 900-foot-deep mass of air simply would not crowd out of a nine-foot opening fast enough for Barbicane's purposes. Instead it would offer such tremendous resistance that the projectile would be crushed between exploding guncotton on one side and the unyielding air on the other. Once again, Verne brushes aside the problems posed by air resistance because if he didn't, he wouldn't have a story.

fourth of an inch [5] in the first second. That is virtual immobility. So it's a question then of progressively conquering the force of gravity. How can we manage that? Through the propellant force."

"Ay, there's the rub," replied the major.

"There it is, indeed," resumed the president, "but we shall overcome it. The propellant force we need will depend on the length of the cannon and the quantity of powder we use, the latter being limited only by the strength of the former. Today then let us work out the dimensions of the cannon. I think we can agree: we may design it on the assumption it will have infinite strength, since it is not intended to be maneuvered." [6]

"All that is obvious," replied the general.

"Up to now," Barbicane said, "our longest cannons, the enormous Columbiads, have not exceeded twenty-five feet in length. We're going to astonish people with the dimensions we're forced to adopt."

"Of course!" exclaimed J. T. Maston. "For my part, I want a cannon a half-mile long at least!"

"Half a mile!" cried the major and the general.

"Yes, half a mile, and it will still be too short by half!"

"Come on, Maston," replied Morgan. "You're exaggerating."

"Not a bit!" replied the ebullient secretary. "And I can't see how you can accuse me of exaggerating."

"Because you're going too far."

"Do not forget," J. T. Maston answered in a high-and-mighty voice, "an artilleryman is like a cannonball: he can never go too far."

The argument was getting too personal, so the president cut in.

"Let's keep calm, friends, let's reason it through. Obviously we need a cannon with a long chase,[7] since the length of the piece increases the explosive force of the gases accumulated under the shell. But we know there is no advantage in going beyond certain limits."

"Exactly," said the major.

"What are the rules of thumb in such cases? Usually the length of the cannon is twenty to twenty-five times the diameter of the shell, and the cannon's weight is 235 to 240 times the shell's weight."

"Not enough," J. T. Maston cried impetuously.

"I agree, my good friend. If we followed those ratios, for a shell nine feet in diameter weighing 20,000 pounds we would build a cannon only 225 feet long weighing only 4,800,000 pounds." [8]

"Ridiculous," said J. T. Maston. "Might as well use a pistol!"

"I think so too," Barbicane went on. "That's why I propose we quadruple that length and build a cannon 900 feet long."

The general and the major posed some objections.[9] Nevertheless Barbicane's motion, vivaciously supported by the secretary, was finally carried.

"Now," said Elphiston, "how thick do we make the walls?"

"Six feet," Barbicane answered.

"You're not thinking of mounting a mass like that on a gun-carriage?" asked the major.

"That would be great!" said J. T. Maston.

"But not practical," replied Barbicane. "No, I'd like to sink this gun into the Earth itself, bind it with hoops of wrought iron, surround it with a massive layer of stone and cement, so that the Earth itself will strengthen its resistance. Once the piece is cast, we must carefully bore and calibrate the cylinder, so as to preclude any vent or windage.[10] Thus there will be no loss of gas, and all the expansive force of the powder will be used for propulsion."

"Hurrah! hurrah!" said J. T. Maston. "We have our cannon."

"Not really," replied Barbicane, quieting his impatient friend with a wave of his hand.

"Why not?"

"Because we haven't discussed its shape. Should it be a cannon, a howitzer, or a mortar?"

"A cannon," replied Morgan.

"A howitzer," said the major.

"A mortar!" cried J. T. Maston.

Another spirited argument was in the making, each man pushing his favorite weapon, when the president cut it short.

"Friends," he said, "I can give you something to agree on. Our Columbiad can be all three guns at once.[11] It will be a cannon, since the powder chamber will be the same diameter as the bore. It will be a

10. *vent or windage* That is, any space between the projectile and the bore.

11. *favorite weapon . . . at once* Keeping in mind how these three types of artillery differ can enhance our enjoyment of Verne's story. When the target is far away, Morgan's *cannon* would be preferred. This is a long-barreled weapon that uses a heavy charge of powder to fire its projectile at great velocity into a long "flat" trajectory. When the target is far away but cannot be reached with low-angle fire—maybe the foe are behind a fortress wall or on the other side of a hill—the major's *howitzer* would be brought into play. This weapon has a shorter barrel and uses a smaller charge to propel its projectile with medium velocity at a higher elevation. And if the target is nearby, Maston's *mortar* might do the job: a thick stubby weapon that uses a light charge to lob its projectile at low velocity through a high arc, a "vertical" trajectory. In reassuring his friends that their Columbiad *can be all three guns at once,* Barbicane gets beyond these distinctions to mention other technical details.

"I want a cannon a half-mile long at least!" The ideal sketch of Maston's gun as it appeared in the first illustrated edition (1872).

howitzer, since it will launch a shell. Finally, it will be a mortar. That is, it will be aimed at a high angle—90°—and being immovably fixed in the Earth, it will be unable to recoil; and so it will give to the shell all the propellant power accumulated behind it."

"Motion carried," said the committeemen.

"Just a thought," said Elphiston. "Will our *can-how-mortar* [12] be rifled?"

"No," replied Barbicane. "No, we need an enormous initial velocity. You know that the projectile escapes more slowly from a rifled barrel than from a smooth bore."

"True."

"So at last we've got it!" repeated J. T. Maston.

"Not quite yet," replied the president.

"Why not?"

"Because we still don't know what metal it should be made of."

"Let's decide right now."

"I was about to suggest it."

The four committeemen paused only to swallow a dozen sandwiches each, washing them down with bowls of tea, before resuming the discussion.

"Esteemed colleagues," said Barbicane, "our cannon must be extremely tough, extremely hard, infusible by heat, indissoluble and inoxidizable by the corrosive action of acids."

"There can be no question of that," replied the major, "and since we'll need a vast amount of metal, we don't have a wide range of choices."

"Well then," said Morgan, "for manufacturing our Columbiad I propose the best alloy yet known: that is to say, one hundred parts copper, twelve parts tin, six parts brass."

"Friends," replied the president, "I admit that that combination has given excellent results. But in our case it would be very costly and difficult to use. I think we should adopt a good low-priced metal, like cast iron. Don't you agree, major?"

"Completely," answered Elphiston.

"Actually, cast iron costs ten times less than bronze; it's easy to melt; it's easy to cast in sand molds; it can be worked quickly; it saves both time and money. This stuff is first-rate. I remember that during the war, at the siege of Atlanta, [13] some cast-iron cannons fired a thousand shots each at twenty-minute intervals, without being the worse for wear."

"Still, cast iron is very brittle," replied Morgan.

"Yes, but still very strong. We shall not burst, I assure you."

"One can burst and still be an honest man," J. T. Maston said sententiously.

"Obviously," replied Barbicane. "I ask our worthy secretary to calculate the weight of an iron cannon 900 feet long, with a nine-foot bore, and six-foot walls."

"Right away," J. T. Maston said.

And, just as he had done the evening before, he worked his equations with marvelous facility, and said after a minute:

"This cannon will weigh 68,040 metric tons (68,040,000 kilograms)."

---

12. *can-how-mortar* Verne is going one step further in a direction already taken by artillerists in his day. Some types of heavy ordnance—like the Columbiad—are hybrids, combining the qualities of *gun* (what Verne calls a *cannon*) and *howitzer*. For example, U.S. field artillerymen sometimes refer to a certain "light gun" by its official name, the "gun-howitzer."

13. *siege of Atlanta* This famous action is all recent news to Verne's original readers. By 1864, Atlanta had become a major Confederate rail, supply, and manufacturing center. When General William Sherman invaded Georgia, President Jefferson Davis chose General John Hood, famous for vigorous attack, to protect Atlanta. Although he built strong defenses and launched three counterattacks over a wide area, Hood was forced to evacuate the city on September 2. Sherman then used Atlanta as his base for his march to the sea.

"And at two cents (10 centimes) a pound, it will cost?"

"Two million, five hundred and ten thousand, seven hundred and one dollars (13,608,000 francs)."[14]

J. T. Maston, the major, and the general all turned nervously to Barbicane.

"But gentlemen," said the president, "I repeat what I said yesterday. Keep calm. We'll have millions to work with."

And with this assurance from their president, the committee agreed to hold their third meeting on the very next day, and they adjourned.

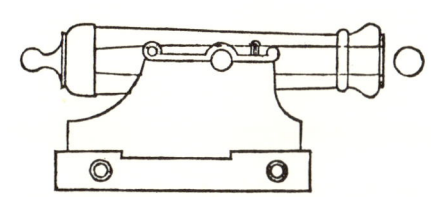

Elevation of the carronade, from the *American Supplement to Encyclopaedia Britannica* (1889). Because of its short range, the carronade was retired from the U.S. Navy in 1845. But some 32- and 42-pounder carronades have been trundled out of the mothballs during the Civil War.

14. *Two million . . . dollars (13,608,000 francs)* It's not easy to convert the cost of the Columbiad into today's dollars. But Professor Irwin Unger, economic historian in the Faculty of Arts and Sciences at New York University, has given us some basis for a rough conversion. Wholesale prices on certain staple items were then about one-third what they are now. He estimates that the late 1860s' dollar was worth two and a half to three and a half times today's dollar. Hence we can assume that Barbicane's cannon would now cost at least $7,532,103. But Roger Greaves, a French-to-English translator, reckons an 1865 franc as worth somewhat more than a 1978 dollar. That would put the cost of the cannon today at about $15,000,000.

CHAPTER IX

The Powder Question

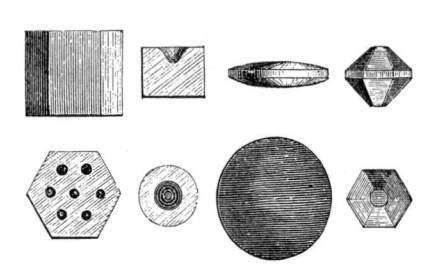

Forms of gunpowder (left to right): prismatic grain, English pellet, lenticular, and Rodman's hexagonal prism. From *The American Cyclopaedia* (1874).

1. *Schwarz . . . Middle Ages* Berthold Schwarz, or Berthold the Black, might well have earned that name for dabbling in the black art of alchemy. He might well have experimented with black powder and indeed have blown himself up. But if he did it *in the fourteenth century* that was too late for him to become the inventor of gunpowder; by then thousands of persons, from China to England, already knew the formula. Still, Schwarz might well have had a part in developing firearms: maybe he met his death when one of his weapons burst. Firearms are frequently mentioned in records surviving from his day. For example, there were shipments of guns and powder from Ghent to England as early as 1314.

2. *"Greek fire" . . . saltpeter* When a Saracen fleet approached Constantinople in A.D. 673, they were met by Byzantine galleys armed with strange bronze tubes mounted on their prows. Suddenly these tubes sprayed liquid fire: the Saracen ships were set aflame and Constantinople was saved. Again in 717–718 another Saracen fleet suffered the same fate.

The exact nature of *Greek fire* was a carefully guarded state secret of the Byzantine Empire. Attributed to the genius of an architect named Callinicus, this secret mixture ignited

The committee had only one more question to take up: the powder. The public waited with great anxiety for this final decision. Now that the size of the shell and the length of the cannon were known, how much powder would be needed to provide the propellant force? This terrible agent, which man has somehow mastered, was now to be called on to play its greatest role in history.

It is widely believed and often repeated that gunpowder was invented in the fourteenth century by the monk Schwarz who paid for his great discovery with his life. But now we are almost certain this story must be regarded as a mere legend of the Middle Ages.[1] Gunpowder was not invented by any one person. It derives directly from "Greek fire," which—like gunpowder—was also composed of sulphur and saltpeter.[2] The only difference is that the ancient mixture, which was simply an incendiary composition, has now become an explosive one.[3]

But while scholars are well aware of the pseudo-history of gunpowder, few people realize the truth about its mechanical power. And that is exactly what we must make clear in order to understand the importance of the question now before the committee.

A liter[4] of powder weighs about two pounds (900 grams). When ignited, it produces 400 liters of gas. Released, and under the action of a temperature of 2,400 degrees, this gas will expand to a volume of 4,000 liters. Thus the ratio of the volume of the powder to the volume of the gas produced by its combustion is 1 to 4,000. It is now easy to understand the frightful force of that gas when it is confined in a space 4,000 times too small for it.

This is the kind of knowledge the committeemen had at their fingertips when they met again the next day. Barbicane gave the floor to Major Elphiston, who had been director of powder production during the war.

"My dear comrades," said the distinguished chemist, "I shall begin with some incontrovertible figures on which we can base our discussion. The twenty-four-pound shell, of which the honorable J. T. Maston spoke in such poetic terms the day before yesterday, is expelled from the gun by only sixteen pounds of powder."

"You're sure of that figure?" asked Barbicane.

"Absolutely certain," the major replied. "The Armstrong cannon uses only seventy-five pounds of powder to launch an 800-pound projectile, and the Rodman Columbiad needs only 160 pounds of powder to fire a half-ton cannonball six miles. These facts are beyond dispute. I got them myself from the files of the Artillery Board."

"Quite right," said the general.

"So," the major continued, "the conclusion to draw from these figures is that the amount of powder does not increase in direct proportion to the weight of the ball. We may need sixteen pounds of powder to fire the twenty-four-pounder—in other words, with an ordinary cannon, we need an amount of powder that's two-thirds the weight of the projectile—but that ratio is not a constant. Figure it out for yourself—to fire the half-ton cannonball, we do not use 667 pounds of powder but we reduce the amount to only 160."

"And what are the implications for us?"

"Yes, my dear major," J. T. Maston said, "your theory seems to imply that if we just make our projectile big enough, we shan't need any powder at all."

. . . the monk Schwarz . . . paid for his great discovery with his life. Engraving from the 1872 edition.

when it was wetted, and its fire could not be extinguished with water. As Verne indicates, his contemporaries thought "sea fire," as it was also called, might have been *composed of sulphur and saltpeter*. Today chemists believe that Callinicus' secret ingredient was either a distilled petroleum fraction or quicklime, which gives off heat when mixed with water. In any event, Callinicus was the inventor of the flamethrower, as it was called when the idea was revived in twentieth-century warfare.

3. *an explosive one* As a popularizer of science, Verne assumes responsibility for tackling such questions. And here he's gambling on a shaky hypothesis. We have no proof that the Byzantine Greeks, or anyone in their part of the world, knew of saltpeter as early as the seventh century. And Greek fire, as we have seen, is better explained in terms of other chemicals. The Chinese, on the other hand, were well acquainted with saltpeter at that time and surely were compounding it into black powder by the ninth century. As early as 1000, Chinese forces were firing explosive grenades and bombs from catapults. At the Battle of Kai-fung-fu in 1232, the Chinese made effective use of powder-propelled "fire arrows," and about that time they were loading powder into bamboo tubes to launch stone projectiles. Meanwhile the thirteenth-century Arab writer al-Hasan al-Rammah discusses "the sending of fire" in his *Treatise on Horsemanship and War Stratagems*. His recipes for gunpowder include solid advice on how to prepare the saltpeter which, significantly, he calls "Chinese Snow." In 1248, the Arabs sent a triple rocket across the Nile into the ranks of the French knights of the Seventh Crusade.

By the thirteenth century, all Europe knew of black powder. Its properties and preparation were described in the writings of Marcus the Greek (fl. 1250?), the German Albertus Magnus (1193–1280), and the Englishman Roger Bacon (1214–1292). Some historians have thought that Europeans discovered black powder independently of the Chinese. But Joseph Needham, in his definitive studies (see Bibliography), concludes emphatically that Western "gunnery and gunpowder resulted from direct Chinese transmission to Europe."

The events and dates we have reviewed here make it clear that Verne is right at least about Berthold the Black: Verne was among the first to discount the efforts of nineteenth-century German historians to identify Schwarz as the father of gunpowder.

4. *A liter* The metric system equivalent of .908 dry quart or 1.056 liquid quart.

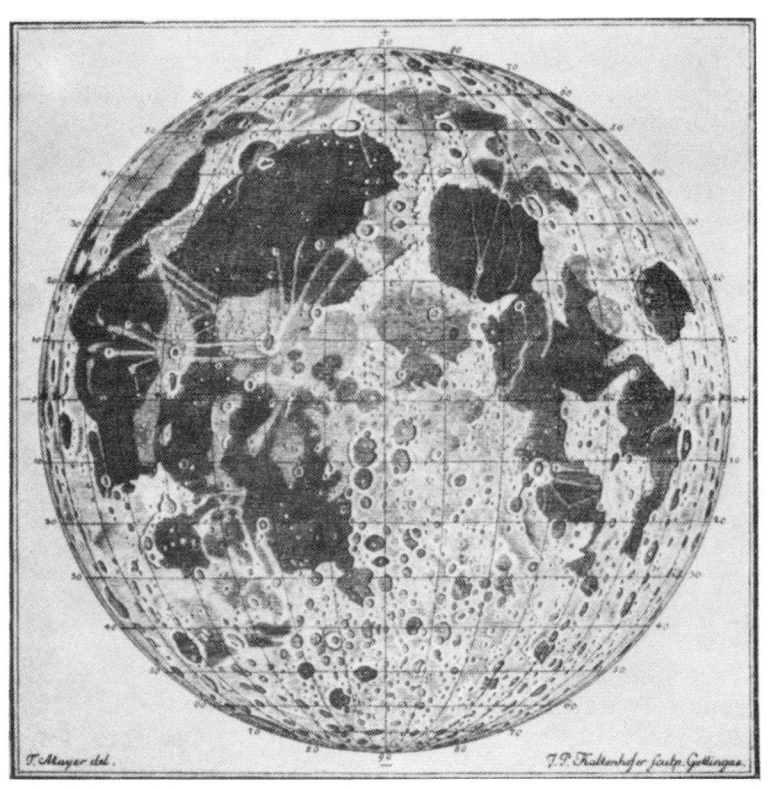

Tobias Mayer (1723–1762), professor of mathematics at Göttingen, made this map of the moon which was published posthumously (1775).

"My friend Maston jokes even about serious things," replied the major, "but I reassure you, I shall soon propose quantities of gunpowder that will satisfy your artillerist's pride. I just want to point out that during the war, the amount of powder used in the biggest guns was reduced, through trial and error, to a tenth of the weight of the projectile."

"Nothing could be closer to the truth," said Morgan. "But before we decide on the amount of powder necessary for our shot at the moon, I think we should agree on the type of powder."

"We shall use coarse-grained powder," the major answered. "It ignites faster than fine-grained powder."

"No doubt," replied Morgan, "but when it explodes, its shattering effect is so great it ultimately damages the bore of the piece."

"But what would damage a cannon designed for long service is no threat to our Columbiad. We do not run the risk of bursting the barrel, and we must ignite the powder instantaneously to get the best mechanical results."

"We could make several touch-holes," J. T. Maston said, "and ignite the powder in several places at once."

"Of course," replied Elphiston, "but that would just make the job more difficult. I'll stick by my coarse-grained powder and avoid such problems."

"So be it," agreed the general.

"Now to charge his Columbiad," the major went on, "Rodman used powder grains as big as chestnuts, made with willow charcoal that was simply roasted in cast-iron boilers. His powder was hard and glossy, it left no smudge on the hand, it contained a high proportion of hydrogen and oxygen, it ignited instantly, and although it had a high degree of brisance,[5] it did not do much damage to the barrel."

"Then it seems to me," J. T. Maston said, "we have no reason for hesitating. The choice has been made for us."

"Unless you prefer gold powder." The major's laugh earned him a mean gesture from his touchy friend's iron hook.

Until now Barbicane had remained aloof from the discussion, listening, maybe working on an idea of his own. Now he contented himself with a question:

"Well, my friends, what quantity of powder do you suggest?"

The three members of the Gun Club looked at each other for a moment.

"200,000 pounds," Morgan said at last.

"500,000," the major answered.

"800,000!" J. T. Maston cried out.

This time Elphiston did not dare accuse his colleague of exaggeration. After all, it was a matter of sending a 20,000-pound projectile all the way to the moon, and with a muzzle velocity of 12,000 yards per second. A moment of silence followed this triple proposition made by the three colleagues.

At last it was broken by President Barbicane.

"Worthy comrades," he said in a calm voice, "I assume that if our cannon is built according to our specifications, it will possess infinite strength. So I shall surprise the honorable J. T. Maston when I tell him he has been timid in his calculations. I propose to double his 800,000 pounds of gunpowder."

"1,600,000 pounds?" exclaimed J. T. Maston, jumping out of his chair.

"Exactly."

"But then we have to go back to my idea of a half-mile cannon."

"Obviously," the major said.

"1,600,000 pounds of powder," the committee secretary went on, "would occupy 22,000 cubic feet. Now your 900-foot cannon would comprise only 54,000 cubic feet. It would be almost half-full of powder. The bore would not be long enough for the expanding gases to give the shell sufficient push—"

There was no answer. J. T. Maston had hit on the truth. Everybody looked at Barbicane.

"Still," the president said, "I stand by my figure. Think, 1,600,000 pounds of gunpowder will give birth to 6,000,000,000 liters of gas. Six thousand million! Imagine!"

"But how can we do it?" asked the general.

"Simple. We must reduce the mass of powder without reducing its mechanical power."

"Good. But how?"

"I'm going to tell you," Barbicane said quietly.

His interlocutors stared at him.

"Actually nothing could be easier than reducing this mass to one-

5. *brisance* This is the technical name for the *shattering effect* of a sudden release of energy that Morgan has mentioned five paragraphs ago. The *grains as big as chestnuts* that the major describes are Rodman's mammoth powder, noted in Chapter I. Pressing ordinary black powder into special dies, Rodman shaped it into hexagonal prisms with perforations parallel to the edges. As the outer surfaces of the prism burned, they shrank. This expanded the inner surfaces provided by the perforations, and this in turn promoted progressive burning rates as the projectile moved through the bore.

6. *Braconnot . . . guncotton* Henri *Braconnot* (1781–1855) did pioneering work in the analysis of carbohydrates, including sugars, starches, and cellulose. It was T. J. *Pelouze* (1807–1867) who discovered that cotton could be converted into a violently inflammable substance by the action of concentrated nitric acid. And it was Christian F. *Schönbein* (1799–1868), discoverer of ozone, who improved Pelouze's method by adding sulphuric acid to the nitric acid. Schönbein is credited with being the first to describe guncotton as such and to demonstrate its use as an explosive and a propellant for firearms.

7. *Maynard . . . Boston* In 1847 J. Parkers Maynard used this method to produce the syrupy stuff called collodion.

8. *fuming nitric acid* "So called because, on contact with humid air, it gives off thick whitish fumes," Verne explains in a footnote.

9. *Nothing could be simpler.* With guncotton, as with aluminum, Verne is extrapolating from current events, and once again, he's gambling against the prevailing opinion. As he writes this scene in 1865, guncotton is not yet regarded as a safe substitute for gunpowder. If it doesn't blow up spontaneously and mysteriously in the arsenal, it might well destroy the gun it's used in. "How far the repeated disasters . . . are due to the carelessness of those who have it in charge, is unknown, for it leaves no witnesses," a standard reference book reports. Then in 1868, three years after Verne writes this chapter, Sir Frederick Abel will diagnose the trouble: guncotton is chemically unstable because it retains some of the acids in its fibers. He devises a more thorough method for removing them. "It was for a time supposed that the ingenious process of Mr. Abel had removed the causes of distrust; but a terrible and unexplained explosion at Stowmarket in 1871 revived the feeling, which still prevails," *The American Cyclopaedia* will conclude in 1874. But later investigators will add chemical stabilizers to guncotton. Then at last the confidence that the Gun Club has in nitrocellulose will be justified: and another Verne prediction will come true.

10. *instead of the usual 240* This figure is not to be confused with the 2,400 degrees mentioned earlier by Verne himself. 240 degrees is the temperature needed to ignite ordinary gunpowder, and 2,400 is the temperature of the released gases after the powder is burnt.

fourth its size. You all know that curious substance that constitutes the elemental tissue of plants, called cellulose."

"Ah!" said the major. "Now I see what you're driving at."

"This substance," the president resumed, "can be found in an absolutely pure state in many bodies, especially in cotton, which is nothing more than the fiber covering the seeds of the cotton plant. Now cotton, when combined with cold nitric acid, is transformed into a substance eminently insoluble, eminently combustible, eminently explosive. In 1832, a French chemist, Braconnot, discovered this substance and called it 'xyloidine.' In 1838 another Frenchman, Pelouze, studied its properties, and in 1846 Schönbein, a chemistry professor at Basel, saw its military value. That powder is nitric cotton—"

"Or pyroxylin," Elphiston added.

"Or guncotton,"[6] Morgan added.

"But isn't there an American name associated with this discovery?" J. T. Maston's question was prompted by his great national pride.

"Unhappily, no," the major replied.

"Yes, I can make you feel better, Maston," the president said. "We could say that one of our countrymen has done work that is related to the study of cellulose. Collodion, one of the basic chemicals used in photography, is simply pyroxylin dissolved in ether with alcohol added. And collodion was discovered by Maynard, at that time a medical student in Boston."[7]

"Hurrah for Maynard and guncotton!" cried the ebullient secretary of the Gun Club.

"Let me get back to pyroxylin," Barbicane said. "You can see the properties that make it valuable for our purposes. It can be prepared with the greatest of ease: you soak cotton for fifteen minutes in fuming nitric acid,[8] you wash it with water, dry it, and it's ready."

"Nothing could be simpler,"[9] said Morgan.

"Furthermore, humidity has no effect on pyroxylin, and that's important for us, since it will take us several days to load the cannon. Pyroxylin ignites at 170 degrees instead of the usual 240.[10] And it burns so fast that when you ignite it on top of ordinary powder, it goes off before the ordinary stuff can catch fire."

"Perfect," observed the major.

"The only trouble is, it costs more."

"And who cares?" cried J. T. Maston.

"Finally, it gives the shell four times more speed than ordinary powder does. And if it's mixed with a quantity of potassium nitrate equal to eighty percent its weight, its explosive power is increased again."

"Is that necessary?"

"I guess not," Barbicane conceded.

"So, instead of 1,600,000 pounds of powder, we'll have a mere 400,000 pounds of guncotton. And since 500 pounds of cotton can safely be compressed into twenty-seven cubic feet, our powder will fill only thirty fathoms of the Columbiad. Our projectile, driven by the expansive force of six billion liters of gas, will have more than 700 feet of bore to travel through before taking wing toward the moon!"

At this point, J. T. Maston could no longer contain his feelings. He launched himself into his friend's arms with the force of a projectile.

Fortunately, Barbicane was built strong enough to stand up to any cannonball.

This incident ended the third session of the committee. Barbicane and his daring cohorts, to whom nothing seemed impossible, had resolved the very thorny questions of the projectile, the cannon, and the powder. Their plans were complete. It remained only to put them into practice.

"A mere detail," J. T. Maston said, "a bagatelle."

AUTHOR'S NOTE. At this meeting, President Barbicane credited one of his compatriots with the discovery of collodion. With due concern for the feelings of J. T. Maston, we must point out that this was a mistake, and it grew out of the similarity between two names.

In 1847, Maynard, who was studying medicine in Boston, got the idea of using collodion to treat wounds, but collodion had been discovered as early as 1846. And the honor of that discovery belongs to a Frenchman, a truly distinguished mind, a scholar who was also a painter, poet, philosopher, hellenist, and chemist—M. Louis Ménard.[11]

—J. V.

11. *Louis Ménard* This has been a chapter rich in jokes, not all of them on the surface, and two of them on Verne himself. The best has been Verne's joke on the four artillerists. They start off seriously talking about how scientific they have become in calculating how much powder to use. They wind up seriously making wild guesses. Then there's Barbicane's touching effort to assuage Maston's wounded national pride. Verne cleverly withholds the information about Barbicane's confusion of *Maynard* with *Ménard* until he can use it as his own curtain line. Meanwhile, he himself has been guilty of a similar confusion of words and, ironically, is a bit hasty, perhaps out of his own national pride, in giving *Ménard* main credit for discovering collodion. Notice that early in the chapter Verne himself says that one liter of gunpowder, which weighs about two pounds, will expand into 4,000 liters of gas. Later Barbicane enthusiastically concludes that 1,600,000 pounds of gunpowder will *give birth to* 6,000,000,000 liters of gas: he mistakenly multiplies not the liters but the pounds by 4,000. 1,600,000 pounds, being about 800,000 liters, should *give birth to* a mere three thousand million liters of gas (we're following Barbicane's penchant for rounding off his figures). Barbicane's error would not be worth mentioning—it affects no other calculations, it's simply part of Verne's satiric exaggerations—except that here Verne himself has confused *liters* with *livres* (French for pounds) just as surely as Barbicane confused *Maynard* with *Ménard*. And that too boomerangs on our author. For *Ménard* is not, in the hindsight of history, regarded as the sole discoverer of collodion, simply as one of its early investigators. Today *Schönbein* is considered to have been the first to describe collodion as well as guncotton.

CHAPTER X

One Enemy out of Twenty-Five Million Friends

The American people were taking a lively interest in every last detail of the Gun Club enterprise. They were following the committee's deliberations day by day. They were tremendously excited by the simplest preparations for this great experiment, by the mathematical questions to be solved, by the mechanical problems to be overcome, in short, by every aspect of the operation.

More than a year would pass between the start of the work and its completion, but this would not be a period without excitement. The search for the proper site for the gun-emplacement, the construction of the mold, the casting of the Columbiad, the highly perilous loading, every step was sure to arouse public curiosity. Once the projectile was launched, it would be out of sight in a few tenths of a second. After that, only a few privileged scientists would be able to see with their own eyes how it behaved in outer space, how it reached the moon. All the more reason, then, for the people at large to take passionate interest in the part they could follow closely: the exact details of the preparatory work.

But the drama was not destined to be purely scientific in nature: it was soon heightened by an unexpected development in the realm of human relations.

Barbicane's project, as we have seen, had won him legions of admirers and friends. Still, it must be admitted that however honorable, however extraordinary his vast following was, it fell short of unanimous support. One solitary individual, one person alone in all the states of the Union, took issue with the Gun Club's plans; he attacked them violently on every occasion. Human nature is so constituted that Barbicane was affected more by this one man's opposition than by all the others' praise.

Yet he knew well the motives behind that antipathy, why it was so personal and long-standing, what circumstances had given birth to that solitary resentment, that jealous rivalry.

The president of the Gun Club had never seen this pertinacious enemy. This was fortunate, because a meeting of these two men would certainly produce dire results. This rival was a scientist like Barbicane himself, a man fiery, bold, determined, and violent, a pure Yankee.

His name was Captain Nicholl. He lived in Philadelphia.

Everyone has heard about the strange struggle that developed during the Civil War between the projectile and naval armor, the former designed to pierce the latter, the latter built to resist the former. This struggle led to radical changes in the navies of two continents. The projectile and armor plate fought with unprecedented intensity, the former growing bigger, the latter growing thicker. Warships bristling with awesome armament moved into battle covered with invincible armor. The *Merrimac,* the *Monitor,* the *Tennessee,* the *Weehawken* first protected themselves against projectiles, and then hurled huge projectiles at their enemy. They did unto others what they would not have others do unto them, an immoral principle that is the basic premise of the art of war.[1]

Now, while Barbicane became a great caster of projectiles, Nicholl became a great forger of armor. The one cast night and day in Baltimore, the other forged day and night in Philadelphia. Each one pursued an ideal diametrically opposed to the other.

As soon as Barbicane invented a new cannonball, Nicholl produced

1. *art of war* With this bitter parody on the beliefs of Christian war-makers, Verne criticizes not only the Americans but also the hypocritical policies of the ruling monarch of France, Emperor Louis Napoleon. A Christian, married to a pietistic Spanish Catholic, declared supporter of the Pope and the Church, the Emperor has nevertheless violated the Golden Rule in precisely Verne's sense. "The Empire means peace," Napoleon III said when he assumed imperial power in 1852. Two years later, France was at war with Russia in the Crimea, in 1859 declared war on Austria, and in 1862 invaded Mexico. As Verne writes, the Mexican adventure is in serious trouble (more of that in Chapter XII), and Napoleon's intrigues in Europe are luring France into catastrophe. A few years after this novel is published, Verne will write to his father complaining that Napoleon's militaristic policy "takes us back to the times of the Huns and Visigoths" and offers "the prospect of a series of stupid wars." Verne will command a coast-guard unit in the last of the Emperor's series.

In this 1872 illustration, the artist represents the saturnine Captain Nicholl with his attributes: battered armor plates and a picture of an ironclad.

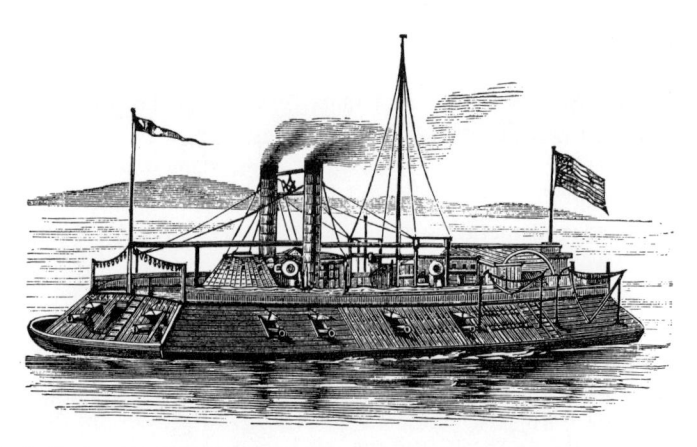

The *St. Louis,* one of the "turtleback" ironclads built by James B. Eads. It was plated with iron slabs two and a half inches thick and eleven inches wide, rabbeted together and laid on a four-inch oak backing inclined at a 45° angle. The ship's *awesome armament* comprised thirteen nine- and ten-inch guns. Engraving from *The American Cyclopaedia* (1874).

2. *cut right through him* Verne is well known among family and friends for his naughty jokes, and his very first play was labeled *risqué* by at least one reviewer. Hence we could assume that Verne is well aware of the sexual overtones in this passage, what with Barbicane compulsively *penetrating,* Nicholl seemingly in terror of *penetration.* But a Freudian would say that if Verne is unconscious of the sexual implications, then they betray even more about the author himself. In either event, it is significant that the relationship Verne is mocking in this fashion is one between men. Verne's fiction offers a world almost entirely devoid of women. Notice that not one major character in this novel seems to need female companionship. All Verne's men save their most profound feelings for other males. Notice too how Verne will develop the relations between Barbicane and Nicholl. Very correctly Verne senses that they do protest too much: more significant than their rivalry is the fact that they are so emotionally involved with each other. Verne's masterful development of this insight, partly in terms of their dreams, is one of many ways in which his fiction anticipates the psychoanalytic approach to characterization.

better armor plate. The president of the Gun Club spent his life penetrating, the captain spent his preventing penetration. This professional rivalry soon became personal. Nicholl appeared in Barbicane's dreams as an unperforable carapace against which he splattered himself, and Barbicane appeared in Nicholl's nightmares as a cannonball that cut right through him.[2]

Although they were pursuing divergent courses, these scientists had inevitably to meet each other, all the axioms of geometry to the contrary: but that meeting would have to be on the dueling ground. Fortunately for these citizens who were so useful to their country, they were separated by some fifty or sixty miles, and their friends had taken great pains to keep them from running into each other.

Now which inventor had bested the other was a moot question; the results achieved had made it difficult to find the answer. It did seem though as if, in the long run, armor plate would give in to the projectile.

Nevertheless, men qualified to judge the matter had their doubts. In the final trials, Barbicane's new cylindro-conical projectiles simply stuck like pins in Nicholl's armor. That day the Philadelphia forger thought he had won forever and he heaped scorn on his rival. But that worthy then substituted ordinary 600-pound shells for the conical shot, and Nicholl was reduced to silence. Although they were fired with only medium velocity, the 600-pounders pierced, cracked, and shattered the captain's best plate.

That was how things stood: apparently the projectile had won. Then on the very day when Nicholl had perfected new armor made of steel plate, the war ended! It was the greatest armor ever, and it defied all the projectiles in the world. The captain had it shipped to the artillery range near Washington, he challenged the president of the Gun Club to shatter it. But the war was over, and Barbicane declined.

Now Nicholl, furious, offered to expose his plate to the impact of projectiles of any conceivable kind: solid or hollow, spherical or conical. Again he was turned down by the president, who clearly did not want to take any chances when he was ahead.

Infuriated by the president's adamancy, Nicholl began to offer every inducement. He would place his new armor only two hundred yards from the cannon. Barbicane still declined. A hundred yards? Not even seventy-five.

"Fifty yards then!" the captain announced to the newspapers. "Twenty-five! And I'll even stand right behind my plate!"

Barbicane announced that even if Captain Nicholl were to stand out in front of his armor, he would not shoot.

When Nicholl heard this, he could no longer contain himself: he resorted to personal insult. He said that a coward in one way is a coward in every way. That the man who refused to fire a cannon must be frightened by it. That artillerists who now fought at a distance of six miles had replaced personal courage with mathematical formulas. That it took more courage to wait calmly behind armor plate for the shock of the cannonball than it took to fire it by the numbers.[3]

To these insinuations Barbicane responded not at all. He might not even have known about them. He was already totally immersed in the complex calculations for his grand experiment.

When Barbicane delivered his famous message to the Gun Club, Captain Nicholl went into paroxysms of rage. Of course his supreme jealousy alternated with feelings of absolute impotence. How could he invent something bigger than this 900-foot Columbiad![4] What armor plate could stand up against a 20,000-pound projectile! At first he was floored and crushed by this salvo of news, but he recovered, he resolved to bury Barbicane's proposal under a landslide of arguments.

He began systematically to attack the work of the Gun Club by writing a series of letters which the newspapers did not refuse to print. He tried to demolish the scientific basis of Barbicane's project. Once he had declared war, he felt that the end justified the means, and so, to tell the truth, he argued speciously and in bad faith.

First he violently assailed Barbicane's figures, trying to prove by A + B that Barbicane's formulas were incorrect, that he was ignorant of the basic principles of ballistics. Then Nicholl, using his own calculations, demonstrated that it was absolutely impossible to give any object at all a velocity of 12,000 yards per second. And, algebra in hand, he maintained that even if such a velocity could be attained, such a heavy projectile could never be lifted beyond the limits of the Earth's atmosphere! It would never reach even an altitude of twenty miles (eight leagues). And furthermore! Even if such a speed could be attained, even if it would suffice, the shell could not withstand the pressure of the gases produced by igniting 1,600,000 pounds of powder. And even if it could resist the pressure, it could not withstand the temperature, it would melt as it left the Columbiad, and a red-hot rain would fall down on the heads of the foolish spectators.[5]

Barbicane did not even wince at these attacks; he simply got on with his work.

Now Nicholl approached the question from different angles. Passing over the uselessness of the project, he considered the extreme danger both for citizens who condoned the wretched experiment by watching

3. *by the numbers* Verne doubtless got the idea for this Nicholl-Barbicane feud from a series of experiments culminating in the famous Armstrong tests of 1861–1862. Back in the days of wooden ships, naval architects had learned, through actual trials, that they had to build their hulls two feet thick to prevent penetration by cannonballs. As early as 1812, John Stevens of Hoboken, New Jersey, had proposed to Congress that American warships be armored with iron plate. In 1841, the Stevens family fired continually at wrought-iron plates in an effort to determine the exact thickness required to withstand the projectiles then in use. In 1857, the English experimented at Woolwich with iron and steel plates four inches thick. They discovered that some plate offered good resistance to 68-pound solid shot fired from 600 yards, but that most plate would break up if subjected to rapid-fire bombardment. They found too that simple wrought iron was better than steel for absorbing the energy of the shot. Projectiles that would only dent or batter iron plate would actually crack the steel.

These experiments, of course, were intended to *perfect* naval armor. But gun-and-projectile manufacturers conducted their own tests with the opposite aim: to develop artillery that could *destroy* armor plate. The American Civil War, the first to feature iron-clad vessels on a big scale, led Sir William Armstrong (we met him in Chapter I) to update and refine these experiments. He concluded that shot fired at a moderate distance by muzzle-loading smooth-bore cannon of large caliber possesses greater power to penetrate and crush iron plates than shot fired from breech-loading rifled ordnance. "This result has excited much comment from eminent artillery officers," remarked one military writer. Enter: Verne the satirist.

4. *900-foot Columbiad* Notice how this passage continues the sexual imagery introduced earlier: Verne describes Nicholl's feelings as *jealousy, impotence,* because he cannot create something bigger than Barbicane's 900-foot phallic symbol.

5. *foolish spectators* To suit his own literary needs, Verne follows up Nicholl's wild arguments with some very sane ones. Nicholl is wrong on two matters: it certainly is possible to give an object *a velocity of 12,000 yards per second* and to lift *such a heavy projectile* into Outer Space (but through the use of rocketry not gunfire). Nicholl is correct, however, in his other objections: *the shell could not withstand the pressure of the gases;* as we have noted in Chapter VIII, the great mass of air trapped in the 900-foot gun-barrel would not crowd out of the nine-foot opening fast enough; the projectile would be crushed between the exploding guncotton and the unyielding air. And as for Nicholl's *red-hot rain,* A. C. Clarke puts it this way: "Only a cloud of vaporised aluminum would have emerged from the muzzle." Verne, as we noted earlier, cannot meet these objections on the scientific level. And so he disposes of them on the dramatic level: he puts them in the mouth of an unpopular character.

Nicholl writing a series of letters which the newspapers did not refuse to print. Engraving from the first illustrated edition (1872).

6. *safety of the commonwealth* Throughout his writing, Verne worries over the possible excesses of technology, especially technology under private control as opposed to technology for the common good. In his very first science-fiction novel, *Five Weeks in a Balloon* (1863), Dick Kennedy, a big-game hunter, says:

"By dint of inventing machinery, men will someday be eaten up by it. I have always thought that the end of the earth will come when some enormous boiler, charged to three billion atmospheres, will blow up and destroy the world."

Joe, a servant, adds:

"And I bet the Yankees will have a hand in that."

Dr. Samuel Ferguson, leader of the balloon expedition and Verne's first science-fiction hero, agrees:

"Yes, they *are* great boiler-makers. . . ."

One of the motifs of *Twenty Thousand Leagues under the Sea* (1870) is the conflict between secret (Faustian) science and public (Baconian) science. (For a full discussion see *The Annotated Jules Verne* edition, pp. 158–159.) This contrast is the dominant theme in *The Begum's Fortune* (1878), in which Prussian perversion of technology is dramatized, and in *Master of the World* (1904) in which a Yankee is again the villain.

it, and for towns unlucky enough to be situated near the deplorable gunsite. He also pointed out that if the projectile could not reach its target—and it certainly could not—then obviously it would fall back onto the Earth, and the fall of such a mass, multiplied by the square of its velocity, would cause great damage to some point on the globe. Under these circumstances, it was necessary to prevent such interference with the rights of free citizens: this was a case calling for government intervention, so that the safety of the commonwealth [6] would not be sacrificed to the whim of one man.

Obviously Captain Nicholl allowed himself to be carried away by such exaggeration. He stood alone in his views. No one took heed of his dire prophecies. He was allowed to shout himself hoarse, since that seemed to be what he wanted. He made himself the defender of a cause doomed to failure; he was heard but he was not listened to, and he did not alienate one single admirer from the president of the Gun Club. Barbicane did not even take the trouble to answer his rival's arguments.

Nicholl was fighting a last-ditch battle. Unable to risk his life for his cause, he resolved to risk his fortune. In the columns of the *Richmond Enquirer* he announced that he was willing to lay a series of bets involving increasing sums of money.

He bet:

1. That the Gun Club would not be able to raise the money needed for its experiment.   1,000 dollars
2. That the casting of the 900-foot cannon was impracticable and would not succeed.   2,000 dollars
3. That it would be impossible to load the Columbiad, and that the weight of the projectile would ignite the guncotton prematurely.   3,000 dollars
4. That the Columbiad would burst the first time it was fired.   4,000 dollars
5. That the shell would go no more than six miles and would fall back to earth a few seconds after the launching.   5,000 dollars

In his great obstinacy, the captain was risking a sizable sum of money. He had no less than $15,000 at stake.[7]

But in spite of the magnitude of the wager, on October 19 he received a sealed envelope containing this superbly laconic reply:

                                      Baltimore, October 18

Taken.

                                                BARBICANE[8]

Dick Kennedy, Dr. Samuel Ferguson, and their servant Joe crossing the Niger in their balloon *Victoria*. Engraving from the 1867 French edition of *Five Weeks in a Balloon*.

7. *$15,000 at stake* If we use the conversion methods proposed in our note on *Two million . . . Dollars* in Chapter VIII, we see that Nicholl has somewhere between $45,000 and $90,000 at stake in today's money.

8. *Taken. BARBICANE* Once again, this time to heighten his suspense, Verne makes Nicholl the spokesperson for some real objections to Barbicane's project. Nicholl, who has figured in the enormously expensive Civil War, knows well how his country manages to underwrite such gigantic enterprises as the building of the Erie Canal and the transcontinental railroads. Hence if Nicholl doubts that Barbicane can raise the money for his moonshot, it shows how really expensive it will be and makes even bigger the question: Just how will Barbicane do it? Again, Nicholl, as a major designer of armor plate, is quite familiar with his country's genius in metallurgy. If he doubts that Barbicane can cast his 900-foot Columbiad, that again intensifies our curiosity about the techniques Barbicane will employ. And if Nicholl believes the loading of the guncotton will lead to disaster, that reminds Verne's original readers of all the tragedies so far caused by the handling of pyroxylin and raises interest in the special precautions Barbicane will take. Nicholl's fourth bet effectively reminds the reader of a very serious problem much in the news in Verne's day, as we explained in Chapter I. Nicholl's fifth bet is comical, given the fact that the four failures he has already predicted would guarantee that the shell would never get to the launching stage. But if it did, "Nicholl's bet 5 has no chance," says our technical adviser, Dr. David Woodruff.

Notice that in Chapter X, Verne has fully recovered his literary power. This is dynamic, dramatic use of science, in terms of characters, far better than the static exposition Verne offered us in Chapters V and VI.

CHAPTER XI
Florida and Texas

1. *declare war on Mexico* This is one of Verne's most ingenious, most complex political jokes. He is satirizing what he regards as the phony excuses that two major powers have given for conquering Mexican territory. He uses a direct attack on American expansionism to cover an indirect attack on French imperialism. And he slyly warns his countrymen that Napoleon has made France vulnerable to military reprisal by the United States.

Officially, the U.S.A. declared war on Mexico in 1846 because Mexico disputed the American annexation of Texas, which had seceded from Mexico ten years before. In actuality, Washington was using the Texas conflict as a makeshift excuse for also annexing Mexico's California: her seaports would give the U.S.A. a strong strategic and commercial position on the Pacific. Officially, President James Polk asked Congress to declare war because "American blood has been shed on American soil." In actuality, he had provocatively sent troops into an area the Texans had not controlled and the Mexicans still claimed.

Predictably, an American unit clashed with a Mexican patrol. As the Mexicans saw it, Mexican blood had been shed on Mexican soil. An additional irony: the U.S.A. went to war to uphold Texas' right to secede from her mother country, a right that Washington denied her own states. The war was widely regarded as immoral by such different people as Henry David Thoreau, Lieutenant Ulysses S. Grant, Congressman Abraham Lincoln, and Jules Verne. Mexicans—man and boy—fought bravely for their homeland but were overwhelmed by superior technology. By 1848 the war allegedly fought over Texas had also netted what is now California, Arizona, Nevada, Utah, Colorado, and New Mexico.

As Verne writes, his own country is the current offender in this matter of *legitimate* causes of war: that is the more immediate association for his liberal French readers in 1865. By December 1860, Mexican President Benito Juarez had set up a revolutionary government, sepa-

Meanwhile, one question remained: it was necessary to select a suitable site for the experiment. According to the advice from the Cambridge Observatory, the cannon would have to be pointed perpendicular to the plane of the horizon, that is to say, toward the zenith. Now the moon rises to the zenith only in places situated between 0° and 28° of latitude; in other words, its declination is only 28°. The Gun Club had to determine exactly the place on the globe where the huge Columbiad would be cast.

Therefore the Club held a general meeting on October 20. Barbicane arrived with a copy of Z. Belltrol's magnificent map of the United States. But before he had time to unfold it, J. T. Maston demanded the floor with his usual vehemence and said:

"Honorable colleagues, the question we're going to take up today is truly one of national importance, and it will give us a chance to perform a great act of patriotism."

The members of the Gun Club looked at each other, wondering what the orator was driving at.

"No one here," he went on, "would ever think of compromising the glory of our country, and if there's one right the Union is entitled to, it's the right to place our formidable cannon within our own borders. Now, under present circumstances—"

"My dear Maston," the president began.

"Let me finish," replied the orator. "Under the circumstances, we are forced to find a place near the equator, and in order to have the proper conditions for our experiment—"

"One moment, please," said Barbicane.

"I insist on free discussion of ideas," said the ebullient J. T. Maston, "and I maintain that the soil from which we launch our glorious projectile must belong to the Union."

"Of course! Without a doubt!" several members said.

"Well then, since our frontiers are not extended far enough, since the sea poses an impassable barrier to the south, since we must find that twenty-eighth parallel beyond our borders but in a neighboring country, I see this as a legitimate *casus belli*. I therefore move that we declare war on Mexico!"[1]

"But no! No!" came from every quarter of the hall.

"No?" replied J. T. Maston. "That's a word I am astonished to hear within these walls."

"But listen then!"

"Never! Never!" cried the fiery orator. "Sooner or later that war will be fought, and I demand it be declared this very day."

"Maston," Barbicane sounded his detonating bell, "you no longer have the floor."

Maston wanted to protest, but several of his colleagues held him back.

"I agree," Barbicane said, "that our experiment can not, ought not, be performed anywhere except on American soil. But if my impatient friend had let me speak, if he had cast his eyes upon a map, he would have realized it is perfectly pointless to declare war on our neighbors, for certain frontiers of the United States do extend beyond the twenty-eighth parallel. You see, we have at our disposal the entire southern portions of Texas and Florida."

The incident was closed. But it was not without regret that J. T. Maston let himself be convinced. It was the sense of the meeting that the Columbiad would be cast in the soil of either Texas or Florida. But this decision was to create a rivalry without precedent between the towns of those two states.

The twenty-eighth parallel, when it reaches the American coast, crosses the peninsula of Florida and divides it into two nearly equal parts. Then, plunging into the Gulf of Mexico, it subtends the arc formed by the coasts of Alabama, Mississippi, and Louisiana. Skirting Texas, from which it cuts a corner, it continues over Mexico, crosses Sonora, strides over Lower California, and loses itself in the waters of the Pacific. And so it was only those portions of Texas and Florida situated below the twenty-eighth parallel that met the conditions of latitude prescribed by the Cambridge Observatory.

The southern part of Florida comprises no major cities. It bristles with forts raised against the roving Indians. There was only one town in the area that could put in a claim for the Gun Club project: Tampa.[2]

In Texas, though, there are many important towns, Corpus Christi in Nueces County, and all the cities located on the Rio Bravo,[3]

Catching wild horses on the prairies of Texas. From *Mitchell's School Geography* (1863).

rated church from state, appropriated vast church holdings to the service of the people, and suspended payments on heavy foreign debts for two years. British, Spanish, French troops landed at Vera Cruz presumably to enforce these financial claims. Satisfied with Juarez's promise of a portion of the customs receipts, the British and Spanish withdrew. But once on Mexican soil, the French refused to negotiate a settlement of the debts. They were there under false pretenses. They moved inland. Their (Napoleon's) real aims were to overthrow Juarez, restore the conservatives and church to full power over Mexican life, and set up a hereditary monarchy with the Austrian archduke as Emperor Maximilian I. As Verne's original readers chuckle over his parody of a phony *casus belli,* the French are paying dearly for their own. Juarez is fighting a guerrilla war against Napoleon's occupying army; the U.S.A., having won its own Civil War, is preparing, on behalf of Juarez and the Monroe Doctrine, to take action against the French.

For Verne and other liberal-minded Europeans, both the American and the French conquests of Spanish-speaking people have been gross violations of the *principle of nationalities* (discussed in Chapter I). The final irony—Napoleon III pays lip service to that principle.

2. *roving Indians . . . Tampa* Like several other Florida cities, Tampa sprang up around a military base: Fort Brooke was activated on Tampa Bay in 1824 to keep tabs on the Seminoles, especially to prevent their receiving arms from Cuba. By 1830 Fort Brooke comprised sixteen square miles of barracks, guardhouse, arsenals, stables, training grounds, and wharves. So many civilians were settling in the area that they could incorporate the city of Tampa and the county of Hillsborough in 1834.

When the federal government pressured the Seminoles into moving west, the Indians resisted. On December 28, 1835, two companies marched out of Fort Brooke headed for Fort King. They walked into an ambush near Bushnell and only three men out of 111 escaped. It was the first of several engagements in a war that raised international outcries against American methods. United States generals, for example, twice captured Indian leaders who had approached the American lines under a flag of truce, and General Zachary Taylor used bloodhounds to track down Seminole families. After the Americans lost 1,700 men—including 215 career officers—the great majority of the Seminoles agreed to leave Florida. "Thus ended a war which had lasted nearly seven years," writes the poet Sidney Lanier, "had taxed the resources of six or seven generals, and had cost the Government more than nineteen million dollars."

But again in 1851 a sizable remnant of Seminoles, who had been living in almost inaccessible marshlands, resisted new efforts to drive them out, and in 1855 full-scale war was resumed. This time the international outcry was over the Americans' bounty system, which sent men out to capture Indian males at $500 per head, females at $250, children at $100. This war petered out with several hundred Seminole survivors scattering into the Everglades where they still support themselves in Verne's day "by hunting, fishing, cattle-driving, and scanty planting," according to Lanier.

European interest in the Florida Indians is based largely on William Bartram's sympathetic accounts of them in his *Travels* (1791). But Verne the voracious reader doesn't come to Bartram until Chapter XIII.

3. *Rio Bravo* Verne uses the official Mexican name for the Rio Grande. In Spanish "bravo" means wild, brave, a name given to the river presumably because of the turbulent flash floods common in its lower course.

4. *Homer's birthplace* Since birth certificates were unknown in the eighth century B.C., and since rhapsodes like Homer were constantly on tour, he was easily identified with numerous places. Perhaps, for public-relations purposes, he even allowed himself to be called a native of several of his major ports of call. Significantly, his alleged birthplaces were widely scattered: Smyrna and Colophon on the west coast of Asia Minor; island cities on Chios, Rhodes, Cyprus; Argos and Athens on the Greek mainland. Another Greek island, Ios, claimed to be the place he died. "Obviously, Homer was an extremely popular poet who traveled wherever Greek was spoken. In many places, he stopped long and often enough for the proud natives to consider him as one of themselves," says Miller in his edition of Homer's *Odyssey* (see Bibliography).

5. *vomito negro* This is the black vomit of yellow fever in its most virulent form. Florida's yellow fever problem is much in the news in Verne's day. In the very year in which his readers are enjoying this novel, the dread scourge hits Florida's Fort Jefferson, an island fortress where the Union still keeps up to 700 prisoners of war. Two hundred seventy men out of 1,400 at the fort contract the fever, and 58 die.

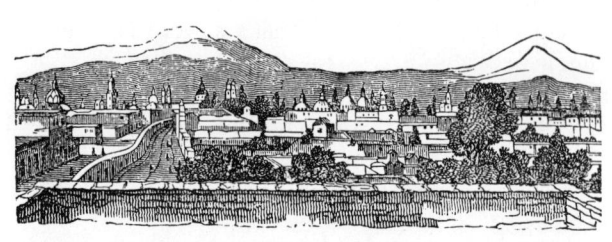

The city of Mexico as pictured in *Mitchell's School Geography* (1863). S. Augustus Mitchell describes the city as "situated in a delightful valley, . . . distinguished for the beauty of its architecture, the regularity of its streets, and the extent of the squares and public places."

Laredo, Comalites, San Ignacio in Webb County, Roma and Rio Grande City in Starr County, Edinburgh in Hidalgo County, Santa Rita, El Panda, Brownsville in Cameron County, all forming an imposing league against the pretensions of Florida.

So, as soon as the Gun Club decision became known, representatives of Texas and Florida began pouring into Baltimore. From that day on, President Barbicane and other influential members of the Club were besieged day and night by formidable claims. Maybe seven Greek cities disputed the honor of having been Homer's birthplace,[4] but now two entire states were threatening to come to blows over a gunsite.

These "fierce brothers" armed themselves and paraded the streets. Every time rival gangs met there was a chance of a conflict with disastrous results. Fortunately Barbicane's prudence and poise calmed the situation. Personal animosities found an outlet in the newspapers of the several states. The *New York Herald* and the *Tribune,* for example, supported Texas, while the *Times* and the *American Review* espoused the cause of the champions of Florida. The members of the Gun Club did not know which to listen to.

Texas boasted her twenty-six counties which she seemed to strut in battle formation; but Florida replied that twelve counties meant more than twenty-six in a state only one-sixth the size.

Texas plumed herself on her 330,000 natives, but Florida, with much less territory, boasted of being more densely populated with 56,000. Moreover, Florida accused Texas of specializing in malarial fevers which, year in and year out, took thousands of lives. And that was true.

In its turn, Texas replied that when it came to fevers, Florida could not be surpassed, and that it was imprudent to call other areas unhealthful when one had the honor of suffering chronically with *vomito negro*.[5] That was true too.

"Besides," the Texans were quoted as saying in the *New York Herald,* "some attention is owing to a state that produces the best cotton in all America and the best green oak for ship building, a state with superb coal fields and iron mines that yield fifty-percent pure metal."

To which the *American Review* replied that the soil of Florida, while not so rich, offered better conditions for molding and casting the Columbiad, since it is composed of sand and clay.

"But," the Texans countered, "before you cast anything in a place, you've got to get there first. Now communications with Florida are difficult, while the Texas coast offers Galveston Bay, with a circumference of thirty-five miles, enough to shelter all the fleets in the world!"

"Some offer!" replied the papers in favor of Florida. "Your Galveston Bay is situated well above the twenty-ninth parallel. Instead we offer the Bay of Espiritu Santo,[6] which opens right onto the twenty-eighth parallel, by which ships can sail straight to Tampa."[7]

"You call that a bay!" the Texans charged. "It's half silted up!"

"Silted up youself!" cried Florida. "Are you trying to say we're uncivilized?"

"You still have the Seminoles prowling your prairies!"

"Oh great! So your Apaches and Comanches[8] are civilized now?"

This dispute went on for several days. Then Florida tried to shift the ground of the argument. One morning the *Times* insinuated that an "essentially American" experiment ought to be conducted on "essentially American" soil.

To these words Texas responded: "American! We're as American as you! Weren't Texas and Florida admitted into the Union at the same time, in 1845?"

"No doubt," the *Times* replied, "but we have belonged to the U.S.A. since 1820."

"Sure," the *Tribune* remarked. "After having been Spaniards or Englishmen for two hundred years, you were sold to the United States for five million dollars!"

"That's nothing to blush over," the Floridians said. "Wasn't the Louisiana Territory bought from Napoleon in 1803 for sixteen million?"

"Scandalous," cried the representatives from Texas. "A miserable patch of land like Florida dares compare herself to Texas which—far from selling herself—declared her own independence, drove out the Mexicans on March 2, 1836, and declared herself a republic after Sam Houston's men defeated Santa Anna's troops on the banks of the San

A Mexican scene as depicted in *Mitchell's School Geography* (1863), showing (left to right): the Pyramid of Cholula, two Indians, several Creoles, and the maguey plant. Maguey, S. Augustus Mitchell says, is "cultivated for the sake of its juice, of which the liquor called pulque, the favorite drink of the lower order of Mexicans, is made." By "the lower order" he means Indians and mestizos, or persons of mixed blood, or anybody who drinks pulque.

6. *Espiritu Santo.* Now called Tampa Bay. In Chapter XIII, Verne explains the system of names he uses.

7. *straight to Tampa* "Here," writes the poet Sidney Lanier, "is a noble harbor." It is forty miles long and navigable by the largest vessels of the day.

8. *Apaches and Comanches* The Indians made repeated incursions into the Republic of Texas in the late 1830s. "In 1840 the Texans pursued them after one of their forays, penetrated into their country, and inflicted summary and severe punishment," reports an encyclopedia of the time.

A Comanche warrior, one of "a roving race, . . . with no fixed villages," as pictured and described in *The American Cyclopaedia* (1874).

It was necessary to keep the partisans under strict surveillance. Engraving from the 1872 French edition.

9. *scared of the Mexicans!* Texas lived on a war footing for most of her ten years as a republic. Mexico refused to recognize her independence and, after Santa Anna's defeat, made several efforts to fit out new armies to reconquer Texas. In 1841–1842 Mexico sent marauding expeditions into the republic and twice captured and plundered San Antonio. Private gangs of Texans mounted retaliatory expeditions which were uniformly unsuccessful: many Texans were captured and executed. In 1843 Santa Anna agreed to an armistice, but Mexico terminated it one year later and threatened to renew hostilities. In 1845, the Lone Star State was annexed to the Union, leading, as we have seen, to the Mexican War (1846–1848).

Jacinto! In other words, an independent country that voluntarily joined the United States of America!"

"Because it was scared of the Mexicans!" [9] Florida said.

"Scared!" From the very day that word was pronounced, things went from bad to worse. Bloody street fights between the two parties now seemed inevitable. It was necessary to keep the partisans under strict surveillance.

President Barbicane did not know which way to turn. Notes, messages, threatening letters rained down on his house. Which side should he take? All things considered—suitability of the soil, communications facilities, rapidity of transportation—the two states seemed about evenly matched. As for the politicians and their pressures, they should not count.

This dilemma, Barbicane decided, had persisted for too long, and he determined to resolve it. He convened his colleagues, and the solution he proposed was profoundly sensible.

"Consider what's going on now between Florida and Texas," he said. "Obviously the same kind of competition will develop among the cities of whichever state we favor. The rivalry will simply descend from the genus to the species, from state to city, and so on down. Now Texas comprises eleven towns that meet our needs, and they would all fight for the project and create new problems for us. But Florida has only one town that qualifies. So let's go for Florida and Tampa!" [10]

When it was announced, this decision floored the representatives from Texas. In a great rage, they sent letters to each Gun Club member challenging him to a duel.[11] The Baltimore authorities saw only one course to take and took it. They chartered a special train, herded the Texans aboard willy-nilly, and sent them out of the city at a speed of thirty miles an hour.

Still, from the train window the Texans managed to fling one last sarcastic threat at their rivals.

Alluding to the narrowness of Florida, a mere peninsula stretched out between two seas, they predicted that it would not survive the firing of the cannon, it would blow up at the very first shot.

"So let it blow up!" The Floridians' laconism [12] was worthy of ancient times.

State seal of Florida. From *The American Cyclopaedia* (1874).

State seal of Texas. From *The American Cyclopaedia* (1875).

10. *Florida and Tampa* "It cannot be a mere matter of coincidence," Colonel Frank Borman will write to Jules Verne's grandson in 1969. "Our space vehicle was launched from Florida, like Barbicane's. . . ." Tampa is about 120 miles from Cape Kennedy.

11. *challenging him to a duel* In Verne's day America is notorious for her duels. While the custom of settling personal disputes with sword or pistol is dying out in most civilized countries, it has enjoyed a bloody renascence in nineteenth-century America, especially in the South. Most Southern gentlemen practice at arms as a matter of simple prudence; they might be challenged at any time; thousands of them have died on the "field of honor." Each county has its dueling hero whom no one, so the story goes, dare jostle on the streets. Indeed, defenders of the *code duello* maintain that it encourages courtesy and peace. Known duelists have included governors, congressmen, the attorney-general of Georgia, Henry Clay, John Randolph, Sam Houston, and the dean of them all, Andrew Jackson.

Almost any Southern city has its dueling ground outside of town: New Orleans has its field "under the oaks," Vicksburg its sand bar along the Mississippi, Memphis its special grove. Until 1857 one of the most famous dueling grounds is a fifteen-acre tract, enclosed by hills on three sides, near Bladensburg, Maryland, just a short carriage ride from Washington, and about forty miles from Verne's scene of action. There political foes have often repaired. There at least two hundred men have defended their personal honor (or a lady's). There in 1820 Commodore James Barron killed Commodore Stephen Decatur; and in 1819 General Armistead Mason and Colonel John McCarty, cousins, faced each other with shotguns at four paces. "For several days afterwards," a contemporary report has it, "the grass and bushes, for some distance around, were bespattered with blood and hung with shreds of clothing and fragments of flesh blown from Mason's body. . . ."

Reminding his readers of the American penchant for dueling, Verne not only enhances his Texas-Florida conflict but also prepares the way for his extraordinary Chapter XXI.

12. *laconism* With their classical education, Verne's original readers are well aware of the origin of this term. Inhabitants of ancient Sparta, metropolis of *Laconia,* were known for the brevity of their speech, their succinct expression. In composing his famous epitaph for the Spartans who fell at Thermopylae, Simonides (556?–468? B.C.) appropriately demonstrated the laconic style:

Tell them in Lakedaimon, passerby,
That obeying their orders, here we lie.

CHAPTER XII
Urbi et Orbi

Now that the astronomical, mechanical, and geographical problems had been solved, there loomed the question of money. This project would cost an enormous sum. No private individual, and no national treasury, could afford to finance this experiment.

And so, although it was an American experiment, President Barbicane decided to make it a global enterprise, and to ask for the financial cooperation of all peoples.[1] It was both the right and the duty of the whole Earth to intervene in the affairs of her satellite. The collection of funds for this purpose, which would begin in Baltimore, would extend to the entire world—*urbi et orbi*.[2]

This subscription was to succeed beyond all reasonable expectation, even though it was a question of giving, not lending. It was a purely disinterested operation in the most literal sense of the word, since it offered not the slightest chance of profit.

The impact of Barbicane's announcement was not confined within the frontiers of the United States; it crossed the Atlantic and the Pacific, invading simultaneously Asia and Europe, Africa, and Oceania. The observatories of America established communications with the observatories of other lands. Those at Paris, St. Petersburg, Capetown, Berlin, Altona, Stockholm, Warsaw, Hamburg, Buda, Bologna, Malta, Lisbon, Benares, Madras, and Peking sent their compliments to the Gun Club. The others maintained a prudent silence, waiting for developments.

As for the Greenwich Observatory, it strongly denied any possibility of success, favoring the theories of Captain Nicholl. And the Greenwich position was endorsed by twenty-two other astronomical establishments in Great Britain. Thus, while the various learned societies were deciding to send delegations to Tampa, the staff at Greenwich held a meeting, bluntly voted against Barbicane's proposal, and passed on to other business. It was English jealousy, pure and simple. Nothing else.[3]

On the whole, though, the reaction was excellent in the scientific world, and from there it passed on to the general public who took a passionate interest in the question. That was important, since the masses were expected to subscribe huge sums.

---

1. *cooperation of all peoples* Verne is following the recent precedent set by another American scientist, the oceanographer Matthew Fontaine Maury (1806–1873). In 1839 Lieutenant Maury took over the U.S. Navy depot of charts and instruments. Reviewing regular reports on winds and currents that naval ships submitted, he realized the value of coordinating and correlating these data. He was soon issuing his "Wind and Currents Charts" and his *Sailing Directions* which made available to a navigator the cumulative experience, as Maury put it, "of a thousand vessels that had preceded him on the same voyage." Maury's early charts proved to be such a boon to captains in choosing speedier, safer routes that Maury had no trouble drawing their attention to the "blank spaces" still to be filled in. He offered all captains who sent logs to Washington copies of the improved charts and directions that could thus be compiled and shared. Next Maury made it officially a *global enterprise*. He organized the International Maritime Conference, held at Brussels in 1853, at which his work won the *cooperation of all peoples*. Typical of international benefit: in 1854 the president of the British Association estimates that Maury's *Sailing Directions* have cut passage from Britain to Australia by 20 days, to California by 30. In 1855 Maury collects all his wisdom on sea and atmosphere into one fat volume, *The Physical Geography of the Sea and its Meteorology*, which has become one of the most popular scientific works in Verne's day. For more on Maury and the ways he inspires Verne, see *The Annotated Jules Verne: Twenty Thousand Leagues under the Sea*, pages 69–70, 88–89.

2. *urbi et orbi* Verne uses Church Latin for its ironic effect. On special occasions, like Christmas and Easter, the Pope appears on the balcony of Saint Peter's in Rome and gives his blessing *urbi et orbi:* to the city and to the world. Now on the special occasion of Earth's intervention *in the affairs of her satellite,* Verne has the blessing originate from the *urbs* of Bal-

On October 8 President Barbicane had issued an enthusiastic manifesto in which he appealed to "all men of good will on Earth." Translated into all languages, it met with great success.

Subscription books were opened in all the major cities of the Union with the main office at the Bank of Baltimore, 9 Baltimore Street. Subscriptions were also taken by commercial firms on other continents, as follows:

Vienna, S. M. von Rothschild
Petersburg, Stieglitz and Co.
Paris, Crédit Mobilier
Stockholm, Tottie and Arfuredson
London, N. M. Rothschild and Son
Turin, Asdouin and Co.
Berlin, Mendelssohn
Geneva, Lombard, Odier, and Co.

timore, with a sly hint there has been a shift of power from the spiritual to the technological.

3. *Nothing else* Well, something else does figure here: Verne's anglophobia. His plots often put the English in a bad light. He never misses a chance to attack them as the arch-villains of imperialism. In *Captain Grant* (1867) and *Mistress Branican* (1891) he accuses Britain of genocide in her treatment of the Hottentots and the Australian and Tasmanian aborigines. In *Family without a Name* (1889) and *Foundling Mick* (1893) he makes capital of French-Canadian and Irish resistance to English domination. His greatest hero, Captain Nemò, proves to be a victim of English oppression of India. In *Hector Servadac* (1877) Verne has all the temporary inhabitants of a comet—French, Spanish, Russian, Italian—working together for the common good while the English keep aloof. Verne sees to it that while all the other nationalities manage to return to Earth, the English "revolve in space forever."

Verne's anglophobia is perfectly illustrated in *Hector Servadac* (1878). Here an English commander pompously reassures his French and Russian visitors: "You're on English ground, protected by the British flag." Actually they are off on a comet that captured them as it swiped the Earth. The English, through their failure to cooperate with the other nationalities, will never get home.

4. *subscription was closed* Notice how in this chapter, with first its list of the world's leading financiers and now its roster of nations contributing, Verne wallows in the Romanticist's love of cataloguing. He enjoys the very variations in the exotic names associated with national currencies: *cruzados, piastres, florins*. And the roll-call gives him a chance to review his own typology of national traits, as well as his own political opinions.

5. *paid after singing* Another snide reference to the two Emperors Napoleon. One day in 1792, the mayor of Strasbourg told some soldiers they needed a marching song for their campaign against Austria. That night Captain Claude Joseph Rouget de Lisle composed both words and music for a "Battle Hymn of the Army of the Rhine." The stirring song caught on immediately. It was sung with such enthusiasm by volunteers from Marseilles on their march to Paris that it came to be called "La Marseillaise." The National Convention adopted it as the national anthem and the French sang it as they carried the message of republicanism to other lands. But their messianic fervor in spreading the Revolution led to formation of powerful coalitions against France: they *paid after singing*. And when he became Emperor, Napoleon banned "La Marseillaise" because of its revolutionary character. After the July Revolution of 1830, Frenchmen could again enjoy the song for some twenty years, and then they have *paid* again: with their civil liberties when Napoleon III has suppressed "La Marseillaise" and all other expressions of republicanism.

Just two years after writing this passage, Verne will experience some public embarrassment over Napoleon III's ban. While he and his brother Paul are en route to New York on the *Great Eastern,* English passengers will sing "God Save the Queen." Americans in the salon will call on Paul to sing the French national anthem. He will render Napoleon III's imperialistic "Partant pour la Syrie." The Americans will insist on the *real* anthem. With a knowing look from Jules, Paul will clear his throat and sing the song forbidden in his native land.

6. *a little gaiety* Verne often twits the French for their occasional conservatism in scientific matters. For example, in 1861, the crew of the dispatch boat *Alecton* discovered a monstrous squid in the waters off Tenerife. They grappled with it for hours, but it was too huge and heavy to bring abroad. Their captain made a detailed report to the government. To their astonishment, the French Academy discredited their experience. One Academician, Arthur Mangin, warned scientists against stories of creatures like "the giant squid . . . existence of which would be some sort of contradiction of the great laws of harmony and equilibrium that rule over living nature. . . ." Mangin suggested that the crew had actually grappled with a sea plant and then became victims of mass hysteria! For the rest of the century the Academy will eat crow,

Subscription books were opened in all major cities . . . Engraving from the first illustrated edition (1872).

Constantinople, The Ottoman Bank
Brussels, S. Lambert
Madrid, Daniel Weisweller
Amsterdam, Netherlands Credit
Rome, Torlonia and Co.
Lisbon, Lecesne
Copenhagen, The Private Bank
Buenos Aires, Bank Maua
Rio de Janeiro, the same bank
Montevideo, the same bank
Valparaiso, Thomas La Chambre and Co.
Mexico City, Martin Daran and Co.
Lima, Thomas La Chambre and Co.

Three days after President Barbicane's manifesto had been issued, $4,000,000 had been collected in the various cities of the Union. With such solid initial support, the Gun Club could begin operations.

But a few days later, word came in from some foreign cities that their people were also subscribing eagerly. Certain countries distinguished themselves by their generosity; others were less liberal. It was a matter of temperament.

Figures speak better than words, so let us consult the official tabulation of deposits credited to the Gun Club account after the subscription was closed.[4]

Russia contributed the enormous sun of 368,733 rubles, about $273,000. This will surprise no one aware of the Russians' strong interest in science, especially their progress in astronomical research, thanks to their numerous observatories, the greatest of which cost two million rubles.

France started out by laughing at the Americans' pretensions. The moon served as the pretext for a thousand stale puns and a score of vaudevilles in which bad taste vied with ignorance. But, just as once the French had paid after singing,[5] now they paid after laughing. They contributed 1,253,930 francs, about $240,000. At that price they had the right to a little gaiety.[6]

Austria did pretty well for a country in financial troubles. She raised 216,000 florins, about $95,000, a nice little windfall.

Fifty-two thousand riks-dollars, about $55,000, were contributed by Sweden and Norway, a large amount for the size of their population. But the figure would have been much larger if a subscription office had been opened in Christiana as well as in Stockholm. For some reason or other, Norwegians don't like to send their money to Sweden.[7]

Prussia endorsed the experiment by sending 250,000 talers, about $175,000. Her observatories especially contributed large sums and were the most enthusiastic in encouraging President Barbicane.

Turkey behaved generously, but then she had a vested interest in the project: the moon actually regulates the cycle of her years and determines the time of her fast of Ramadan.[8] She could not do less than donate 1,372,640 piastres, about $65,000, and she gave with an eagerness that betrayed a certain pressure from the government of the Sublime Porte.[9]

Belgium distinguished herself among the smaller nations with a gift of 513,000 francs, about $95,000, roughly two cents per person.

Holland and her colonies were interested in the experiment to the extent of 110,000 florins, about $43,000, asking only for a five-percent discount, since they paid in cash.

Denmark, a bit cramped in her territory,[10] still gave 9,000 ducats, about $22,000, demonstrating once again the Danes' fondness for scientific expeditions.[11]

The Germanic Confederation pledged 34,285 florins, about $13,000; it was impossible to ask for more, and anyhow, she would not have given it.

Financially embarrassed, Italy managed to find 200,000 lire, about $37,000, by turning her children's pockets inside out. If she had had Venetia, she would have done better; but she did not have Venetia.[12]

The Papal States felt duty-bound to send no less than 7,040 Roman crowns, about the same number of dollars, while Portugal demonstrated her devotion to science to the tune of 30,000 cruzados, roughly $21,000.

as giant squid from 32 to 57 feet long will be sighted and caught repeatedly first off Newfoundland, later off New Zealand. And Verne will make mocking allusions to Mangin's attitudes in Chapter I of his masterpiece, *Twenty Thousand Leagues* (1870). For more details, see *The Annotated Jules Verne* edition, pages 321–322.

7. *money to Sweden* The reason, of course, is *the principle of nationalities,* violated by the Congress of Vienna (1815) when it bound Norway into a "union" with the Crown of Sweden. The Swedes have frequently treated the Norwegians as a conquered people; Swedish influence has prevailed in all questions where the interests of the two nationalities differ. As Verne writes, the Swedes are pressing for revisions in the Act of Union which would codify the supremacy of Sweden. In his *Lottery Ticket* (1886), which features the plight of Norway, Verne observes that "so marked was the difference between the two peoples that the Swedish flag was flown over neither Norwegian buildings nor ships." Norway will not achieve her independence until 1905.

8. *fast of Ramadan* The twenty-nine days of Ramadan constitute the fifth month of the Moslem year, the month when "the Koran was sent down as a guidance for the people" (*Koran* II, 181). Ramadan begins when one trustworthy witness testifies to the authorities that he has sighted the new moon. Then for the entire lunar month, from dawn to sunset—from the moment that "so much of the dawn appears that a white thread may be distinguished from a black" until at nightfall the two again become indistinguishable (II, 183)—the faithful abstain from food, drink, medicine, and sexual intercourse.

Since it is the moon, as Verne says, that *regulates the cycle of* [*Turkey's*] *years;* and since the lunar year, based on lunar months of twenty-nine and a half days each, does not coincide with the solar year, Ramadan will, over a period of time, occur at different seasons.

Verne will use Europeans' misunderstanding of the Turks' Ramadan customs as the basis for a comic scene in *Keraban the Inflexible* (1883).

9. *Sublime Porte* This is the European version of the Turkish *babiali,* or Gate of the Eminent, the official name of the gate to a block of buildings in Istanbul which, in Verne's day, houses the foreign ministry and other departments of government of the Ottoman Empire.

10. *cramped . . . territory* Just shortly before this novel appears, Denmark has lost one-third of her land to Prussia and Austria, whose forces crushed the Danes in two swift campaigns.

11. *Danes' . . . scientific expeditions* In Verne's day the Danes are famous for their oceanographic expeditions. In 1845, for example, Steen Andersen Bille, naval officer, took his corvette *Galathea* on a two-year trip around the world during which the scientists aboard made several important contributions to marine biology. Bille has published a three-volume account of the voyage (1849–1851).

12. *not have Venetia* Another dig at Napoleon III. Posing as liberator of Italian territory under foreign control, he declared war on Austria in 1859. After he and his Italian allies won victories at Magenta and Solferino and were on the verge of entering Venetia, he suddenly, without consulting the Italians, made a separate peace. The Austrians agreed to relinquish Lombardy but not Venetia. Italy will *not have Venetia* until 1866.

13. *empires . . . short of cash* Still another dig at still another feckless enterprise of Napoleon III. His troops, as we have seen, landed in Vera Cruz allegedly to collect Mexico's debt to France. Instead they have taken over the country and installed the Austrian archduke as Emperor Maximilian, and his wife, a Belgian princess, as Empress Carlotta. But even after three years of military management, the Mexican treasury is still so bare the Emperor is supporting himself out of his own private funds. Soon the U.S., citing the Monroe Doctrine, will demand that Napoleon recall his troops. Napoleon will expect that Maximilian will leave with the army. But poor Maximilian—who has been led by Mexican reactionaries and by Napoleon to believe that the Mexican people actually "voted" him the throne!—will refuse to desert "his people." Juarez will capture, courtmartial, shoot him. His Empress will go permanently insane after vainly seeking help from Napoleon and the Pope. Is it any wonder that Verne can't keep Louis Napoleon out of his fiction? As we shall see, the ruler of France will prove to be the only real villain in this book.

. . . the foundry at Cold Spring, New York, as pictured in the French edition of 1872.

A Russian silver ruble. From *The American Cyclopaedia* (1874).

As for Mexico, it was the old story of the widow's mite—a mere 86 piastres, or about $300. But then, empires in the making are always short of cash.[13]

Two hundred and fifty-seven francs, about $50, was Switzerland's modest donation to the American project. We must say it outright, Switzerland could not see any practical value in the experiment. She could not imagine that sending a projectile to the moon would stir up any business there. It did not seem wise to sink any capital in so risky a venture. And after all, maybe she was right.

As for Spain, she could not possibly scrape together more than 110 reals, about $11. She gave as her excuse the fact that she had to finish her railroads. The truth is, science is not held in high esteem in that country. She is still a bit backward. Moreover, there were some Spaniards, and by no means the least educated ones, who had the wrong idea about the ratio between the mass of the projectile and the mass of the moon. They were afraid the shell would wrench the moon out of her orbit and, ending her role as a satellite, bring her crashing down to

Earth. In that case, it was better to abstain from the subscription, which they did, except for a few reals.

That leaves England. We have already seen how she belittled Barbicane's project. The English have but one soul for the 25,000,000 inhabitants of the British Isles. They implied that the Gun Club enterprise was contrary to "the principle of non-intervention," and so they subscribed not one farthing.

When they heard this news from England, the Gun Club members shrugged their shoulders and returned to their great mission. And when South America—that is to say, Peru, Chile, Brazil, the provinces of La Plata, Colombia—handed more than $300,000 to the Gun Club, Barbicane's men found themselves in possession of a considerable capital sum, as follows:

Subscriptions from the United States	$4,000,000
Subscriptions from foreign countries	$1,446,675
Total	$5,446,675 [14]

Let no one be surprised at the size of the sums that flowed into the coffers of the Gun Club. The members estimated that casting and boring the cannon; the masonry; relocating the workers, housing them in a still uninhabited area; building furnaces, workshops, and plant; buying the powder and the shell; and paying all the operating, maintenance, and incidental expenses would easily absorb most of the five and a half million dollars subscribed. Certain cannonades in the Civil War had cost one thousand dollars a shot. President Barbicane's shot, unique in the annals of gunnery, might cost five thousand times as much.

On October 20, the Club signed a contact with the foundry at Cold Spring, New York, which had furnished Parrott with his largest cast-iron cannon.

The contracting parties agreed that Cold Spring would send to Tampa, in southern Florida, all materials required for casting the Columbiad. This operation was to be completed, at the latest, by October 15 of the following year. The cannon was to be turned over to the Club in good working condition under penalty of an indemnity of one hundred dollars a day until the time when the moon would once again present herself in the same conditions, that is to say, eighteen years and eleven days later! Cold Spring also agreed to recruit and manage the work force.

Executed in duplicate, the contract was signed by I. Barbicane, president of the Gun Club, and J. Murchison, superintendent of the Cold Spring Foundry, who had worked out the terms of the agreement.

A Spanish 100-reals gold piece with a likeness of Isabella II. From *The American Cyclopaedia* (1874).

14. *$5,446,675* Using once more the Unger and Greaves ratios proposed in Chapter VIII, we see that today's equivalent of the Gun Club's costs would be somewhere between $16,500,000 and $33,000,000. Verne's estimate, then, falls far below the actual cost of the Apollo project: about $20,000,000,000.

Three French coins of Barbicane's day: (top) a twenty-franc gold piece or "Napoleon," (middle) a ten-franc gold piece, and (bottom) a silver franc. From *The American Cyclopaedia* (1874).

The Prussian silver taler. From *The American Cyclopaedia* (1874).

CHAPTER XIII
Stony Hill

1. *everybody can read* Well, nearly everybody, especially among the younger generations. Verne's exaggeration is politically inspired. He is reminding his readers that in America free, compulsory, secular education is well-nigh universal, that freedom of the press prevails and *everybody can read*—that is, whatever he wants. These things simply cannot be said about France under the Second Empire. "Napoleon III has sometimes been seen as the first of the modern dictators, as a protofascist," say Crane Brinton and his colleagues in their *History of Civilization: 1815 to the Present* (1976).

2. *Bartram's Travels* Verne attracts attention to his list by heading it with a title well known to his readers, one of the first great classics to come out of America. When he was a young man, William Bartram (1739–1823) accompanied his father, a Philadelphian, who bore the title of "American Botanist to the King of England," on a scientific expedition to Florida. Then in 1773 William led his own expedition through Florida, Georgia, and the Carolinas. His book about the trip described and illustrated many flora hitherto unknown and provided the fullest list of American birds then available.

But his influence on natural history is at least equaled if not surpassed by his impact on the Romanticist movement in literature and philosophy. His descriptions of the Florida Indians have helped shape the Romanticist notions of the Noble Savage, of the perversion of natural man by civilization. Bartram said outright that the "moral duties" associated with the Golden Rule, which Europeans believe must be instilled in the individual by society, come naturally to the Indian. "The visage, actions, and deportment of the Siminoles [*sic*] form the most striking picture of happiness in this life," the Philadelphia explorer reported back to the civilized world. ". . . Joy, contentment, love, and friendship, without guile or affectation, seem inherent in them. . . . How are we to account

After the Gun Club had decided against Texas, everybody in America—a country where everybody can read[1]—felt duty-bound to study the geography of Florida. Never before had the bookstores sold so many copies of Bartram's *Travels*[2] *in Florida,* Romans' *Natural History of East and West Florida,* Williams' *Territory of Florida,* Cleland's *On the Culture of Sugar Cane in East Florida.* The publishers rushed new editions into print.[3] They sold like mad.

But Barbicane had better things to do than read. He wanted to locate and mark out the gunsite with his own eyes. Therefore, losing not a moment, he advanced the Cambridge Observatory the money needed to build the telescope,[4] he contracted with Breadwill and Company in Albany for the manufacture of the aluminum shell, and then he left Baltimore accompanied by J. T. Maston, Major Elphiston, and the superintendent of the Cold Spring iron works.

The next day, the four fellow travelers arrived in New Orleans. There they immediately embarked on the *Tampico,* a naval dispatch boat which the government had placed at their disposal. Barbicane ordered full speed ahead, and soon they lost sight of Louisiana.

It was a short trip. Two days after they lifted anchor, the *Tampico,* having sailed 445 miles, sighted the coast of Florida. Barbicane could see a low, flat land, seemingly barren. After coasting along a series of coves rich in oysters and lobsters, the *Tampico* entered the Bay of Espiritu Santo.

This bay is divided into two deep harbors, Tampa Bay and Hillsborough Bay. Now the four travelers could see the low batteries of Fort Brook, and then the town of Tampa, spread out nonchalantly around the small natural port formed by the mouth of the Hillsborough River.

That was where the *Tampico* dropped anchor at seven o'clock in the evening of October 22. The four passengers disembarked at once.

Barbicane felt his heart pounding violently when he first stepped on Florida soil.[5] He seemed to be testing it with his foot as an architect does when he gauges the solidity of a house. J. T. Maston scratched the earth with the end of his hook.

"Gentlemen," Barbicane said, "we have no time to spare. Tomorrow morning we must explore the area on horseback."

As soon as Barbicane had landed, three thousand residents of Tampa came out to meet him, to honor the president of the Gun Club who had selected their town. They welcomed him with enthusiastic shouts and cheers. But he shied away from every ovation. He engaged a room in the Hotel Franklin and, locking the door, refused to see anyone. He did not relish the role of celebrity.

The next morning, October 23, some small Spanish horses, full of vigor and fire, were pawing the ground beneath his windows. But instead of four, there were fifty steeds, with their riders. Barbicane came downstairs, accompanied by his three companions, and he was astonished to find himself in the midst of a cavalcade. He commented on the fact that every horseman had a rifle slung across his shoulders and pistols in his holsters. The reason for this display of strength was given by a young Floridian who said:

"Sir, there are Seminoles where you're going."

"What do you mean, Seminoles?"

"Savages who roam the prairies. We thought it best to escort you."

"Pooh!" cried J. T. Maston as he mounted his horse.

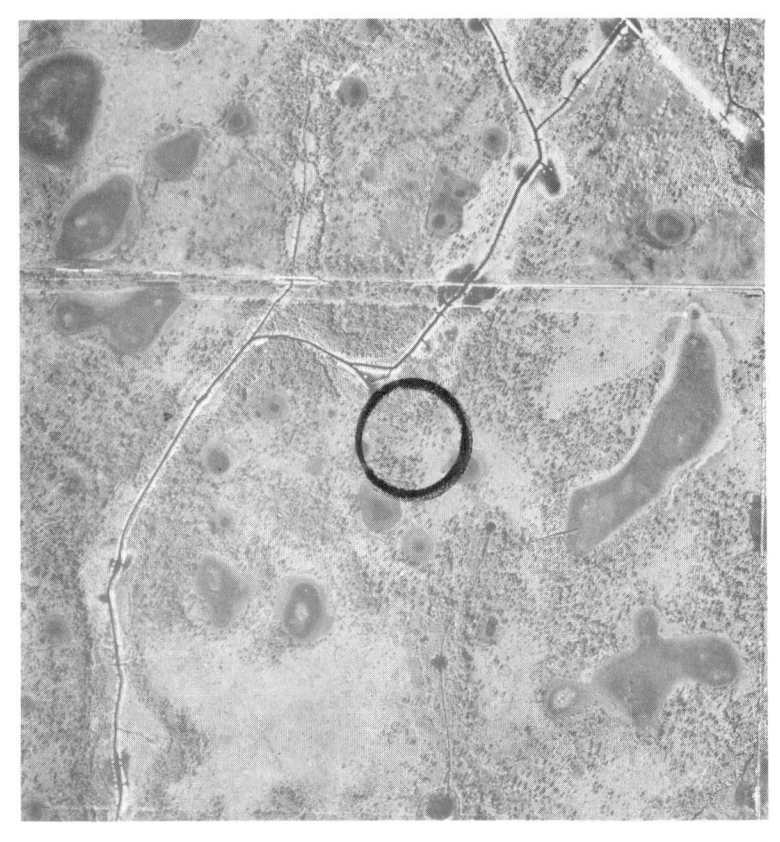

Bartram's own drawing of "a new and most beautiful species of Annona. . . . the very dwarf decumbent annona pigmaea," as he described it in his *Travels* (1791).

for their excellent policy in civil government; it cannot derive . . . from coercive laws, for they have no such artificial system. Divine wisdom dictates, and they obey. . . . As moral men they certainly stand in no need of European civilization." Here was dramatic proof of the doctrines of Jean Jacques Rousseau, who had taught that man is virtuous by nature and learns evil only from his contact with social institutions.

Bartram's ideas spread rapidly because they were couched in rich, sensuous, often sublime prose. His book inspired many of the brightest images and concepts in the poetry of William Wordsworth and Samuel Taylor Coleridge. Bartram's influence has survived into the third generation of Romanticists. "All American libraries ought to provide themselves with that kind of book; and keep them as a future *biblical* article," Thomas Carlyle (1795–1881) has written to Ralph Waldo Emerson (1803–1882). Verne, as we shall see, makes good use of Bartram's information about birds, alligators, and spiders; but he has mixed feelings about the Noble Savage.

3. *new editions into print* Even without the help of Barbicane's project, three of these books have enjoyed a good publishing history. Bartram's *Travels through North & South Carolina, Georgia, East & West Florida* was first issued in Philadelphia in 1791, in London in 1794, and in a two-volume French translation in 1801, going through nine European editions by 1804. In 1928 Mark van Doren edited a facsimile edition of the Philadelphia original which has been kept in print in paperback since 1955, and in 1958 Yale University Press issued a "Naturalists Edition" with commentary by Francis Harper. Bernard A. Romans' *Concise and Natural History* (1775) and John Lee Williams' book (1837) were both reissued in 1962 by the University of Florida Press.

Barbicane's launching site lies within the circle drawn on this 1973 aerial photograph of the northern portion of the city of North Port. When this picture was made for the Florida Department of Transportation, the site was located in a clump of scattered pine and palmetto.

4. *build the telescope* The Cambridge Observatory staff does not manufacture telescopes, but probably Barbicane is trusting their judgment in designing and ordering one for the Gun Club's needs, since the new instrument will be manned by Cambridge people. Cambridge's own 15-inch telescope was, as we have seen, ordered from Merz and Mahler of Munich in 1843. But since then Clark and Sons of Boston also have been manufacturing large lenses of superior quality (see Chapter IV).

5. *on Florida soil* Touching land after having been afloat is always a poignant moment to Verne. This is probably related to a childhood anxiety. As a boy he lived on the Ile Feydeau, an island in the Loire River off Nantes. The Ile was ship-shaped, pointed at one end, rounded at the other. In spring the flood-swollen Loire would smash against the quays of Feydeau, spill over the isle, pour into the cellars. Jules and his brother Paul would watch from an upstairs window. Jules imagined that the island would be torn from its anchorage and float out to sea. In real life he comes to love yachting and lives and even writes on board for weeks at a time. But in his fiction he always lingers over this moment of touching solid ground once more.

6. *Pascua Florida* "It seems . . . ruthless to break up the popular superstition that Florida was named so because of its floweriness," writes poet Sidney Lanier. "But truth is, after all, the most beautiful thing under heaven; and there does not seem to be the least doubt that Ponce de Leon named this country Florida because the day on which he made the land was called in his calendar *Pascua Florida*, or Palm-Sunday."

Bartram's drawing of the Florida great softshell tortoise. From *Travels* (1791).

"Really," the Floridian insisted, "it's safer this way."

"Gentlemen," Barbicane replied, "I'm grateful for your concern. But it's time to be off."

The little troop left at once and disappeared in a cloud of dust. It was five o'clock in the morning. The sun was shining and the thermometer already registered 84°. But cool sea breezes moderated this excessive temperature.

Leaving Tampa behind, Barbicane made his way south along the coast toward Alifia Creek. This little stream feeds into Hillsborough Bay about twelve miles below Tampa. Barbicane and his escort followed its right bank eastward. Soon the waves of the bay disappeared behind a rise in the ground, and now they could see only the Florida countryside.

Florida is divided into two sections. The northern part, more heavily populated, less primitive, includes Tallahassee, the state capital, and Pensacola, one of the principal naval bases of the United States. The southern part, pressed between the Atlantic and the Gulf of Mexico, is only a narrow peninsula gnawed at by the Gulf Stream, its point of land losing itself in the middle of a small archipelago, rounded by numerous ships on their way through the Bahama Channel. This is the Gulf's outpost against hurricanes.

Florida comprises 38,033,267 acres. Barbicane's problem now was to find one situated below the twenty-eighth parallel that was suitable for his project. And so, as he rode along, he was studying the lay of the land and the composition of the soil.

Discovered by Juan Ponce de Leon on Palm Sunday, 1512, Florida was originally called *Pascua Florida*.[6] Certainly its dry, parched coasts did not deserve such a charming name. But a few miles inland, the nature of the terrain changes bit by bit and the country comes to earn its designation. The land is interspersed with networks of creeks, rivers, waterways, ponds, little lakes. At first glance, a visitor might think he was in Holland or Guiana. But then the countryside rises gently to plains where all kinds of northern and southern crops are cultivated, to immense fields where the tropic sun and the water held in clayish soil do most of the farmer's hard work, finally to prairies of pineapples, yams, tobacco, rice, cotton, sugar cane, stretching to the horizon, displaying their riches with insouciant prodigality.

Barbicane seemed very pleased that the ground was rising. When J. T. Maston asked him about this he said:

"We have a very good reason for wanting to cast our cannon on high ground."

"To be closer to the moon?" guessed the secretary of the Gun Club.

"Not exactly," Barbicane smiled. "What difference could a hundred feet make? But the higher the ground, the easier the work. We won't have to contend with water. No pumps, no long and expensive hoses. That's a serious consideration, for we have to sink a well some nine hundred feet deep."

"Right," said Murchison, who was an engineer. "As much as we can, we should avoid water when we're digging. But if we do run into some underground springs, we can handle them. We've got the equip-

Mico Chlucco, King of the Seminoles, as pictured by William Bartram in his *Travels* (1791).

. . . flamingos simply stared The American flamingo as pictured in *The American Cyclopaedia* (1874).

ment. We'll pump them dry or change their course. We're not digging an artesian well, narrow and dark, where the drill, the casing, the sounding rod, and all the other digging tools work blind. No. We'll work in the open air, in broad daylight, pick and shovel in hand, and with the help of blasting powder, we'll get down there fast."

"Even so," replied Barbicane, "if the level of the ground, or the nature of the soil, can help us avoid a struggle with underground water, we'll do the job faster and better. So let's try to sink our shaft into ground that's a hundred fathoms or so above sea level, if we can."

"By all means, Mr. Barbicane. Unless I'm mistaken, we'll soon find a suitable spot."

"Then I'll want soon to hear the first stroke of the pickaxe," said Barbicane.

"And I'll want soon to hear the last," cried J. T. Maston.

"We'll do it, gentlemen," the engineer replied. "Believe me, Cold Spring won't owe you a nickel's indemnity for lateness."

"By Saint Barbara, you better be right!" exclaimed J. T. Maston. "One hundred dollars a day until the moon returns to the same conditions—which won't be for eighteen years and eleven days—do you realize that would add up to $658,000?"

7. *crab-eaters . . . gems* A good example of Verne's use of Bartram's *Travels*. The Philadelphia naturalist identifies a "speckle-crested heron," *maculata cristata,* as a "crabcatcher." He describes it as spending part of the year in Florida to breed and rear its young.

8. *alligators . . . long* Bartram has seen them twenty feet long and has heard of them longer. He was once attacked "on all sides" by these "subtle, greedy" creatures. He describes one in particular: "Behold him rushing from the flags and reeds. His enormous body swells. His plaited tail brandished high, floats upon the lake. The waters like a cataract descend from his opening jaws. Clouds of smoke issue from his dilated nostrils. The earth trembles with his thunder."

9. *phaetons* These particular teal (ducks) are probably specimens of Bartram's *Phaethon aethereus,* the tropic bird, a yellow-billed migrant from the south.

10. *swift horses* Bartram admires Seminole horses as "the most beautiful and sprightly species of that noble creature perhaps any where to be seen."

11. *show of hostility* Perhaps Verne has got the idea for this martial display from Bartram's description of some Florida Indians as "brave and valiant in war, restless and perpetually exercising their arms." Verne is never able to resolve his contradictory views of "savages." Here, as in *Around the World in Eighty Days* (1873), he represents the Indians as standing in the way of the inevitable expansion of "civilization": on his great scientific mission, Barbicane needs an armed escort because of the unfortunate existence of "backward" peoples. But in other works Verne is more the Rousseauist, the Bartramite, viewing the savage as "noble." Thus in *The Chancellor* (1875) he will speak admiringly of "that insuperable strength of will, that power of self-control which is one of the privileges of the free Indians of the New World." And in *The Adventures of Captain Hatteras* (1866) his mouthpiece-character, Doctor Clawbonny, will observe that "the Esquimaux are happier than the working people of our great cities." It's Verne the lover of James Fenimore Cooper at war with Verne the lover of "progress."

12. *1,800 feet above sea level* "Verne was having a little joke," thinks Arthur C. Clarke, "when he discovered an eighteen-hundred-foot high hill in Florida." The highest spot in the state is 350 feet above sea level. In his book on Florida, Lanier feels bound to warn potential visitors about its "levelness," as he calls it: "the State is not remarkable for beauty of landscape, and . . . persons—particularly those from hill countries—who should go to Florida for this sole end would certainly be disappointed."

13. *5° 7′ west longitude* "From the meridian of Washington," Verne explains in a footnote, for in those days many nations reckoned longitude from their own capitals. The Washington meridian was 77° 03′ west of Greenwich. That puts Barbicane's launching site in what we now call 82° 10′ west longitude, 27° 7′ north latitude. And so it's east of the Myakka River, in an area of scattered pine and palmetto, about twenty miles from the Gulf of Mexico. In Barbicane's day this is a belt of sparsely cultivated land, with great cattle ranges further inland.

Today Barbicane's site lies within the city of North Port, one of Florida's fastest growing developments, with a population nearing 10,000. According to Joseph F. Dracup, of the National Geodetic Survey, the latitude and longitude could be in error by ±30″, or a distance of 3,000 feet. And according to Jon S. Beazley, state topographic engineer, who asked his computer, the distance from Barbicane's site to the Vertical Assembly Building at Cape Kennedy is only 137.218 miles.

"No sir, we do not realize it," the engineer answered, "and we'll never have to."

By ten in the morning the little troop had ridden a dozen miles or so inland, over the fertile plains and into a region of forests. Trees of many varieties and masses of vines flourished in tropical profusion. The fruits and the blossoms of pomegranate, orange, lemon, fig, olive, apricot, and banana trees rivaled one another in color and scent. In their fragrant shade, a whole world of birds of brilliant plumage fluttered and sang. Among them our travelers especially noted the crab-eaters, whose nests would have to be jewel-boxes to be worthy of these feathered gems.[7]

J. T. Maston and the major were full of admiration for the splendid beauty all around them. But Barbicane seemed indifferent to these wonders. He was in a hurry. This fertile country annoyed him precisely because of its fertility. He was no dowser surely, but he could sense water underfoot, and he kept looking for incontestable signs of *in*fertility: arid land.

They pressed on, fording several streams, not without danger, for these were infested with alligators fifteen to eighteen feet long.[8] J. T. Maston threatened them with his formidable hook, but he managed to scare only the pelicans, teal, phaetons,[9] wild denizens of these banks, while the big red flamingos simply stared stupidly at him.

Finally these swamp-dwellers disappeared in their turn, the trees became smaller, the thickets thinner, until there were only small patches of wood on a vast plain where the riders startled a herd of deer.

"At last," Barbicane stood in his stirrups, "we've come to pine country."

"And Indian country too," the major observed.

Indeed, some Seminoles had just appeared on the horizon. They charged back and forth on their swift horses,[10] brandishing long spears, firing muskets into the air. But they contented themselves with a mere show of hostility,[11] and Barbicane and his troop were not alarmed.

They were crossing a rocky plain, an open space of many acres, scorched by a brilliant sun. They were on fairly high ground, which seemed to offer the members of the Gun Club all the conditions required for setting up their Columbiad.

"Halt!" Barbicane reined in his horse. "What's the name of this place?"

"Stony Hill," one of the Floridians said.

Without saying a word, Barbicane dismounted, set out his instruments, and began to determine his position with scientific care. The little troop formed a circle around him and waited in deep silence.

As soon as the sun reached the meridian, Barbicane figured the results of his observations and announced:

"This place is situated 1,800 feet above sea level[12] in 27° 7′ north latitude, 5° 7′ west longitude.[13] Its dry and rocky character makes it a good site for our experiment. So, right on this plain is where we'll build our magazines, workshops, furnaces, houses for the work crew, and from this very spot"—he stamped his foot on the summit of Stony Hill—"we'll launch our projectile into the lunar world!"

CHAPTER XIV

Pickaxe and Trowel

Barbicane and his companions returned to Tampa that same evening. Murchison the engineer set sail on the *Tampico* for New Orleans. He was going to recruit an army of workers and bring back the greater part of the materials. The Gun Club members remained in Tampa to organize the preliminary work with the help of local talent.

Eight days later, the *Tampico* sailed back into Espiritu Santo Bay with a flotilla of steamships. Murchison had signed up fifteen hundred workmen. In the evil days of slavery, he would have been wasting his time and effort. But now that America, the land of liberty, counted only free men within her borders, they were willing to go anyplace where there were good-paying jobs. Since the Gun Club was not short of money, they offered their men high pay and very attractive bonuses. Any man who worked on the project until its completion could count on having a large sum deposited in his name in the Bank of Baltimore. Therefore Murchison had had many applicants to choose from and was able to set high standards of intelligence and skill. Hence it is easy to see that his work force comprised the finest mechanics, stokers, foundrymen, lime-burners, miners, brickmakers, laborers, and artisans of all kinds, white and black, chosen without regard to race or color.[1] Many of them brought their families along. It was a real emigration.

At ten o'clock in the morning, October 31, this legion disembarked on the quays of Tampa. It is not hard to imagine the bustle and excitement that reigned in that little town whose population was doubled[2] in one day. Indeed, Tampa was to profit enormously from the Gun Club project, not because of the number of new workers, who were soon moved to Stony Hill, but because of the influx of the curious who trickled in to the Florida peninsula from all parts of the globe.

The first few days were spent unloading the cargo of the steamships: machinery, food supplies, and a great number of parts for sheet-iron houses that had been numbered for easy assembly. At the same time Barbicane was busy laying out the route of a railroad to run the fifteen miles between Stony Hill and Tampa.

The way an American railroad is built is well known. Capricious in its curves, foolhardy in its slopes, scornful of guard-rails and other

1. *race or color* Verne is understandably hasty in assuming that the end of the Civil War means the end of racial discrimination in America. After all, he could never imagine how long it will take to achieve the conditions he describes. And since he regards America as the land of freedom, he is eager to see its one major blemish—its treatment of the black man—removed. And again, he oversimplifies to stress his own political beliefs. For most of his life up to this point (he is 37 as he writes this novel), slavery has been a world-wide issue. In his boyhood, slave traders still operated in the eastern Mediterranean. His attitude toward slavery in America is summed up in *North against South* (1887): he has been on the side of the ''Northerners, anti-slavers, abolitionists, federalists,'' against the ''Southerners, slave owners, secessionists, confederates.'' Later in this novel he will write one of the most touching descriptions of the anti-slavery attitude to be found anywhere in his entire *oeuvre*.

2. *population was doubled* In real life, Tampa's population won't rise above 720 until the 1880s.

3. *jump the track* In Verne's day, America is notorious for her slapdash railroad engineering. Writers often note the crudity of America's railways compared with Europe's. In *American Notes* (1842), for example, Charles Dickens writes: "Occasionally the rails are laid upon the extreme verge of a giddy precipice; . . . the traveller gazes sheer down, without a stone or scrap of fence between, into the mountain depths below." And *The American Cyclopaedia* (1875) explains it this way: "In England," the plan has been to build railroads "in the most solid and substantial manner from the start, and to supply them with every appliance necessary for their operation; while in America the general rule has been to build upon the cheapest possible plans, with light rails, narrow banks, heavy gradients, wooden bridges, and less expensive cars, buildings, and machinery, and to depend upon future earnings with which to bring the works up to the standard required by the increasing business of the line." Also, Congress' good intentions have been subverted by some dishonest builders. To encourage railroad construction across the Territories, the Federal government pays subsidies of, say, $16,000 per mile over level ground, $32,000 over hilly terrain. So some contractors avoid open, flat areas and run their line over every hill in sight!

The bitterest denunciation of irresponsible railroad building will soon come from the distinguished engineer Arthur Mellen Wellington, who will blame it all on "general negligence" and "incompetence." In his classic, *The Economic Theory of the Location of Railways* (1877), he will complain that in the West especially, "the fatal ease with which a . . . line . . . may be run from almost anywhere to anywhere, by using heavy enough grades, has brought the average train load lower than in the rugged regions of the East, and caused perhaps a . . . more discreditable aggregate of thoroughly bad location than in any other . . . region of the world."

4. *miner . . . artillerist* In Barbicane's day it is common for an engineer to function as a generalist, practicing what would today be considered the separate fields of military, civil, mechanical, mining and metallurgical engineering, and even architecture. For example, many of the "civil" engineers who earned their credentials working on the Erie Canal (1817–1825) moved right on into railroad or electrical engineering in later decades. Verne draws his best picture of this Leonardo da Vinci type of generalist in *The Mysterious Island* (1874–1875): Captain Cyrus Smith is an applied scientist, period. He navigates a balloon; starts a fire with watch lenses; maps an island; makes bows and arrows; discovers clay, coal, various ores with which to build an oven and a forge; manufactures iron and steel; derives chemicals, including nitroglycerine, which he uses as an explosive to redirect the island's waterways; constructs an elevator and an electric telegraph; and engages in scientific agriculture.

Edward Roth's map of "The Scene of the Operations" as it appears in some early editions of his 1874 translation.

such luxuries as it climbs hills and plunges into valleys, the railroad runs blindly along with no concern for a straight line. It's not costly, it's no inconvenience, it's only that trains do jump the track.[3] The line from Tampa to Stony Hill was a mere bagatelle; its construction took little time, little money.

Barbicane was the guiding spirit of this world that had answered his call. He inspired his people, he gave them enthusiasm and conviction. As though gifted with ubiquity, he made his presence felt everywhere. Always he had J. T. Maston, his buzzing fly, at his elbow. Out of his practical genius flowed a thousand inventions. He overcame every obstacle, saw no difficulties, was never befuddled. He was miner, mason, mechanic as well as artillerist,[4] with answers for all questions, solutions for all problems. He carried on regular correspondence with the Gun Club and the Cold Spring iron works. Day and night, its lights burning, its boilers stoked up, the *Tampico* awaited his orders out in the roads of Hillsborough harbor.

On November 1, Barbicane left Tampa with a crew of workmen and the next day they put up a village of sheet-iron houses around Stony

Hill. They enclosed it with palisades. In its activity and its excitement, at least, it soon resembled a major American city. Life was purposeful, and work was conducted according to a regular schedule.

After scientific boring had revealed the nature of the soil, they began to dig on November 4. On that day, Barbicane called his foremen together and told them:

"You know, my friends, why I have brought you to this primitive part of Florida. It is our job to cast a cannon with an inside diameter of nine feet and walls six feet thick, surrounded by a stone revetment nineteen and a half feet thick. So we must dig a shaft sixty feet wide to a depth of 900 feet. That's a big task to complete in eight months. You must excavate 2,543,400 cubic feet[5] of earth in 255 days, or in round numbers, 10,000 cubic feet a day. That's not much of a job for a thousand men working with plenty of elbow room, but it won't be so easy in a relatively tight space. Nevertheless, it must be done, and it will be done. And I'm counting on your courage as well as your skill."

At eight o'clock that morning, the first blow of the pickaxe sounded in the Florida soil, and from that moment that valiant tool never rested in the hands of the excavators. The work gangs relieved each other in four shifts a day.

Colossal though the operation was, it was not beyond the limits of human strength. Far from it. Many a more difficult project has been completed, often involving direct struggle with the elements. To mention some comparable works, let us consider "Father Joseph's Well," constructed near Cairo by the Sultan Saladin at a time when machines had not yet increased man's strength a hundredfold: it goes down to the very level of the Nile itself, to a depth of 300 feet! Or consider that other well dug at Coblenz by Margrave Johann von Baden, six hundred feet down! And what was the problem in Florida? To dig a shaft three times deeper and ten times wider with that greater width[6] actually making the digging easier! There was not one foreman, not one laborer, who doubted the success of the operation.

Murchison the engineer made an important suggestion which, when approved by President Barbicane, speeded up the work considerably. A clause in the contract had required that the Columbiad be reinforced with hoops of wrought iron put in place when they were still hot. This was a needless precaution; it was clear now that the gun-barrel could do without these hoops, and so they canceled that clause.

This saved a lot of time, for now they could use the new system of digging adopted for the construction of wells: the masonry is built in as the hole is dug down. Thanks to this simple procedure, it is no longer necessary to shore up the earth with braces: the wall of masonry holds it back with unshakable strength,[7] and lowers itself by its own weight.

This technique would not be used until the pickaxe had got down to hard ground.

On November 4, at the very center of the enclosure, that is to say, at the summit of Stony Hill, fifty men started digging a circular hole sixty feet in diameter.

First the pick hit a layer of black vegetable matter, half a foot thick, which they got through quickly. Then they came to two feet of a fine

5. *2,543,400 cubic feet* In reckoning the volume of the cylinder he describes, Barbicane is using the convenient round figure of 3.14 as the value of π. If he were to carry π to, say, five decimal points—3.14159—he would arrive at a greater result, in this case, 2,544,690 cubic feet.

6. *greater width* Father Joseph's Well, dug in the twelfth century, was 20 feet by 12 feet in its horizontal dimensions. The Italian engineer San Gallo, working for Pope Clement VII in 1527, dug another deep-and-wide well at Orvieto: 180 feet down, 46 feet in diameter, all of it scooped out of solid rock. San Gallo also constructed two spiral staircases to the bottom: one for descent, the other for ascent.

7. *unshakable strength* That is, being circular, the wall functions as an arch: the more it is compressed, the more it resists the pressure.

The work progressed with great regularity. From the first illustrated edition (1872).

8. *chalk of England* The English call it *marl*.

sand which they removed very carefully, since it would prove useful in the casting of the inner mold.

After the sand appeared a compact white clay, resembling the chalk of England,[8] which extended down to a depth of four feet.

Then the iron picks struck sparks on the hard bed of the soil, a kind of rock composed of petrified shells, very dry, very solid, which they would encounter from here on. At that point, the excavation was six and a half feet deep, and now the masons began their work.

On the floor of the excavation they built a "wheel" of oak, a disk firmly bolted and tremendously strong, with a hole in the center equal in diameter to the exterior diameter of the Columbiad. On this wheel they laid the first courses of masonry, binding the stones together with a hydraulic cement of inflexible tenacity. After laying the stones from the circumference to the center, the masons were enclosed in a pit twenty-one feet in diameter.

When this was done, the excavators got busy with their picks again, cutting away the rock from under the wheel, taking care as they advanced outward, to support the disk with thick props. Every time they gained another two feet of depth, they would successively remove the supports. The oak wheel then sank by degrees,[9] and with it the massive ring of masonry, on top of which the masons were always at work, laying more courses, but leaving an occasional vent-hole for the gas to escape through during the casting.

This kind of work required great skill and unflagging attention. More than one man digging under the wheel was seriously hurt by falling stones, and some were killed. But their morale never dimmed as they worked night and day: by night, under the glow of electric lamps;[10] by day, under a sun that would in a matter of months raise the temperature to 99° on that parched plain. The sounds of picks on the stone, the explosions of blasting powder, the clank of machinery, the ribbons of smoke winding into the air, all this forged a ring of terror around Stony Hill: herds of buffalo and bands of Seminoles stayed far away.

The work progressed with great regularity. Steam derricks removed

9. *sank by degrees* This is a miner's technique; now we see why Murchison has recruited miners to dig this shaft. Before they *remove the supports,* his men supplement them with a second set of iron studs a few inches shorter. Then they remove the first set, allowing the mass above to subside just a few inches onto the second set. They reposition the first set of irons a few inches lower, take out the second set and so on. John A. Roebling will use a similar technique in building the towers of the Brooklyn Bridge (1869–1883).

10. *electric lamps* With his flair for pioneering and his vast financial resources, Barbicane can afford these in the 1860s. But they are expensive and short-lived and hence not widely used. The basic principle has been known for decades: electricity passing through a resisting medium will give off light. In 1802 Sir Humphrey Davy demonstrated that strips of platinum could be heated to incandescence electrically. In 1809 he used a battery of 2,000 cells to pass a current through two charcoal sticks placed four inches apart. The flame that leaped the gap described an arc and so this second type of electric luminary has been dubbed the arc lamp. In 1856 the French engineer C. de Chagny has developed a platinum-filament lamp for miners; in 1857 an arc lamp has been installed in the lighthouse at Dungeness, England.

But so far only visionaries like Verne can imagine electric illumination in general use. Aside from the prohibitive cost, electric light as developed in Barbicane's day is not very comfortable to work with. "It is . . . so very intense," says a standard reference book as late as 1874, "that the eye is dazzled, and vision becomes much more indistinct than with the same quantity of light given off from an oil lamp with large concentric wicks."

As Verne writes this passage, scientists and inventors the world over are hunting for cheap filaments that will not burn out fast and not dazzle the eye. In October 1879 Thomas Alva Edison will light a glass bulb using a carbonized thread for the filament, and two months later will demonstrate the first complete incandescent lighting system at his laboratory in Menlo Park, New Jersey.

Barbicane the generalist is typical of Verne's heroic applied scientist who can solve any practical problem. Here Captain Cyrus Smith, hero of *The Mysterious Island* (1875), operates an elevator he has constructed to lift the castaways to their dwelling high in the cliffside. He is taking the injured Herbert to safety indoors.

11. *thirty-foot cube . . . of rock.*

12. *cyclopean labors* Some translators have said *herculean,* presumably because they could not count on their readers' having as good a knowledge of mythology as Verne's French audience has. But *herculean* does not have the same connotations as *cyclopean.* Around the fourteenth century B.C., the early Greeks built the walls of Mycenae and Tiryns by piling huge masses of irregularly shaped rocks one on top of the other. Later Greeks, finding it hard to understand how normal men had been able to move such masses, assumed the walls had been build by *Cyclopes,* the one-eyed giants that Odysseus encounters in the *Odyssey:* the Cyclops whom Odysseus blinds casts huge boulders great distances. In architecture, *cyclopean* signifies rude polygonal masonry. But Verne uses the term in its fullest literary sense: to signify the rearrangement of vast masses of natural materials—in this case two and a half million cubic feet of soil and rock—seemingly accomplished by giants.

13. *humanity . . . in particular* This engineering emphasis on the benefits to mankind-at-large, as opposed to the sacrifice of particular individuals (usually of the working class), does not originate with the Americans. It finds full expression in engineering literature as early as Georgius Agricola's classic *De Re Metallica* (1556). In his introduction, Agricola takes on the critics of "the metallic arts" who condemn mining as a perilous occupation: miners may be slowly killed by pestilential air that rots their lungs or instantly crushed by falling rock. But Agricola insists that "since things like this rarely happen, and only in so far as workmen are careless, they do not deter miners from carrying on their trade any more than it would deter a carpenter from his because one of his mates has acted incautiously and lost his life by falling from a high building." Oddly enough, much later Agricola notes that in the Carpathian mines "women are found who have married seven husbands, all of whom this terrible [occupational] consumption has carried off to a premature death." Eager as Agricola is to insist that mining is no more fatal than carpentry, his own encyclopedic coverage of the facts allows the reader to conclude for himself that no woman is likely to marry seven carpenters each of whom has fallen to a premature death. Obviously, Barbicane's men *digging under the wheel* have been in greater peril than the Agricolas care to acknowledge.

14. *200,000 francs of work* American engineers will use a similar rule of thumb for decades to come: in the twentieth century, they will expect to lose one life for every million dollars invested. But laborers have more poetic ways of expressing much higher ratios: for example, Irish immigrants who build railroads through mountain, desert, malaria, and Indian country say that an Irishman lies buried under every tie.

the rubble. There were very few unexpected problems: most difficulties had been anticipated and were handled according to plan.

At the end of the first month the excavators were right on schedule: they were 112 feet down. In December, they doubled this depth, and in January, tripled it. During February the men had to contend with an underground spring they had exposed. They used powerful pumps and compressed-air machines to drain it dry, and then they stopped up the opening with concrete, just as they would plug a leak in a ship. Finally they had eliminated these undesirable waters, but because a section of the soil had been washed away, the wheel sank unevenly, and some of the masonry caved in. It's easy to imagine the crushing weight of a cylinder of masonry almost 400 feet high. This accident took the lives of several workers.

Three weeks were consumed shoring up the stone revetment, building a support under it, restoring the cylinder to its original condition. But thanks to the talent of the engineer and the power of his machinery, the structure, once thrown off-balance, now recovered its aplomb, and digging could be resumed.

The work suffered no more setbacks, and on June 10, twenty days before the date set by Barbicane, the shaft, completely lined with stonework, attained its depth of 900 feet.

The bottom of the stone cylinder now rested on a massive thirty-foot cube,[11] while its top was level with the surrounding terrain.

President Barbicane and other members of the Gun Club showered praises on Murchison the engineer; he had finished his cyclopean labors[12] with extraordinary rapidity.

During those eight months Barbicane had never for one moment left Stony Hill. Keeping close watch on the excavation, he had been concerned with the well-being and the health of his workers, and he had been lucky enough to avoid those epidemics that often plague crowded communities, especially in the tropics.

Several workmen, it is true, had paid with their lives for the rashness inherent in such dangerous projects. But these fatal accidents are impossible to prevent, and Americans worry very little about such details. They show more concern for humanity in general than for individuals in particular.[13] Barbicane, however, professed contrary principles, and tried to carry them out at every opportunity. Because of his concern, his intelligence, his effective intervention in threatening situations, his prodigious and humane sagacity, the accident rate did not exceed that of countries overseas noted for their extreme precautions, France among others, where they reckon one casualty for every 200,000 francs of work.[14]

CHAPTER XV

The Festival of the Casting[1]

Digging the pit was not the only task accomplished during these eight months. Preliminary work on the casting was done at the same time and with great speed. A stranger arriving at Stony Hill would have been astonished at the sight.

At a distance of 600 yards from the pit, forming a circle around it, 1,200 reverberatory furnaces had been set up, each one six feet wide and three feet apart. In other words, the circumference of the circle was more than two miles long. All the furnaces were built on the same plan, with a tall rectangular chimney, and they created a singular spectacle. J. T. Maston saw it as a superb architectural arrangement. It reminded him of the monuments in Washington. For him there was nothing more beautiful,[2] not even in Greece, where, he admitted, "I've never been anyhow."

At their third meeting, the executive committee had decided to use cast iron, specifically "gray iron," for the Columbiad. This metal is durable, ductile, and malleable, easy to bore, hence suitable for all casting operations. Processed with coal, it proves to be a superior material for making cannons, steam-engine cylinders, hydraulic presses, and other pieces of equipment requiring great powers of resistance.

But iron melted only once is not likely to be sufficiently homogeneous. It takes a second fusion to refine it completely, to rid it of its last impurities.

So, before it was shipped to Tampa, the iron ore, melted in the furnaces at Cold Spring and placed into contact with carbon and silicon heated to a high temperature, was carburized and transformed into cast iron. When this first operation was completed, the metal was sent on to Stony Hill. But it would have cost too much to send 136,000,000 pounds of iron by rail. The price of transportation would have doubled the price of the material. It seemed better to charter ships in New York and to load them with the iron in the form of bars. This required no less than sixty-eight ships of 1,000 tons each, a veritable fleet, which left New York on May 3, headed out to sea, followed the American coast, sailed through the Bahama Channel, rounded the tip of Florida, and, on May 10, entered the Bay of Espiritu Santo, dropping anchor in the port of Tampa.

1. *The Festival of the Casting* The French title—*La Fête de la Fonte*—better emphasizes the ironic religious overtones that Verne first sounded with his use of the papal phrase *urbi et orbi*. In French, *fête* can mean not simply *holiday* but also *saint's day* or *parish feast*. Again the suggestion is there that man now celebrates the technological rather than the spiritual. Note how later in this chapter, there is a disquieting feeling that technology may be overshadowing nature as well.

2. *nothing more beautiful* Verne is passionately concerned with the esthetics of technology. As we sense from his sarcasm here, he believes man need not settle for an ugly environment as the price of technical progress. But the Mastons are legion. In later works Verne develops the contrast between harsh, crude design and beautiful use of modern materials. And he comes to see that architectural arrangement of living and working quarters is an expression of the political relationships among the inhabitants. In *The Begum's Fortune* (1879) he portrays Stahlstadt (Steel City) as ugly, black, and gloomy like Pittsburgh: a city of clangor and smog that birds bypass. No one there can remember having seen a butterfly. The regimented work force lives in barrack-like buildings. The entire city is organized around a Central Block—Verne calls it "the dragon's cave"—which is the secret brain-center of technics and politics. Stahlstadt is Verne's extreme form of some cities created by the Industrial Revolution in which, according to J. L. and B. Hammond, "all diversions were regarded as wrong, because it was believed that successful production demanded long hours, a bare life, a mind without temptation to think or to remember, to look before or behind." For this reason, some English magistrates in industrial towns have refused to license public music and concert halls.

By contrast, Franceville, a rival community in the same novel, is a "radiant city" of hygiene and happiness, organized entirely on humanistic principles. There is a prescribed ratio between residential and garden space. To prevent air-pollution, the city planners conduct industrial smoke into underground pipes. All major questions are decided by "a show of hands" in "an immense building" called the Town Hall.

Verne will continue in many works—*Propeller Island* (1895), for example, and *The Day of an American Journalist in 2889 A.D.* (1889)—to stress the possibility of a beautiful technology. But in real life he becomes more and more pessimistic. In 1887 he will travel to Nantes to settle his mother's estate. He will visit the cottage in nearby Chantenay where he and Paul had played as boys. He will find it surrounded by factories. The leaves of the few remaining trees will be covered with soot. He will write: "The air, once full of perfume of flowers and fruit trees, is now vitiated by a pall of black smoke. What can we do? Apparently civilization must adopt the harsh guise of necessity."

There the cargo was transferred from the ships to the cars of the Stony Hill railway and, by the middle of January, this enormous mass of metal had reached its destination.

Now we can see why it was necessary to build 1,200 furnaces: those 68,000 tons of iron had to be melted all at once. Each furnace could hold about 114,000 pounds of metal. They were all built on the model of those used for casting the Rodman cannon. They were low and trapezoidal in shape. The hearth and the chimney were located at opposite ends of the furnace so that it was heated evenly throughout. Constructed of fire brick, these furnaces consisted simply of a grate for burning the coal and a "sole" or flat bottom on which the bars of iron were placed. These "soles" or hearths were inclined at an angle of twenty-five degrees to permit the metal to flow into basins and thence—through tapholes—into 1,200 conduits converging on the central pit.

The day after the excavators and the masons had completed the pit, Barbicane set to work on the inner mold. His object now was to build, in the center of the well, and in a direct line with its axis, a solid cyl-

Since morning, 12,000 chimneys had been belching torrents of flame . . . Engraving from the 1872 French edition.

The Indian on the periphery of the white man's world is a favorite theme of nineteenth-century writers and artists. *Mitchell's School Geography* (1863) features this drawing of "Indians viewing the improvements of white men." Mitchell's caption implies that the red men are impressed if not envious, maybe ripe for conversion. But Verne's variation on the theme rings truer. He reports that the *Seminoles stayed far away* from the project (Chapter XIV); he imagines they see the casting as a natural disaster; they seem repelled by the white man's "improvements."

inder 900 feet high and nine feet wide which would exactly occupy the space reserved for the bore of the Columbiad. This cylinder was composed of a mixture of clayish earth and sand, with hay and straw added. The space remaining between the mold and the masonry would be filled with the molten metal, which thus would form the walls of the cannon, six feet thick.

To maintain the shape of this cylinder, they reinforced it with iron bands and braced it with crosspieces firmly embedded in the stone revetment. After the casting, these iron crosspieces would become a part of the solid metal and hence would pose no problem at all.

That operation was completed on July 8, and the casting was set for the following day.

"This casting will be a great ceremony, a true festival," J. T. Maston said to his friend Barbicane.

"Oh yes," Barbicane agreed, "but it can't be a festival open to the public."

"What! You're not going to open the gates to everybody?"

"I wouldn't dream of it, Maston. The casting of the Columbiad is a delicate operation, not to speak of the dangers involved, and I prefer to do it in private. When we finally launch the projectile, then you may have your festival, but at this stage—no."

The president was right. The operation might lead to unexpected dangers. A large crowd of spectators would make it difficult to take the proper measures. It was necessary to maintain complete freedom of movement. No new persons were admitted inside the enclosure except a delegation from the Gun Club, who had made the trip to Tampa. Among these were the dapper Bilsby, Tom Hunter, Colonel Blomsberry, Major Elphiston, General Morgan, and others who had a personal interest in the casting of the Columbiad. J. T. Maston served as their cicerone.[3] He overlooked not one detail, guiding them through the powder magazines, the work shops, the machine shops, and then

3. *cicerone* In choosing this word to describe Maston's service as a tour guide, Verne slyly reminds us of Maston's pompous efforts at *Ciceronian* oratory (as in Chapter VII). Both words derive from the name of the Latin author and orator, Marcus Tullius *Cicero* (*Cicéron* in French). From medieval times on down, writers like Edward Gibbon and orators like Edmund Burke have striven to achieve a *ciceronian* style: Cicero is their guide. Meanwhile, in Italy, a learned antiquarian, who could guide people through ruins and classics, came to be known as a *cicerone* (the Italian form of Cicero).

Niagara Falls as pictured in the 1872 illustrated edition of Verne's *A Floating City,* a novel based on his 1867 trip to America.

to each and every furnace! By their twelve-hundredth visit they were played out.

The casting was set for noon. The day before, each furnace had been charged with 114,000 pounds of iron bars stacked crosswise to each other so that the hot air could circulate freely among them. Since morning, 1,200 chimneys had been belching torrents of flame into the air, and the ground was shaking with dull tremors. For every pound of metal to be cast, a pound of coal had to be burned. Thus there were 68,000 tons of coal sending a thick curtain of smoke across the face of the sun.

Inside the circle of furnaces the heat soon became unbearable; their roar resembled the rumble of thunder. Powerful fans added the noise of their continuous blast as they fed fresh oxygen to the glowing hearths.

To guarantee success, the operation had to be carried out very swiftly. The firing of a cannon would be the signal for releasing the liquid metal, for emptying every furnace.

When the preliminaries were completed, the foremen and all hands waited for the signal with impatience and mounting excitement. There was no one inside the circle now. Each foundry master stood at his post ready to open the tapholes.

Barbicane and his colleagues, stationed on a nearby rise of land, supervised the operation. They were ready to fire a cannon as soon as the engineer gave the signal.

Shortly before noon, the first drops of metal began to flow. The basins filled up gradually. When the iron was entirely molten, it was allowed to stand for a few moments to facilitate the separation of impurities. At noon the cannon fired abruptly, sending a tawny flash into the air. Twelve hundred tapholes were opened simultaneously, one thousand two hundred fiery serpents unfolded their incandescent coils and crept toward the central pit. There with a terrific noise they dropped nine hundred feet. It was a moving, magnificent spectacle. The ground trembled as these cascades of molten metal, sending whirls of smoke toward the sky, volatilized the moisture in the core-mold and sent it through the vent-holes in the stone revetment in the form of dense vapors. The artificial clouds spiraled toward the zenith, reaching a height of 3,000 feet. A savage, wandering on the other side of the horizon, would have thought some new crater was being formed in the heart of Florida, but there was neither eruption, nor tornado, nor tempest, nor clash of the elements, none of those terrible catastrophes nature is capable of producing. No! It was man alone who had created these reddish vapors, these gigantic flames worthy of a volcano, these loud tremors like the shock of an earthquake, these reverberations rivaling the sound of hurricanes. It was his hand that had flung—into an abyss he had created—a whole Niagara of molten metal.[4]

4. *Niagara of molten metal* Nothing in this novel so far has moved Verne so much as this metallurgical feat. Note how he consummates his description with images that marry nature and technology. He seems most inspired when he can portray the works of man and the great natural wonders on the same scale. And such imagery signals a definite turning point in man's relations with Mother Earth. Until now, even for Verne, Niagara has stood mainly as a symbol of the powerful forces of nature with which pioneers must cope. But here Verne makes Niagara serve as a metaphor not for the forces of nature but for the forces of man.

Partly because of the financial success of this book, Verne will be able in 1867 to afford a trip to New York on the *Great Eastern*. With his brother Paul he will take the paddle steamer north up the Hudson and then the train west through the Mohawk Valley to Buffalo. Later he will tell in an article in *The Youth's Companion* how he has "marveled at the Niagara Falls from the top of Terrapin Tower with a lunar rainbow showing in the spray. . . ."

Verne's fascination with metallurgy began when his father took him and Paul to visit the Indret iron works, where the boys gaped at the steam hammers pounding glowing chunks of iron into shape for France's new, mechanized Navy. Throughout his career, Verne researches metallurgy so well that in *The Begum's Fortune* (1879) he can describe in convincing detail how his hero works first as a "puddler" in a "monster forge" and later as a "caster" in a casting "gallery." And in *The Mysterious Island* (1875) his hero starts with the extraction of the minerals from the earth and goes right on through to the production of finished metal implements.

CHAPTER XVI

The Columbiad

Had the casting operation succeeded? They were reduced to mere conjecture. There was good reason to be optimistic, since the mold had absorbed the entire mass of metal melted in the furnaces. In any event, it would be quite some time before they could be absolutely sure of the results.

Now when Major Rodman had cast his 160,000-pound cannon, it actually took fifteen days to cool. How long, then, would this new monstrous Columbiad, crowned with clouds of vapor and defended by its terrific heat, remain hidden from its admirers' gaze? It was difficult to predict.

Members of the Gun Club suffered from unbearable impatience. But they could do nothing. J. T. Maston's concern almost caused him to be roasted alive.[1]

Fifteen days after the casting, an immense column of smoke was still rising in the open sky, and for at least two hundred feet all around the summit of Stony Hill, the ground was too hot to walk on.

Days added up to weeks. There was no way to hasten the cooling of the immense cylinder. It was impossible even to get near it. For the Gun Club members, it was a period of fretful anxiety.

"Today is August 10," said J. T. Maston one morning. "We're only four months away from December 1! We still have to remove the mold, bore the cannon, load it, and we don't have that much time! We can't even approach it! Suppose it doesn't cool on time? What a cruel joke that would be!"

They tried to calm the impatient secretary and without success. Barbicane said nothing, but his silence hardly muffled his irritation. Their advance had been halted by time itself, a formidable enemy under the circumstances, and to be at the mercy of such a foe was hard on these veteran campaigners.

But now, in their constant vigil, they began to notice a change in the state of the soil. By August 15, the clouds of vapor began to diminish in their intensity and thickness. A few days later the ground exhaled only a thin wisp of smoke, the last gasp of the monster enclosed in its circle of stone. There were no more tremors in the earth, and the ring of heat shrank little by little. The more impatient of the

---

1. *roasted alive* Many readers experience some puzzlement or disappointment here. They expected this sentence would lead to some anecdote about *how* Maston risked being cooked. They wonder, has a passage been dropped from the text? No, this is the way it reads even in the first edition.

spectators were able to get closer, one day ten feet more, the next day, twenty. On August 22, Barbicane, his colleagues, and the engineer were able to stand on the outcrop of iron that now served as the summit of Stony Hill. It seemed to be a healthful place, for no one could get cold feet there.

"At last!" Barbicane heaved a great sigh of relief.

And they got back to work that same day. In order to clear the bore of the piece, they had to remove the interior mold. The clayish earth and sand had been greatly hardened by the heat of the casting, but with the help of machinery, they dug out that mixture, still hot from contact with the cast-iron walls, and loaded it rapidly onto railroad cars. They worked so hard, their morale was so high, and Barbicane's bonuses were so persuasive, that all traces of the mold had disappeared by September 3.

Now they were ready to bore the cannon. Powerful reaming machines were installed without delay, and their cutting edges attacked the iron. Within a few weeks the interior surface of the immense tube was perfectly cylindrical, and the bore of the piece had acquired a smooth polish.

Tampa before Barbicane arrived. Engraving from the 1872 edition.

2. *some modern Erostratus* This allusion seems so puzzling that one early translator assumes Verne really means *some modern Curtius*. In the fourth century B.C. *Erostratus* set fire to the Temple of Artemis at Ephesus. Apprehended, asked why he had done it, he said, "To make my name immortal." And he succeeded. His story appears in dozens of reference books. Is Verne saying then, that if Maston fell down into the tube he would gain an ironic immortality? An allusion to Curtius seems slightly more relevant, more complimentary to Maston. One day in ancient Rome, the legend goes, the ground in the Forum suddenly split open. Soothsayers declared that Rome would have to sacrifice her chief strength before the chasm would close. A soldier, Marcus Curtius, decided that Rome's greatest asset was her arms and valor. He had both. He mounted his horse, unsheathed his sword, and plunged into the chasm which, of course, magically closed. Is Verne thinking, then, that Maston is the Gun Club's "chief strength"? Verne already knows, from his story outline, that later in the book Maston will declare his willingness to sacrifice himself. But why would Maston risk doing anything that would close this particular hard-won chasm?

It's obvious since the start of the chapter that Verne has been troubled by a possible death for Maston. Would his *impatience* cause him to be *roasted alive,* or would he plunge into the chasm like Curtius, gain immortality like *Erostratus?* But underlying these surface concerns is the basic fact that the chasm, at first unapproachably torrid and later dangerously deep, is a powerful sexual symbol. Maybe Verne suffered from unconscious confusion here, because the thought of Maston's disappearance in that chamber could trigger neurotic anxiety about being swallowed up in the vagina. That would suffice, in a misogynist at least, to cause the indecisiveness and the slip of the pen that figure in these scenes.

3. *ten fathoms thick* Sixty feet. Verne assumes that as a designer of naval armor, Nicholl is thinking in nautical terms. Officially, a *fathom* is a distance of six feet, but in actual practice, it's the distance between the fingers of the right and left hands when a seaman stretches his arms wide. For example, as he hauls up his sounding line, this is the maximum convenient length he can pull in with each movement. As he counts each pull, he's adding up the depth in *fathoms*. Of course he often estimates horizontal distance this way too.

4. *population and business* Verne's predictions-to-come-true are adding up. So far, he has correctly prophesied that the United States will channel some of its military-industrial talents into a space effort, and that its space center will be built in Florida. Here he correctly anticipates the effect on the demographic and economic growth of that state. Brevard County, Florida—which will house the space personnel, their families, and the business and professional people who will service them—will increase in

Tampa after Barbicane arrived. Engraving from the 1872 edition.

Finally, on September 22, less than a year after Barbicane had delivered his famous speech, the enormous mechanism, its calibration and verticality absolutely verified by the most delicate instruments, was pronounced fit for service. Now they had only to wait for the moon. But no one doubted that she would keep her rendezvous.

The joy of J. T. Maston knew no bounds, and he nearly suffered a frightful fall as he looked down the 900-foot tube. But for the right arm of Blomsberry, which the colonel luckily still had, the secretary of the Gun Club, like some modern Erostratus,[2] would have found his death in the depths of the Columbiad.

There could no longer be the slightest doubt, the casting of the cannon had been a complete success, and so on October 6 Captain Nicholl paid off his bet and Barbicane deposited two thousand dollars in his account. The captain's wrath was so great it made him sick. But he still had three bets of three, four, and five thousand dollars, and if he won just two of these, he could emerge, if not victorious, at least not disgraced. But it wasn't the money that made him so sick, it was the fact that his rival had cast a cannon that not even armor ten fathoms thick[3] could resist.

Since September 23, the gates of Stony Hill had been open to the public, and it is easy to imagine the influx of visitors that resulted.

Hordes of sight-seers and curiosity-seekers, hailing from all parts of the country, converged on Florida. The town of Tampa had grown prodigiously during this year devoted to the Gun Club project, and it now counted a population of 150,000 souls. After surrounding Fort Brooke with a network of streets, Tampa now extended out onto the tongue of land that divides the Bay of Espiritu Santo. New neighborhoods, new squares, whole new forests of houses had grown up on these formerly uninhabited shores, under the warm American sun. Companies had been founded to build churches, schools, and private homes, and in less than a year the city's area had increased tenfold.

Everyone knows that Yankees are born businessmen; wherever fate may lead them, to the frozen north or the torrid south, their talent for business must assert itself in some useful way. That is why mere curiosity-seekers, people come to Florida simply to see what the Gun Club was up to, drifted into business just as soon as they had caught their breath in Tampa. The ships chartered to bring in men and materials had made the port a very busy place. Soon other ships of every type, of every tonnage, loaded with food, supplies, merchandise, plied the bay and its two harbors. Large shippers' and chandlers' offices were opened in the city, and every day the *Shipping Gazette* reported new arrivals at the port of Tampa.

While new roads were stretching in every direction, the city, in view of its prodigious increase in population and business,[4] was finally linked by rail with the Southern states of the Union. One railroad ran from Mobile to Pensacola, the great naval base of the South; from that important point, it went on to Tallahassee. Here there was a short section of track, twenty-one miles long, which linked Tallahassee with Saint Marks, on the coast. And it was this line that was now extended to Tampa, awakening or reviving the sleeping or dead parts of central Florida.[5] Hence Tampa—thanks to those technological wonders that grew out of an idea hatched one fine day in the head of one man—could now put on airs as a great city. She was nicknamed "Moon City," and she threw the capital of Florida into a total eclipse, visible all over the world.

And so we can see why such intense rivalry had developed between Texas and Florida, why Texans were so irritated when their claims were turned down by the Gun Club. With the wisdom of foresight, they had understood what a region might gain from Barbicane's experiment, all the benefits that such a cannon-shot might bring. In effect, Texas had lost a vast center of commerce, railroads, and a great increase in population. All these advantages had devolved upon that miserable peninsula of Florida, stretching out like a mere breakwater[6] between the billows of the Gulf and the waves of the Atlantic. Hence Barbicane now shared the hatred that Texans had heretofore reserved for General Santa Anna.[7]

Despite its business boom and its industrial excitement, the new population of Tampa never forgot the interesting operations of the Gun Club. Quite the contrary. They relished news of every detail of the

population from 23,653 in 1950 to 111,435 in the 1960s, with corresponding increases in the number of schools and bowling alleys.

5. *awakening . . . Florida* This is an early statement of Verne's theory that nature has no real existence until man enters the scene. In a very deep religious sense, Verne sees the natural and the human worlds as consubstantial. He puts a fuller statement of these ideas in the mouth of the philosophical Doctor Clawbonny in *The Adventures of Captain Hatteras* (1866): "It is a general law of Nature that countries where people have never lived are unhealthful and sterile, like those where man no longer lives. . . . Little by little, by the mere act of breathing, man changes and improves the exhalations of the soil and the conditions of the atmosphere." This of course ties in with the observation we made earlier that Verne is most inspired when he can describe nature and technology in terms of each other. Major French critics—M. Butor, P. Machery, J. Chesneaux—all stress the point that man's relationship with nature is the basic theme of Verne's *oeuvre.* And the Romanticist notion that man and his artifacts *awaken . . . the dead parts* of the natural world persists into contemporary writing. For example, the poet Miller talks, in his *Making an Angel,* of:

. . . the hill where our tent has brought
Fulfillment to the unawakened curve.

6. *a mere breakwater* No point in Florida is more than seventy miles or so from either the Atlantic Ocean or the Gulf of Mexico; what Verne's Texans think of as *that miserable peninsula* is never much more than 140 miles wide. Compared with Texas, that could seem like a *mere breakwater,* Some Texas land is almost 700 miles from the sea, and she's almost that in width as well.

7. *hatred . . . for . . . Santa Anna* This is the second time Verne need simply allude to *Santa Anna* to make his point: his original audience is well aware of the Mexican's dubious exploits. By 1865, this opportunistic soldier and politician has been a storm center in Mexican affairs for forty years. His notoriety extends far beyond Texas: to Spain, France, the U.S.A., and throughout Mexico itself. His career provides a summary of those peoples' relations that Verne has been playing on for several chapters now.

Born in 1794 in Veracruz, where his father served as a Spanish colonial official, Antonio Lopez de *Santa Anna* became a cadet in the Spanish army at the age of sixteen. He fought against the Mexicans in their War of Independence, but near the end of that conflict he switched sides, joining forces with Augustin Iturbide, who won and declared himself Emperor of Mexico. Iturbide considered Santa Anna to be a dangerously insubordinate soldier and refused him the advancement he expected. Santa Anna switched to the republican faction and drove Iturbide from power. As Mexican commander-in-chief when Spain made a tardy effort to reconquer Mexico in 1829, Santa Anna decisively defeated the invaders. After leading two more insurrections, he became President in 1833, ruling with a high hand, squandering the national income. He abolished the federal constitution and placed the provincial governments under his personal control.

In 1836 the province of Texas rebelled: she had been settled largely by proud Americans who could not stomach his unconstitutional rule. President Santa Anna took the field in person, rushing north with 6,000 troops. They massacred 200 Texans at the Alamo and hastened to attack the main Texan Army under General Sam Houston, who routed the Mexicans at San Jacinto and captured the President-General. Houston let Santa Anna go only after he signed a treaty granting Texas her independence. In Mexico City the treaty was disowned and Santa Anna expelled from office. In 1838 he took command when the French attacked Veracruz: he lost a leg, became a hero again, President again, and was soon ousted again. In 1846 he returned from exile to command the Army in the war with the U.S. He was defeated first by General Zachary Taylor, then by General Winfield Scott. In 1853 he fomented a new revolution, declared himself President for life with the title of His Most Serene Highness: and his turbulent despotism earned him exile again.

During the recent French occupation, he has offered his services to Emperor Maximilian while simultaneously seeking help from the U.S.A. with which to oust Maximilian. By now nobody trusts Santa Anna: both proposals are rejected. As Verne writes, Santa Anna has been dictator-president five times, has identified at different periods with opposite factions in Mexican politics: reactionary to liberal, and has done more than any other man to create an unfortunate stereotype of the ruthless Latin American despot.

The feast was lively, even noisy. Engraving from the 1872 edition.

8. *number in the millions* Another Verne prophecy which will be verified by history. We'll save the details for *the actual day.*

work, of every stroke of the pick. There was a constant coming and going between the town and Stony Hill, a procession, or better still, a pilgrimage.

It was obvious that on the actual day of the experiment, the spectators would number in the millions,[8] for they were already descending on this narrow peninsula from all over the world. Europe was emigrating to America.

But so far, it must be admitted, the curiosity of these numerous newcomers had been poorly satisfied. Those who had counted on seeing the casting had seen only its smoke. That was mighty little for hungry eyes, but Barbicane had refused to admit spectators to that operation. There was much grumbling, discontent, dark murmuring: they accused the president of dictatorial conduct, they called his behavior "un-American." A riot almost erupted outside the stockade around Stony Hill. But Barbicane stood by his decision.

When the Columbiad was completed, however, it was no longer possible to keep the gates shut. It would have been ungracious, even unwise, to stir up public resentment. Barbicane opened the enclosure to all comers. But true to his practical bent, he resolved to coin money out of public curiosity.

Of course it was something just to contemplate this immense Columbiad, but to descend into its depths, that seemed to Americans to be the *ne plus ultra* [9] of happiness on earth. There was not one curiosity-seeker who did not want to give himself the pleasure of visiting the interior of that iron abyss. A small carriage, let down by a steam-winch, made it easy for them to satisfy their curiosity. They went wild. Women, children, elderly people, everybody assumed the duty of penetrating the mysteries of the colossal cannon. The fare for the descent was five dollars per person, and despite this high price, during the two months preceding the launching, the influx of visitors enabled the Gun Club to pocket nearly five hundred thousand dollars.

Needless to say, the first visitors inside the Columbiad were members of the Gun Club, a privilege justly reserved for that illustrious body. The ceremony took place on September 25. President Barbicane, J. T. Maston, Colonel Blomsberry, Major Elphiston, General Morgan, the engineer Murchison, and others—about ten in all—descended in a special carriage. It was still rather hot at the bottom of that long iron tube. They sweltered. But oh what joy! What ecstasy! A table had been set for ten on the massive stone that supported the Columbiad, which was illuminated *a giorno* [10] by a beam of electric light. Dishes exquisite and numerous, which seemed to descend from the sky, were placed before the guests, and the finest French wines flowed generously during this banquet served nine hundred feet beneath the surface of the Earth.

The feast was lively, even noisy. Toasts were proposed back and forth. They drank to the terrestrial globe, to her satellite, to the Gun Club, to the Union, to the moon, to Phoebe, to Diana, to Selene, to the celebrity of the night, to the "peaceful courier of the firmament!" All these hurrahs, carried on the sound waves of the immense acoustic tube, arrived like a crescendo of thunder at the upper end, and the crowd gathered around Stony Hill joined their cheers with those of the ten revelers hidden at the bottom of the gigantic Columbiad.[11]

J. T. Maston seemed to have lost all self-control. It would have been difficult to decide whether he shouted more than he gesticulated, or ate more than he drank. In any case, he would not have given up his place [12] for an empire, not even, as he put it, if the cannon were to be loaded and fired at that very moment, blowing him piecemeal out into "the planetary spaces."

9. *ne plus ultra* Latin for the extreme, utmost point, or the height of achievement. Literally, it means *no more beyond*. Ancient legend had it that these words were inscribed on the Pillars of Hercules to warn mariners not to sail out into the unknown Atlantic.

10. *a giorno* Italian for *as by day, like daylight*.

11. *bottom of the . . . Columbiad* This banquet held inside an iron tube might have been suggested to Verne by a New Year's Eve party staged inside a famous telescope in 1839. We come to the details in Chapter XXIV.

12. *his place* In addition to their technical triumph, Verne's asexual boys are celebrating fulfillment of perhaps their greatest fantasy. Deep inside Mother Earth, well insulated from the shocks of the outside world, well nourished through a slender but trustworthy umbilical cord, they actually have succeeded in *returning to the womb*. This symbolic satisfaction completely offsets the terror raised earlier in the chapter by Maston's near-fall into the chasm. Then the chasm represented the threat a mature woman poses for an immature man: he could be swallowed by her. Here the chasm represents the woman as total reassurance, total maternal protection for the permanent boy. This scene helps explain why most of Verne's main characters are—and remain—bachelors.

CHAPTER XVII
A Telegram

1. *when she leaves* With this sentence, Verne approaches the political crisis of his novel. The symbolism is magnificent: the telegram asks that instead of sending a cannonball, a warlike message, to the moon, Barbicane send a vehicle carrying a passenger, a peaceful emissary. Until now, the Gun Club has been concerned mainly with finding an outlet for their untapped military talents: they have thought in terms of inanimate objects like cannon, powder, projectile. The telegram challenges them to face the fully humanistic possibilities of their moonshot: to redesign their equipment for a manned space probe, that is, for the safety and adventure of a space voyager. Chesneaux gives the broadest possible interpretation to the alteration Ardan proposes: "He . . . accuses the Gun Club of militaristic tendencies, . . . appeals for the reconversion of American industries to peaceful uses."

Notice that Ardan does not need at this point to explain the technical reasons for the change of shape: Barbicane knows them. Not discussing them until later adds to the suspense.

2. *Michel Ardan* The 1865 French reader already senses that Verne is modeling *Ardan* on a great celebrity: *Ardan* is a transparent anagram for *Nadar*, pseudonym of Verne's friend Felix Tournachon. Who else would send a telegram at four A.M.? Who but the builder of the balloon *Géant* would drop everything and offer to go to the moon? So long as no one has done it before!

Cartoonist, caricaturist, traveler, author, Nadar is presently a well-known, sensitive portrait photographer: he has already given the world its permanent images of Charles Baudelaire, Gioacchino Rossini, Jules Verne, other major figures of his day. In a balloon ride over Paris in 1858, Nadar has pioneered in aerial photography. He has helped Verne with the technical innovations that launched him on a new career with *Five Weeks in a Balloon* (1863). As Verne was fabricating his fictitious craft, Nadar was building his real *Géant*: as tall

The great engineering work undertaken by the Gun Club was, practically speaking, finished, and yet it would be two months before they could launch their projectile toward the moon. To the impatient public, these two months would seem like two years. Until now the minutest details of the project had been reported in the daily press, which the public devoured passionately with eager eyes. But now it seemed that this "dividend of interest" distributed to the public would be greatly reduced. Everyone was afraid he would no longer collect his daily share of excitement.

Everyone was wrong. For the most unexpected, extraordinary, incredible and improbable development was yet to come, one that would carry public excitement to new heights and throw the entire world into a state of keen anticipation.

One day, September 30 to be exact, at three forty-seven in the afternoon, a telegram, sent via the underwater cable laid between Valentia, Ireland, and Newfoundland and the American coast, was delivered to President Barbicane.

President Barbicane ripped open the envelope and read the message; in spite of his great powers of self-control, his lips grew pale, his eyes looked troubled as he read the twenty words of the telegram.

Here is the text, now preserved in the archives of the Gun Club:

FRANCE, PARIS

September 30, 4 a.m.
To Barbicane, Tampa, Florida, U.S.A.

   Replace the spherical shell with a cylindro-conical projectile. I shall be inside when she leaves.[1] Arriving on steamer Atlanta.

Michel Ardan [2]

as Notre Dame, with a two-story gondola. His spectacular flights have included a 400-mile trip in October 1863: the *Géant* dragged through the country near Hanover, demolishing everything in its path, badly bruising Nadar and his wife. And Nadar is the founder of the Society for Aerial Locomotion, which aims to develop a heavier-than-air flying machine.

What Verne's audience expects, now that they sense the real identity of Ardan, is irrepressible energy. Nadar is a showoff who produces: he makes exorbitant boasts so he will have to live up to them. He takes fortune as it comes, and with style. Broke, he stays in bed for weeks at a time because he has no clothes to wear. In the money, he buys oysters by the barrel and litters his floor six inches deep with shells. Notice that no character in this novel— not even Barbicane—will merit anything like the care that Verne will lavish on Ardan-Nadar.

Nadar's photograph of Jules Verne taken in 1854 in the writer's twenty-fifth year.

CHAPTER XVIII

The Passenger on the *Atlanta*

1. *French . . . American telegraphers* This is the second time that Verne traces the route of Ardan's message. But as he writes in 1865, the Atlantic cable is, in effect, only a prediction, and a real gamble at that. In 1857–1858, and again in 1863, Cyrus Field's project has ended in failure. There is now widespread belief that it will never be possible to complete and maintain such a lengthy (2,000-mile) underwater telegraph cable. Not until July 1866, a year after this novel becomes a best-seller, will Field be able to lay an Ireland-to-Newfoundland cable that proves to be a permanent success.

In his 1863 and 1866 projects, ex-paper-salesman Field uses the *Great Eastern,* the only ship afloat big enough to carry the whole cable on one trip. In 1867 Verne and his brother will board the *Floating City,* as he will call it in his novel of that name (1871), for their voyage to America. For Verne one of the unexpected joys of the journey will be the discovery that Field is on the passenger list. Verne will interview Field, as well as crew-members involved in the cable project, and use much of the material so gained in his *Twenty Thousand Leagues under the Sea* (1870). For the full story, see *The Annotated Jules Verne* edition, pages 337–339.

2. *each . . . to his disposition* In this ironic reversal, the bold, innovative Gun Clubbers suddenly become the backward ones, standing in the way of progress. Verne is stressing his point that these artillerists can see the moonshot only in very limited terms: to them it's mainly a chance to engage in target practice on a cosmic scale. This heightens the contrast with Ardan's broader conception of the project.

If this astonishing news, instead of flying over the wires, had only come by mail in a sealed envelope, if the French, Irish, Newfoundland, and American telegraphers [1] were not aware of the contents of the message, Barbicane would not have hesitated for a moment. He would have kept quiet about it, out of prudence in order not to discredit his experiment. This telegram might be a cover for a hoax, especially since it came from a Frenchman. What chance was there that any man could be rash enough even to think of such a journey? And if such a man did exist, he must be a lunatic who should be shut up not inside the projectile but in the asylum.

However, the telegram was surely known, since the telegraphic system is not discreet by nature: yes, news of Michel Ardan's proposal was running through all the states of the Union. It would do no good for Barbicane to keep quiet about it. He called together those of his colleagues who happened to be in Tampa, and without letting them know his own opinion, without even raising the question of the good faith of the telegram, he simply read them its laconic text.

"Impossible!"

"That's unrealistic!"

"Pure facetiousness!"

"He's mocking us!"

"Ridiculous!"

"Preposterous!"

Thus they ran through the whole vocabulary of doubt, incredulity, scorn, and derision, accompanying the words with the usual gestures, each man grinning, laughing, or shrugging his shoulders, according to his disposition.[2] Only J. T. Maston had a good word for Ardan's message.

"What a great idea!" he exclaimed.

"Yes," the major agreed, "it's all right sometimes to have ideas like that, so long as you don't try to carry them out."

"And why not?" the secretary of the Gun Club replied warmly, all set for an argument. But no one pursued the matter.

Meanwhile the name of Michel Ardan was going the rounds in Tampa. Strangers and natives exchanged glances, questions, and jokes, not about the European—a myth, a chimerical individual—but about J. T. Maston, who actually believed in the existence of this legendary being. When Barbicane first proposed sending a projectile to the moon, everyone had greeted it as a natural and practicable undertaking, a simple question of ballistics. But for a sane man to offer to go aboard the projectile as a passenger, to offer to make such an improbable voyage, that was a fantastic proposal, a joke, a farce, and, to use a word for which the French have an exact equivalent in their everyday speech, a "humbug."[3]

The joking persisted without interruption until evening. The entire Union was seized with a laughing fit. This was strange in a country where any impossible enterprise can always drum up its strong advocates, supporters, and partisans.

Nevertheless, Michel Ardan's proposal, like all new ideas, did trouble a few minds. It upset their usual patterns of thought. "How is it that no one ever thought of it before!" The incident soon became an obsession precisely because it was so strange. People couldn't get it out of their heads. How many things are denied one day only to become realities the next! Why shouldn't somebody go to the moon someday? But, in any case, the man willing to risk his life that way would have to be crazy, and obviously, since the project could not be taken seriously, he should have kept quiet, instead of upsetting a whole population with this idle stuff.

But did the man really exist, in the first place? What a question! The name "Michel Ardan" was not unknown in America! It belonged to a European often cited for his bold feats. And look, this telegram flashed across the bottom of the Atlantic, that actual naming of a ship the Frenchman said he was coming on, the implication that its arrival was imminent, all these circumstances gave the message a certain aura of plausibility. They had to get this thing straight. Soon scattered individuals were forming into groups, the groups combining under the influence of curiosity like atoms responding to molecular attraction, and finally, there was a compact crowd on its way to the residence of President Barbicane.

He had made no statement at all about the telegram. When J. T. Maston had expressed his opinion, Barbicane neither agreed nor disagreed. He remained silent, waiting to see what would happen. But he had not considered the impatience of the public, and he looked with small satisfaction on the population of Tampa crowding beneath his windows. Their mutterings, their clamor soon forced him to make an appearance. It was obvious he had all the duties, hence all the vexations of the celebrity.

When silence fell over the crowd, one citizen came straight to the point:

"The man mentioned in the telegram, Michel Ardan, is he on his way to America? Yes or no?"

"Gentlemen," Barbicane replied, "I know as much about it as you do."

"But we've got to know," others cried impatiently.

"Time will tell," the president said dispassionately.

"Time has no right to keep a whole nation in suspense," the spokesman replied. "Are you redesigning the projectile, as the telegram requested?"

3. *"humbug"* In a footnote, Verne gives the *exact equivalent* in French as *mystification,* or hoax.

The Great Eastern is the only ship big enough to carry the Atlantic Cable on one trip. Here the gigantic vessel is seen in the 1872 edition of Verne's novel *A Floating City*.

"Not yet, gentlemen; but you are right, we do need more information. The telegraph raised all these questions, and the telegraph should settle them."

"On to the telegraph office!" shouted the crowd.

Barbicane came down and led them there.

A few minutes later, they sent a telegram to the ship-brokers of Liverpool. They requested answers to the following queries:

"Is there a vessel called the *Atlanta?* If so, when did she leave Europe? Does she have on board a Frenchman named Michel Ardan?"

Two hours later, Barbicane received intelligence of such a precise nature that it left no room for further doubt.

"The steamer *Atlanta,* of Liverpool, put to sea on October 2, bound for Tampa, with a Frenchman on board carried on the passenger list under the name of Michel Ardan."

At this confirmation of the first telegram, the president's eyes lighted up with a sudden flame, his fists clenched violently, and they heard him mutter:

"It's true then! It's possible! This Frenchman exists, and within two

. . . he looked with small satisfaction on the population of Tampa crowding beneath his windows. Engraving from the first illustrated edition (1872).

weeks he will be here! But he is a crazy man, a hothead! Never will I consent—"

Nevertheless, that very evening, he wrote to the firm of Breadwill and Co., asking them to postpone the casting of the projectile until further notice.

Now, to try to describe the emotion that gripped all of America; how this new excitement was ten times greater than that caused by Barbicane's original proposal; what the Union newspapers said, the way they treated the news and celebrated the arrival of that Old World hero; to depict the feverish state in which everyone lived, counting the hours, counting the minutes, counting the seconds; to give some idea, however faint, of the haunting obsession of all those minds dominated by one single thought; to show how all occupations gave way to one preoccupation, work halted, trade suspended, ships delaying their departure so as not to miss the arrival of the *Atlanta,* trains arriving full and leaving empty, Espiritu Santo Bay incessantly ploughed by steamers, packet boats, pleasure yachts, fly-boats of all dimensions; to count the thousands of curiosity-seekers who in two weeks' time quadrupled the population of Tampa and were obliged to camp out in tents like an army in the field: this would be a task beyond human strength, one that would appeal only to the reckless.

On October 20, at nine in the morning, the signal posts in the Bahama Channel reported thick smoke on the horizon. Two hours later, they exchanged recognition signals with a big steamer. At once the name of the *Atlanta* was flashed to Tampa. At four o'clock, the English ship entered Espiritu Santo, and at five she steamed into Hillsborough Bay. At six she dropped anchor in the port of Tampa.

But before the anchor could hit the sandy bottom, five hundred boats had surrounded the *Atlanta,* and the steamer was taken by storm. Barbicane was the first to land on deck, and in a voice whose emotion he tried in vain to control:

"Michel Ardan!" he cried.

"Here I am!" said an individual standing on the poop deck.

Barbicane, arms crossed, lips tight, eyes interrogating, fixed his gaze on the passenger of the *Atlanta.*

He was about forty-two, tall but a bit bent, like the caryatids that hold balconies on their shoulders.[4] He had a head powerful like a lion's, and he tossed his long fiery hair like a mane. A short face, broad at the temples, adorned with a moustache bristling like cat's whiskers, little patches of yellow beard on the cheeks, and round eyes a bit wild and myopic, completed this definitely feline physiognomy. But his nose was boldly drawn, his mouth particularly humane, his forehead high, intelligent, furrowed like a field never fallow. Finally, a well-developed body fixed firmly on long legs, muscular arms, powerful and well attached, and a determined look, all combined to make of this European a strapping fellow, "forged not cast,"[5] if we may borrow a phrase from the metallurgist.

Disciples of Lavater and Gratiolet[6] would have had no trouble detecting on his skull and face the unmistakable signs of combativeness, that is to say, of courage in the face of danger and a tendency to overcome obstacles; signs too of benevolence and a sense of wonderment, the instinct that leads certain temperaments to attempt the superhuman;

4. *caryatids . . . shoulders* These are fully draped statues of women who support, on their heads, the roof of some ancient buildings. The most famous examples are the six *caryatids* who held up the entablature of the Erechtheum on the Acropolis of Athens. In Verne's day, the explanation given in Vitruvius' *De Architectura* (first century B.C.) is still widely accepted. He says the caryatids represent women of Caryae doomed to such hard labor because their town had sided with the Persians after Thermopylae (480 B.C.). But sculptors were using caryatids in lieu of columns long before that. A better explanation is that the *maidens of Caryae* (the meaning of the Greek *Karyatides*), when they performed ritual dances at the annual festival of Artemis, sometimes assumed the attitude we now associate with a caryatid: strong, easy, somewhat resigned acceptance of a burden.

Verne means Ardan to display that attitude: in his case, as we soon see, acceptance of the burden of being endlessly innovative and messianic. It's significant that Verne chooses the *caryatids* for his analogy rather than the *Atlantes,* the male type: Atlas, holding up the world, is an example. In architecture, the Atlantes are usually represented as supporting greater weights, or at least showing greater strain, than the caryatids do. The Atlantes are not so beautiful.

5. *"forged . . . not cast"* A metal object that is *forged* has been individually heated, beaten, hammered into shape: it is unique. An object that has been *cast* has been made in a mold, which can be used to make many such identical objects.

6. *Lavater and Gratiolet* Johann Kaspar Lavater (1741–1801), whose notions Verne used in analyzing Barbicane's profile (Chapter II), was the founder of physiognomics. He was convinced that the interaction between mind and body would inevitably leave "traces of the spirit on the features." His theories so intrigued one of the greatest writers of the age, Johann Wolfgang von Goethe, that Goethe helped Lavater compose his classic *Physiognomische Fragmente* (1775–1778). Louis-Pierre *Gratiolet* (1815–1865) is a French physician and naturalist whose studies in the Lavater tradition are keeping physiognomy very much alive in Verne's day.

Verne overlooks the work of Sir Charles Bell (1774–1842), who was credited with the first *scientific* correlations between facial movements that express certain feelings and the specific muscles that produce those movements. Hence the muscles in a person's face that are most strongly developed would reveal the dominant emotions or traits of his character. In *Essay on the Anatomy of Expression* (1806), Bell said "there are even muscles in the human face to which no other use can be assigned than to serve as the organs of this language" of emotions.

7. *hyperbole . . . superlatives* Verne himself never grows out of this age. Verne's and Nadar's mutual love of *hyperbole* as a necessary way of life constitutes one of the strongest ties between the two friends.

8. *"a sublime ignoramus"* That's what Voltaire called Shakespeare.

9. *Land of Mountains and Marvels* The land where everything comes true. In French, the proverbial expression *promettre monts et merveilles* means *to promise the Earth*.

10. *paid with himself* Nadar has risked his life many times in his experiments with balloons. He "was ready for anything, the crazier the better," says Verne's grandson. "So Nadar, rechristened anagramatically Ardan, would be the world's first astronaut." At a costume ball that the Vernes will give in 1877, Nadar will show up dressed as Ardan.

11. *Phaëthon . . . Icarus . . . Agathocles* Now Verne's schoolboy lessons in mythology and history are serving him better than they did in his *Erostratus* allusion. *Phaëthon* was the impetuous, *daredevil* son of Helios, the sun-god. He asked his father to let him drive the sun-chariot for a day. In spite of Helios' warning that the job might be too big for him, he tried it. He proved to lack the great strength required to guide the horses of the sun. They bolted from their course and flew so close to the Earth that civilization was in danger of being burnt up. Zeus hurled a thunderbolt at *Phaëthon,* tumbling his body into a river. In his eagerness to ride the Gun Club projectile, Ardan could have more than one resemblance to Phaëthon.

Icarus was the son of the famous artificer Daedalus; they were imprisoned in Crete in the Labyrinth they had built for King Minos. To escape, Daedalus made wings for himself and Icarus out of wax and feathers. But Icarus flew too close to the sun: the wax melted, he plunged into the sea, and drowned. Verne's qualification here is important: while Ardan would be so reckless as to venture too close to the sun, he would also take the precaution of carrying spare parts.

Agathocles was an ancient Syracusan adventurer and despot who conducted himself in war and peace in a very unorthodox manner, in a kind of calculated recklessness. After he became dictator of Syracuse, in 317 B.C., he abolished all debts and distributed the property of the rich among the people. The oligarchic Carthaginians besieged his town and surrounded him on land: so he escaped by sea to carry the war to the Carthaginians' own soil in Africa! On landing there, he *burned his ships* so they could not fall into enemy hands and so his soldiers would fight more desperately to capture a new fleet. He was on the verge of making Sicily a great naval power when he died in 289 B.C.

but the bumps of acquisitiveness, the need to possess and acquire, were totally lacking.

To complete this portrait of the passenger on the *Atlanta,* we should comment on his loose, easy-fitting clothes, his trousers and his coat so full that Michel Ardan had described himself as "death on fabric," his flowing cravat, his shirt collar open wide to reveal a robust neck, his cuffs unbuttoned to give his restless hands full play. He gave the impression that in the freeze of winter, at the chilling prospect of danger, he would never look cold.

Right now, on the deck of the steamer, in the midst of the crowd, he was marching back and forth, never staying in one place, "dragging his anchor," as the sailors put it, gesticulating, friends with everybody, eagerly, nervously biting his nails. He was one of those originals that the Creator invents in a capricious moment, only to break the mold immediately thereafter.

Indeed, Michel Ardan's personality offered a fertile field of study for the analyst. This astonishing man lived in a perpetual state of hyperbole and had not yet passed the age of superlatives:[7] objects regis-

. . . a well-developed body fixed firmly on long legs . . . and a determined look . . .
Engraving from the first illustrated edition (1872).

tered on his retina with outsized dimensions; hence even his ideas were gigantic; he tended to magnify everything, except problems and men.

His was a luxuriant nature. He was an artist by instinct, a wit, not one of those who keep up a running fire of clever remarks, but a sharpshooter. In discussion, he cared little for logic and rebelled against the syllogism, which he would never have invented; he fought his battles his own way. A true iconoclast, he could hurl *ad hominem* arguments with deadly effect, and he loved to fight tooth and nail for hopeless causes.

Among his other idiosyncracies, he proclaimed himself "a sublime ignoramus,"[8] like Shakespeare, and professed contempt for scholars and scientists: "people," he said, "who can only keep score while we play the game." He was, in short, a bohemian from the Land of Mountains and Marvels,[9] adventurous but not an adventurer, a daredevil, a Phaëton driving the chariot of the sun at top speed, an Icarus with extra wings. For the rest, he paid with himself[10] and paid well, he threw himself into the wildest schemes, he burned his ships behind him with greater eagerness than Agathocles,[11] and, always ready to break his back, he invariably landed on his feet, like those little wooden acrobats, "pith figures," that children play with.

In short, his motto was: "What of it!" Love of the impossible was his "ruling passion," to use Pope's fine phrase.[12]

But this enterprising fellow also had the faults that went along with his virtues! Nothing ventured, nothing gained, so they say. But Ardan ventured much and gained little! He was a spendthrift, he was truly the jar of the Danaids![13] A perfectly unselfish soul, he followed his heart as often as his head; helpful, chivalrous, he would never have signed a death warrant for even his cruelest enemy, and he would have sold himself into slavery in order to free one Negro.[14]

France, Europe, all the world knew him, that brilliant, ebullient man. Weren't the hundred voices of Fame getting hoarse talking on his behalf? Didn't he live in a glass house, making the whole world privy to his most intimate secrets? But he also had an admirable collection of enemies from among the many he had more or less offended, bruised, or knocked down without pity as he elbowed his way through the crowd.

However, he was generally liked; he was treated like a spoiled child. He was, as the saying goes, "a take-me-as-I-am man," and most people took him. Everyone was interested in his daring projects and kept an anxious eye on him. They knew him as imprudently audacious! Whenever some friend would try to stop him by predicting imminent disaster, he would smile amiably and say: "The forest cannot be burned except by its own trees," never once realizing that he was quoting the most pleasing of all Arab proverbs.

Such was the *Atlanta*'s passenger, always agitated, boiling over from some inner fire, always excited, not because of what he had come to do in America—he was not even thinking about that—but because of his own feverish constitution. If ever two persons offered a sharp contrast to each other, these two certainly were the Frenchman Michel Ardan and the Yankee Barbicane;[15] this is not to deny that each was enterprising, fearless, and bold in his own way.

12. *Pope's fine phrase* Verne's reference to Alexander Pope's *Essay on Man* (1723–1734) justifies Ardan's eccentricities and ties in with Verne's love of typology. The concept of the *ruling passion* dates back to the medieval theory of humors. Each man's personality was determined by his body fluids. If he had an excess of rich blood, he was merry, sanguine; too much phlegm made him phlegmatic. Later both Francis Bacon (1561–1626) and Michel de Montaigne (1689–1762) spoke of such a dominant trait as necessary for organizing a personality, for giving it direction. But Pope's treatment of this idea is regarded as the fullest. He sees God as giving each person a *ruling passion* so he may have a distinctive personality: what he does with it, whether he uses it for good or evil, depends on his own artistry. Thus each person's character is partly his own creation "built out of chaos as God built the world," as Maynard Mack sums it up in his definitive edition of *Essay*. And so Verne draws attention to Ardan's successful use of his particular *ruling passion* to create this celebrated self. Here is the exact passage Verne has in mind (Epistle II, lines 131–138):

> . . . one master Passion in the breast,
> Like Aaron's serpent, swallows up the rest.
>   As Man, perhaps, the moment of his breath,
> Receives the lurking principle of death;
> The young disease, that must subdue at length,
> Grows with his growth, and strengthens with his strength:
> So, cast and mingled with his very frame,
> The Mind's disease, its ruling Passion came. . . .

13. *jar of the Danaids* Previous translators have rendered this as "a bottomless pit" or simply a "spendthrift." Presumably they feared their readers would not know their Greek mythology so well as Verne's generation did. But in reducing the number of mythological allusions, they help create the conditions they fear.

The mythic King Danaus of Argos was forced to give his fifty daughters in marriage to the fifty sons of King Aegyptus of Egypt. But Danaus advised the girls to stab their grooms on their wedding night. Forty-nine of the *Danaids* obeyed. Zeus sentenced them in Hades to try forever to fill with water a *jar* with holes in the bottom.

14. *free one Negro* This is the "touching description" of Verne's and Nadar's anti-slavery attitude that we promised in Chapter XIV. In politics, Nadar wavered between socialism and anarchism.

15. *contrast . . . Ardan . . . Barbicane* In real life, the contrast would be between Verne's friend Nadar and Verne's father, Pierre, who have served as models for Ardan and Barbicane.

The contemplation in which the president of the Gun Club had lost himself[16]—in the presence of a rival who threatened to push him into the background—was interrupted now by the hurrahs of the crowd. Their cries became so frenetic, their enthusiasm became so personal, that Michel Ardan, having shaken thousands of hands at the risk of losing his ten fingers, at last had to take refuge in his cabin.

Barbicane, not yet having said a word, followed him.

"You are Barbicane?" Michel Ardan asked, when they were alone, in a tone of voice in which he might speak to a friend of twenty years.

"Yes," answered the president of the Gun Club.

"Then hello, Barbicane! How do you do? Very well? That's splendid!"

"Now," said Barbicane, getting right to the point, "are you still determined to go?"

"Absolutely determined."

"Nothing will stop you?"

"Nothing. Have you redesigned your projectile as I suggested in my telegram?"

"I was waiting for your arrival. But," he insisted, "have you thought this thing through?"

"Thought it through! Do I have time to kill? I have a chance to take a trip to the moon, and I'm taking it, and that's all there is to it. What's there to think through?"

Barbicane stared hard at this man who spoke of this voyage so lightly, with such complete nonchalance, such perfect freedom from anxiety.

"But at least," he said, "you have a plan, some idea of how to proceed—"

"An excellent idea, my dear Barbicane. But let me say one thing: I would like to tell my story just once, to everybody at the same time, so I don't have to repeat myself. So, if you don't mind, call your friends together, your colleagues, the whole town, all of Florida, all of America, if you like, and tomorrow I shall be ready to explain my plans and meet any objections that may be raised. Don't worry, I can do it. Don't you think so?"

"All right," Barbicane replied.

The president left the cabin and informed the crowd of Michel Ardan's proposal. His words were received with stamping of feet and shouts of joy. The Frenchman's proposal made everything easier. The next day everyone would be able to contemplate the European hero at his leisure. Still, some of the more stubborn spectators refused to leave the deck of the *Atlanta;* they spent the night on board. Among others was J. T. Maston, who screwed his hook into the poop-rail, and it would have taken a windlass to pull him away.

"He is a hero! A hero!" he cried out again and again. "We are nothing but a lot of silly, weak women compared to that European!"[17]

As for the president, after asking the visitors to leave, he went back to the passenger's cabin and stayed there till the ship's bell summoned the midnight watch.

Then the two rivals in popularity shook hands warmly, and Michel Ardan wished President Barbicane a friendly good night.[18]

---

16. *lost himself* It's Verne more than Barbicane who has lost *himself.* Back on page 99, Barbicane *fixed his gaze on the passenger.* Verne proceeded to exploit this device, giving us a good picture of Ardan as he appears to a stranger. But then on page 101, Verne gets carried away; he pours out hundreds of words of information about Ardan that Barbicane could never gain at first glance. This violation of point of view is more noticeable to the modern critic than to Verne's audience: Verne is writing this book long before Henry James teaches the modern fiction-writer all about such niceties. Here Verne is following his own great teachers, James Fenimore Cooper and Walter Scott. Cooper, for example, has an unsophisticated frontiersman walking through the forest thinking of the shadows in terms of a Rembrandt painting! Cooper's audience accepted the fact that the author would blend his own meditations with those of his character. That's exactly what Verne has done here. And Scott will have a knight walking through an archway when suddenly Scott stops the action for a static 1,000-word briefing on the man's background. By putting at least some of Ardan's attributes into the form of Barbicane's impressions, Verne does a bit better than Scott at his worst.

17. *weak women . . . European* Male chauvinist as this remark may be, it represents some real growth for Maston. Less than a year ago (Chapter IX), he was unable to believe that any foreigner could surpass an American. Now he can judge Ardan by his merits, not his nationality. Verne means this as a tribute to both their characters: one can teach through sheer force of personality, the other can open himself to learn.

18. *friendly good night* And so Verne gives us the definite impression that Barbicane has been won over to Ardan's broader conception of the project. Thus Barbicane, like Maston, stands out from the other Gun Clubbers: Barbicane and Maston are capable of growth. Throughout his novel, Verne will continue to use Ardan as a catalyst, as a humanizing force.

CHAPTER XIX

A Mass Meeting

The next day the sun rose too late to please the impatient public. They felt it was acting quite indifferent for a sun that would light up such an occasion. Barbicane, fearing they might ask Michel Ardan indiscreet questions, would have preferred to limit the audience to a small number of informed persons, to his colleagues, for example. It would have been easier to try to dam up Niagara Falls. He had to give up the idea and let his new friend take his chances in a public confrontation. The floor of the new Tampa Stock Exchange, despite its colossal dimensions,[1] was obviously too small for this occasion, which was taking on the character of a mass meeting.

Instead the site selected was a vast plain on the outskirts of town. In a few hours it was protected from the intense sunlight; the ships in port, well-supplied with canvas rope, spare masts, and yards, provided materials for erection of a colossal tent. Soon an immense canvas ceiling was spread over the parched prairie, shielding it from the direct rays of the sun. There three hundred thousand people braved high temperatures for several hours while waiting for the Frenchman. Of this crowd of spectators, a third perhaps could see and hear; another third could see poorly and hear nothing; and the rest could neither see nor hear, but they were the loudest in their applause.

At three o'clock Michel Ardan arrived with the leading members of the Gun Club. On his right strode President Barbicane, on his left J. T. Maston, more radiant than the sun at noon and almost as ruddy. Ardan mounted the platform, from which height he looked out over a sea of black hats. He seemed not at all shy, he was gay, familiar, amiable, right at home. He acknowledged the cheers of the crowd with a graceful bow and then, raising his hand, asked for silence, silence, and began to speak in perfectly correct English:

"Gentlemen," he said, "in spite of this intense heat, may I take a few moments to tell you of my plans, which seem to interest you. I am not an orator, not a scientist, and I hadn't counted on speaking in public, but my friend Barbicane tells me it would please you, and I am glad to be of service. So then, lend me your six hundred thousand ears, and please overlook my shortcomings as a speaker."

This unpretentious beginning was quite effective, and the crowd

---

1. *colossal dimensions* When ex-stockbroker Jules Verne, refugee from the Bourse of Paris, faces a need to create a big building in his boomtown Tampa, he makes it not an opera house but a money-market: *Bourse de Tampa-Town,* he says in French. In his *Propeller City* (1895), Verne will talk of "American towns which have the happiness and misfortune to be modern—happiness on account of the facilities for communication, misfortune on account of the artistic side, which is absolutely wanting."

2. *law of progress* One of the dominant ideas of the French Age of Reason: it greatly influences philosophy and sociology in Verne's day. And coupled with Ardan's sentence about the audience's freedom of dissent, this reference to the idea of progress constitutes another oblique attack on Emperor Louis Napoleon. The theory of progress largely inspired the revolutionary

French *Encyclopédie,* finished in 1765, but it was brought to its fullest expression in *Sketch for a Historical Picture of the Progress of the Human Mind* (1795) by the Marquis de Condorcet. From his survey of "nine epochs" of human history, Condorcet infers a general *law* of man's progression toward perfection. In the future, the "tenth epoch," man will destroy all inequalities between classes and nations, and individuals themselves will be greatly improved—morally, intellectually, physically. Ardan's very mention of the *law* reminds Verne's French audience of Condorcet's intense aversion to monarchy, which he sees as inevitably doomed.

3. *cannonballs . . . Creator* Now that Ardan also makes use of Newton's idea that heavenly bodies and projectiles are essentially similar (see Chapter VII), we wonder whether it was Nadar who first made Verne aware of the notion. But they are both members of the *Cercle de la Presse Scientifique* where such ideas are typical topics of conversation.

4 *all mixed up* As we know from the Cambridge Observatory letter in Chapter IV, Verne himself stresses the fact that learned men are able to *express* themselves in both the metric and Anglo-American systems. But here Verne is dramatizing the difficulty in international communication when a speaker is unable to convert readily from one system to the other.

5. *Neptune . . . Mercury, 52,520* In Chapter IV Verne has identified his league as four kilometers long, or 2.485 miles. If Ardan were able to convert, then he would give his miles-per-hour speeds for the planets as listed in the left column below. His memory is serving him fairly well here: his figures are reasonably close to the 1865 values, except for Uranus and Mercury. Their speeds are well known in his day to be closer to 15,000 and 107,000 miles per hour, respectively. Astronomers determine a planet's speed from the length of time it takes to orbit the sun and its distance from the sun. Today's figures are listed in the right column.

Neptune	12,425	12,150
Uranus	17,395	15,210
Saturn	22,012	21,570
Jupiter	29,012	29,210
Mars	54,697	53,970
Earth	68,338	66,620
Venus	79,992	78,340
Mercury	130,512	107,100

Today Ardan would have to add Pluto, moving at 11,000 mph.

6. *certain comets . . . perihelion* This would be 3,480,000 miles per hour. Ardan is bluffing. The sun's gravity cannot make a comet go faster than 1,300,000 miles per hour. And at that speed, the comet would be drawn into the sun and cease to be a comet: hence if any comet remains in orbit, it is traveling less than 1,300,000 miles per hour even at perihelion.

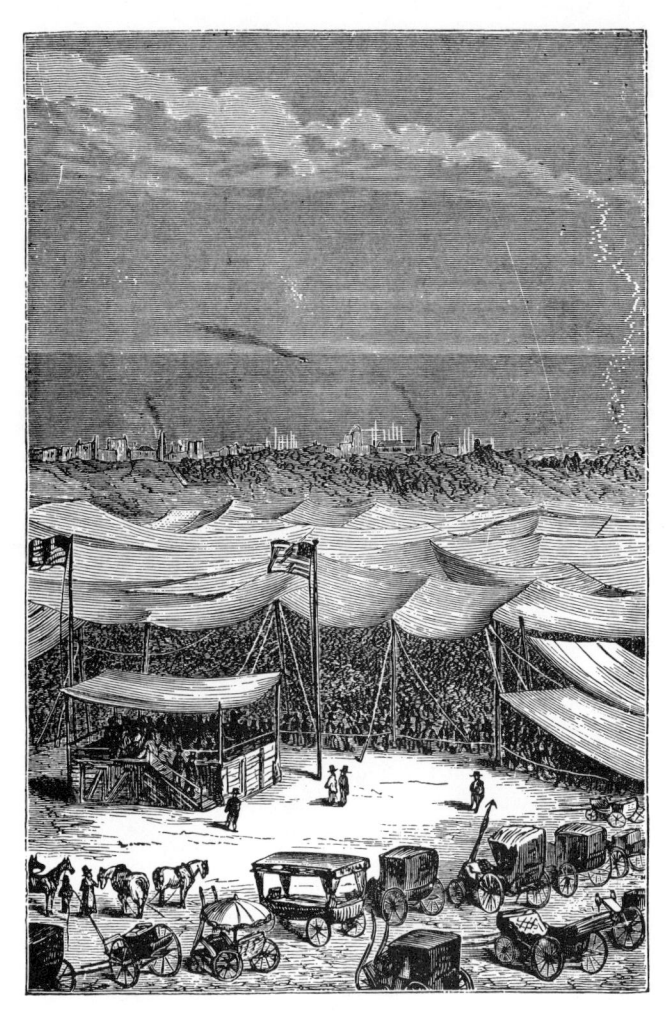

Soon an immense canvas ceiling was spread over the parched prairie . . . The scene of the mass meeting as pictured in the 1872 edition.

expressed their appreciation with an immense murmur of satisfaction.

"Gentlemen," he said, "if we first agree that you are free to express your reactions to what I say, I shall begin. First of all, do not forget you are dealing with an ignoramus, but his ignorance has this advantage: he does not even know enough to fear the difficulties. And so it seemed to him to be a simple, natural, easy thing to book passage in a projectile and go to the moon. This voyage must be made sooner or later, and as for the means of locomotion, that simply follows the law of progress.[2] Man started to travel on all fours, then one fine day, on two feet, then in a cart, then in a wagon, then in a stage-coach, then in a railroad car, and now! The projectile is the vehicle of the future, and, to tell the truth, the planets themselves are nothing but projectiles, cannonballs launched by the hand of the Creator.[3] But let's return to our own vehicle. Some of you gentlemen may believe that the velocity with which it will depart is excessive. That's not so. All the heavenly bodies go faster, and the earth itself, in its movement around the sun, is carrying us three times as fast. Here are a few examples. Only I ask your permission to express myself in leagues, since I am not very familiar with American measurements, and I could get my figures all mixed up [4] if I used them."

His request seemed to meet with no objections. The orator resumed his discourse.

"Here then are the speeds of the several planets. I confess that, despite my ignorance, I do know these little astronomical details fairly well, and in two minutes you will be a savant like me. Know then that Neptune travels at 5,000 leagues an hour; Uranus, 7,000; Saturn, 8,858; Jupiter, 11,675; Mars, 22,011; Earth, 27,500; Venus, 32,190; Mercury, 52,520;[5] certain comets, 1,400,000 leagues an hour at their perihelion![6] As for us, veritable loafers, people taking it easy, our speed will never exceed 9,900 leagues an hour, and it will always be decreasing! I ask you if that's anything to be upset about, and isn't it obvious that this speed will someday be surpassed by even greater speeds, probably with light or electricity as the mechanical agent?"[7]

No one seemed to question Michel Ardan's prediction.

"My dear listeners," he went on, "if we are to believe certain narrow-minded people,—and what else can we call them?—humanity is confined within a circle of Popilius[8] from which there is no escape, condemned to vegetate on this globe, never able to venture into interplanetary space! That's not so! We are going to the moon, we shall go to the planets, we shall travel to the stars just as today we go from Liverpool to New York, easily, rapidly, surely, and the oceans of space will be crossed like the seas of the moon! Distance is only a relative term, and ultimately it will be reduced to zero."

The audience, although generally in favor of the French hero's ideas, were obviously quite taken aback by this bold theory, and Ardan seemed to sense that.

"My dear hosts, you do not seem convinced," he acknowledged with a friendly smile. "Very well, let's talk it over. Do you know how long it would take an express train to reach the moon? Three hundred days. No more! A distance of 86,410 leagues, but what is that?[9] That is only nine times around the earth, and any sailor or traveler expects to do more than that in his lifetime. Now consider that I shall be en route for only ninety-seven hours! You may feel that the moon is a long way from the Earth and that a man ought to think twice before attempting it! But what would you say if it were a question of traveling to Neptune, which moves in an orbit 1,147,000,000 leagues from the sun![10] There's a trip not many people could afford to take, even if it cost only five sous a kilometer! Even Baron Rothschild, who's worth a billion francs, would not be able to pay the fare, he'd be 147 million short, he would not be able to go the whole way!"

This approach seemed to please the audience. Warming up to his subject, Michel Ardan threw himself into it with superb enthusiasm. Sensing that he had their avid attention, he went on with admirable assurance:

"Still, my friends, the distance from Neptune to the sun is nothing compared to the distances from us to the stars. And to consider those distances, we must enter into that dazzling arithmetic in which the smallest number has nine figures, and use the billion as our basic unit.[11] Forgive me for being so well versed in this area, but I find it

Comets have frequently made the news during Verne's lifetime. In 1862, for example, a bright comet appeared which was observed to follow the path of the mid-August showers of meteors. As Ardan speaks, then, astronomy buffs are abuzz with a theory that comets are the parents of shooting stars. This theory is widely accepted today. The trajectories of most meteors coincide with the orbits of known comets. For example, the meteor shower that occurs each year around October 21 is produced by a swarm of particles detached from the tail of Halley's Comet.

7. *light . . . as . . . mechanical agent* Verne is right on top of new developments in physics and racks up two more successful predictions. James Clerk Maxwell (1831–1879) has recently discovered that *light* exerts a pressure on surfaces. Today astrophysicists believe this pressure could propel spacecraft just as wind pressure drives sailboats. This "solar wind" would be too weak to lift a ship off the Earth, but once the craft is out in the airless and weightless conditions of space, the astronauts could unfurl a huge sail and get a free but slow ride. And *electricity* may also figure *as the mechanical agent:* charged particles can be used as the exhaust gases that propel a rocket. Shot out of an electric gun like the one that produces images on the TV screen, a stream of charged particles leaving the rocket is really an electric current flowing out into space.

8. *circle of Popilius* Verne counts heavily on his audience's solid knowledge of the classical world. In 168 B.C King Antiochus of Syria invaded Egypt. An envoy from Rome, Gaius *Popilius* Laenas, publicly asked Antiochus to cease hostilities. He said he would think it over. Popilius then drew a circle in the earth around Antiochus and told him not to step beyond it until he had made his decision. Antiochus got the point: he ordered his army out of Egypt. As we have noted before, translators fudge over Verne's more difficult allusions. Lewis calls the Popilian circle "some magic circle," and Roth calls it "a vicious circle," while Bair settles for "a circle."

9. *but what is that?* 214,815 miles. An express train that takes 300 days to go that far would be chugging away at 30 miles an hour: good time in Ardan's day.

10. *Neptune . . . sun* 2,850,295,000 miles. By 1913 astronomers figure this distance as 2,795,276,800 miles, and by 1961, as 2,794,078,300.

11. *billion . . . basic unit* In the French, Ardan says *le milliard pour unité.* We have translated *milliard,* or *one thousand million,* into its American equivalent, *billion.* But British readers, who follow the French practice, and who reserve the word *billion* to mean *a million million,* should simply read *milliard* whenever our Ardan says *billion.*

12. *Capella 170,000 billion* Again, if Ardan were nimble at conversion, he'd give these distances in billions of miles as listed in the left column below. In Ardan's day, as we shall see, astronomers have not yet perfected their methods for measuring stellar distances, so we are not surprised to find that today's figures, given in billions of miles in the right column, differ considerably.

Alpha Centauri	20,000	25,000
Vega	120,000	155,000
Sirius	120,000	51,000
Arcturus	130,000	240,000
Polaris	290,000	2,700,000
Capella	420,000	256,000

A star's distance was first measured in 1838, by F. W. Bessel, director of the Königsberg Observatory. We can understand the basics of his approach by performing a simple experiment. We hold a pencil a foot away, close the left eye, and note the position of the pencil against its background objects: a picture on the wall, for example. We close the right eye and see that the pencil's position has apparently shifted to the right. This apparent shift is known as *the parallax effect*. If we extend the pencil to full arm's length and repeat the sightings, we discover that the apparent shift is not so great. In other words, the amount of parallax is a measure of the distance of the pencil. If we substitute a star for the pencil, we do what Bessel did, on a cosmic scale. We illustrate his technique with two diagrams from Arthur Berry's classic, *A Short History of Astronomy* (1898). Here σ represents a nearby star in the Constellation Cygnus, 61 *Cygni;* a and b are distant stars in the background; E is Earth in its orbit around S, the sun. Notice that SE is already known: 93,000,000 miles. So is the angle SE: it's 90°. Hence if Bessel could measure the angle EσS, he could then use simple trigonometry to find the distance Sσ. He observed the position of σ against the two background stars when Earth was at E, and again at frequent intervals as Earth moved around S. Since these observation points are as far apart as 186,000,000 miles, *the star seemed to shift its position perceptibly,* describing a small ellipse as the distances a and b varied. Using a micrometer, Bessel estimated the angle of that shift in seconds of arc. Dividing by two gave him his needed angle EσS, the star's *annual parallax,* which he first calculated to be ⅓". Later investigators recalculated it as closer to ½". Hence Sσ, or 61 *Cygni's* distance from our sun, was reckoned to be 37,200 billion miles.

Berry reports that by 1898, "some 50 stars have been ascertained with some reasonable degree of probability to have measurable, if rather uncertain, parallaxes. . . ."

Giving these distances in miles soon proved to be cumbersome. Astronomers decided to express stellar distance in terms of the time light takes to travel from the star to us. At its rate of 186,000 miles per second, light goes approximately six trillion miles a year. Berry says: ". . . light takes more than six years to

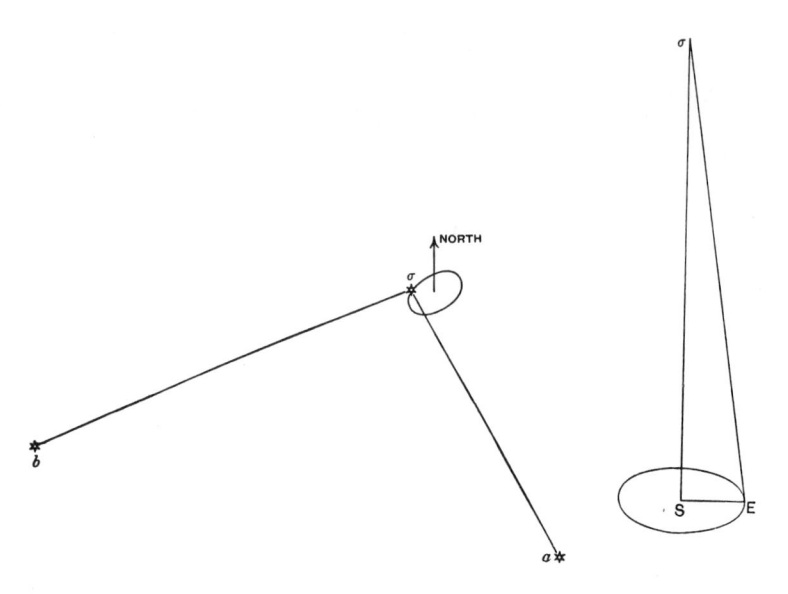

Berry's diagrams discussed in Annotation 12.

fascinating. You be the judge! Alpha Centauri is 8,000 billion leagues away, Vega 50,000 billion, Sirius 50,000 billion, Arcturus 52,000 billion, Polaris 117,000 billion, Capella 170,000 billion;[12] and other stars are thousands and millions and billions of billions of leagues away! So how can anyone speak of the distance that separates the planets from our sun! How can anyone claim that such a distance exists! What an error! What a fallacy! What an aberration of the senses! Do you know what I think about the system that begins with the sun and ends at Neptune?[13] Would you like to hear my theory? It's very simple. To me, the solar system is a solid, homogeneous body; the planets that compose it are touching, pressing against, adhering to each other, and the space between them is no more than the space that separates the molecules of the most compact metal, silver or iron, gold or platinum! I have then the right to insist, and I repeat it with a conviction that I hope you will share, 'Distance is an empty word, distance does not exist!' "

"Well said! Bravo! Hurrah!" cried the audience as one man. They were electrified by his gestures, his oratory, and the audacity of his thinking.

"No!" J. T. Maston cried more energetically than the rest. "Distance does not exist!" And, carried away by the violence of his movements, by the physical excitement he was unable to control, he almost fell from the platform to the ground. But he recovered his balance, and thus prevented a fall that would have given him brutal proof that distance is not an empty word. Meanwhile the speaker continued to enchant his audience:

"My friends, I think that settles that question. If I have not convinced everybody, it's because I'm timid in my illustrations, feeble in my arguments, and you will have to put the blame on my inexperience with theoretical studies. Be that as it may, I say it again, the distance from the Earth to its satellite is really insignificant, unworthy of serious consideration. I do not believe I go too far when I say that in the future we shall have trains of projectiles [14] in which people will be able to travel comfortably from the Earth to the moon. There will be no accidents, no jolts, no derailments. Passengers will reach their destination swiftly, with no fatigue, on a straight course, 'in a bee line,' [15] to use the language of your trappers. Within twenty years, half of the Earth's population will have visited the moon!"

"Hurray! Hurray for Michel Ardan!" cried the audience, even those least convinced.

"Hurray for Barbicane!" the orator answered modestly.

This recognition for the promoter of the enterprise was greeted with unanimous applause.

"Now friends," Michel Ardan said, "if you have any questions to ask me, you will obviously embarrass an ignorant man like me, but I'll do my best to answer them."

Up to this point the president of the Gun Club had good reason to be satisfied with the nature of the discussion. It was concerned with spec-

Arden's fantasy, discussed in Annotation 14.

reach us from 61 *Cygni*." But ever more precise measurements of that tiny distant angle EσS will give us today's figure: 61 *Cygni* is just over ten light years. And today Ardan would say that *Alpha Centauri* is more than four, Sirius more than eight, light years away.

13. *ends at Neptune* Few things in this novel can better illustrate the limits of man's knowledge in 1865 than the fact that Verne (Chapter V), Maston (Chapter VII), and now Ardan all talk of Neptune as the outpost of the solar system. Early in the twentieth century Percival Lowell, working at the Lowell Observatory in Flagstaff, Arizona, will contend that there must be a planet beyond Neptune. He will base his hypothesis on irregularities in Neptune's movements which suggest it is being influenced by another, as yet unknown, heavenly body. He will begin searching for it in 1905, the year Verne dies, and will publish his calculations of its predicted position in 1914. In 1929 a young astronomer, Clyde W. Tombaugh, will join the Lowell staff and within a year he will discover an "object" whose motion, he will write, "conformed perfectly to that expected of a trans-Neptunian planet."

Suggestions for a name will pour into Flagstaff from all over the world. An eleven-year-old English girl will suggest Pluto, which will be picked for two reasons. In mythology, Pluto, god of the underworld, was brother of the lord-god Jupiter and the sea-god Neptune: outer planets have already been named after Jupiter and Neptune, and Pluto will now be able to join the family. Also, the first two letters of *PL*uto, which will be used as the symbol of the planet, are the initials of *P*ercival *L*owell.

The new body, whose orbit lies mainly beyond Neptune's but at two points passes inside it, will extend the known boundary of the solar system 880,000,000 miles beyond Neptune: Pluto is 3,670,000,000 miles from the sun. But later astronomers will regard the comets, which they number in the billions, as the real outposts of the solar system: some of them orbit out into space one-fifth of the way to the next nearest star, *Alpha Centauri*. This places the outer limits of the solar system at 5,000 billion miles, almost one light year, away.

14. *trains of projectiles* The artist who illustrates the original French edition takes Ardan literally. He pictures a five-section train heading for the moon—with smoke pouring out of the locomotive and out of the last car! Presumably a chef is preparing dinner. But steam engines and cook stoves need oxygen, of which there is none in the near-vacuum of Outer Space. Probably Verne approved the engraving as illustrating the fantasy of an unscientific man.

15. *a bee line* Popular belief has it that once it's laden with pollen, a bee will instinctively speed back to its hive in a perfectly straight line.

16. *agree with them* Ardan drops the names of three writers of the past who still enjoy great popularity in his day, at least in France. *Plutarch* (A.D. 46?–c. 120) was a Greek biographer and essayist whose fourteen-volume *Moralia* includes more than sixty pleasant essays on questions like "Do Animals Reason?" and the physical and medical problems of living "On the Face of the Moon's Disk." Emanuel *Swedenborg* (1688–1772) was a Swedish genius who enjoyed success in engineering, science, and then theology and mysticism. In his technical writings he proposed new ways to build docks and to determine longitude by the moon; he was the first to indicate the real nature of the cerebrospinal fluid; he predicted the submarine and the airplane and anticipated the basic notions of nuclear physics. After thirty years in scientific pursuits, he resigned a government position to contemplate spiritual matters. Claiming to have conversed directly with God and his angels, he offered a new interpretation of the Scriptures which his followers used to found a new religion in his name. It's in his *Earths in the Universe* (1758) that Swedenborg declares there are "thousands, yea, ten thousands of earths, all full of inhabitants." As a matter of fact, angels, spirits, and devils include ex-inhabitants of many worlds. Jacques Henri *Bernardin de Saint-Pierre* (1737–1814) was a French naturalist and author whose writings, fictional and nonfictional, have influenced the Romanticists. Ardan is probably thinking of Bernardin's *Études de la nature* (1784) in which he sees God's existence demonstrated in the wonders of nature, wonders that include worlds other than ours.

17. *boiling water . . . polar seas* Ardan is prone to exaggeration. These animals can adapt to virtually every fresh-water habitat, from hot springs to cold mountain streams, but not to boiling water and not to the polar regions.

18. *meteorites . . . 'animalized'* On May 15, 1864, a year before this novel appears, a large meteorite fell near Orgeuil, France. Distinguished chemists have analyzed it for any evidence it may have brought of extraterrestrial conditions. They have been astonished to find a considerable amount of organic matter. In articles in scientific journals, they have considered the possibility that living organisms might be thriving on the parent body of the meteorite: that is, on the asteroid or comet from which the meteorite became detached. Of course, other writers have stressed the possibility that the meteorite has been "contaminated" by life on Earth.

In the twentieth century, scientists will take great care to keep meteorites sterile. Still their analyses will show that about two percent are carbonaceous, that is, they do contain significant quantities of organic matter: high molecular weight paraffins, hydrocarbons like tar, fatty acids, and porphyrins, the "building blocks" of chlorophyll. Furthermore, radio astronomers will detect evidence of the existence of organic molecules in Outer Space.

ulation, in which Michel Ardan, with his vivid imagination, was so brilliant. But now Barbicane felt he must prevent the discussion from turning toward technical questions, with which Ardan might not do so well. And so Barbicane hastened to ask his new friend whether he thought the moon or the other planets were inhabited.

"That's a big question that you pose for me, my dear president," the orator replied with a smile. "However, and correct me if I'm wrong, men of great intelligence, Plutarch, Swedenborg, Bernardin de Saint-Pierre, and many others have taken the affirmative view. Looking at it from the standpoint of natural philosophy, I would agree with them;[16] I would tell myself that nothing useless exists in this universe, and, answering your question by extending the question, I would say, friend Barbicane, that if the worlds are inhabitable, then either they are inhabited, or they have been, or they will be."

"Right!" cried the first row of spectators, whose opinion had the force of law for those in the back.

"A logical and fair answer," said the president of the Gun Club. "No one could do better. The question comes down to that: Are the worlds inhabitable? For my part, I believe they are."

"And for mine, I'm sure they are," said Michel Ardan.

"However," a member of the audience joined in, "arguments have been raised against the inhabitability of the worlds. It's obvious that on most of them, the principles of life as we know it would have to be modified. To mention only the planets, we would be burned alive on some of them and frozen to death on the others, depending on their distance from the sun."

"I regret that I don't know my honorable adversary personally," Michel Ardan replied, "because I would try to answer him. His objection is valid, but I believe that this and all other arguments against the inhabitability of the worlds can be met successfully. If I were a physicist, I would tell him that if less heat were generated on planets near the sun, and more on planets far from the sun, that simple phenomenon would suffice to equalize the temperature on those worlds and make it more supportive of creatures like us. If I were a naturalist, I would tell him, as would many illustrious scientists, that nature gives us right here on Earth many examples of animals who live under greatly varied conditions of inhabitability; that fish breathe in a milieu that is fatal for other animals; that amphibians lead a double life that is difficult to explain; that certain creatures live at great depths in the sea, where they withstand pressures of fifty or sixty atmospheres without being crushed; that certain aquatic insects, indifferent to temperature, can be found in springs of boiling water or in the ice fields of the polar seas;[17] and finally, that he must recognize in nature a great diversity of means of action often incomprehensible but none the less real and verging on omnipotence. If I were a chemist, I would tell him that analysis of meteorites, bodies obviously formed outside our planet, reveals that they contain traces of carbon; that that substance owes its origin solely to living organisms, and that according to Reichenbach's experiments, it must of necessity have been 'animalized.'[18] Finally, if I were a theologian, I would say to him that divine redemption seems, according to Saint Paul, to apply not only to the Earth but to all celestial bodies. However, I am not a theologian, not a chemist, not a naturalist, not a physicist. Hence, in my perfect ignorance of the grand laws that regulate the universe, I'll say only this: I do not know whether other worlds are inhabited, and since I do not know, I'll go there and see!"

Did Michel Ardan's adversary have any other arguments to offer? It is impossible to say, for the frenetic shouts of the crowd would have prevented any opinion from being heard. When silence was finally restored in even the groups furthest away, the triumphant orator was content to add just these few remarks:

"You surely realize, my good Yankee friends, that I have hardly touched on this great question; I have not come here to give public lectures and advance any hypothesis. There is a whole series of other arguments in favor of the inhabitability of other worlds. I put them aside. Permit me to emphasize just one point. People who maintain that the other planets are not inhabited should be answered as follows: You may be right, if it can be demonstrated that the Earth is the best of all possible worlds, but that is not the case, no matter what it says in Voltaire.[19] The Earth has but one satellite, while Jupiter, Uranus, Saturn, Neptune have several in their service, an advantage not to be despised. But what makes our globe especially uncomfortable is the inclination of its axis to the plane of its orbit. Hence the inequality of our days and nights, and the unfortunate variation in our seasons. On our unlucky spheroid, it is always too hot or too cold; we freeze in winter, we sweat in the summer; this is the planet of colds, pneumonia, and consumption. But on the surface of Jupiter, for example, whose axis is only slightly inclined,[20] the inhabitants enjoy unvarying temperatures; there they have a zone of perpetual spring, a zone of perpetual summer, one of continuous autumn, and one of permanent winter; each Jovian can choose the climate that suits him and spend all his life free from changes in temperature. In this sense, you must admit, Jupiter is superior to our planet, not to mention the fact that each year there lasts twelve of ours! Moreover, it's evident to me at least that living under such auspices, under such marvelous conditions, the inhabitants of that lucky world are superior beings, that their scientists are more scientific, their artists more artistic, their villains less villainous, their saints more saintly. Alas! What does our globe need in order to achieve this Jovian perfection? Not much! Only an axis of rotation much less inclined to the plane of our orbit!"

"Well, then!" cried an impetuous voice. "Let us unite our efforts, let us invent the machines, and let us correct the earth's axis!"

Thunderous applause greeted this proposal, made of course by no other than J. T. Maston, prompted no doubt by his instincts as an engineer. But it must be said—since it is true—that many others shouted out their agreement with the idea, and without doubt, if they had had the fulcrum first mentioned by Archimedes,[21] the Americans would have fashioned a lever capable of moving the Earth and correcting its axis. That's all those daring mechanics lacked: the proper fulcrum.

Nevertheless, this "eminently practical" idea enjoyed enormous popularity. The discussion was suspended for a good quarter of an hour, and for a long, long time thereafter, the plan put forth so forcefully by the permanent secretary of the Gun Club was seriously discussed all over America.[22]

But in the twentieth century, scientists will also know what Georg von *Reichenbach* (1788–1869) and the chemists at Orgeuil do not know: nature can produce very complex organic molecules in total absence of life. "Thus, in itself, the demonstrations that organic matter exists in the meteorites does not prove that life also exists on the meteorite parent body," I. S. Shklovskii and Carl Sagan will conclude in their *Intelligent Life in the Universe* (1966).

19. *says in Voltaire* Actually, Voltaire's novel *Candide* (1759) is a satire on the doctrine, formulated by the followers of Leibnitz, that "this is the best of all possible worlds."

20. *slightly inclined* "The inclination of Jupiter's axis toward its orbit is only 3° 5′," Verne adds in a footnote.

21. *fulcrum . . . Archimedes* Archimedes of Syracuse (c. 287–212 B.C.), Greek mathematician, inventor, and physicist, is reputed to have explained the principle of the lever by saying: "Give me a place to stand on, and I will move the world."

22. *all over America* These last three paragraphs provide the basis for a novel Verne will write a quarter of a century later. In 1888, Alcide Badoureau, a mining engineer, will spend four months working out the technical details of Maston's plan *to correct the Earth's axis*. Verne will reward Badoureau with 2,500 francs and write *The Purchase of the North Pole* (1889) in which the engineer appears as Alcide Pierdeux. But J. T. Maston is the main character. Coal has been discovered at the North Pole. There is a rush to buy the polar ice cap. A European cartel led by Britain's Major Donellan loses out in the bidding to Barbicane and Co. Barbicane plans to use Maston's idea—to straighten the axis—so the Arctic will become a temperate zone.

"Archimedes," Barbicane says, "just needed a fulcrum to move the world. We have found one. The Syracusan geometrician needed only a lever. We possess one. We shall move the Pole."

"If man cannot go to the Pole," Donellan sums it up, "the Pole is coming to him?"

"Thou sayest," replies Barbicane.

The mechanism is another giant Columbiad, this one tunneled into the south side of Mount Kilimanjaro. The Gun Club will fire a 400-million-pound shell: they expect the recoil to flip the Earth into perpendicularity! The world press becomes uneasy: other scientists predict the slip will raise Europe to too great an altitude to support life while it lowers America below sea level. Barbicane fires the cannon—and nothing happens. Amid world laughter, a French journal publishes the explanation: Maston dropped three zeros when he included the Earth's circumference (40,000,000 meters) in his figuring. Maston suffers such despair he quits mathematics for marriage.

CHAPTER XX

Attack and Riposte

1. *abundant American-type beard* This would include an untrimmed moustache overflowing into full side and chin whiskers. Apparently Verne wants to make it clear this *hard, spare* man is not wearing one of the more dapper styles of the 1860s: the *burnsides,* or *sideburns,* trimmed side whiskers joined to a trimmed moustache, a style popularized by the Civil War General Ambrose Burnsides; the *mutton chops,* a more luxuriant growth of wide whiskers usually without moustache, worn in both the United States and Britain; and the *imperial,* fashionable in France, named after Napoleon III who wears a pointed tuft of chin whiskers and moustache twirled into long thin ends.

2. *up to the front row* Is this the *member of the audience* who *joined in* in Chapter XIX? The question is interesting, as we shall see, for what it reveals of Verne's narrative method.

3. *pulled away by . . . Earth* There are many other explanations given in Ardan's day for the moon's possible "loss" of its atmosphere. Some eminent physicists hypothesize that the lunar "air" has settled into deep cavities in the moon's interior. The moon's low specific gravity leads them to believe that it is in effect partly hollow. Others theorize that not Earth but a passing comet has *pulled away* the lunar atmosphere. Several scientists still follow the classical theories of the Comte de Buffon (1707–1788), author of a thirty-six volume *Histoire Naturelle,* and of the famous astronomer Jean Sylvain Bailly (1736–1793): they believed the moon's air has been solidified by its intense cold. Ardan himself will soon mention still another hypothesis. But all of these theories crumple in the face of a simple truth. A celestial body's ability to retain an atmosphere depends on a balance between its gravitational pull and the temperature at the top of that atmosphere, which indicates the energy available to the gas to escape. Now the moon's gravity is too weak, and its temperature too high on the sunlit side,

That incident, apparently, had closed the discussion. It provided the "last word" on the subject, it could not be improved upon. Yet, as soon as the excitement had died down, a strong and severe voice called out:

"Now that the speaker has indulged his imagination, would he please return to his subject, play less with theories, and face the practical problems posed by this expedition?"

All eyes turned to the person who had just spoken. He was slight, hard, and spare, with an energetic face and an abundant American-type beard.[1] Taking advantage of the movements of the crowd, he had worked his way up to the front row.[2] There, arms crossed, he fixed his bright, bold gaze on the hero of the meeting. After posing his question, he listened for an answer, unaffected by the thousands of eyes focused on him or by the murmur of disapproval provoked by his words. Getting no reply, he repeated his question with the same sharp and precise enunciation, adding:

"We are here to discuss the moon, not the Earth."

"You are right, sir," Michel Ardan answered. "We have digressed. Let us get back to the moon."

"Sir," the stranger went on, "you claim our satellite is inhabited. Perhaps. But if there really are any Selenites, they must exist without breathing, because—and I warn you for your own good—there is not a molecule of air on the surface of the moon."

Ardan ran his hand through his tawny mane; he realized this man was going to force him to grapple with basic realities. Trying to outstare the stranger, he said:

"No air on the moon! Would you please cite your authority for that remark?"

"Science."

"Really?"

"Really."

"Sir," Ardan replied, "all jokes aside, I have great respect for scientists who know but deep disdain for those who don't."

"Do you know of any who deserve to be placed in your second category?"

"Oh yes. In France, we have one who can prove 'mathematically' that birds can't fly, and another whose theories demonstrate that the fish was never made to live in water."

"They have no bearing on our question. But to support my argument, I could cite names you would have to respect."

"Sir, you would be embarrassing a poor ignoramus who, indeed, seeks only a chance to learn!"

"Then why tackle scientific problems if you're not prepared for them?" the stranger asked bluntly.

"Why?" replied Ardan. "For the simple reason that a man can always be brave if he's unaware of danger. I know nothing, it's true, but it is precisely that weakness that is the source of my strength."

"Your weakness verges on folly," the stranger shouted in irritation.

"All the better," the Frenchman riposted, "if my folly takes me to the moon!"

Barbicane and his colleagues had been studying this intruder who so clearly was trying to discredit the project. None of them knew him, and the president, uneasy about the consequences of such a frank argument, looked at his new friend with some apprehension. The audience seemed concerned, disquieted, for this debate was calling attention to the dangers, maybe even to the impossibilities of the expedition.

"Sir," said Michel Ardan's adversary, "there are many unanswerable arguments against the existence of a lunar atmosphere. I could say, *a priori,* that if the moon ever did have an atmosphere, it was pulled away by the Earth.[3] But I prefer to gainsay you with undeniable facts."

"Gainsay, my dear sir," Ardan said with perfect gallantry, "gainsay all you want."

"You are aware," the stranger said, "that when light rays enter a medium like air, they are bent, in other words, they are refracted. Very well! When stars are occulted by the moon,[4] their rays, as they pass the edge of her disk, never bend, never offer the slightest evidence of refraction. Obviously this means the moon is not enveloped in an atmosphere."[5]

All eyes turned to the Frenchman. If he granted the truth of this observation, the consequences could be drastic.

"Actually," he said, "that is your best if not your only real argument,[6] and a scientific man might be at a loss how to answer it. As for me, I need only say, this argument is not conclusive, because it assumes that the angular diameter of the moon has been precisely determined, and that's not the case. But enough of that.[7] Tell me, my dear sir, do you admit that there are volcanoes on the moon?"

"Extinct volcanoes, yes. Active ones, no."

"I may still assume then, without being illogical, that these volcanoes must have been active at one time or another?"

"Naturally, but since they themselves could have furnished the oxygen required for combustion, the mere fact that they have erupted does not prove the existence of a lunar atmosphere."[8]

"Let's leave that kind of argument and pass on to things that have actually been observed. But I warn you, I shall name names."

"Name them."

so that any primordial gases have long ago wafted away into space.

4. *occulted by the moon* That is, when they are concealed, or blocked from view, by the moon's passing "over" the stars in question.

5. *refraction . . . atmosphere* When stars are occulted by the moon, they disappear instantly. But if the moon had an atmosphere, they would seem to blink out gradually as their rays would continue briefly to bend around the moon's edge.

6. *only real argument* The best argument of all will soon come from spectroscopy, which makes it possible to ascertain the nature of a substance by analyzing the light received from it. Sir William Huggins (1824–1910) is putting the spectroscope to work for astronomy. As Richard A. Proctor, popularizer of science in Ardan's day, will write in 1870, Huggins "has never been able to detect a sign of the existence of any lunar atmosphere, though Mars and Jupiter, so much farther from us, have afforded distinct evidence respecting the atmospheres which surround them."

7. *enough of that* Because Ardan is bluffing. The *angular diameter* is the angle subtended by the visible disk of the moon as observed from the Earth. The mean *angular diameter* is thirty-two minutes of arc, being greater at perigee, less at apogee. Now this certainly has been *precisely determined* by 1865, and anyhow, it is not necessary to know it in order to study refraction effects.

8. *oxygen . . . atmosphere* But part of a volcano's eruption is gaseous, so for at least a brief time after an eruption, there would be some atmosphere, however small. As a matter of fact, just a year after Verne writes this passage, the question will arise: Do lunar volcanoes continue intermittently to issue gas?

In 1866 the astronomer Julius Schmidt will report he can no longer see the Linné crater. When other astronomers describe changes in the appearance of Linné, it will appear there might sometimes be a haze—of gas, dust, or both—over the crater. In 1956, Palomar Observatory will take photographs of the Alphonsus area which will suggest residual outgassing from a rill on a crater floor. Then Dr. N. A. Kozyrev of the Pulkovo Observatory will make a spectrographic study of the Alphonsus region. He will conclude that for about half an hour on the night of November 3, 1958, low density gas, ionized by sunlight, has escaped from the central craterlet. Other astronomers will offer different explanations. For example, are these obscurations the result of lunar minerals flashing in sunlight? Are there materials that glow when hit by nuclear particles in the solar wind or by ultraviolet rays? Still, an authority like Dinsmore Alter will say flatly that this "transient phenomenon" was a discharge of gas (see Bibliography).

"In 1787, didn't Herschel observe a great many points of light on the moon's surface?" Portrait of William Herschel.

9. *what other scientists thought* Both men took the error in their stride. The Chevalier de Louville (1671–1732) went on to write a memoir advancing Newtonian principles, published prestigiously by the Paris Academy of Sciences (1710). Dr. Edmund Halley (1656–1742), already famous for identifying the comet of 1682 as the same one observed in 1531 and 1607, and for being the first astronomer to predict a comet's return (it's named after him), went on to become Astronomer Royal in 1720.

10. *no atmosphere* Now the strange adversary is also bluffing and name-dropping. As Willy Ley puts it, Beer and von Mädler "could not quite believe" that the moon "could be without any atmosphere."

11. *Laussedat* As this novel comes off the press in 1865, Aimé Laussedat is quitting his professorship in astronomy at the École Polytechnique to become professor of geometry in the Conservatoire des Arts et Métiers (crafts). Today he is known as the father of photogrammetry, the science that uses photographs to establish distances in map-making and astronomy, for example.

12. *air . . . rarefied* As late as 1898, Arthur Berry will write: "If there is air its density must be very small, some hundredfold less than that of our atmosphere . . . but with this restriction there seems to be no bar to the existence of a lunar atmosphere of considerable extent. . . ."

"In 1715, the astronomers Louville and Halley, observing the eclipse of May 3, noted certain fulminations of a very bizarre nature. These flashes of light, rapid and repetitive, they attributed to storms raging in the moon's atmosphere."

"In 1715," the stranger replied, "the astronomers Louville and Halley mistook terrestrial phenomena for lunar phenomena. What they actually saw were meteorites or similar objects within our own atmosphere. That's what other scientists thought [9] when Louville and Halley reported their observations, and that's what I think now."

"To get on," Ardan said without taking the trouble to riposte, "in 1787, didn't Herschel observe a great many points of light on the moon's surface?"

"True, but he did not try to explain their origin, and he certainly did not infer that their existence had anything to do with a lunar atmosphere."

"Touché," Michel Ardan complimented his adversary. "You are well versed in selenography."

"I certainly am. Hence I should add that the two most skillful, most experienced observers of the moon, Beer and Mädler, agree that the moon has absolutely no atmosphere." [10]

The crowd became restless, apparently disturbed by the arguments put forth by this strange person.

"We come now to an important fact," Ardan continued calmly. "A talented French astronomer, Laussedat,[11] during the eclipse of July 18, 1860, noticed that the horns of the sun's crescent were rounded and truncated. Now this phenomenon could be caused only by refraction of the sun's rays as they passed through the moon's atmosphere, and there can be no other explanation."

"Are you certain?" the stranger asked.

"Absolutely certain."

The crowd swayed again, this time in favor of the Frenchman, as his adversary remained silent. Ardan said simply, without gloating over his advantage, "You see, my dear sir, we can't afford to rule out the possibility of a lunar atmosphere. It's probably not very dense, it's probably very thin, but science today generally admits it's there."

"Not in the mountains, if you please," the stranger riposted, unwilling to give in entirely.

"No, but it's in the bottom of the valleys, at least to a height of a few hundred feet."

"In any case, you would have to take extreme precautions, because that air would be rarefied." [12]

"Oh my dear sir, there will always be enough for one man; and once I'm up there, I'll live very economically: I'll breathe only on special occasions!"

Laughter thundered in the ears of the mysterious interlocutor, who glared around at the audience.

"Now that we agree there's at least some air on the moon," Ardan said lightly, "we are forced to acknowledge too the presence of a certain amount of water. And that's also good for me. Moreover, my amiable adversary, let me make one further observation. We know but one side of the moon, and if there's very little air on the side we see, it's still possible there's plenty on the opposite side."

"Why?"

"Because the moon, under the pull of earth's gravity, has assumed the shape of an egg, pointing its smaller end toward us. According to Hansen's calculations, this means that its center of gravity is located in the other hemisphere. And so, most of its air and water must have been drawn to the other side of our satellite during the early days of its creation."

"Pure fantasy!"[13] cried the stranger.

"Pure theory, you mean, based on the laws of mechanics, and I think it would be difficult to disprove. I appeal to this assembly, and I call for a voice vote[14] on this question: Is life, as it exists on Earth, possible on the surface of the moon?"

Three hundred thousand people voted by applauding loud and long. Ardan's adversary wanted to speak again, but he couldn't make himself heard. Curses and threats fell on him like hail.

"We've had enough!" some were saying.

"Chase him out!" others shouted.

13. *Pure fantasy!* The theory of the displacement of the moon's center of gravity, set forth by the German astronomer Peter Andreas *Hansen* (1795–1874), is respected in Verne's day because Hansen's celebrated *Tables de la Lune* (1857) are the most accurate so far produced: they will remain in standard use throughout the century. But many astronomers point out that even during the moon's librations, when we can see past the moon's edge to the other side, we still see no evidence of an atmosphere there. And the famous Simon Newcomb (1835–1909), professor in the U.S. Naval Observatory in Washington, questions even the "displacement" on which the "far-side" theory is based. By the 1970s scientists will conclude there is no appreciable lunar bulge, but there *is* a slight displacement: the moon's center of gravity is located in the *nearer* hemisphere, one and a half kilometers this side of its geometric center.

14. *voice vote* Verne's naughty satire on the pretensions of democracy. Of course such a scientific question cannot be settled by universal suffrage. And it's a neat way of pointing up the demagoguery in Ardan's character.

"I won't come back."
At this reply, whose simplicity verged on sublimity, the crowd fell silent.
Engraving from 1872 edition.

15. *squirrel in a cage* At the end of Chapter VII, Barbicane suggested *a round projectile which can rotate if it likes, or behave as it pleases*. But of course that would scramble Ardan's brains. Ardan has asked for *a cylindro-conical shell* because its pointed shape is *more likely to keep it in a stable position*.

16. *only real problem* What the stranger is talking about is discussed today in terms of *gravities* or *gees acceleration*. And what we know today about *gee forces* proves that Ardan's *dear adversary* is absolutely right. A *gee* is a unit for measuring how rapidly a body's speed changes. One gee is the acceleration caused by gravity as a body falls near the Earth's surface: its speed increases by thirty-two feet per second every second. Since weight depends on acceleration due to gravity, the gee is a convenient measure of impact on jet pilots and astronauts. If a jet accelerates with 1 gee, the pilot is pressed back into his seat feeling a force equal to his own weight. If the jet's acceleration is 2 gees, he feels a force twice his weight, and so on. Acceleration over 10 gees gets to be decidedly dangerous especially if it's maintained long enough. Under experimental conditions, with very careful preparations, men have endured accelerations of 35 or even 50 gees and more. In December 1954, Lieutenant Colonel John Paul Stapp was belted and strapped to a rocket sled and shot along a track at record speeds. He accelerated from rest for five seconds, coasted for half a second, then was jerked to a halt in 1.4 seconds. For that 1.4 seconds, he felt a force equal to thirty-five times his own weight. Dust particles hitting him at the speed of sound gave him blood blisters. His eyeballs flattened out against his eyelids to give him two black eyes. But if the 35 gees had lasted for more than ten seconds, he would have lost consciousness, and for more than minutes, his life.

In May 1959, the monkeys Able and Baker were shot 300 miles into space. They survived deceleration forces thirty to forty times their own weight. Still other experiments have shown that men can withstand 50 or more gees. But now here's the rub. According to Dr. David Woodruff, when the Columbiad is fired, the projectile will be subjected to 28,000 gees! Let's assume Ardan weighs 150 pounds. He would be thrown back into his seat with a force of $28,000 \times 150 = 4,200,000$ pounds. He would weigh 2,100 tons. He would be crushed into a smear. Only his ignorance of the *real problem* gives him such confidence it will *be solved*.

Ardan's twentieth-century counterparts don't have to worry about 28,000 gees because they are not fired from a cannon. As television viewers the world over are well aware, today's astronauts are lifted into space gently, slowly, gradually—by rocketry.

17. *no time at all* In August 1966, when Apollo 3 will move through the atmosphere at 19,000 miles per hour, the temperature on its heat shield will reach 2,700° F. The tempera-

"Out with the intruder!" cried the furious crowd.

But he held on to the platform, he would not budge, he let the storm pass. It would have assumed alarming proportions if Ardan had not restored peace with a gesture. He was too chivalrous to abandon his adversary in such a situation.

"Would you like to add a few words?" Ardan asked the stranger.

"Yes, a hundred, a thousand. Or better yet, only a few. To persevere in this enterprise, you must be—"

"Imprudent! But how can you say that to me? Haven't I asked my friend Barbicane for a cylindro-conical shell so I won't tumble about like a squirrel in a cage?" [15]

"But you unhappy man, the dreadful impact of the explosion will crush you at the very start!"

"My dear adversary, you have put your finger on the only real problem; [16] but I have too great an opinion of American industrial genius to believe it won't be solved."

"But the heat the projectile will generate as it speeds through the air?"

"Oh, its walls will be thick, and I'll get beyond the atmosphere in no time at all!" [17]

"But food? And water?"

"I figure I can take along a year's supply, and the trip will last only four days!"

"But air to breathe on the way?"

"I'll make it chemically."

"But your fall on the moon, if you ever get there?"

"It will be six times slower than a fall on the Earth, since the force of gravity is only one-sixth as great on the surface of the moon."

"But that will still be great enough to shatter you like glass!"

"And why can't I slow down my descent by firing rockets?" [18]

"But—suppose all these problems can be solved, all these obstacles overcome, suppose everything does work out in your favor, suppose you do arrive safe and sound on the moon—then how can you get back?"

"I won't come back."

At this reply, whose simplicity verged on sublimity, the crowd fell silent. But its silence was more eloquent than its applause. The stranger took this opportunity to make one final appeal.

"You're sure to kill yourself," he cried, "and your death, which will be the death of a madman, won't even have served science!"

"Go on, my generous stranger, you predict such wonderful things for me!"

"Ah! this is too much," the adversary cried, "and I do not know why I engage in a discussion so lacking in dignity! Persist in your folly! You're not the one to blame!"

"Now don't restrain yourself!"

"No, another man will be fully responsible for your actions!"

"And who is that, if you please?" Michel Ardan asked in an imperious voice.

"The ignoramus who organized this impossible and ridiculous experiment!"

This was a direct attack. Barbicane, since the intrusion of the

. . . a hundred strong arms had lifted the platform. Engraving from the first illustrated edition (1872).

stranger, had made violent attempts to contain himself, to "burn his smoke," as certain boiler furnaces are said to do; but as soon as he heard this outrageous reference to himself, he rose suddenly and rushed over to the adversary who glowered at him. Then all at once they were separated.

What had happened was that a hundred strong arms had lifted the platform. Barbicane had to share triumphal honors with Ardan. This particular shield was heavy, but the bearers[19] came in continuous relays as each man argued, wrestled, struggled for the privilege of lending his shoulder to this demonstration.

Meanwhile the stranger did not take advantage of the confusion to escape. But could he have slipped through that dense crowd? Probably not. In any event, he kept his place in the very first row, arms folded, eyes fixed on Barbicane.

And Barbicane never took his eyes off the stranger. The two men's looks crossed like two quivering swords.

The immense crowd shouted constantly at their highest pitch

ture inside will remain at 70° F. Now Barbicane's design does not provide for a heat shield. And so, as his projectile passes through the atmosphere at meteoric speeds, he should expect most of its parts to melt, vaporize, or otherwise disintegrate.

18. *by firing rockets* Here we have one of Verne's greatest—one of his self-fulfilling—prophecies. This passage will directly inspire early space scientists to consider rocketry as the big answer to space travel. And rockets will be used in the twentieth century to brake the descent of spacecraft. The Russian Konstantin Tsiolkovsky (1857–1935), who will create the mathematical theory for rocket propulsion, will say: "Probably the first seeds of the idea were sown by that great fantastic author Jules Verne—he directed my thinking." And the German rocketry pioneer, Hermann Oberth (1894–), will write: "I always had in mind the rockets designed by Jules Verne."

All of which brings us to the big question posed by A. C. Clarke in 1962: Why doesn't Verne himself allow rockets to do the whole job? The "gun concept," Clarke says, "with its impossible accelerations, was so obviously impracticable that it made the whole idea of space-travel seem ludicrous, and it has taken half a century to convince the public that astronauts need not be pulped at take-off."

To which we find two answers. The first comes in Verne's sequel, *Around the Moon,* in which Ardan discovers that his rockets are too weak even for steering the ship. Verne is not alone in the 1860s in believing that rockets will never develop sufficient thrust to launch heavy loads. Or as another space scientist, Wernher von Braun (1912–1977), puts it: "The science in *From the Earth to the Moon* is nearly as accurate as the knowledge of the time permitted." Secondly, in choosing his method of blastoff, Verne has one eye on his needs as a social satirist. What better way to emphasize that the moonshot is a spinoff of U.S. military might than to launch it from a cannon? Especially if he can devise some plausible way for *American industrial genius* to cushion the *dreadful impact* for Ardan? True, a few rockets have been fired in the Civil War, but fecklessly: they could never match the Columbiad as a symbol of U.S. power.

Of course today Verne would not rely on "the gun concept": too many readers know all about gees acceleration. But then today, in using a rocket, he would be using a mechanism that during World War II did come to symbolize the military just as surely as the cannon had in 1865.

19. *shield . . . bearers* The allusion is ironic. In a spontaneous demonstration, soldiers in ancient times might stand a hero on his shield and carry it in triumph on their shoulders. But they also used his shield to carry a dead hero off the field of battle.

20. *don't forget your rifle* This is a good time to appreciate Verne's careful plotting, his pacing of the dramatic movement, his arrangement of his themes. In Chapter X he told us about the professional battles these men had fought at a distance: their friends kept them apart to prevent a fatal duel. Then Nicholl, failing to taunt Barbicane into a gladiatorial combat between shell and armor, did lure him into a wager by mail. In Chapter XI Verne used the Texans' mass challenge to the Gun Club to keep us reminded that Americans do take dueling for granted. Nicholl apparently receded as a threat, becoming simply one who paid his bets. But in Chapter XIX we heard from *a member of the audience,* and Ardan began calling that unidentified man *my honorable adversary.* In this chapter we have heard from someone who *had worked his way up to the front row.* The only clue we have he might be the same man is that again Verne uses the word *adversary.* And now he brings Barbicane and Nicholl face-to-face to arrange for the long-threatened clash on the "field of honor." A duel between two military engineers is arranged right after Ardan has succeeded in convincing everyone that the warlike projectile should be converted into a civilian vehicle. Now notice how in the next chapter Verne will bring all these themes—American penchant for violence, Barbicane-Nicholl feud, militarist-vs.-civilian approach—all to a simultaneous climax.

Notice finally that we had gotten rather fond of Barbicane. In this scene Verne brings to the fore again the less admirable side of the puritanical, self-righteous Yankee's makeup. Much of what we have come to like in him was brought out by Ardan. But Nicholl represents an older, more familiar type of influence. We have a hint in the last sentence of this chapter which influence might gain the upper hand.

throughout this march of triumph. Michel Ardan was obviously enjoying himself. His face glowed. Sometimes the platform seemed to pitch and roll like a weather-beaten ship. But the two heroes of the mass meeting had their sea-legs; they never swayed, and their vessel made it safely to port in Tampa. Michel Ardan disentangled himself from the farewell hugs of his vigorous admirers and fled to the Hotel Franklin, quickly gaining his room and sliding under his covers while an army of a hundred thousand posted watch under his windows.

Meanwhile a short, serious, and crucial scene was in progress between the mysterious stranger and the president of the Gun Club.

Barbicane, finally free, went right up to his adversary.

"Come!" he said curtly.

The man followed him to the waterfront, and the two soon found themselves alone at the entrance to an open wharf near Jones Falls.

There the two enemies, still unidentified, stared at each other.

"Who are you?" asked Barbicane.

"Captain Nicholl."

"So I suspected. Until now chance has never brought us together—"

"*I* have brought us together."

"You have insulted me!"

"Publicly."

"You are ready to give satisfaction for that insult?"

"Right now."

"No. I want everything that passes between us to be secret. There's a woods located about three miles out of Tampa, Skersnaw Woods. Are you familiar with it?"

"I know it."

"Kindly walk into one side of those woods at five o'clock tomorrow morning."

"Yes, if you walk into the other side at the same time."

"And don't forget your rifle,"[20] Barbicane said.

"No more than you'll forget yours," replied Nicholl.

These words coldly pronounced, the captain and the president of the Gun Club separated. Barbicane returned to his house, but instead of trying to get a few hours' rest, he spent the night searching for a way to soften the impact inside the projectile and so solve the difficult problem raised by Michel Ardan at the mass meeting.

CHAPTER XXI

How a Frenchman Settles a Quarrel

While the president and the captain were discussing the conditions for their duel—a terrible, savage type of duel in which each adversary becomes a manhunter—Michel Ardan was resting from the fatigues of triumph. "Resting" is obviously not the right word, for American beds can rival any marble or granite table for hardness.

He was sleeping rather badly, turning over and over between the napkins that served as his sheets, and he was dreaming of installing a more comfortable bed in the projectile when a violent noise awakened him from his fantasies. Frantic blows were shaking his door, blows seemingly made by an iron instrument. Loud shouts mingled with the metallic racket, and all so early in the morning.

"Open the door!" someone cried. "For heaven's sake, open up!"

Ardan could think of no reason to comply with a demand so crudely expressed. Nevertheless, he got up and unlocked the door just as it was about to yield to the obstinate visitor. The secretary of the Gun Club flung himself into the room. A bomb could not have entered with less ceremony.

"Yesterday," J. T. Maston cried *ex abrupto,* "our president was publicly insulted at the mass meeting! He challenged his adversary to a duel—it's none other than Captain Nicholl! They're to fight this morning in Skersnaw Woods! Barbicane told me![1] If he's killed, it's the end of our project! They mustn't go through with it! Now, there's only one man in the world who has enough influence over Barbicane to stop him, and that man is Michel Ardan!"

While J. T. Maston was talking, Michel Ardan, giving up any hope of asking a question or two, jumped into his spacious trousers and in a few minutes the two friends were racing toward the suburbs of Tampa.

On the way Maston told Ardan the whole story; the real causes of the long-standing enmity between Barbicane and Nicholl; why until now, thanks to mutual friends, the captain and the president had never met face to face; he added that it was wholly a matter of rivalry between armor plate and projectiles, and that the mass meeting had finally given Nicholl his long-sought chance to satisfy an old grudge.

Nothing is more terrible than this particular type of American duel, in which each of the two adversaries hunts the other through the brush,

---

1. *Barbicane told me!* Verne develops Barbicane's character by showing that he only *seems* to be ultra-rational. In fact, he operates just like the rest of us, zigzagging, feeling his way through contradictory impulses. First he resolves not to allow a passenger inside the projectile. Then he writes Breadwill to hold up the design. First he resolves to shoot it out with Nicholl and to keep the duel a secret. Then he tells Maston, knowing full well Maston might not keep the secret and might try to stop the shootout.

2. *hour after hour* Verne is describing what is known as "a Kentucky duel." As late as 1874 a Philadelphia teacher will complain that "this terrible species of duel, so common in the South and West thirty or forty years ago, is not yet . . . extinct." Both North and South Americans are notorious in Verne's day for their variations on the European *code duello*. In the West, for example, helpful townspeople might link the duelists neck to neck with a chain three feet long, place keys to the lock in their pockets, hand each a Bowie knife, and go away to let them settle their dispute. In one such *terrible, savage . . . duel,* both men flailed about so much that the winner could find neither key. Bleeding from slashed arms, he had to carry his dead opponent back to the town blacksmith. A South American variation is used in Jorge Luis Borges' "The End of the Duel." Two gauchos are famous—like Barbicane and Nicholl—for a long-standing antagonism that everyone knows must end on "the field of honor." When war comes, they are both drafted into the same militia troop, both captured, both sentenced to execution. But their understanding captors allow these two to settle their affair before they die. They are allowed to run a race—after their throats are slashed. Gallantly they dash forward, tumble. One stretches out his arms as he falls. "Perhaps never aware of it," Borges concludes, "he had won."

lies in wait for him in a thicket or a coppice, and tries to shoot him down like a wild beast. Each of them is trying to emulate those wonderful traits so natural to the prairies Indians: their swift intelligence, their cunning ingenuity, their ability to track and even scent the enemy. One mistake, a moment's hesitation, one false step can mean instant death. On these dueling expeditions the Yankee will often take his dogs along; at once the hunter and the hunted, he stalks his prey hour after hour.[2]

"What devilish people you are!" cried Michel Ardan, after J. T. Maston had explained the whole sordid procedure.

"That's how we are," J. T. Maston said modestly, "but let's hurry."

Although he and Michel Ardan had raced over plains still wet with dew, crossed rice fields, forded creeks, and taken every shortcut, they still were unable to reach the edge of Skersnaw Woods before half past five. Barbicane was supposed to have gone in half an hour before.

They saw an old backwoodsman who was splitting logs with an axe. Maston ran up to him and cried:

The secretary of the Gun Club flung himself into the room. Engraving from 1872 edition.

"Have you seen a man armed with a rifle go into the woods, Barbicane, the president—my best friend?—"

The secretary of the Gun Club naively thought its president would of course be known to the whole world. But the backwoodsman didn't understand.

"A hunter," Ardan said.

"A hunter, yes," the man replied.

"How long ago?"

"An hour or so."

"Too late!" cried Maston.

"And have you heard any rifle shots?" asked Michel Ardan.

"No."

"None at all?"

"Not a one. Your hunter doesn't seem to have much luck."

"Now what?" said Maston.

"Go into the woods and risk getting a bullet not intended for us."

"Ah!" cried Maston, in tones that revealed his deep sincerity. "Better ten bullets in my head than one in Barbicane's!"³

"Then let's hurry!" Ardan grabbed his friend's arm.

A few seconds later the two had disappeared into the woods. It was a dense forest of giant cypresses, sycamores, tulip trees, olive trees, tamarinds, oaks, magnolias. The branches of these various trees were so thickly tangled it was difficult to see very far. Michel Ardan and Maston walked silently side by side through tall grass, cutting a path through strong vines, looking behind bushes and under branches hidden in the thick, shadowy foliage, expecting at any minute to hear the crack of a rifle. If Barbicane had come through here, they were unable to detect any signs of it; they walked blindly where an Indian would have been able to trail his enemy step by step.

After an hour of searching in vain, they paused, more apprehensive then ever.

"It must be all over by now," Maston sounded discouraged. "A man like Barbicane wouldn't use any tricks, or lie in ambush, or try to outmaneuver his enemy. He's too open, too honorable. He went straight ahead, right into the danger, and he must have gone so deep that the wind prevented the backwoodsman from hearing the shot."

"But how about us?" asked Michel Ardan. "In all the time we've been in the woods, we should have heard—"

"And if we came too late?" said J. T. Maston in despair.

Michel Ardan couldn't find a word to say. They resumed their search. Now and then they would shout out, now calling Barbicane, then Nicholl, but neither of them answered. Joyous flocks of birds, startled by the noise, disappeared among the branches, and a few frightened deer fled through the thickets.

They kept it up for another hour. They had already explored the greater part of the forest and seen no trace of the combatants. They were beginning to doubt the information the backwoodsman had given them, and Ardan was about to give up the search as useless, when all of a sudden Maston stopped.

"Shh!" he said. "There's someone down there."

"Someone?"

"Yes! A man! He's standing still. He doesn't have a rifle in his

---

3. *ten bullets . . . Barbicane's* A convenient stock character in Verne is the man so devoted to his leader or his employer that he will lay down his life for that superior being. In *Five Weeks in a Balloon* (1863), when their punctured craft is losing altitude over a lake, the three occupants throw their supplies overboard in an effort to lighten the ballast.

"Go on, throw out something else," says Doctor Ferguson, the expedition leader.

"There is nothing else," says Kennedy the big-game specialist.

"Yes, there is," says Joe the servant as he vanishes over the side. Relieved of his weight, the balloon shoots upward.

In *Twenty Thousand Leagues* (1870), when Conseil the servant and Ned the harpooner have only a few whiffs of oxygen left, they give them to Aronnax the scientist.

"Your life is worth more than ours," Ned explains.

hands. What is he doing?"

"But do you recognize him?" asked Michel Ardan, whose nearsightedness was little help at a time like this.

"Yes! Yes! He's turning," said Maston.

"And who is it?"

"Captain Nicholl!"

"Nicholl!" cried Michel Ardan, feeling a violent contraction in his chest.

Nicholl unarmed! He had nothing to fear then from his adversary?

"Let's go ask him what happened," said Michel Ardan.

But he and his companion had not taken fifty steps when they paused to watch the captain more attentively. They had expected to find a bloodthirsty man absorbed in his vengeance. They were stupefied at what they did see.

A strong, closely meshed net was stretched between two gigantic tulip trees, and in the middle of this snare a little bird, its wings entangled, was struggling and crying out pitifully. The bird-catcher who had arranged this trap was not a human being, but a venomous spider indigenous to the area, as big as a pigeon's egg, and provided with enormous legs. This hideous creature, about to pounce on its prey,[4] instead beat a hasty retreat into the upper branches of the tulip tree, because a formidable enemy now threatened him in turn.

It was Captain Nicholl, who had set his rifle on the ground and, forgetting the danger he was exposing himself to, tried gently to release the victim from the monstrous spider's web.[5] At last the bird was free, and Nicholl held it up high and it fluttered its wings and flew away.

Nicholl was watching it disappear into the foliage when he heard these words spoken with strong feeling:

"You are a brave man, you—"

He turned around. Michel Ardan was there, saying in a different tone:

"—are a kind man."

"Michel Ardan!" cried the captain. "What are you doing here, sir?"

"I'm here to shake your hand, Nicholl, and to prevent you from killing Barbicane or being killed by him."

"Barbicane," cried the captain. "I've been looking for him for two hours and can't find him. Where is he hiding?"

"Nicholl," said Michel Ardan, "that's not very polite! You should always respect your adversary. Don't worry, if Barbicane is alive, we shall find him; it will be all the easier since, if he hasn't stopped to rescue a bird, he's out looking for you too. But when we do find him, I, Michel Ardan, assure you there will be no question of a duel between you."

"Between President Barbicane and me," Nicholl said gravely, "there is a rivalry so great that only the death of one of us—"

"Come, come, now!" replied Michel Ardan. "Good men like you two may dislike each other but you must respect each other too. You must not fight."

"I will fight, sir."

"Not at all."

"Captain," said J. T. Maston with heartfelt emotion, "I am the

---

4. *hideous creature . . . prey* Verne doesn't give enough detail for us to be sure, but this could be one of several spiders known by the name tarantula: some of them weave huge webs to snare big insects and even small birds. Verne might be partly influenced here by Bartram, who watched "a remarkably large spider," his body about the size of *a pigeon's egg,* stalk and eat "a large fat bomble bee."

5. *monstrous spider's web* One of the artistic triumphs of this chapter is the way this animal scene symbolizes the human situation. Nicholl has in effect hoped to be the *venomous spider . . . about to pounce on its prey. One mistake, . . . one false step,* and Barbicane would be *the victim.* Throughout the chapter Verne describes the conditions of the duel and the spider-bird situation with words that can apply to both: *lies in wait, lies in ambush, this snare, this trap.* When their primitive instincts are in control, Barbicane and Nicholl operate on the level of *this hideous creature.*

. . . in the middle of this snare a little bird . . . was struggling and crying out pitifully. Engraving from first illustrated edition (1872).

friend of the president, his *alter ego*,[6] his second self; if you want desperately to kill someone, kill me, it will be exactly the same thing."

"Sir," said Nicholl, seizing his rifle convulsively, "these bad jokes—"

"My friend Maston wasn't joking," said Michel Ardan, "and I understand his willingness to die for the man he admires. But neither he nor Barbicane will die in your sights, because I am going to make a proposal to you two rivals so attractive you'll both be eager to accept it."

"And what could that be?" asked Nicholl with obvious incredulity.

"Patience!" replied Ardan. "I can tell you only in the presence of Barbicane."

"Then let's find him," cried the captain. The three men set off at once. Uncocking his rifle, Nicholl shouldered it and marched with an irregular step, without a word.

For still another half-hour, the search proved fruitless. Maston was

6. *alter ego* In Verne's own life, his "other self" is his brother Paul, who is what Jules always wanted to be: a man of action. In August 1897 Paul will die and Jules will say, "I never thought I could outlive my brother." *The Kip Brothers* (1902) will be Jules' memorial to Paul. One Kip pursues his career on land, the other at sea. They always understand each other without words.

oppressed by sinister thoughts. He watched Nicholl intently, asking himself whether the captain hadn't already satisfied his vengeance, whether the unfortunate Barbicane, surprised by a bullet, was not already lying dead in some blood-stained thicket. Ardan seemed to be suffering from similar fantasies. They had both been casting suspicious glances at Captain Nicholl when suddenly Maston stopped.

Twenty paces away, half-hidden in the grass, the head and shoulders of a man rested, motionless, against a gigantic catalpa tree.

"There he is!" said Maston.

Barbicane remained motionless. Ardan looked straight into the eyes of the captain, who did not flinch. Ardan stepped forward shouting:

"Barbicane! Barbicane!"

No response. Ardan flung himself toward his friend, but, at the very moment he was about to shake him, he stopped short and uttered a cry of surprise.

Barbicane, pencil in hand, was scribbling formulas and sketching geometric figures in a notebook, while his rifle lay uncocked on the ground.

Absorbed in his work, the scientist had forgotten all about the duel and his vengeance; he had seen nothing, heard nothing.[7]

But when Michel Ardan put his hand on Barbicane's arm, he looked up and gaped at the Frenchman.

"Ah," he said at last, "it's you. Here, I've got it, my friend, I've got it."

"Got what?"

"My plan!"

"Which plan?"

"My plan for softening the shock inside the projectile when the cannon is fired."

"Really?" said Michel, looking at the captain out of the corner of his eye.

"Yes! Water! It's simply water, which can serve as a spring [8]—Ah! Maston!" cried Barbicane, "you're here too!"

"In person," Ardan said, "and allow me at the same time to introduce the good Captain Nicholl."

"Nicholl!" cried Barbicane, jumping to his feet. "I'm sorry, captain, I forgot—I'm all set—"

Michel Ardan stepped between them before they could resume hostilities.

"Good heavens," he said, "we're lucky you two couldn't find each other. If you had, we'd be mourning for at least one of you right now. But thank God, who interfered in this matter, we have nothing more to worry about. When a man can put his hatred aside to outwit a spider or solve a problem in mechanics, that hatred isn't so dangerous after all."

And Michel Ardan told the president the story about the captain.

"And now I ask you," he said in conclusion, "can't two good men like you find something better to do than blast each other's head off with a rifle?"

This whole situation had something so ridiculous, so unexpected about it, that Barbicane and Nicholl no longer knew how to look on

7. *seen . . . heard nothing* The absent-minded savant, so engrossed in his work he forgets all danger, is one of Verne's favorite people. In seven years, he will try another version of this scene in *Measuring a Meridian* (1872). An international expedition ceases its geodetic work to hunt for its mathematician, Nicholas Palander. When they finally locate him—at the edge of a lagoon, sitting motionless on a tree root, notebook on his knee—they also spot some crocodiles "crawling up to their prey." They fire at the "monsters" and actually gain Palander's attention.

"I've found it," he exclaims.

"Found what?" asks Sir John.

"A decimal error in the hundred and third logarithm in James Wolston's *Tables*."

Verne remarks that not even André Marie Ampère, "the most absent-minded savant in the whole world," could have done better. Verne himself can't do any work at all when there is even the slightest noise.

8. *water . . . as a spring* Barbicane's plan to use water as a shock absorber is one more Verne prophecy that will come true. In the twentieth century, space scientists will discover that when a man is cushioned by water, he can survive very high accelerations, maybe more than 50 gees. Still, no cushioning device can work for Ardan. The object of such devices is to spread the impact evenly over parts of the body so no part takes more stress than any other. But even when it's so distributed, 28,000 gees is more than Ardan could survive. In 1865, however, readers are not yet thinking in terms of gees acceleration, so Barbicane's plan will have at least a faint ring of plausibility.

each other. Michel Ardan sensed this, and decided to embarrass them into making peace.

"My brave friends," he said, breaking out his best smile, "there has never been anything between you but a misunderstanding. Nothing else. So now! To prove that that is all over between you, and since you're both so willing to risk your hides, accept the proposal that I am going to make."

"Make it," said Nicholl.

"Friend Barbicane believes his projectile will go straight to the moon."

"Yes, of course," said the president.

"And friend Nicholl believes it will fall back to Earth."

"I am absolutely certain it will," cried the captain.

"Now I can't make you agree with each other, but I can suggest this: Come with me, and see for yourselves how far we get."

"What!" J. T. Maston was stupefied.

The two rivals, hearing this unexpected proposal, raised their eyes

"Come with me, and see for yourselves how far we get." Engraving from 1872 edition.

and studied each other carefully. Barbicane waited for the captain's response. Nicholl watched for some sign from the president.

"Well?" said Michel in his most charming voice. "Now that there's no more problem about initial impact?"

"All right!" cried Barbicane.

But as he pronounced these words, Nicholl said them too.[9]

"Hurrah! Bravo! *Vivat!*[10] Hip hip hip!" cried Michel Ardan, holding out his hands to the two adversaries. "And now that that's settled, let me treat you the French way. Let's go have breakfast."

9. *Nicholl said them too* At first this sounds incredible. If Nicholl is *absolutely certain* Barbicane's shell *will fall back to Earth,* why is he willing to be inside it? How could he collect on his bet after he won it? Then we realize that Ardan functions like an expert psychologist. He has sensed that what has really motivated Nicholl's conduct is his fury at being *excluded* from Barbicane's project. Whether Nicholl has been conscious of it or not, the real function of the wager, of the public debate, of the duel has been to get himself involved in this spectacular event. Since that is his basic need, he can answer without thinking: Ardan's proposal, as he promised, is *so attractive* that Nicholl is *eager to accept it.*

10. *Vivat!* While the Italian cry of approval, *bravo!* ("fine! brave!"), has been naturalized into English, the French *vivat* ("hurray!") remains a foreign word.

The American deer was a familiar sight in Florida in the days when the Gun Clubbers tramped the woods. Illustration from *The American Cyclopaedia,* 1874.

CHAPTER XXII

The New Citizen of the United States

That very day, all America heard about the duel between Captain Nicholl and President Barbicane and its unique resolution. The role played in that situation by the chivalrous Frenchman, his unexpected proposal which had put an end to the difficulty, the simultaneous acceptance by the two rivals, the fact that now France and the United States would set off together[1] to conquer the lunar continent,[2] everything combined to make Michel Ardan more popular than ever.

All the world knows how Yankees can become passionately devoted to one individual. In a country where solemn magistrates harness themselves to a dancer's carriage and pull it in a triumphal march, it is easy to imagine how passionately the populace reacted to the daring Frenchman! If his horses were not unhitched,[3] it is probably because he did not have any, but all other tokens of public enthusiasm were accorded him. There was not a citizen who did not identify with him, body and soul. *E pluribus unum,* says the official motto of the United States.

From that day on, Michel Ardan never had a moment of peace. Delegations from all corners of the country harassed him without intermission. He had to see them all, willy-nilly. How many hands he shook, how many people he had to pass the time of day with, is beyond counting; soon his teeth were on edge; his voice, made hoarse by numerous speeches, escaped his lips only in unintelligible sounds, and he was getting symptoms of gastroenteritis from all the toasts he had to drink to all the counties in the Union. Anyone else would have gotten disgracefully drunk from such success, but he managed to stay in a steady state of witty, charming semi-tipsiness.

Among the deputations of all types that assailed him were the "lunatics," who especially acknowledged their debt to the future conqueror of the moon. One day, several of these poor people, quite numerous in America, visited him to ask whether they could return with him to their "native land." Some of them claimed to be able to talk "Selenese" and volunteered to teach it to Michel Ardan. He played along with their harmless self-delusions, agreeing for example to take messages to their friends on the moon.

"Strange, this lunacy," he said to Barbicane after the delegation left, "and it's a type of madness that often hits the best minds. One of

1. *set off together* The United States, as we have seen, is the ideal setting for any futuristic project, and in 1865 it gives Verne good materials for his talents as a social satirist. But there are excellent reasons for also involving a Frenchman. Verne is still writing primarily for a French audience. He loves to compare national temperament: Ardan's Gallic wit, nonchalance, Old World mellowness, and esthetic preferences (soon to come) provide good contrast to the Gun Clubber's work-ethic grimness, puritanical ambition, and stress on results at the expense of style. Finally, Verne likes to emphasize the inherent internationalism of exploration and experiment.

2. *conquer . . . lunar continent* Ever since Barbicane spoke of annexing the moon as the thirty-seventh state, Verne has stressed the imperialist nature of the project (Chapters II, III, VI, XXII). And so he actually anticipates the sentiments of the British magnate and arch-colonialist Cecil Rhodes (1853–1902), who will later write: "The world is nearly all parcelled out . . . what there is left . . . is being divided up, conquered, and colonised. To think of these stars that you see overhead at night, these vast worlds which we can never reach! I would annex the planets if I could; I often think of that. It makes me sad to see them so clear and yet so far." Rhodes' unethical, dictatorial methods in building Britain's African empire will earn him the censure of the House of Commons in 1897. But well before that Verne will have made him the gin-drinking villain in *The Southern Star Mystery* (1884).

3. *horses . . . unhitched* On the American frontier, the arrival of a woman in an all-male town has provoked many such displays of enthusiasm, bridled and unbridled.

4. *famous . . . Arago* Verne has met the charming, popular Dominique-François Arago (1786–1853) in the early 1850s at the home of Jacques Arago, Dominique's younger brother and Verne's friend. François was director of the

Paris Observatory, where he lived, and permanent secretary of the Academy of Sciences. He became *one of* France's *most famous scientists* for his original work in electromagnetism and the wave theory of light, and for his genius as a public lecturer on scientific subjects. "All ranks flocked to hear him, fascinated by his graceful eloquence and his crystalline clearness of explanation," the *World-Wide Encyclopedia* (1899) will report. "He used to remark, what many lecturers often forget, that *'clearness is politeness in public speakers.'* His manner in lecturing is said to have been to fix his eye on some one of his audience whose intellect had apparently the minimum of development, and to keep it fixed till the face should brighten up with intelligence." In intellectual circles François is remembered for his courageous refusal to take an oath of loyalty to Louis Napoleon, who did not dare punish such a popular savant. Although he is dead for twelve years when this novel appears, François is still very much in the public mind: his collected works, including *Astronomie Populaire,* have been appearing posthumously, volumes I to XVII, from 1854 to 1862.

The Arago family has had much to do with young Verne's growing excitement over scientific adventure. Jules was a frequent visitor to Jacques' house, a meeting place for scientists and explorers. Jacques' is where Verne first met Nadar-Ardan: surely that is where one or both of them heard the remark by Dominique that Ardan is presently building up to. Jacques, himself an author, was more concerned with the geographical sciences. He almost induced the twenty-two-year-old Jules to accompany him on a gold-hunting trip to America; Jacques died on an expedition to Brazil in 1855.

5. *moon possesses them* Apparently today's scientists don't often take up the question of the moon's influence on man's behavior. But security guards on campus, attendants in mental hospitals, and desk sergeants at the police station can often be heard expanding on this old maxim of their calling: the full moon provokes certain "types" to *behave incredibly.*

6. *Bacon . . . clear* Philosopher of science Francis Bacon (1561–1626) would faint not only during an eclipse of the moon: he would pass out during the slightest change in the weather. Like Verne, Bacon was a prophetic writer. In his (unfinished) philosophical novel *New Atlantis* (1627), for example, he describes a scientific utopia whose wise men have developed flying machines, "boats for going under water," pipes for conveying sounds over long distances:

7. *Charles VI . . . full moon* Nominal ruler of France from 1379 to 1422, he earned the popular nickname of Charles the Beloved before he became better known as Charles the Mad. The first of his *bouts of madness* was brought on when he was violently frightened by the sudden appearance of a "ragged maniac" who stopped his horse and cried: "Do not go

our most famous scientists, Arago,[4] told me that many perfectly sane and respectable people will experience great excitement and behave incredibly whenever the moon possesses them.[5] Now would you believe that the moon could affect people's health?"

"Hardly," said the president of the Gun Club.

"Neither would I, yet history has recorded some facts that make you think about it. For instance, in 1693, during an epidemic, a great number of people died on January 21 at the very moment of an eclipse. The celebrated Bacon always fainted during an eclipse of the moon and he would revive only when it was entirely in the clear.[6] King Charles VI suffered six bouts of madness in 1399, every one during the new moon or the full moon.[7] Some medical doctors classify epilepsy as an illness affected by the moon, and nervous disorders seem to be in that class too. Mead speaks[8] of a child who had convulsions whenever the moon went into opposition. Gall reported that sick people became much more excited at two periods during the month: the new moon and the full.[9] And there have been thousands of observations of this kind about vertigo, malignant fevers, somnambulism, all suggesting that the celebrity of the night exerts a mysterious influence on terrestrial illness."

"How? Why?" demanded Barbicane.

"Why?" said Ardan. "I can only give you the same answer Arago repeated nineteen centuries after Plutarch: 'Perhaps it's because it is not true!' "

In the midst of his triumph, Michel Ardan could not escape any of the duties imposed on a celebrity. Exploiters of success wanted to exhibit him. Barnum offered him a million dollars to be allowed to cart him from town to town all over the United States to display him like a freak. Ardan dubbed him a "mahout"[10] and dismissed him.

If Ardan refused to satisfy public curiosity in person, his portraits at least circulated all over the world and occupied the place of honor in everybody's album; they came in all dimensions, some as big as life, others as tiny as a postage stamp. Everybody was able to have his hero in any pose imaginable, portrait, bust, full-length, from the front, in profile, three-quarter view, or from the back. More than a million and a half copies were made, and he was offered a chance to sell bits of himself as relics, but he did not take it. If he had sold his hairs at a dollar apiece, he would have made a fortune!

To tell the truth, this popularity by no means displeased him. On the contrary. He made himself available to the public and answered letters from all over the world. His witticisms were repeated and widely circulated, especially those he had never made. They were lent to him, according to the custom of lending only to the rich.

Not only men were "for" him, but women too. How many "good marriages" he might have contracted, if only he had been ready to settle down! Old spinsters, especially those who had been waiting for forty years, dreamed night and day over his photographs.

He would have had no trouble finding hundreds of wives, even if he had imposed the condition that they go to the moon with him.[11] Women are absolutely fearless when they are not afraid of everything. But it was not his intention to cross-breed a race of French and Americans. He declined.

"I'm not going up there to play the role of Adam with a daughter of Eve," he said. "No thank you, I might encounter a serpent—"

As soon as he could get away from the demands of his public, he went with his friends to visit the Columbiad. He felt it was the least he could do. Besides, he had become well versed in ballistics since he had been living with Barbicane, J. T. Maston, and *tutti guanti*.[12] His greatest pleasure came in telling these artillerists they were nothing but cheerful, learned murderers. He was always making jokes like that. The day he visited the Columbiad, he admired it greatly and descended to the bottom of the gigantic tube destined to send him to the moon.

"At least," he said, "this cannon isn't meant to hurt anybody, and that's quite astonishing for a cannon. But as for your guns that destroy, burn, smash, and kill, let's not talk about those, don't tell me that they have 'a soul'[13] because I just won't believe it."

Here we must report a proposal made by J. T. Maston. When the secretary of the Gun Club heard Barbicane and Nicholl accept the proposal made by Michel Ardan, he resolved to join them and make it a foursome. One day he asked to be included. Barbicane, pained at having to say no, said the projectile could carry only so many passengers. J. T. Maston, in despair, sought out Michel Ardan who told him he had to resign himself, adding some *ad hominem* arguments.

"Good old Maston," he said, "I hope you won't take this in the wrong spirit, but the truth is, just between you and me, you are too incomplete to make an appearance on the moon."

"Incomplete!" cried the valiant invalid.

"Yes, my good friend. Suppose we meet inhabitants up there on the moon. Would you want to give them a depressing picture of what happens down here, telling them what war is, that we spend our time devouring each other, breaking each other's arms and legs, and all that on a globe that could nourish one hundred billion inhabitants, and right now has one billion two hundred million? Come, come now, my good friend, you'd make them throw us out!"

"But if you land there in pieces," J. T. Maston retorted, "you'll be as incomplete as I am!"

"True," answered Michel Ardan, "but we won't land there in pieces!"

In fact, a preliminary experiment, made on October 18, had produced excellent results and given them good grounds for optimism. Barbicane, wanting to test the effect the explosion would have on life inside the projectile, had procured a thirty-two-inch mortar from the arsenal at Pensacola. They positioned it on the shore of Hillsborough Bay so that its shell would fall into the water, and thus the shock would be cushioned. But their main purpose was to test the shock of departure, not of arrival. They carefully prepared a hollow projectile. They lined the inner walls with a network of springs made of the finest steel, over which they laid a thick padding. The result was a kind of carefully wadded nest.

"Too bad I can't get into that!" said J. T. Maston, regretting that he was too big to participate in the trial.

Into this charming projectile, which could be closed with a cover screwed into place, they put a large cat, then a squirrel belonging to on, noble king, you are betrayed." Charles had good reason to be frightened: since his childhood he had been surrounded by relatives eager to rule in his name. Their continuous machinations, not the phases of the moon, probably determined his periods of derangement.

8. *Mead speaks* As we saw in Chapter VI, this famous physician died in 1754, and he's still being quoted in 1865.

9. *Gall . . . full* Dr. Franz Gall (1758–1828) specialized in such simplistic correlations. As a boy, he concluded that his classmates who were good at memory-work all had large eyes. As a physician, he studied the heads of people with peculiar mental traits: professors, prisoners, patients in asylums. He decided character could be read from the bumps on the skull. His lectures on his new "science"—phrenology—caused a sensation in Vienna. But in 1802 they were interdicted by the government as "dangerous to religion." So Dr. Gall moved to Paris.

10. *mahout* In referring to P. T. Barnum as a keeper of an elephant, Ardan is kindly emphasizing the more legitimate aspects of the showman's activities. He launched his career in 1835 by buying an eighty-year-old slave and exhibiting her as "the 161-year-old ex-nurse of George Washington." In 1842 he opened his Museum in Manhattan where he displayed, alongside real "freaks" like the thirty-three-inch "General" Tom Thumb, fakes like the "Fiji Mermaid": a stuffed upper half of a monkey joined to the stuffed lower half of a fish.

As Ardan's remark makes clear, Barnum is already famous in 1865 for his animal exhibits. But he will not acquire Jumbo, his huge African elephant, until 1882. And so Ardan's remark has its prophetic side.

On April 9, 1867, Jules and Paul Verne will arrive in New York on the *Great Eastern*, check in at the Fifth Avenue Hotel, eat at Delmonico's, and sit through the play *New York Streets* at Barnum's Theatre (in Barnum's American Museum). Barnum's sensational theatrics is typified by what will happen in Act IV. As part of the scripted action, a blazing fire is put out by "firemen" who rumble out of the wings on the latest-model steam-driven fire-engine. His one night at Barnum's will surely influence Verne in his 1874 stage version of *Around the World in Eighty Days*. The cast will include a live elephant; and the props, a real railway engine.

11. *to the moon with him* Verne cannot suspect as he writes this passage that it contains a prophecy about his personal life. As *De la Terre à la Lune* appears serially in *Journal des Débats*, Verne's fan mail will contain many offers from young men eager to embark on his spaceship—and from *women too*. Many of the letters will contain locks of hair. "The Parisiennes are certainly intrepid," Jules will write to Paul. "Some of them are determined by hook or crook to board my projectile."

12. *tutti guanti*   Italian meaning "all the people."

13. *have 'a soul'*   It's a much better joke in the French. Guns *do* have a soul in that language, because the French for soul, *âme*, is also the word for bore (of a gun).

14. *martyrology*   Verne's third satiric reference in this novel to the fact that science may be taking on the authority of a religion. The Martyrology is the official calendar of martyrs and saints of the Roman Catholic Church, arranged by the dates of their anniversaries and giving some biographical details. The name indicates that the earliest calendars extant—like that for the year 354—listed only martyrs.

15. *this experiment*   The Gun Club's trial shot anticipates two features of twentieth-century space experiments: the use of animals to measure the effect of space travel on living creatures, and the splashdown to cushion the landing. In November 1957 the Soviets will launch Sputnik 2, the first inhabited space capsule, carrying the dog "Laika." Four years later the United States will launch its first orbital flight carrying a living being: the chimpanzee "Enos." And landing in the water—with ships standing by, divers on the alert—will become a standard feature of the American space effort.

While Verne deserves credit for seeing the value of these procedures, he should not be considered the originator. There are precedents in both science fiction and science. In Bishop Francis Godwin's *The Man in the Moone* (1638), as we saw in Chapter II, the hero sends a lamb aloft in the first trial of his space "engine," and in his first manned flight steers over water to take advantage of the soft fall should anything go wrong. On September 19, 1783, Joseph Michel Montgolfier and his brother Jacques Étienne sent up a balloon over Versailles with a sheep, a rooster, and a duck as passengers before they themselves risked the first manned flight over Paris a month later.

16. *la fayette . . . America*   Verne's identification of Ardan with la Fayette is effective because in France the Marquis is called "the hero of two worlds." Not generally known in America is the fact that la Fayette made good practical use of his honorary U.S. citizenship. After serving as a major general in the American Revolution (he commanded the élite Light Division), he was awarded the same rank in the French Army. Becoming unpopular with the Jacobin dictatorship, he fled France in 1792 and on his way to Holland was captured by an Austrian patrol. After five years in prison, he succeeded in getting himself delivered to the U.S. consul in Hamburg—because he was an American citizen. In 1824–1825 he revisited the United States where he was feted as the last surviving major general of the Revolution. His direct descendants, the Chambrun family, still enjoy honorary American citizenship.

the permanent secretary of the Gun Club, of which he was particularly fond. They wanted to know how this little animal, which is not subject to vertigo, would be affected by this experimental voyage.

They loaded the mortar with one hundred and sixty pounds of powder and then placed the shell in the piece. They fired it.

The projectile rose rapidly into the air, described a majestic parabola, reached an altitude of about a thousand feet, and curved gracefully down until it plunged into the waves.

Without losing a moment, they rushed in an open boat to the spot where the shell had fallen. Skilled divers went down into the water and attached cables to the ears of the projectile, which they swiftly hoisted into the boat. Only five minutes had elapsed between the loading of the animals and the unscrewing of the cover of their prison.

Ardan, Barbicane, Maston, Nicholl were watching the operation with understandable concern. As soon as the mortar-shell was opened, the cat leaped out, slightly ruffled, but full of life, acting not at all like one who has just returned from an aerial expedition. But no squirrel. They looked again. Not a trace. They finally had to face the facts: the cat had devoured his fellow traveler.

Deeply grieved over the loss of his pet squirrel, J. T. Maston proposed that his name be inscribed in the martyrology[14] of science.

After this experiment,[15] all hesitation, all fear vanished; besides, Barbicane planned to work further to perfect the projectile and to eliminate entirely the internal effects of the firing. Soon there would be nothing more to do but go!

Two days later, Michel Ardan received a message from the President of the Union, an honor he fully appreciated. Following the precedent set in the case of his chivalrous compatiot, the Marquis de la Fayette, the government had conferred on Ardan the title of citizen of the United States of America.[16]

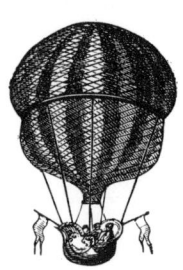

The first balloons made by J. M. and J. E. Montgolfier, as represented in *The American Cyclopaedia* (1873).

CHAPTER XXIII

The Vehicle-Projectile

Once the famous cannon was completed, public interest shifted to the projectile, the new type of vehicle destined to carry the three bold adventurers into space. No one had forgotten that in his telegram of September 30, Michel Ardan had asked that the plans drawn up by the executive committee be changed.[1]

Barbicane had had good reason for thinking that the shape of the projectile was not very important, for, after passing through the atmosphere in a few seconds, it would be moving in a total vacuum. The committee had adopted the spherical shape so that the projectile could turn on itself and behave as it saw fit. But if it was going to be used as a vehicle, that was another matter. Michel Ardan did not care to travel like a squirrel; he wanted to keep his head up and his feet down, with the dignity of a man standing in the basket of a balloon, although of course traveling much faster. He was not interested in capriole or somersault.[2]

New plans were therefore sent to the Albany firm of Breadwill and Co. with the request that they be carried out as soon as possible. The new design[3] was cast on November 2 and immediately shipped to Stony Hill by rail. It arrived safe on November 10. Michel Ardan, Barbicane, and Nicholl were waiting impatiently for their "vehicle-projectile" in which they would go to discover a new world.

No one could deny that it was a beautiful piece of metal, a metallurgical product that was a great credit to the industrial genius of the Americans. It was the first time aluminum had been obtained in such a considerable quantity, and this alone was a prodigious feat. The precious projectile scintillated in the sunlight. Its imposing form, topped by a conical cap, could be taken for one of those thick turrets, shaped like pepper-pots, which medieval architects used to place at the corners of their citadels. All it lacked was loopholes and weather-vane.

"I keep expecting," Michel Ardan cried, "to see a man of arms come out of it, carrying an arquebus and wearing a steel breastplate. Inside that, we'll feel like feudal lords, and, with some artillery, we could hold off all the Selenite armies, if there are any."

"So this vehicle tickles your fancy," Barbicane said to his friend.

1. *plans . . . be changed* And the way the nature of the project has changed—from militarist to civilian—is clear from a comparison of the titles Verne has given two of his chapters. He heads VII *L'Hymne du Boulet* (The Hymn to the Cannonball) and XXIII *Le Wagon-Projectile* (The Vehicle-Projectile).

2. *capriole or somersault* Almost every word here has its delicious side-effects. The phrases *dignity of a man standing in . . . a balloon* of course remind the 1865 reader of Nadar himself and then, hilariously, of Daumier's cartoon in which Nadar is hardly *standing . . . with dignity*. The word *capriole* reinforces the animal imagery begun with *travel like a squirrel:* a trained horse can do a *capriole,* that is, leap upwards without going forward, and with all feet in the air. Continental readers also see the Italian *capriola,* leap of a goat, and English readers might sense *caper,* a short form of *capriole.*

3. *new design* If it calls simply for a cylindro-conical shape, the *new design* is not enough. As we noted in Chapter XX, this shape is more likely to keep the craft stable, but it would still need additional stabilizers of some kind. Otherwise the craft could still spin or even tumble. Ardan would first suffer disorientation from dizziness, then a jellying of his softest tissue: his brain.

"Yes, yes, no doubt of that," Michel Ardan replied, looking at it like an artist. "I only regret that it isn't slenderer, that its cone isn't more graceful. It could use at its top a cluster of metal ornaments, like a chimera, a gargoyle, a salamander coming out of the flames with wings spread and mouth open—"

"What for?" said Barbicane, whose practical mind was not very sensitive to artistic beauty.

"What for, my friend? Alas, if you have to ask that question, I'm afraid you wouldn't understand the answer."

"Tell me anyhow, my dear fellow."

"Well as I see it, it's always better if we do everything artistically. Are you familiar with an Indian play called *The Child's Wagon?*"

"Not even by name," Barbicane admitted.

"That doesn't surprise me," Michel Ardan answered. "Then listen: in that play a burglar, who is about to cut a hole through the wall of a house, wonders whether he should shape the hole like a lyre, like a flower, like a bird, or like an amphora. Now tell me, friend Barbicane, if you had been a member of the jury, could you have condemned that burglar?"

"Without a moment's hesitation," said the president of the Gun Club; "it was housebreaking aggravated by burglary."

"And I would have voted for acquittal, friend Barbicane! And you would never understand why!"

"I wouldn't even try, my valiant artist."

"But at least," said Michel Ardan, "since the exterior of our vehicle-projectile leaves much to be desired, you might permit me to fur-

Verne's passage on Ardan's desire to travel *with . . . dignity* surely reminds his 1865 readers of Honoré Daumier's satiric cartoon, "Nadar Raising Photography to the Status of a Fine Art." In this engraving Daumier pokes fun at Nadar—who pioneered in aerial photography—for his frenetic energy and his flair for publicizing his enterprises.

nish the interior with all the luxury befitting the ambassadors from Earth!''

"In that department, my dear Michel, we shall give free rein to your imagination."[4]

Barbicane was ready to discuss interior decorating only because he had completed his last task of a practical nature: his plan for lessening the impact inside the projectile was working out very well.

Barbicane had told himself, and rightly so, that no spring would be strong enough to withstand the initial shock and, during his famous walk in the Skersnaw Woods, he had solved this problem in an ingenious way. He would count on water to perform this special service. And this is how:

They would fill the projectile with three feet of water over which they would place a water-tight wooden disk fitted snug against the walls but able to slide up and down. The voyagers would be stationed on this raft at the moment of firing. The water beneath them would be divided by horizontal partitions which would successively absorb the initial shock. Each sheet of water, from the lowest to the highest, would in its turn be driven upward through pipes toward the top of the projectile, thus acting like a spring, and the disk, provided with buffers, would not drop to the bottom until each of the partitions had been broken. Of course the voyagers would still experience a violent shock after all the water had escaped, but they expected that the initial impact would be greatly diminished by this very strong spring.[5]

It was true that three feet of water over a surface of fifty-four square feet would weigh close to 11,500 pounds: but the thrust of the gases exploding in the Columbiad would, according to Barbicane, overcome this increase in weight; moreover, in just one second all that water would be driven out and the projectile would be back to its normal weight.

That was the president's plan for solving the problem of impact. And the Breadwill engineers had carried it out with great intelligence. Once the initial shock had been absorbed and the waters driven out, the passengers could dispose of the broken partitions and dismantle the sliding disk on which they had been stationed for the firing.

The upper walls of the projectile were lined with thick leather padding fastened over coils of fine steel, flexible as watch springs; the padding also covered the pipes through which the water would escape.

Thus every conceivable precaution had been taken to lessen the initial shock. Now they could be crushed, according to Michel Ardan, only if they themselves were made "of inferior materials."

The projectile measured nine feet in outside diameter and twelve feet in height:[6] in order not to exceed the assigned weight, they had slightly reduced the thickness of the walls. They reinforced the floor, which would have to take the violent thrust of the gases produced by the explosion of the pyroxylin. The bottom is always the thickest part in cylindro-conical bombs and projectiles.

They would enter this metal tower through an opening in the wall of the cone; it resembled the manhole in a steam boiler. They could close it hermetically with an aluminum plate bolted from the inside. Thus they would be able to leave their mobile prison at will when they reached the moon.

4. *your imagination* This kind of casual, meandering conversation is totally new for Barbicane. Under Ardan's tutelage, the Gun Club president is learning how to relax and enjoy people as much as artifacts.

5. *very strong spring* Ingenious, and to most of Verne's original readers, probably plausible. But today's readers, conversant with the gees-acceleration concept, would see that this still won't work, for several reasons. The purpose of cushioning is to support the body equally in all areas, an effect that can be approached on a water-bed but not on a *water-tight wooden disk*. Then, the projectile will undergo all its acceleration in 0.04 seconds. It's doubtful that all that water can crowd out that fast through those *pipes*. And the wooden raft would slam against the three men with a velocity of 12,000 yards a second, or 28,000 gees, or squash. Also, the water will increase the projectile's weight by one and a half times: Barbicane should increase the powder. But as we noticed in Chapter IX, the decision about powder was mainly a farce on the "science" of overkill.

6. *twelve feet in height* "Our space vehicle . . . had the . . . same height" as Barbicane's, Frank Borman the astronaut will write to Jules Verne's grandson in 1969.

But it was not enough simply to get there, they had also to see en route. Nothing could be easier. Under the padding were four portholes fitted with thick biconvex panes, two in the circular wall, a third at the bottom, and a fourth in the conical cap. On their trip then, the passengers would be able to observe the Earth they were leaving behind, the moon they were approaching, and the stars in the sky. For protection against the initial impact, these portholes were covered with tight-fitting plates that could be unscrewed from the inside and swung outward.[7] In this way, they could look out in any direction without permitting air to escape.

These mechanisms were neatly installed and easy to use; and the engineers had been equally ingenious in laying out the interior of the vehicle-projectile.

There were built-in containers for their food and water, and a special reservoir for compressed gas provided them with a six-day supply for heat and light. They had only to open the tap. They lacked nothing essential for life or even for well-being. Moreover, thanks to Michel Ardan's good taste, the useful was supplemented by the beautiful in the form of *objets d'art;* if space had permitted, he would have turned

7. *swung outward* In nautical terminology, these plates or shutters would be called deadlights.

no one could deny . . . it was a beautiful piece of metal. Engraving from 1872 edition.

the projectile into an artist's studio.[8] Still it would be wrong to suppose that three people would be crowded in that metal tower. They had an area of fifty-four square feet, a height of about ten feet, which allowed them a certain freedom of movement. They would not have been any better off in the most comfortable railway car in the United States.

Once the question of food and light was settled, there remained the question of air. It was obvious that the air enclosed in the projectile would not be enough to keep three men breathing for four days. Actually every person consumes in one hour just about all the oxygen contained in one hundred liters of air. Barbicane, his two companions, and the two dogs they planned to take along would consume about two thousand four hundred liters of oxygen, or seven pounds, every twenty-four hours.[9] Clearly they would have to be able to renew the air inside the projectile. But how? By a very simple process, developed by Reiset and Regnault,[10] which Michel Ardan had mentioned at the mass meeting.

We know that for practical purposes, air is composed of 21 parts oxygen and 79 parts nitrogen. Now what happens when we breathe? A very simple phenomenon. We absorb the oxygen in the air, which is essential for sustaining life, and exhale the nitrogen intact. The air exhaled has lost about five percent of its oxygen and contains an almost equal volume of carbon dioxide, the end product of combustion of the elements of the blood by the oxygen inhaled. It follows then that in an enclosed space, after a certain period of time, all the oxygen in the air has been replaced with carbon dioxide, an essentially noxious gas.[11]

The question then could be reduced to this: with the nitrogen kept intact, first, to replace the oxygen consumed; second, to destroy the carbon dioxide exhaled. This could be done easily with potassium chlorate and caustic potash.

Potassium chlorate is a salt that comes in the form of white flakes. When heated to a temperature above 400°, it changes into potassium chloride and gives off its oxygen content. Now eighteen pounds of potassium chlorate will produce seven pounds of oxygen, which is to say, the amount the passengers needed in a twenty-four-hour period. So much for replenishing the oxygen.

As for the caustic potash, it has a great affinity for carbon dioxide present in the air; the passengers would need only to shake the caustic potash to make it combine with carbon dioxide and form potassium bicarbonate. So much then for absorbing the carbon dioxide.

By combining these two processes, it was possible to restore to the vitiated air all of its life-sustaining properties. This was what the two chemists, Reiset and Regnault, had shown experimentally. But, it must be acknowledged, the experiment had so far been performed only on animals. Scientific and precise as the experiment had been, it still had not yet been tried out on human beings.

This was pointed out at the meeting called to consider this grave question. Stressing the importance of proving that man could also live on that artificial air, Michel Ardan offered to try it out himself before their departure. But J. T. Maston energetically claimed for himself the honor of making the test.

8. *an artist's studio* Nadar's studio in Paris is described as "ornate" and crowded with photographer's "properties."

9. *every twenty-four hours* Converting, we find that in one hour every person consumes the oxygen contained in about 27 U.S. gallons (about 3½ cubic feet) of air. Every twenty-four hours, the five passengers would consume about 600 U.S. gallons of oxygen, or the oxygen contained in about 3,000 gallons (about 400 cubic feet). Since the interior of the cylindro-conical craft has a floor surface of 54 square feet and a height of about 10 feet, it cannot contain more than 540 cubic feet of air to start with.

10. *Reiset and Regnault* Verne enhances the credibility of his futuristic projects by referring continually to the ongoing work of scientists whose successes are a matter of record. In 1865, Henri Victor *Regnault* (1810–1878) is director of the celebrated porcelain works at Sèvres, where he carries on his famous researches on the properties of gases. He is a professor of chemistry and author of a four-volume treatise already translated into many languages. But his life, which began with a long struggle against poverty, will end in tragedy. On January 19, 1871, his son Henri the painter will fall in combat. And Regnault's laboratory at Sèvres, together with all records of his latest researches, will also be destroyed by the Prussians. Never able really to work after this double blow, he will die on the seventh anniversary of his son's death.

Jules *Reiset* (1818–1896), well-known chemist and agronomist, has been Regnault's associate in his analyses of gaseous mixtures. They are co-authors of *Chemical Studies of the Respiration of Animals* (1849).

11. *noxious gas* Carbon dioxide is not a poison. But *if all the oxygen in the* spaceship's *air were replaced by carbon dioxide,* then the space-voyagers would suffocate.

"Since I'm not to go," said the brave artilleryman, "at least I could be allowed to experiment with living in the projectile for a week or so."

It would have been unkind to refuse him, so they granted his wish. They supplied him with enough potassium chlorate, caustic potash, and food and water for eight days. On November 12, at six in the morning, he shook hands with his friends, reminded them not to open his prison until November 20, at six in the evening, slipped into the projectile, and hermetically sealed it from the inside.

What was happening during that "week or so"? No one could tell. The thickness of the projectile's walls prevented any sound from reaching outside.

On November 20, at six o'clock exactly, the aluminum plate was swung outward. J. T. Maston's friends had been in a state of anxiety. But now they were promptly reassured when they heard a jolly voice shouting a loud "hurrah!" There, at the top of the cone, the secretary of the Gun Club was striking a triumphant pose. He had put on weight!¹²

12. *put on weight* Apparently because he has had nothing to do except eat. We learned at the banquet in Chapter XVI that it would be difficult to say whether Maston *drank more than he ate*. Which raises a serious question that Verne, living in the period of Queen Victoria and Louis Napoleon, would never have raised: How about waste disposal? After a week in that sealed metal tower . . . But looking back over the chapter, we see that such vital matters must be covered in the sentence: *They lacked nothing essential for life or even for well-being*. Under the circumstances, this sentence qualifies as one of the great euphemisms of all time.

What was happening during that "week or so"? . . . J. T. Maston . . . had put on weight! Engraving from the 1872 edition.

CHAPTER XXIV

The Telescope in the Rocky Mountains

At the close of the subscription, on October 20 of the preceding year, the president of the Gun Club had turned over to the Cambridge Observatory the money required for construction of an enormous telescope. Barbicane had specified that this apparatus—whether it would be a reflecting telescope or a refracting telescope had yet to be determined—must be powerful enough to detect an object nine feet wide on the moon's surface.

There is a significant difference between these two types of telescope, and it would be best to review it here. A refracting telescope is a tube equipped at its upper end with a convex lens called the objective, and at its lower end with a second lens called the ocular, to which the observer puts his eye. Rays emanating from a distant object pass through the first lens and, by refraction, form an upside-down image at the focal point.[1] The observer, peering through the ocular, which acts exactly like a magnifying glass, sees that image greatly enlarged. The tube of the refracting telescope, then, is closed at each end by an objective or an ocular.[2]

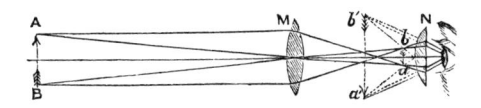

By contrast, the reflecting telescope is open at its upper end. Rays from the distant object enter the open end and without distortion go on to strike a concave—that is to say, convergent—metal mirror. From there they are reflected to a smaller mirror that relays them to the ocular, which magnifies the image.[3]

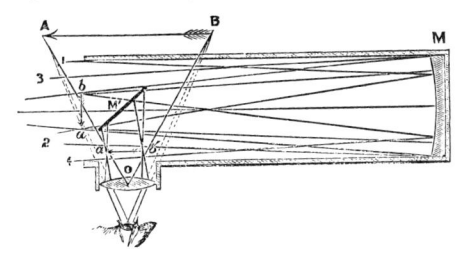

1. *the focal point* "The point where the refracted rays are reunited," Verne says in a footnote. This awkward after-thought illustrates a basic uncertainty under which the science popularizer works. How much does his audience already know? Should he add more explanation and risk being too elementary and hence boring? Some of Verne's notes show that he—or his publisher—was often unsure. There's no problem when Verne has his characters discussing such matters: even basic facts are more interesting when cast in dialogue. But he gets nervous when, as here, he fails to dramatize his material and gives a lecture instead.

2. *objective of an ocular* The workings of *the refracting telescope* are illustrated in this schematic diagram from *The American Cyclopaedia* (1876). *M* is *the objective*, *N* is *the ocular*. *AB* is the distant object under observation. The five lines emanating from *AB* represent paths that light rays can take as they proceed through the lenses. They *form an upside-down image at the focal point*, at *ba*. The observer peering through *N* sees that *image greatly enlarged* at *b'a'*.

3. *magnifies the image* The workings of *the reflecting telescope* are shown in this 1876 schematic diagram of Newton's 1671 instrument. *M*, the objective, is a *concave . . . metal mirror* at the lower end of the tube. Since rays *1* and *2* would be reflected toward *a*, and rays *3* and *4* toward *b*, *an upside-down image* would normally be formed at *ba*. But *a smaller mirror*, *M'*, is interposed at a 45° angle to *relay the image* to *a'b'*, and the *ocular*, *O*, *magnifies the image* into *AB*.

4. *Hence . . . refractor . . . reflector* To us, this sentence seems to be an elaboration of the obvious because in Enlish the two types always have parallel names: *refracting* and *reflecting telescopes* are often called *refractors* and *reflectors*. But in French the original names are not so self-explanatory: since refracting telescopes are known as *lunettes* and reflecting telescopes as *telescopes,* they really undergo a change when they become *refracteurs* and *reflecteurs*.

5. *Galileo . . . at the most.* Actually, in his famous year 1609, Galileo made at least three telescopes. The first magnified only three times; the second more than doubled that, and presumably the second is the one Verne calls *his poor refractor*. But Galileo's third instrument achieved a magnification of thirty powers. The way it worked is shown in this 1876 encyclopedia drawing. The objective *M*, focused on *AB*, would normally form an inverted image at *ba*, but Galileo's double-concave ocular, *N*, refracts the rays, which are produced backward to form an upright image at *a'b'*. With this instrument, Galileo estimated the altitudes of lunar mountains, found the sun spots, resolved the Milky Way into distinct stars, and saw the satellites of Jupiter.

6. *Pulkovo . . . objective.* "It cost 80,000 rubles," or about $60,000, Verne adds in a footnote. Ten miles south of St. Petersburg, Pulkovo Observatory is one of the reasons Verne has so highly praised the Russians in Chapter XII. In Verne's day, Pulkovo is considered the best endowed and most perfectly organized of all European observatories. Its first director, Friedrich Georg Wilhelm Struve, measured the annual parallax of Vega in 1840 and has since observed some 2,640 double and multiple stars. His papers and books, published in French or Latin, rank among the major astronomical works of the period. As Verne writes, Struve has just died, and now Pulkovo is under the management of his son Otto.

7. *optician Lerebours* His instrument is mounted in the Paris Observatory.

8. *Cambridge . . . diameter.* See Chapter IV, Annotation 1. Apparently Verne does not know that the Cambridge instrument is a twin of the Pulkovo refractor.

9. *Herschel . . . diameter* Sir William's discovery of Uranus in 1781 prompted King George III to finance the construction of this celebrated reflector, finished in 1789 at Slough near Windsor. It was actually *forty feet long,* its mirror *four feet in diameter.*

10. *This tube . . . diameter* Verne is having trouble with his phallic figures in this paragraph. Rosse's *tube* was actually almost *sixty* feet long. Now Verne's strange difficulties in granting Herschel's and Rosse's tubes their full length could be related to an unconscious discomfort over the sexual parallels. This is further suggested by the footnote he adds to this paragraph, in which he feels constrained to dis-

Hence, the major role is played by refraction in one type, and by reflection in the other, for which reason the refracting telescope is often simply called the refractor; the reflecting telescope, the reflector.[4] The entire difficulty in making these apparatus lies in making the objectives, whether they be lenses or metallic mirrors.

Now at the time when the Gun Club was setting up its great experiment, these instruments had reached a high degree of perfection and were giving magnificent results. Astronomy had come a long way since Galileo had observed the celestial bodies with his poor refractor which had a magnification of only seven powers at the most.[5] Since the sixteenth century, astronomical telescopes had grown considerably in length and width, making it possible to probe the interstellar spaces to depths previously unknown. Among the refractors in use at that time were the one at the Pulkovo Observatory in Russia, with its fifteen-inch (thirty-eight-centimeter) objective,[6] another of the same size made by the French optician Lerebours,[7] and finally the Cambridge Observatory refractor, equipped with an objective nineteen inches (forty-eight centimeters) in diameter.[8]

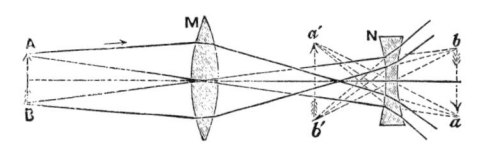

Among the reflectors, there were two of remarkable power and gigantic size. The first, constructed by Herschel, was thirty-six feet long with a mirror four and a half feet in diameter;[9] it had a magnification of 6,000 powers. The second had been set up in Ireland, at Birrcastle, in Parsonstown Park, and belonged to Lord Rosse. This tube was forty-eight feet long, and its mirror was six feet in diameter;[10] it had a magnification of 6,400 powers. They had to build an immense structure, of brickwork and masonry, to house the apparatus for maneuvering this instrument, which weighed 28,000 pounds.[11]

Still despite these colossal figures, it is easy to see that magnifications obtained did not surpass 6,000 powers, in round numbers; now, a magnification of 6,000 brings the moon to an apparent distance of thirty-nine miles (sixteen leagues), and this makes it impossible to detect any object less than sixty feet in diameter, unless it happens to be very long.

Now the projectile had a diameter of only nine feet, a length of twelve; this made it necessary to bring the moon to an apparent distance of no more than five miles (two leagues), and to do this, they would need a telescope with a magnification of 48,000 powers.

That was the problem faced by the Cambridge Observatory; it was a question not of money but of material difficulties.

First of all, they had to choose between a refractor and a reflector. Refractors have certain advantages over reflectors. With the same size objective, the refractor provides greater illumination; less light is lost by absorption when it passes through lenses than is lost by reflection when it is bounced off a metal mirror. But the thickness that can be given to a lens is limited, for if it is made too thick, it does not transmit rays at all. Furthermore, construction of these vast lenses is exceedingly difficult and requires considerable time, measured in years.

Therefore, even though the image is illuminated better in the refractor—a considerable advantage in observing the moon, whose light is only reflected light—they decided to use a reflector, which can be made more rapidly and has greater magnifying power. Only, since light rays lose a great deal of their intensity as they pass through the atmosphere, the Gun Club decided to set up their instrument on one of the highest mountains in the Union; this would reduce the thickness of the layer of air that the light would have to pass through.

In reflectors, as we have seen, it is the ocular, that is, the magnifying glass that the observer puts his eye to, which gives the instrument its powers of magnification; and the objective that helps provide max-

credit certain "longer" telescopes: "We often hear talk of refractors of much greater length. One in particular, 300 feet long, was installed at the Paris Observatory by Dominique Cassini; but we should remember that such telescopes had no tube. The objective was suspended in the air by means of masts, and the observer, holding the ocular in his hand, positioned himself as close to the focus of the objective as possible. It is easy to see how difficult it was to use these instruments, and how difficult it was to center two lenses under these conditions." And it's just as easy to see how difficult it was for Verne to write these passages.

11. *weighed 28,000 pounds* Finished in 1845, Lord Rosse's telescope, "the most stupendous instrument known," as one writer says, is moved by a windlass, strong chains, pullies, and heavy counterpoises. Rosse has used it to discover the spiral form of several nebulae and to "resolve" several others into star clusters.

Lord Rosse's famous drawings of spiral nebulae, reproduced in Arthur Berry's *A Short History of Astronomy* (1898).

12. *Léon Foucault* (1819–1868) is known especially for determining the speed of light in air, water, and other transparent media. He has invented the gyroscope and the Foucault Pendulum, which he has used to give a new and striking demonstration of the rotatory motion of the Earth.

13. *hoist himself to the upper end* In other words, as Berry's illustration (1898) makes clear, Sir William Herschel had to work at a considerable height above the ground. He had to climb ladders fifty feet long to reach the station where he would *peer into the enormous cylinder.* His sister Caroline, who specialized in comets and discovered eight of them, often expressed in her journals great anxiety about his safety. In 1839 his son, Sir John Herschel, dismantled the telescope and on New Year's Eve his family assembled in the tube and sang its requiem. Has this Herschel party given Verne the idea for the banquet held at the bottom of the gun tube in Chapter XVI?

14. *The image was less weakened.* This 1876 encyclopedia drawing shows *the method devised by Herschel.* His mirror M was slightly *inclined* so that the image of the object was formed at ba, near the ocular O, which magnified it into $b'a'$. Such reflectors, Verne tells us in a footnote, are called "front view telescopes." Notice how much simpler Herschel's is than Newton's. Unfortunately, the *inclined mirror* could not keep its polish for more than two years at a time, and finally it succumbed to the weather and "went blind," as Verne's English biographer, Kenneth Allott puts it.

15. *sixteen feet in diameter* Another Vernean prediction come true. For in 1948 the Mount Palomar Observatory, in southern California, will install its reflecting telescope: 55 feet long with a 16-ton mirror more than *sixteen feet* in diameter. Its magnifying power will be 12,000, a far cry from the 48,000 Verne expects. Colossal as such an instrument will be, the Palomar 200-inch reflector will remain the world's largest for less than three decades. In January 1976 the Soviet Special Astrophysical Observatory in the northern Caucasus will unveil a reflecting telescope with a tube more than 78 feet (24 meters) long and a mirror more than *nineteen feet* (6 meters) *in diameter.* In September 1976 the French astronomer M. J. Heidmann, of the Observatory of Meudon, will become the first foreigner to use the 236-inch mirror. He will write in *Sky and Telescope* (July 1977) that other foreign scientists will "be applying for telescope time in the near future." Verne, with his admiration for internationalism in science, would like this even more than Pulkovo.

16. *a few years ago* Apparently a kind of figure of speech for "how time flies": Robert Hooke lived in the seventeenth century. In Verne's day Hooke is still disparaged for being "jealous of all other inventors, and . . . involved in continual disputes concerning different inventions, generally pretending . . . they were all taken from ideas of his own," as one writer puts it. Nevertheless historians today do find Hooke's claims to be just: he *had* anticipated Newton's law of universal gravitation and *had* invented, independently of Huygens, the hair spring of watches.

17. *orographic system* Orography is the

Herschel's *great apparatus* as pictured in Berry's *Short History of Astronomy* (1898).

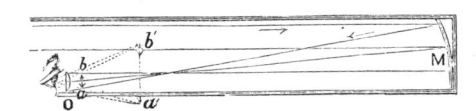

Herschel's method as discussed in Annotation 14.

imum magnification is the one with the greatest diameter and greatest focal distance. To achieve a magnification of 48,000 powers, they would have to exceed by far the size of Herschel's and Lord Rosse's objectives. That was the problem, for the casting of these mirrors is a very delicate operation.

Fortunately, just a few years earlier a scientist at the Institut de France, Léon Foucault,[12] had made it easier and faster to polish the objective by replacing the metal mirror with one made of silvered glass. All they had to do was cast a mass of molten glass of the desired dimensions and plate it with silver. This was the process, which gives excellent results, that they would use in the manufacture of the objective.

In putting their telescope together, they would follow the method devised by Herschel. In the great apparatus set up by the astronomer of Slough, the image of the object, reflected by an inclined mirror at the bottom of the tube, was formed at the other end where the ocular was situated. Thus the observer, instead of stationing himself at the lower end of the tube, would hoist himself to the upper end [13] and there, with his magnifying glass, he would peer into the enormous cylinder. This combination had the advantage of eliminating the little mirror designed to reflect the image to the ocular. Thus the image was subjected to only one reflection instead of two. Hence less light was lost by absorption. The image was less weakened.[14] In short, they could achieve greater clarity, a precious advantage in the kind of observations the Gun Club would have to make.

When all such decisions had been made, they began the actual work. According to the Cambridge Observatory's calculations, the tube of the new reflector would have to be 280 feet long, and its mirror would have to be sixteen feet in diameter.[15] Colossal as such an instrument would be, it could not begin to compare with the 10,000-foot (three-and-a-half-kilometer) telescope that the astronomer Hooke proposed building a few years ago.[16] Nevertheless its construction posed some great difficulties.

The question of location was quickly solved. They had to pick a high mountain, and high mountains are not very numerous in the United States.

In effect, the orographic system[17] of that huge country can be reduced to two ranges of only medium elevation; between them flows the magnificent Mississippi which Americans, if they could entertain any ideas of royalty at all, would surely call "the king of rivers."

In the East there are the Appalachians, whose highest summit, in New Hampshire, reaches an altitude of only 6,600 feet.[18]

In the West, on the other hand, there are the Rocky Mountains, part of an immense chain that begins at the Straits of South America under the name of the Andes or Cordilleras, crosses the Isthmus of Panama, and runs up through North America all the way to the polar seas.

These mountains are not very high; the Alps or the Himalayas would look down on them with supreme disdain. Their highest summit is only 10,701 feet above sea level, while Mont Blanc rises to 14,439, and Kinchinjunga, the highest peak in the Himalayas, to 29,454.[19]

But, since the Gun Club wanted their telescope, as well as their Columbiad, to be situated within the boundaries of the states of the Union, they had to settle for the Rocky Mountains. And so all the necessary materials were dispatched to the summit of Longs Peak, in Missouri Territory.[20]

Neither tongue nor pen could describe the difficulties of every kind that the American engineers had to overcome, or the feats of courage and skill that they accomplished. It was truly a tour de force. They had to raise enormous stones, heavy forged parts, corner clamps of prodigious weight, immense sections of the cylinder, the objective, itself weighing almost 30,000 pounds—all this they had to raise up above the snow line, to an altitude of more than 10,000 feet, after having transported it across deserted prairies, through dense forests, over fearful rapids, far from centers of population, into wild regions where almost every detail of life poses a serious problem. But the American genius overcame a thousand such obstacles. Less than a year after the work was started, in the last days of September, the gigantic reflector pointed its 280-foot tube into the sky. It was suspended from an enormous iron framework; an ingenious mechanism made it possible for

science that studies mountains and mountain ranges.

18. *Appalachians . . . 6,600 feet* In Verne's day, Mount Washington in New Hampshire is widely believed to be the *highest summit* in the Appalachians. But today it is calculated to be 6,288 feet tall, while Mount Mitchell in North Carolina, with an altitude of 6,684, is known to be the *highest summit* in the range.

19. *10,701 . . . 29,454* "Up to 1865, no portion of the great Rocky Mountain region had been examined with such care and detail as to render the maps anything more than approximately correct," *The American Cyclopaedia* will say in 1875. And as he writes this novel in 1865, Verne apparently does not know that there are dozens of peaks in the Rockies rising 14,000 feet or more above sea level. Longs Peak, which he selects for his observatory, reaches 14,225 feet, and is today known to be surpassed by Mount Elbert, 14,431. And after Verne calls Kinchinjunga the *highest peak in the Himalayas,* the orographers will correct that too. By 1875, the *Cyclopaedia* will report that the Himalayan Mount Everest, 29,002 feet high, is "believed to be the highest summit on the globe." And today Everest is credited with another twenty-six feet.

Today Verne would enjoy pointing out that Everest is the "highest summit" only if you measure height from sea level. If you figure altitude from the center of the earth, then Chimborazo, a peak in the Ecuadorian Andes, becomes the *real* tallest mountain. Reason: The earth is not round but bulges out at the equator. Sea level there is actually 14 miles farther from the earth's center than it is at the North Pole. Although Chimborazo rises only 20,561 feet above sea level, it is much closer to the equator than Everest is; it juts two miles farther out into space, and hence—according to this mode of measurement—is two miles higher than Everest.

20. *Missouri Territory* The Rockies once were the western frontier of the old Missouri Territory, but since 1861, *Longs Peak* is in the Colorado Territory.

21. *volcanic nature* We know from the Ardan-Nicholl debate (Chapter XX) that neither of them believes there are any live volcanoes on the moon. And we noted in Chapter V that the moon did undergo a long period of volcanism and lava flooding. If that's what Verne's astronomers are *able absolutely to verify,* then Verne racks up another prediction come true. But if he's harking back to the (Chapter V) implication that the moon's *craters* are all volcanic in origin—that is, that they are at the top of conical mountains built up by lava eruptions—then he is backing the wrong theory: relatively few lunar craters seem to be the vents of volcanoes.

22. *diameters . . . distant stars* The angle of arc that the star's diameter occupies in the observer's eye is called *the apparent diameter.*

Unfortunately, astronomers will prove Verne's prediction to be impossible of fulfillment. The *greater accuracy* that the Longs Peak telescope would achieve would still be insufficient to give the staff anything like the true measurement of that angle. Rays of light from a distant point object that hit the edge of a lens are bent. What the eye sees then is a blurred, enlarged image of the actual object. True, the larger the telescope, the smaller this image—called the *diffraction disk*—will be. But even Verne's 16-foot-wide lens at Longs Peak will still create a diffraction disk around a star that is greater than the star's true *apparent diameter*. And then there's a second difficulty. Atmospheric disturbance also enlarges stellar images. "Therefore," says Jean Dufay in his 1964 book on astrophysics, "no hope exists for obtaining the apparent diameter of stars from direct measurement by observing their images at the focus of a telescope, no matter how large it is." But if the telescope were mounted in Outer Space, wherever there is no atmosphere, it could measure these *apparent diameters*—if it had a lens 90 feet wide!

In the twentieth century, astronomers use indirect techniques to measure the apparent diameter of a few of the closest, largest stars. They find these apparent diameters to be less than .05 seconds of arc. And the diffraction disk for the Longs Peak telescope (with a 16-foot lens) would be .057 seconds!

23. *resolved . . . Crab Nebula* Another Verne prediction that will not come true. A remote nebula, or foggy patch of light in the heavens, may consist of a densely packed swarm of stars ("star cluster") so far away that the light of individual stars is lost in the mass. Or it may consist of a vast cloud of gas and dust ("gaseous nebula"). If an astronomer points a new, more powerful telescope at a nebula whose nature is still in doubt, and begins to see separate stars, then he is said to have *resolved the . . . nebula*. But the opposite has happened with *the Crab Nebula:* astronomers now know it's gaseous and cannot be resolved.

Still, Verne has picked a fascinating nebula to observe. The Crab is an expanding cloud ejected by a star that exploded in A.D. July 1054. Chinese astronomers who observed the explosion rated it as brighter than Venus: the supernova remained visible in daylight for twenty-three days. The resulting nebula was first noted telescopically in 1731 by the British astronomer John Bevis (1693–1771); later it became the first object (M1) in the catalog of nebulae compiled by the French astronomer Charles Messier (1730–1817). Lord Rosse discovered its long, tenuous filaments. His 1844 drawing of M1 roughly resembled the pincers of a crab, and so the nebula acquired its name. We now know the Crab emits powerful radiation at all wavelengths, from radio to gamma rays. Its huge output—25,000 times the luminosity of our sun—is maintained by a pulsar at its center which rotates thirty times a second, the fastest rotating pulsar known, and the first to be observed optically.

the observer to maneuver it easily toward any point in the heavens and to follow the celestial bodies from one horizon to the other during their march across space.

It had cost more than $400,000. The first time the observers trained it on the moon, they experienced both curiosity and anxiety. What would they discover in the field of that telescope which magnified objects 48,000 times? Populations, herds of lunar animals, villages, lakes, oceans? No, nothing not already known to science, although in all areas of the moon they were able absolutely to verify its volcanic nature.[21]

Still, the telescope in the Rockies, before taking up the Gun Club duties for which it was built, rendered great service to astronomy. Thanks to its prodigious power, its staff was able to probe deeper into space than man had ever seen before; they were able to measure with greater accuracy the apparent diameters of a vast number of distant stars,[22] and Mr. Clarke of the Cambridge Observatory was able to achieve what Lord Rosse's telescope had failed to do—he resolved the Crab Nebula[23] in Taurus.

. . . the gigantic reflector pointed its 280-foot tube into the sky. Engraving from the 1872 illustrated edition of *From the Earth to the Moon.*

CHAPTER XXV

Final Preparations

It was November 22. Departure was scheduled for ten days later. They had only one more task to complete to bring the project to its climax, an operation delicate and perilous, requiring infinite precautions. Indeed, Captain Nicholl had laid his third bet against its success. This was the task of loading the cannon, of putting 400,000 pounds of guncotton into it. Nicholl thought, perhaps not without good reason, that in handling such a huge quantity of pyroxylin they would trigger off a catastrophe, and that in any case, this exceedingly explosive mass would ignite itself under the pressure of the projectile.

The hazards involved were greatly increased by the notorious nonchalance of American cannoneers; during the Civil War, they had actually loaded their guns with cigars in their mouths. But Barbicane, determined to succeed, did not intend to sink within sight of port; he selected his best workmen, he supervised them in person, never once taking his eyes off them, and through prudence and precaution, he enlisted luck on his side.

First of all, he took the precaution of not storing all the powder in the Stony Hill enclosure at the same time. He had it brought in bit by bit, always in tightly sealed ammunition-wagons. They put the 400,000 pounds of guncotton into 800 bags, holding 500 pounds each, made by the best artificers in Pensacola. They loaded ten bags to the wagon and shipped the wagons, one at a time, by rail from Tampa; thus they were sure never to have more than 5,000 pounds of pyroxylin in the enclosure at any given time. As soon as each wagon arrived, it was unloaded by men working in bare feet;[1] they carried each bag to the orifice of the Columbiad and lowered it with cranes operated by hand. All steam engines had been moved far away, and indeed no flames at all were permitted within a two-mile radius. Even in November, they took pains to protect that mass of guncotton from the heat of the sun. They preferred to work at night by light produced in a vacuum, that is, by the Rühmkorff apparatus,[2] which created artificial day in the very depths of the Columbiad. There they stacked the bags in perfect order, connecting them with wires that would bring an electric spark to all of them at the same time.

In other words, they were going to use a battery to set off the gun-

1. *working in bare feet* Shoe-nails could strike sparks on Stony Hill.

2. *Rühmkorff apparatus* Heinrich Daniell Rühmkorff (1803–1877) is a German instrument-maker living in Paris in Verne's day. He is noted mainly for his development in 1851 of his induction coil, a type of transformer that generates high-tension discharges. His *Rühmkorff apparatus* consists of a Bunsen battery, a Rühmkorff coil, and a spiral glass tube containing only a small amount of carbonic gas in a partial vacuum. When the worker, who carries this apparatus on his belt, presses a switch, electric current passes through the gas and gives off a steady white light.

. . . They had to load the vehicle-projectile with all the things they needed for the trip. The interior of the projectile as illustrated in the 1872 edition of *From the Earth to the Moon.*

3. *Bunsen battery* Until 1842, most batteries comprised one zinc and one platinum cathode. Then Robert Wilhelm *Bunsen* (1811–1899) substituted cheap retort carbon for the platinum, creating the first inexpensive cell. When Barbicane orders his *powerful . . . battery,* composed maybe of hundreds of Bunsen cells, Professor Bunsen heads the celebrated chemistry department at Heidelberg University. And the Bunsen burner, the Bunsen photometer, and the Bunsen pump as well as the *Bunsen battery* are regarded as indispensable equipment in every laboratory.

powder. All of the wires, which were insulated, joined into one cable which went first through a hole cut in the cannon wall at the point where the projectile would rest, then through one of the vents created in the revetment for this purpose, and on up to the surface of the earth. When it reached the summit of Stony Hill, the cable was carried on poles for two miles, until it passed through a switch and finally connected with a powerful Bunsen battery.[3] They had only to close the switch to make the current flow instantaneously and thus ignite the 400,000 pounds of guncotton. It goes without saying, they would not activate the battery until the very last moment.

All 800 bags had been stacked at the bottom of the Columbiad by November 28. This part of the operation was a complete success. But poor President Barbicane, what confusion, what anxieties, what pressures he had suffered! In vain he had closed the gates to Stony Hill; every day curiosity-seekers scaled the fences, and some of these, pushing imprudence to the point of folly, smoked cigars while standing near the bales of guncotton. Barbicane was in a perpetual state of fury. J. T. Maston helped out as best he could, chasing trespassers with great vigor and picking up the lighted cigar butts the Yankees had tossed here and there. A hard job, for there were 300,000 people milling around the enclosure. Michel Ardan had offered to escort the powder-wagons to the Columbiad; but Barbicane once caught Ardan with an enormous cigar in his mouth, even as he was chasing away visitors to whom he himself offered such a bad example; the president of the Gun Club, seeing he could not count on this bold smoker, put him under special surveillance.

But since there is a God for artillerymen, nothing blew up, and the loading was completed. Captain Nicholl now stood to lose his third bet. But they still had to put the projectile in the cannon and lower it onto its thick couch of guncotton.

But before they did that, they had to load the vehicle-projectile with all the things they needed for the trip. And these were numerous. If Ardan had had his way entirely, there would have been no space left for passengers. What that amiable Frenchman wanted to take to the moon! A veritable collection of useless items! But Barbicane intervened, weeding out everything not absolutely necessary.

In their instrument compartment they stored several thermometers, barometers, and telescopes.

The type of barometer Verne's astronauts store in *their instrument compartment* is probably the aneroid barometer, illustrated here with an engraving from *The American Cyclopaedia* (1873).

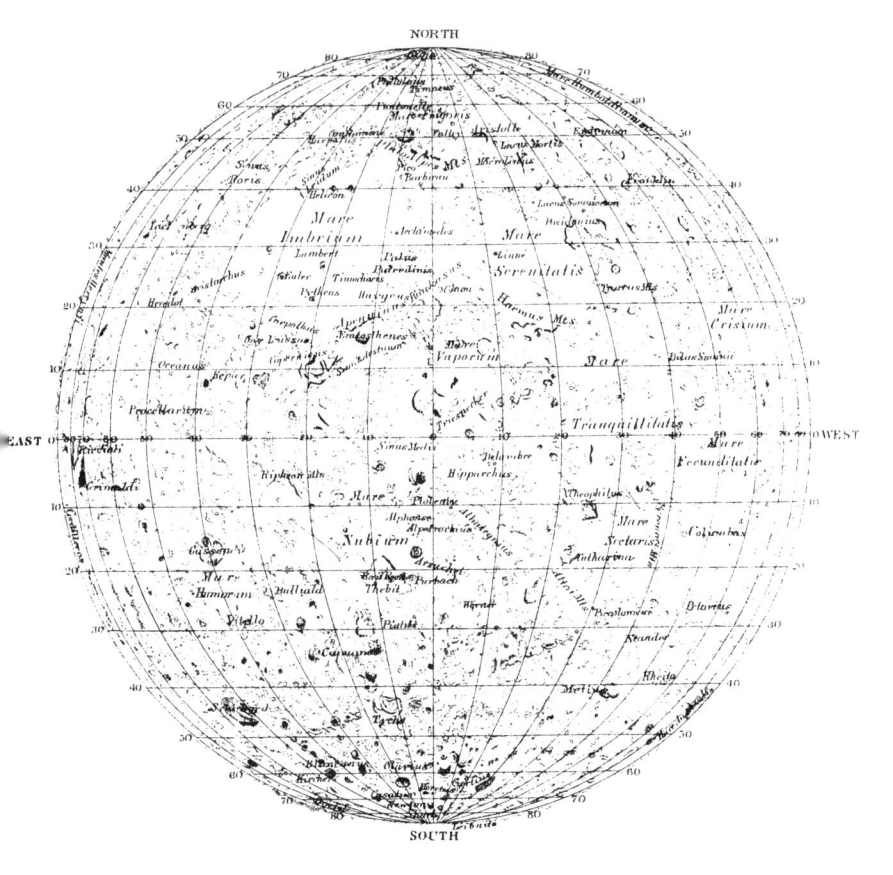

Beer and Mädler's *Mappa Selenographica* as reduced by Joseph S. Ward for Edward Roth's 1876 translation of Verne's *Round the Moon*.

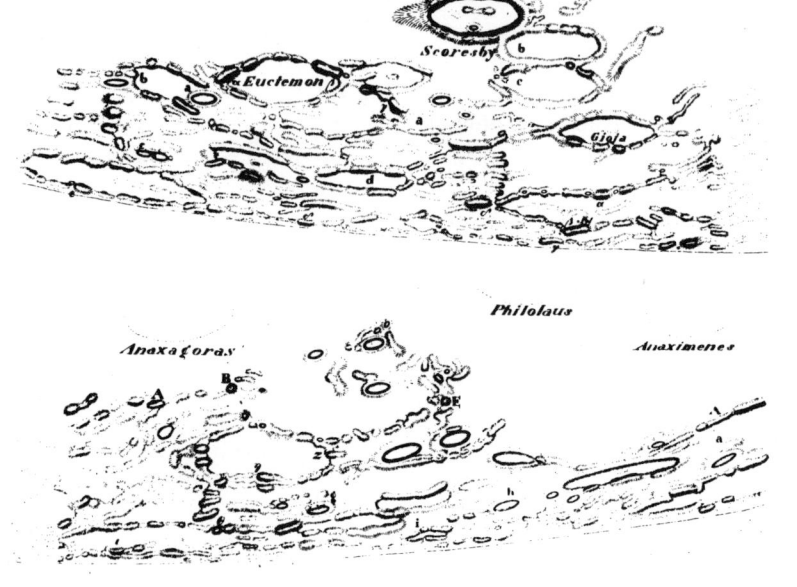

Details from Beer and Mädler's original map, as reproduced in their book *Der Himmlischen Körper im Sonnensysteme* (1841). Photographs courtesy of the Harvard College Observatory.

4. *Doerfel and Leibnitz Mountains* When the Flemish mathematician Michael Florent van Langren mapped the moon in 1628, he started a 200-year controversy: How shall we name the lunar features? Langren's answer was to use biblical names. But when John Hevel of Danzig prepared his celebrated *Selenographia* (1647), he rejected Langren's designations. Hevelius, as he called himself in Latin, decided to name lunar areas after their assumed counterparts on Earth: for example, he called the chief mountain ranges on the moon the Apennines and the Alps, and gave similar titles to single mountains and craters. But then John Baptist Riccioli (1598–1671), in his fat treatise *New Almagest* (1651), introduced the practice of calling the single features after leading men in science and philosophy, and even after some politicians he was hoping to please. Riccioli left many areas unnamed, and as other mapmakers continued to play favorites, confusion piled on confusion. Finally, because of the patent superiority of Beer and Mädler's *Mappa Selenographica* (1837), the names they used—many old, some new—became standard.

The *Doerfel Mountains* are named after a seventeenth-century German clergyman, Georg Samuel Doerfel. In one of his nine astronomical writings, he suggested that the path of a comet "is a parabola, the focus of which should be in the center of the sun." Astronomers found this assumption worked in charting the path of several comets. But in 1759, Halley's comet returned, confirming his prediction that it follows a long elliptical orbit. For a century and a half, then, it was assumed there are two types of comets: parabolic comets, one-time visitors from remote Outer Space, and elliptical or "periodic" comets which return at predictable intervals. Today it is believed all comets are periodic, some following such elongated elliptical paths that they take millions of years to return around the sun.

The *Leibnitz Mountains* are named after the rationalist philosopher Gottfried Wilhelm Baron von Leibnitz (1646–1716). He regarded the universe as one single context in which each occurrence must be seen in its relation to every other: if we find some particular event or condition inharmonious or evil, it is only because we do not know its place in the overall divine plan. And since the universe is an expression of di-

Since they intended to study the moon carefully, they packed Beer and Mädler's excellent *Mappa Selenographica,* published in four parts, rightly considered to be a masterpiece of scientific observation. With scrupulous fidelity, this map gave every detail of that portion of the moon that faces the Earth; mountains, valleys, cirques, craters, peaks, rills were all shown with their exact dimensions, positions, and names, from the Doerfel and Leibnitz Mountains,[4] whose summits stand in the eastern side of the disk, to the Mare Frigoris,[5] located in the north circumpolar regions.

This was a valuable document for the voyagers, making it possible for them to study the country before setting foot on it.

In their gun-rack they placed three rifles and three hunting-pieces that could fire explosive bullets, along with a good supply of powder and ammunition.

"Who knows whom or what we will have to deal with," said Michel Ardan. "Men or beasts might take a dim view of our visit. And so we must take every precaution."

In addition to these weapons they stowed away some picks, shovels, hand saws, and other necessary tools, not to mention clothing for every climate, from the cold of the polar regions to the heat of the torrid zone.

Michel Ardan had hoped to take on their expedition a certain number of animals, although not necessarily a pair of every known species, for he did not see any need to populate the moon with serpents, tigers, alligators, and other harmful creatures.

"But some beasts of burden, an ox or a cow, a mule or a horse, they would add a nice touch to the landscape, and they would prove useful to us."

"Yes, my dear Ardan," replied the president of the Gun Club, "but our vehicle-projectile is not Noah's Ark, it has neither the same capacity nor the same purpose. Let's stay within the confines of the possible."

At last, after lengthy discussion, they agreed to limit themselves to an excellent hunting dog belonging to Captain Nicholl and a vigorous, prodigiously powerful Newfoundland.[6] They also considered certain seeds to be essential, and they took several boxes. If Michel Ardan had had his way, he would have taken bags of soil to plant them in. In any case, he did stow in a corner of the projectile a dozen shrubs carefully wrapped in straw.

There was still the important question of food, for suppose they landed in a barren region of the moon? Barbicane actually managed to take a full year's supply. If this sounds impossible, we must explain that these victuals consisted of preserved meats and vegetables which had been greatly reduced in volume under hydraulic pressure.[7] Hence they would enjoy much nourishment if not much variety, but they could not afford to be fussy on such an expedition. They also found

The *powerful Newfoundland* (left) and the *excellent hunting dog* (right) as they are pictured in the 1872 edition of Verne's *Round the Moon*.

vinity, Leibnitz's followers called it "the best of all possible worlds." Ardan, like Voltaire, as we have seen, takes a dim view of this philosophy. Today, Leibnitz's reputation rests more on his attainments in mathematics. He developed his infinitesimal calculus before Newton developed his, and Leibnitz manuscripts published in our time establish him as the founder of symbolic logic.

The *Doerfel and Leibnitz Mountains* are situated to the east and west, respectively, of the lunar south pole. Apparently Verne had named two *eastern* ranges in an early draft, then later saw the advantage in sweeping from one polar region to the other, and substituted these two southern ranges, but he forgot to change *eastern* to *southern* side.

5. *Mare Frigoris* Latin for "The Sea of Coldness." When Galileo, the first person to study the moon through a telescope, turned his *poor refractor* on the lunar features in 1609, he thought the dark areas were oceans. He called them *maria,* seas. Taking a cue from Galileo, Hevelius named some of the lunar "seas" after terrestrial oceans, for example the Mare Serenitatis, or Pacific Ocean. Many astronomers today—like Jastrow and Thompson—believe these dark flat areas were once seas of lava that solidified some three billion years ago.

6. *powerful Newfoundland* The "Newf" is the perfect animal for this trip, as Verne's audience can well imagine: the breed is very popular in his day. The "Newf" does not romp or bounce when not encouraged to. And he enjoys a reputation as the strongest work-dog, good, for example, in hauling loads. He has a massive build, a height of up to 28 inches, and is described by Verne's contemporaries as highly intelligent, trusty, kind: one writer says that anecdotes about "the sagacity of this well known breed are innumerable." And the "Newf" won't be hard to look at in the crowded projectile: he's handsome, with a large broad head, decided stop, squarish muzzle, drooping ears, long coarse hair disposed to curl. Usually he's black, maybe black and white, or he's bronze. He's called Newfoundland because it's believed he was developed by fishermen who crossed European breeds with Newfoundland dogs.

7. *under hydraulic pressure* In Verne's day, several firms have earned an international reputation for their dehydrated or condensed foods. In New York, the American Desiccating Company preserves a variety of foods by removing the moisture. In England, the Liebig Extract of Meat Company—named after the German chemist, Baron Justus von Liebig (1803–1873)—produces compressed meat biscuits. Perhaps most famous are the Gail Borden (1801–1874) establishments which have supplied condensed milk to the Union Army during the Civil War. Borden, after whom Borden, Texas, is named, has invented "pemmican," a meat biscuit carried on Arctic expeditions; he also produces beef extract and condensed fruit juices, tea, coffee, and cocoa.

room for fifty gallons of brandy, but took enough water for only two months, because they expected, in accordance with the latest observations by astronomers, to find a certain amount of water on the surface of the moon.[8] As for provisions generally, it would have been insane to think that men from the Earth would not know how to find nourishment on the moon. Michel Ardan never entertained the slightest doubt about this. If he had, he would have decided not to go.

"Besides," he said one day to his friends, "we shall never be completely abandoned by our comrades on Earth; they will take care not to forget us."

"Surely not," answered J. T. Maston.

"What do you have in mind?" Nicholl asked.

"Nothing could be simpler," Ardan replied. "Won't the Columbiad always be there? So! Whenever the moon meets our conditions so far as the zenith—if not the perigee—is concerned, that is to say about once a year, why couldn't they send us projectiles loaded with supplies, which we would be expecting on a certain day?"

"Hurrah! hurray!" cried J. T. Maston like a man who has just been hit by a good idea. "What a good idea! Rest assured, friends, we shall not forget you!"

"I'm counting on you! So we'll get news from the Earth regularly, and, for our part, we'll be awfully inept if we can't figure out some way of getting news to you!"

He spoke with such confidence, such an air of determination, such superb aplomb, that he could at that moment have convinced the whole Gun Club to go along. What he said seemed so simple, so elementary, so easy and sure to succeed, that only a man with sordid reasons for staying on Earth could have hesitated to join the three voyagers on their lunar expedition.

Once these various supplies had been stowed in the projectile, they pumped into the partitions the water that would serve as a spring, and they compressed their illuminating gas into its tank. As for the potassium chlorate and caustic potash, Barbicane, worried about possible delays en route, took enough to replenish the oxygen and absorb the carbon dioxide for two months. He installed an ingenious apparatus, which worked automatically, to purify the air and restore its life-sustaining properties. The projectile was all ready, but it still had to be lowered down into the Columbiad. An operation fraught with perils and difficulties.

The enormous shell was transported to the summit of Stony Hill. There powerful cranes seized it and held it suspended over the metal pit.

It was a terrifying moment. If the chains were to break under this enormous strain, the fall of such a mass could trigger off the guncotton.

Fortunately that did not happen, and a few hours later, the vehicle-projectile, having been let down slowly into the bore of the cannon, was resting on its couch of guncotton, on its explosive eiderdown. Its weight had no other effect than to ram down the charge of the Columbiad.

"I have lost." The captain handed President Barbicane three thousand dollars.

---

8. *water . . . on . . . the moon* They surely cannot expect to find much. Richard A. Proctor, popular lecturer on astronomy in Verne's day, puts it this way: if there were any large bodies of water on the moon, the high temperatures of the lunar day would cause enormous quantities of it to evaporate. "Not only would the effects of this process be distinctly recognizable in the telescope," he says, "but the spectroscope would exhibit in an unmistakable manner the presence of the aqueous vapor thus formed."

In 1969, when the Apollo 11 astronauts Neil Armstrong and Edwin Aldrin will step onto the moon, they at first will think the dark, shiny particles in the dust look "wet." But their careful search for moisture will lead to the conclusion that the moon is bone-dry. Rock samples they will bring back will be analyzed in the laboratory: they will contain neither free moisture nor minerals with water molecules in their structure.

Barbicane did not like to take money from a fellow traveler, but he did so when Nicholl insisted that he wanted to meet all his obligations before leaving the Earth.

"Then," said Michel Ardan, "I can wish only one thing more for you, my brave captain."

"And that is—?" asked Nicholl.

"That you lose your other two bets as well! If you do, then we can't fail to complete our mission."

Testing the *illuminating gas*. Engraving from the 1872 edition of Verne's *Round the Moon*.

CHAPTER XXVI

Fire!

1. *Turenne . . . slept* Comparing Ardan first with General la Fayette, and now with Marshal Turenne, Verne characterizes well by parallel. Henri de la Tour d'Auvergne, Viscount of Turenne (1611–1675), is one of France's perennial heroes. Even when he was supreme commander, Turenne lived with his troops. They loved him as a comrade. Physically weak as a boy, he decided at the age of 12, after his father died, to exercise himself into strength. At 14 he studied war in Holland in the camp of his uncle, Maurice of Nassau, winning a captaincy in the Dutch forces at 15, then a colonelcy in the French army at 19, a marshalcy at 24. In all of his numerous victories he combined the personal bravery of a young front-line soldier with the skill and caution of a seasoned general. He excelled in "chess board" maneuvers, waiting patiently to get the superior position, then mounting a swift surprise attack. He would for example overtake his foe by a secret march in the dead cold of winter. "His genius grew bolder as it grew older," Napoleon said.

In 1675, Turenne asked for retirement. But in a war with the Dutch and their allies, the king had no other marshal capable of outguessing the Italian general, Raimondo, Count of Montecucculi. In four months of large-scale maneuvers, Turenne finally forced Montecucculi into a position near Sasbach where he would have to fight at a disadvantage. Turenne had another triumph in the palm of his hand. On the eve of battle, July 27, he went out to supervise the final preparations. A stray bullet felled him. Demoralized, his troops retreated across the Rhine. He was buried with the kings of France. Although he had been a royalist, even the extreme revolutionists of 1793 respected him. When they tossed the bones of the kings to the winds, they preserved Turenne's remains. In Verne's day (as in ours) he lies in the Church of the Invalides at Paris.

As Verne views Ardan-Nadar, the astronaut-balloonist shares with Turenne the ability to act decisively without recklessness, to gain popularity without losing respect, to remain forever young.

The first day of December had arrived, the fateful day, for if they did not launch the projectile that very evening, forty-six minutes and forty seconds after ten o'clock, they would have to wait for eighteen years before the moon would once again offer the same simultaneous conditions of zenith and perigee.

The weather was magnificent. Despite the approach of winter, the sun was shining brightly on that Earth which three of its inhabitants were about to abandon for a new world.

How many people had slept badly during the night that preceded this long-anticipated day! How many breasts were heavy with anxiety! Every heart was beating apprehensively except the heart of Michel Ardan. Undisturbed, he came and went with his habitual hustle and bustle; nothing in his manner betrayed any unusual concern. He had slept peacefully, as Turenne had slept,[1] on a gun carriage, before a battle.

Since dawn vast crowds had covered the plains that extended as far as the eye could see around Stony Hill. Every fifteen minutes the Tampa railroad unloaded more curiosity-seekers; this immigration reached fabulous proportions and, according to the *Tampa Town Observer,* on that memorable day five million spectators[2] trod the soil of Florida.

For a month the better part of this multitude had camped around the enclosure, laying the foundations for a city that is now known as Ardanton. Huts, sheds, lean-tos, and tents dotted the plains, and these makeshift dwellings housed a population large enough to make the biggest cities of Europe green with envy.

All the peoples of the Earth were represented there; every language could be heard at the same time. They spoke a confusion of tongues as in the biblical days at the Tower of Babel. All the various classes of American society mingled in absolute equality. Bankers, farmers, sailors, buyers, brokers, cotton planters, merchants, bargemen, magistrates all rubbed elbows with pristine casualness. Louisiana creoles fraternized with Indiana farmers; Kentucky and Tennessee gentlemen, elegant and haughty Virginians, chatted with half-savage trappers from the Great Lakes, with cattle merchants from Cincinnati.[3] They sported the broad-brimmed white beaver [4] or the classic panama, [5] blue cotton trousers from the mills of Opelousas, [6] elegant jackets of unbleached linen, boots of bright colors, shirts ruffled with batiste. And on their shirts, cuffs, cravats, on their ten fingers and in their ears, they wore an assortment of rings, pins, diamonds, chains, trinkets, whose high value was matched only by their bad taste. Women, children, servants, all in equally opulent dress, accompanied, followed, preceded their husbands, fathers, masters, who looked like tribal chieftains surrounded by their enormous households.

At mealtime it was a sight to behold when they fell to work on delicacies peculiar to the South and devoured, with an appetite that menaced the food supply of Florida, dishes that would have turned a European stomach, like fricasseed frog, stuffed monkey, fish chowder, roast sarigue, very rare opossum, and grilled raccoon. [7]

And what a variety of liquors and other beverages came to the aid of that indigestible food! What exciting cries, what inviting shouts resounded in the barrooms and taverns decorated with glasses, tankards,

. . . vast crowds . . . covered the plains . . . around Stony Hill. Engraving from the 1872 edition.

2. *five million spectators* When history catches up with Jules Verne on the morning of July 16, 1969, and three Americans—Neil Armstrong, Edwin Aldrin, Michael Collins—will be getting dressed for a trip to the moon, about *one million spectators* will gather around the space center at Cape Kennedy. Automobiles on the roads outside will be "backed up for hours in lines 10 miles long," *The New York Times* will report. Many more millions of people all over the world—except in mainland China—will be staring at their TV screens counting the minutes until launch time: 9:32 A.M.

3. *Louisiana . . . Cincinnati* We realize more than ever at this point that the idealistic Verne has invented a situation that has reunited the North and South. Certainly in 1865 nothing could accomplish such a miracle so fast as a "space effort" that would appeal to the pride and imagination of every state.

4. *white beaver* In Barbicane's day, the beaver underfur used in making top hats is in such great demand it has sparked exploration of the West: trappers have pushed far into unknown territory seeking out these industrious little builders of dams, canals, and dome-shaped homes. Frontiersmen use beaver hides, trimmed and stretched, as money. Soon after this novel appears, the beaver becomes so scarce that U.S. hat-makers start importing coypu (nutria) furs from South America, dyeing the olive-gray hair to resemble the beavers' brown, tan, or white underfur. And by 1881, when Verne publishes *Mistress Branican,* he can have a character say: "Now . . . beaver hats are never manufactured but with rabbit skins. . . ."

The industrious little builder of dams whose underfur is used in making top hats, as pictured in *The American Cyclopaedia* (1873).

5. *Classic panama* Hand-made panamas will stay in style long after machine-made beavers vanish because the jipijapa plant can grow new leaves but a beaver habitat can be hunted dead in a few years. In Barbicane's day, Indian women, children, men in Ecuador, Colombia, and other parts of Central and South America gather the fanlike leaves before they unfold; shred, boil, and dry them in the shade; plait the straw upon a block of wood they hold between their knees, working from the apex of the crown to the edge of the brim, then back up, and down again; pare the ends; pound the hood with a wooden mace to smooth it; and wash and dry it in the sun. They finish an ordinary panama in two or three days, but they devote weeks or even months to making a truly fine hat that can last a lifetime. Panama hats get their name from the port through which they are shipped.

6. *mills of Opelousas* The capital of Saint Landry Parish, Louisiana, Opelousas is situated in picturesque rice and cotton country and enjoys considerable trade. Maybe Verne singles out this particular cotton-mill town because French fur traders had settled there in 1628: Opelousas is still known for the *joie de vivre* that marks the French-accented approach to life.

7. *fricasseed frog . . . grilled raccoon* Verne is chiding his European readers as well as Americans. *Frog would not have turned a European stomach,* much as Verne thinks it should. No country consumes more frogs than France, as he well knows. There frogs are kept alive in "froggeries" until they are wanted on the table. Europeans consider the hind leg of the frog to be as much more delicate than chicken as chicken is better than pork. And the American frog most frequently sought after by American epicures is the shad frog, precisely because it resembles the common frog of Europe.

To enjoy *stuffed monkey* the Tampa eateries would have to import the animal from Guiana or Brazil. But pioneers and frontier people would not turn up their noses at any new dish. American exploration has included discoveries of new foods provided by a new land: yams, for example, wild turkey, and succotash. *Fish chowder* is indeed so foreign to the French that Verne has to footnote it: "Dish composed of various fishes," he says. But he leaves out the salt pork, the vegetables, the milk! *Sarigue* is the French word for *opossum* used in creole as well as in English in Verne's day: it makes it possible for him to offer this pouched mammal well done or rare, as indeed it is often enjoyed in the South. And black Southerners especially like *raccoon,* which they describe as fat and tender, with a flavor of pig.

Americans who suspect that Verne lacks zest for new foods will appreciate his grandson's opinion. "He was certainly no gourmet," says Jean Jules-Verne.

flagons, carafes, and bottles of incredible shape, mortars for pounding sugar, bundles of straws!

"Here's a mint julep!" a bartender would cry.

"Here's a Bordeaux sangaree!" another would yelp.

"A gin sling!" cried the first.

"A cocktail and a brandy smash!" said the second.

"Try a genuine *new*-style mint julep!" a crafty hawker would shout as he shook from glass to glass, like a sleight-of-hand artist, the sugar, lemon, mint, crushed ice, water, cognac, and fresh pineapple that make up that refreshing drink.

Until now, these invitations, addressed to throats made fiercely thirsty by hot spices, were so constantly repeated as to create a deafening hubbub. But not many such shouts were heard on this first day of December. The hawkers would have cried out in vain. No one thought of food or drink, and at four o'clock in the afternoon, there were many spectators who had not yet had their lunch. Even more significant was the fact that many of them had forgotten their violent passion for games. Tenpins were lying on their sides, dice were sleeping in the dice-box, the roulette wheel stood still, the cribbage boards were abandoned, and packs of cards for whist, twenty-one, red-and-black, monte, and faro remained unopened. Clearly, the main event of the day had absorbed all needs and allowed no distractions.

Toward evening, a dull, silent agitation, like the kind that precedes great catastrophes, ran through that anxious crowd. An indescribable uneasiness gripped every mind, a painful torpor, an indefinable feeling that oppressed the heart. Everyone wished that it was over.

But at about seven o'clock this heavy silence was suddenly dissipated. The moon was rising above the horizon. She was saluted with millions of hurrahs! She had kept her rendezvous. Cheers mounted to the heavens; applause sounded from all sides, as pale Phoebe glowed peacefully in a clear sky and cast her most affectionate beams on that feverish crowd.

And at that moment the three intrepid voyagers appeared. At the sight of them, the crowd cheered with greater intensity. Unanimously,

The American frog preferred by epicures is the shad frog (1), shown here with the marsh frog (2) in *The American Cyclopaedia* (1874).

spontaneously, the national anthem swelled from every chest, and "Yankee Doodle," [8] sung by a chorus of five million, rose like a tempest of sound into the far reaches of the atmosphere.

Then, after that irresistible rush of feeling, the anthem subsided, the last harmonies died away bit by bit, and a profound silence moved over the crowd. Meanwhile the Frenchman and two Americans had entered the enclosure around which the immense crowd was pressing. They were accompanied by members of the Gun Club and representatives sent by the leading observatories of Europe. Barbicane, cool and collected, calmly gave his last orders. Nicholl, lips tight, hands clasped behind his back, walked with firm and measured step. Michel Ardan, as flippant as usual, dressed for travel, with leather gaiters, a loose velvet suit, a satchel under one arm, cigar in his mouth, was shaking hands with everybody. He overflowed with inexhaustible energy and gaiety, laughing, joking, poking fun at the dignified J. T. Maston; in a word, he was "French" or, worse yet, "Parisian" to the very last minute.

Ten o'clock sounded. The moment had come for them to take their places in the projectile, for some time would be required for lowering them down the bore, screwing the plate back in place, removing the cranes, and clearing away the scaffolding from the mouth of the Columbiad.

Murchison was charged with igniting the powder with an electric spark. Barbicane had set his chronometer to within a second of the time shown on Murchison's, so that the voyagers enclosed in the projectile could watch the impassive hand that would indicate the moment for departure.

The time had come to say goodbye. It was a touching scene; in spite of his feverish gaiety, Michel Ardan felt deeply emotional. J. T. Maston found under his dry eyelids one old tear which doubtless he had saved for this very occasion. He shed it on the forehead of his dear, brave president.

"Shouldn't I go too?" he said. "There is still time!"

"Impossible, old fellow," Barbicane replied.

A few seconds later, the three traveling companions had settled into the projectile and bolted from the inside the plate that covered the manhole, and the mouth of the Columbiad, entirely cleared, was open to the sky.

Nicholl, Barbicane, and Michel Ardan were now sealed into their coach of metal.

What words could describe the universal emotion that was rising now to a crescendo?

The moon was moving over a sky of pellucid purity, outshining the glittering of the stars in her path. She was crossing the constellation Gemini, approaching the halfway point between the horizon and the zenith. As everyone could understand by now, they were aiming the projectile ahead of the target, just as the hunter aims ahead of the hare he hopes to hit.

An awesome silence fell over the scene. Not a breath of wind on the face of the earth! Not a breath escaped from any chest! Hearts stopped beating. Every anxious eye was fixed on the gaping mouth of the Columbiad.

8. *national anthem . . . "Yankee Doodle"* Here Verne is carried away by his idealism and his own success. And he betrays his tendency to think of the North as the United States. Like most Europeans, he thinks that of course Americans have an official *national anthem*—but at this time they don't. Reference books of the 1860s describe "Yankee Doodle" simply as *one* "of our national airs."

What has happened is that Verne has invented a moon project that has swiftly, miraculously reunited a Civil War–torn country. But that doesn't mean that Southerners in his crowd are going *unanimously* to break out with *"Yankee Doodle,"* anymore than the Northerners would *spontaneously* sing "Dixie." Southerners regard "Yankee Doodle" as a Northern air: South Carolina even outlawed it in 1861! What then would Verne's Tampa crowd really sing, under these extraordinary circumstances? Probably "My Country, 'Tis of Thee," with words by F. S. Smith and melody borrowed from "God Save the Queen." For three decades before the War between the States it was a truly *national* favorite.

The colorful history of the spirited, cocky *"Yankee Doodle"* has made it inevitable that many Europeans regard it as the American anthem. The tune goes back to the 1600s when it was sung in England to the nursery rhyme "Lucy Lockit Lost her Pocket." The words "Yankee Doodle" first appeared in the song when one version of it was used, supposedly, to satirize Oliver Cromwell:

Yankee Doodle came to town
 Upon a Kentish pony. . . .

British bands played the tune in the colonies, adding new verses to ridicule the Revolutionary troops. The Americans responded by adopting "Yankee Doodle" as a marching song. This defiant turnabout was admired the world over. But by the nineteenth century Southerners are using the word "Yankee" to mean Northerner, and even abolitionist, and the song has become regional.

In the twentieth century, the Army and the Navy will prefer to play "The Star-Spangled Banner" as their national anthem, with words by Francis Scott Key of the Gun Club's Baltimore, and music from the British song "To Anacreon in Heaven." But this preference will not be made official until President Wilson issues an executive order to that effect in 1916. Congress will confirm the order in 1931.

9. *Forty! Fire!!!* Even though this is, technically speaking, a count-up, it constitutes a fair prediction of the use of an *out-loud* countdown in the space effort a century hence.

Murchison was following the hand of his chronometer. Forty seconds to go, and each of them lasted as long as a century.

At the twentieth, a shudder ran through the crowd, as it occurred to everyone that the bold voyagers inside the projectile were also counting the terrible seconds.

There were shouts here and there:

"Thirty-five!—Thirty-six!—Thirty-seven!—Thirty-eight!—Thirty-nine!—Forty! Fire!!!" [9]

Murchison closed the switch and sent an electric current into the depths of the Columbiad.

The instantaneous result was a terrifying, incredible, unearthly detonation that could be compared to nothing already known, not to the roar of thunder, not to the eruption of a volcano. An immense geyser of flame shot from the entrails of the Earth as if from a crater. The ground heaved, and only a few of the onlookers could catch a moment's glimpse of the projectile triumphantly cleaving the air through clouds of blazing vapor.

"*. . . thirty-nine!—forty! Fire!!!*" Engraving from 1872 edition.

CHAPTER XXVII
Cloudy Weather

When that incandescent geyser rose to such a prodigious height, the glare of the flames lighted up all of Florida, and, for just an instant, day replaced night over a considerable expanse of the country. The immense plume of fire was visible from a hundred miles out in the Gulf as well as in the Atlantic, and many a ship's captain noted in his log the appearance of a gigantic meteorite.

The detonation of the Columbiad was accompanied by a veritable earthquake. Florida was shaken to its depths. The gases of the powder, expanded by the heat, pushed back the strata of the atmosphere with incomparable violence, and this artificial hurricane, a hundred times swifter than any natural tempest, swept through the air like a tornado.

Not one spectator had remained standing; men, women, children were all flattened like ears of corn by a storm; the result was an indescribable panic. J. T. Maston, contrary to all common sense, had stayed too close, and was thrown back one hundred and twenty feet, passing like a bullet over the heads of his compatriots. Three hundred thousand persons suffered temporary deafness and shock.[1]

The waves of air, after flattening huts, squashing cabins, and uprooting trees over a radius of twenty miles, pushed railroad trains back to Tampa, hit that city like an avalanche, and destroyed about a hundred buildings, among others the Church of St. Mary and the new Stock Exchange, which was split right down the middle.[2] Several small boats in the harbor, thrown one against the other, sank at once, and a dozen ships, anchored in the roadstead, snapped their chains as if they were cotton thread, and washed up on the beach.

But the area of devastation extended much further, beyond the limits of the United States. Aided by the west wind, the concussion was felt out in the Atlantic as much as three hundred miles from the American coast. An artificial storm, which Admiral Fitzroy[3] had certainly not expected, hit his ships with unheard of violence; several vessels, including the *Childe Harold*[4] out of Liverpool, caught in this frightful turbulence before they had a chance to lower their sails, sank under full canvas. This regrettable disaster was to become the subject of fierce recriminations on the part of England.

Finally, to leave nothing unrecorded, we should note that natives in

1. *deafness and shock* "The thunderous blastoff at 9:32 A.M. Eastern Daylight Time sent a tremor through the ground and staccato shock waves beating at an estimated total of one million people," *The New York Times* will report in its account of the July 16, 1969 launching of the Apollo 11 moonshot. But some of the other effects that Verne predicts will be achieved only by hydrogen bomb explosions. Barbicane's Columbiad is charged with only 200 tons of guncotton. The atomic bomb that will hit Hiroshima will have the force of 20,000 tons of TNT, which is more explosive than guncotton. And the force of a hydrogen bomb will be measured in scores of millions of tons of TNT.

2. *Split . . . down the middle* Verne's final revenge on the Bourse, where every weekday for six years he "went . . . reluctantly to earn his living," as his grandson tells it.

3. *Admiral Fitzroy* Often Verne chooses his characters' names for their echo value. As he writes this passage, there is a real Vice-Admiral Robert Fitzroy who for thirty years has figured in the news. In 1831, as commander of H.M.S. *Beagle*, he picked up young Charles Darwin and took him on their famous five-year trip around the world. While Darwin collected evidence for his *Origin of Species* (1859), *Descent of Man* (1871), and other works, Fitzroy surveyed the Straits of Magellan and took notes for his two-volume *Narrative of Surveying Voyages* (1839) to which Darwin added a third volume. In 1855 Fitzroy was chosen as chief of the new meteorological department of the Board of Trade. His *Weather Book* (1863) has expressed bold ideas far in advance of his day. But in biological matters he has been a strict traditionalist: since 1859 he has blamed himself for the way Darwin's ideas have hurt religion. At the sensational 1860 debate on evolution between Bishop Samuel Wilberforce and Thomas Henry Huxley, Fitzroy stalked around defen-

sively with a Bible under his arm. And in the year in which this novel appears, Fitzroy feels so guilt-ridden over his early relations with Darwin that he puts a bullet through his brain.

Verne fans will recall another sea captain named for the echo. Shortly after a certain Admiral D. G. Farragut earns fame at Mobile Bay, Verne sends an American commander in pursuit of the *Nautilus*—a commander named Farragut.

4. *Childe Harold* Verne doesn't like the libertine Lord Byron any more than he likes the materialistic Bourse. *Childe Harold's Pilgrimage* (1812–1818) is the four-canto work that made Byron famous. So Verne names a ship *Childe Harold* and sinks it. His contemporary, Mark Twain (1835–1910), enjoys the same kind of fun in *Huckleberry Finn* (1885). Twain doesn't like Sir Walter Scott. Twain has to give a name to a half-sunken river boat. He calls it *Walter Scott*.

5. *weather . . . naval warfare* This is a common superstition in Verne's day, and a prophetic one. The Philadelphia schoolmaster Edward Roth writes in 1874 that Americans have learned "by the bitter experience of several years, that great battles are always followed by violent atmospheric disturbances." Certain charlatans will capitalize on this belief for decades to come. Traveling through the West equipped with cannon, they offer to fire at the sky in any parched area where farmers are desperate enough to pay the fee. And long after World War I, people will say the fierce cannonading in France has changed the world's weather patterns. Scientists will say there's not a shred of proof. But finally scientists themselves will produce the fission and fusion bombs that will change the nature of precipitation. Nuclear explosions cause a rain of radioactive particles that persists for years. Falling to the soil and into streams, these particles can be taken up by plant and animal tissue. If they accumulate in the human system, they may cause bone cancer, leukemia, and damage to the genes.

6. *impenetrable curtain . . . Earth* Verne's description of the aftereffects of his moonshot somewhat anticipates what will happen when Krakatoa, a volcanic island between Java and Sumatra, explodes in 1883. It will throw so much dust into the atmosphere that Europe will enjoy picturesque sunsets for at least a year afterward.

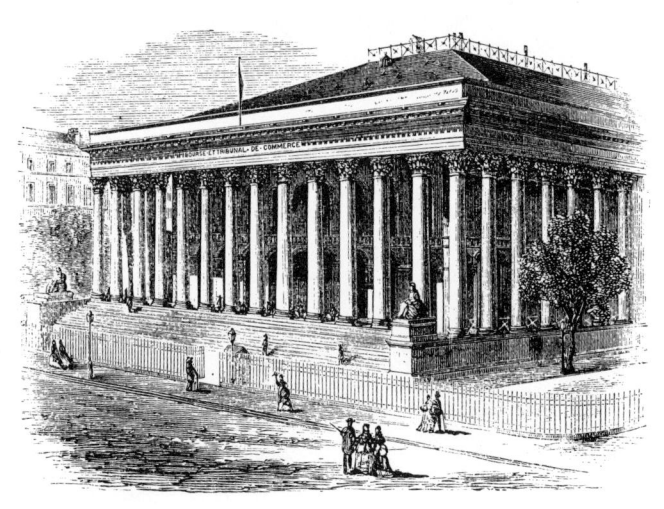

The *Bourse* or Stock Exchange in Paris where author Jules Verne proved to be a mediocre broker. Engraving from *The American Cyclopaedia* (1875).

Gorée and Sierra Leone reported that, half an hour after the launching of the projectile, they had heard a dull boom, the very last displacement of sound waves which, having crossed the Atlantic, died out on the African coast.

But to return to Florida. As soon as the first shock was over, the injured, the deafened, the whole crowd came to life and frenetic cries of "Hurrah for Ardan! Hurray for Barbicane! Hurrah for Nicholl!" rose to the heavens. Several million people, noses in the air, armed with telescopes and opera glasses, were interrogating space, forgetting their contusions and their shock, concerned only with the projectile. But they searched in vain. It was out of sight. They had to resign themselves to waiting for the telegraph to bring the news from Longs Peak. The director of the Cambridge Observatory, Mr. Belfast, was at his post in the Rocky Mountains; he had been entrusted with the task of observing the progress of the projectile.

But a phenomenon that was unforeseen, although easily foreseeable, and about which nothing could be done anyway, now put the public's patience to a severe test.

The weather, superb until now, suddenly changed; the sky became thick with clouds. How could it have been otherwise, after that terrible displacement of the strata of the atmosphere, and that dispersion of enormous quantities of vapors caused by the explosion of 400,000 pounds of guncotton? The whole natural order had been disturbed. This could not really surprise anyone, because it is well known that the weather is often abruptly changed by the firing of big guns in naval warfare.[5]

The following day, the sun rose above a horizon thick with clouds; an impenetrable curtain stretched between the sky and the Earth;[6] unhappily, it extended even to the Rocky Mountains. This was a disaster. A chorus of protests came in from all over the world. But nature was adamant: since men had disturbed the atmosphere with their detonation, they had to suffer the consequences.

During that first day, everyone tried to see through that opaque veil of clouds, but everyone failed, and anyhow, they were all wrong to be looking up since, as a consequence of the Earth's rotation, the projectile was now flying away from the antipodes.[7]

And then, when night fell, it was a night impenetrable and profound, so that when the moon rose over the horizon, it was impossible to see her; she seemed deliberately to be hiding from those men who had had the temerity to shoot at her. No observations were possible, and telegrams from Longs Peak confirmed this contretemps.

However, if the experiment had succeeded, the voyagers, having left at forty-six minutes and forty seconds after ten on the night of December 1, would reach their destination at midnight of December 4.[8] And so, until that time, especially since in such weather it would have been difficult to observe such a small shell, the world just had to be patient.

On the night of December 4, between eight o'clock and midnight, it might have been possible to track the projectile, which might have appeared as a black dot on the bright disk of the moon. But the skies

7. *away from the antipodes* Out from the exact opposite side of the Earth. The word *antipodes* has a lovely exotic ring in Verne's day, the last great age of terrestrial exploration. The word derives from Greek meaning "with the feet opposite"—that is, people who live in the *antipodes* "have their feet against ours." In 1800, British seamen discovered a group of rocky uninhabited islands southeast of New Zealand, just 180°—halfway around the world—from Greenwich, England. They named them the Antipodes. By the time Verne writes this passage, the expression is often used to mean that part of the other side of the globe dominated by Australia.

8. *midnight of December 4* Actually, as we saw in Chapter IV, they would make their rendezvous with the moon *at midnight of December 5*, a correction Verne himself will make in the "Preliminary Chapter" of *Round the Moon* (1870).

The director of the Cambridge Observatory . . . was at his post in the Rocky Mountains . . . Engraving from the 1872 edition of From the Earth to the Moon.

Foucault's telescope is mounted in the Paris Observatory, which is pictured in the 1878 edition of Verne's novel *Hector Servadac*.

9. *telescopes . . . Foucault's* We have already met all three of these scientists (Chapters II, V, XXIV). Sir John Herschel's telescope—the one he took to the Cape of Good Hope—is back home in Slough, England. Lord Rosse's is mounted in his park at Parsonstown, Ireland, and Léon Foucault's is at the Paris Observatory.

10. *Wild schemes . . . clouds* Another successful Verne prophecy: these schemes will approach reality in the twentieth century. American scientists will experiment with ways of "seeding" clouds with chemicals or ice to make them drop their moisture and cease to be clouds. They will use these techniques in an effort to affect the weather adversely in Indochina and Cuba, and to bring rain to drought-stricken farmlands in the states.

were still clouded over, and the public experienced agonies of desperation. Some people flung insults at the moon for not showing her face. A sad state of affairs!

In despair, J. T. Maston went to Longs Peak to see for himself. He never doubted that his friends would reach their destination. Besides, there had been no news of the projectile's having fallen anywhere on any continent or island, and J. T. Maston could not face for an instant the possibility it had fallen in the seas which cover three fourths of the globe.

On December 5, the same weather. The great telescopes of the Old World, Herschel's, Rosse's, Foucault's,[9] were constantly focused on the celebrity of the night, for it so happened that the skies were clear in Europe; but the relative weakness of these instruments made their observations useless.

December 6, same weather. Impatience gripped three quarters of the globe. Wild schemes were being proposed for dissipating the thick collection of clouds.[10]

December 7, the sky changed somewhat. There was hope, but it was short-lived, for by evening thick clouds once again protected the starry skies from scrutiny.

Now the situation was becoming critical. Indeed, on December 11, at eleven minutes past nine in the morning, the moon would enter her last quarter. Thereafter she would be waning, and even if the skies were to clear, the chance of observation would be very slight, for the moon would be showing a constantly decreasing portion of her disk and finally would become a new moon, which is to say, she would set and rise with the sun, whose rays would make her absolutely invisible. They would have to wait until January 3—when there would be a full moon at forty-seven minutes after midnight—to resume their observations.

The newspapers discussed these developments in great detail and with thousands of commentaries, concluding always that the public would have to display angelic patience.

December 8, nothing. On December 9, the sun reappeared for a moment as if to mock the Americans. It was greeted with jeers and hisses, and, offended no doubt by this reception, proved very miserly with its rays.

December 10, still no change. J. T. Maston nearly went out of his mind, and there were fears for this worthy man's brain, which until now had been well protected by his gutta-percha skull.

But on December 11, one of those appalling storms that develop in the semi-tropical regions was unleashed in the atmosphere. Strong east winds cleared away the clouds that had been piled high for so long, and that night the half-wasted disk of the celebrity of the night marched majestically among the clear constellations in the sky.

CHAPTER XXVIII

A New Heavenly Body

1. *passed to one side* Verne begins his big gamble. He takes a chance on frustrating us. We need to know the fate of the spacemen. He needs to create suspense for his sequel, *Round the Moon* (1870). Why has the projectile missed its mark? Was it because of human error? Or has something deflected them from their course? Instead of resolving these questions, Verne will suggest a broad spectrum of possibilities. He makes perfect use now of point of view, in contrast to his flubbing it in Chapter XVIII. Since the astronauts locked themselves in, Verne has told us only what we can know from without. He saves the shift in point of view for his next novel, when we can go inside the spacecraft and find out first-hand what the three men have experienced.

2. *a true satellite* But, if they actually *were* passing the moon, then probably all the moon's attraction could do would be *either* to change their course as they move on into Outer Space, *or* to start them falling back to Earth. *Unless* something has slowed them down as they were nearing the moon. . . . Is it possible they used their retrojets in a successful effort to prevent themselves from hurtling out into the far reaches of the galaxy?

3. *2,833 miles* Assuming the projectile's path is nearly circular, then it would be orbiting the moon about twice a day. Another question for the sequel to answer: Why hasn't Belfast given at least this approximate orbit period?

By contrast, the orbit of the Apollo eleven command module will range from 62 to 75 miles above the moon's surface.

4. *attained their goal* But if the shell really has become *a true satellite*, then lunar gravity could not pull it down. The moon's gravity would be just strong enough to bend the shell's path into a closed orbit, in which it would travel forever—*unless*—again Verne leaves it open to discussion—*unless* the moon has an atmosphere, *or* the astronauts help the moon pull

That very night, the exciting, long-awaited news sounded like a thunderclap over the United States, and then, jumping across the ocean, ran through all the telegraph wires of the world. The projectile had been sighted, thanks to the gigantic reflector on Longs Peak.

Here is the memorandum drawn up by the director of the Cambridge Observatory. It contains his scientific conclusions about that great experiment of the Gun Club.

Longs Peak, December 12

To the Staff of the Cambridge Observatory:

The projectile launched by the Columbiad at Stony Hill was observed by Messrs. Belfast and J. T. Maston on December 12, forty-seven minutes after eight o'clock in the evening, when the moon had entered its last quarter.

The projectile has not reached the moon. It passed to one side [1] of it but close enough, however, to be captured by lunar gravity. Thus its linear motion has been changed to a circular motion of extreme rapidity, and it is following an elliptical orbit around the moon, of which it has become a true satellite. [2]

We have not yet been able to determine the basic facts about this new heavenly body. We know neither the speed of its revolutions nor the speed of its rotation. But we have estimated that its mean distance from the surface of the moon is about 2,833 miles. [3]

And under the circumstances, two hypotheses suggest themselves:

Either the moon will eventually draw the projectile to its surface, and the voyagers will have attained their goal; [4]

Or, in accordance with an immutable law of nature, the projectile will remain in orbit around the lunar disk until the end of time. [5]

Our observations will someday resolve this question, but at the moment, we can report only one result of the Gun Club experiment: it has added a new heavenly body to the solar system.

J. M. Belfast

This unexpected dénouement gave rise to a host of new questions. What great mysteries now lay in wait for scientific investigation! Thanks to the courage and devotion of three men, this project of sending a bullet to the moon, once seen as a futile enterprise, had already produced concrete results, with incalculable consequences. The voyagers, imprisoned in their new satellite, had not reached their destination, but at least they had become part of the lunar world; they were in orbit around the celebrity of the night, and, for the first time, the human eye could penetrate all her mysteries. The names of Nicholl, Barbicane, and Michel Ardan would be forever celebrated in the annals of astronomy, for these bold explorers, eager to widen the circle of human knowledge, had audaciously launched themselves into space, gambling their lives in the strangest undertaking of modern times.

However that might be, once the memorandum from Longs Peak became known a feeling of surprise and fear swept over the world. Was it possible to go to the aid of those bold inhabitants of the Earth? No, not at all, because they had placed themselves beyond the pale of humanity by transcending the limits God had set for his earthly creatures. They had enough air for two months. They had enough food for a year. But then? Even the most hardened hearts beat faster at this terrible question.

them down. Does Belfast believe enough in a lunar atmosphere to think its resistance will slow down the projectile until it falls into the moon? An atmosphere extending 2,833 miles up? Or does Belfast think the same force that maybe slowed down the projectile as it neared the moon will function again?

5. *end of time* Assuming they have been pulled into orbit in the first place. There is a third possibility, but Verne saves it for future use. For the sake of his plot, he makes Belfast and Maston a bit obtuse. And we connive at this literary convention. If Doctor Watson could understand everything as fast as Sherlock Holmes can, then A. Conan Doyle wouldn't be able to create much suspense.

The Gun Club's vehicle-projectile found afloat in the Pacific. Engraving from the 1872 edition of *Round the Moon*.

6. *resolve this situation soon* And so Verne ends his book on a dissonant two-tone chord: a note of triumph and a note of suspense. Man can escape Earth's gravity and cross Outer Space (one of Verne's major prophecies). But what has happened to the first astronauts?

Verne and Garcet will wait three years before they themselves *resolve this situation* in detail. Then Verne will publish *Round the Moon* first in the adult magazine *Journal des Débats* (1869), and the following year as a book. He opens that novel with a "Preliminary Chapter" that reviews the action of *From the Earth to the Moon* (1865). This gives our overworked author a chance to correct his own confusion about the date of rendezvous (he changes it to December 5, as we explained in Chapter IV) and to expand on some of the problems we have raised in this chapter. Belfast, for example, could not give details like the orbit period for the new satellite because with an elliptical orbit, at least three observations are required. (We give our estimate above, based on Belfast's one observation, by assuming a nearly circular orbit.) Then Verne tears into the basic assumptions of the December 12 memorandum: Belfast and Maston were guilty of rushing to conclusions. In assuming the moon could capture the projectile as a satellite, they violated the laws of mechanics; presumably Verne has in mind the point made in our note on *a true satellite*. Only their first hypothesis "could be fulfilled"—and Verne expands on it now—"the one that assumes the voyagers would link their own efforts with the moon's attraction in order to reach the moon's surface." Finally, in addition to their theoretical errors, Belfast and Maston have committed observational errors. Apparently they never actually saw the projectile. Certainly they could not have seen the projectile near the moon on the night of December 11–12. Where was it then?

That's the subject of the sequel, in which Verne brilliantly develops the third possibility that Belfast and Maston overlooked. Without destroying the reader's enjoyment of Verne's chapter-by-chapter suspense, we can simply say this: much against their will, in spite of all their efforts, in helpless obedience to the laws of physics, Ardan, Nicholl, and Barbicane have only looped the moon and then returned to Earth. On the very night when Belfast thought he had the projectile in focus in his telescope, the shell has whooshed down into the ocean 250 miles off California.

For more than a century after *Round the Moon* appears, astronomers and s-f buffs will argue—in *Popular Astronomy* (1942), for example, and in *Bulletin of the Pacific Rocket Society* (1952)—about the astronomical phenomenon that brought about Verne's "third possibility." And in 1969 the astronaut Frank Borman will write to Verne's grandson: "Our space vehicle was launched from Florida, like Barbicane's, . . . and it splashed down in the Pacific a mere two and a half miles from the point mentioned in the novel."

Only one man refused to admit that the situation was hopeless. Only one man was still confident, and that was their devoted friend, audacious and determined like them, the brave J. T. Maston.

He never took his eyes off them. His home was now the Longs Peak Observatory; his horizon, the mirror of the huge reflector. As soon as the moon rose in the sky, he focused her in the field of the telescope, he did not lose her for a moment, and he followed her assiduously in her march across the starry reaches; with everlasting patience he observed the projectile's passage across the silver disk, and truly this worthy man remained in constant communion with his three friends, whom he fully expected to see again someday.

"As soon as circumstances permit," he would say to anyone willing to listen, "we shall communicate with them. We'll get news to them, and they'll get news to us! Yes, I know them, they are ingenious men. Those three have taken with them, out into space, all the resources of art, of science, and of industry. With such resources, they can accomplish anything; you wait and see, they will resolve this situation soon!" **6**

AFTERWORD

Revaluation of
From the Earth to the Moon

Now we can understand why readers and critics on the Continent think of Verne not simply as a science seer but also as a social prophet. For now we have experienced *From the Earth to the Moon* as they know it, as he wanted us to have it—not as the "standard" translators diluted it, not as the myth-making process passed his story down to us.

Going back to the real Verne has paid off in pleasant surprises. It seems he had a better grasp of the problems involved in getting to the moon than the myth gives him credit for. Putting space science in its total human context, he starred as a social satirist, he predicted even some of the economic and political features of the space effort. And he pioneered in what we now call surrealist and psychoanalytic techniques in fiction. Indeed, the fully restored text demonstrates that Verne is a much more sensitive, imaginative, and successful *novelist for adults* than his American reputation would lead us to expect.

Let's first review his score as a science prophet. He was the first fiction-writer systematically to apply the science of ballistics to the problems of putting *man* into space. In the course of his calculations, he hit on what has proved to be a typical flight-time for manned spacecraft en route to the moon. He correctly predicted, for the right scientific reasons, that the American moonshots would be launched from Florida: his launching site was only 137 miles from the pads at Cape Kennedy. He anticipated the approximate weight and size of our manned space capsule. He prophesied the use of rockets for retrojets—a self-fulfilling prophecy, since it inspired early space scientists to think of rockets as doing the whole job. He anticipated experiments with animals to measure the effect of space travel on living creatures, and experiments with the splashdown as a means of cushioning the landing. He predicted that blastoff would send a tremor through the ground and shock-waves beating through the crowd.

Along the way, he anticipated that telescopes—like those installed at Mount Palomar (1948) and in the Caucasus (1976)—would reach diameters of sixteen feet and more; that American scientists would tackle the riddle of the rilles, experiment with water as a shock absorber, and try to control the weather. He gambled against the prevailing views of his day that aluminum, guncotton, and the Atlantic Cable would be expensive failures. He even foresaw that space scientists would someday consider light and electricity as mechanical agents.

While he was scoring so many home-runs, he also struck out a few times. He backed a faulty experiment on the speed of electricity and a shaky hypothesis on the origins of gunpowder; he overestimated what Earth-based telescopes of the future would be able to do. He failed to protect his spacecraft from air resistance and his astronauts from the impact of his kind of blastoff. Indeed he chose the wrong kind of motive power for his moonshot: to hit .966 he should have let rocketry do the whole job. But surely one good reason he chose gunnery rather than rocketry (aside from the piffling impotence of rockets in his day) is that launching his spacecraft from a gun better served his purposes as a social satirist.

So now let's check his score as a social prophet. He not only sensed that arch-imperialists of his own century would, like Cecil Rhodes, cast greedy eyes on the heavens. He also divined that it would be the military-industrial complex—makers and users of weapons—who would launch the Space Age. He predicted that the space effort would provide a peacetime spillover for the pentup energies of the world's military juggernauts. He foresaw the race to reach the moon as a ritualization of war. He so constructed his plot that it becomes an outright plea that space travel be developed as a civilian enterprise, *not* as a glorification of the military. He even calculated the sudden huge economic and demographic growth of Florida during the Age of Space. He anticipated our psychological concerns about meeting extraterrestrials. Indeed, the more of the real Verne we enjoy, the more we realize that the actual space effort—right down to many details of the Apollo and Pioneer projects—has been one long replay of Jules Verne.

Just as his moonshot is his extrapolation of the Earth-bound science of his day, so his social prophecies stem from his shrewd grasp of the world situation. He makes what our critics have narrowly regarded as a science-fiction novel serve also as an all-out satire on militarism. Just think of those Gun Clubbers, a convention of animated prosthetic devices, lamenting the "sterility" of peacetime. Of the way they decorate their meeting hall. Of Maston's two hilarious tries at finding a new justification for war. Of their blind inability to see their project as anything more than target practice on a cosmic scale. Then you realize that no writer—not even Aristophanes, Voltaire, or Joseph Heller—has conceived of better ways to satirize war and the military mind. And think of the theatergoers turned vandals in the swift scene that revolves on clever puns with Shakespearean titles. Of the grim, then poignant melodrama in Skersnaw Woods. Then you realize Verne sees the American love of violence as a strange perversion of democratic freedom.

But Verne doesn't pick on Americans alone. He builds up to an excellent parody of the Golden Rule as practiced by all Christian war-makers including his own Emperor. Maston's comic efforts to find new reasons for invading Mexico serve, as we have seen, to condemn France as well as the U.S.A. Verne so continually draws attention to his own government's shabby foreign and domestic policy that by the end of the novel the only villain left unredeemed is the Emperor Louis Napoleon. No wonder the French critic Chesneaux calls Verne a writer of political fiction.

To develop these diverse concerns, Verne designs a seemingly simple plot. Actually it combines the powerful appeal of two archetypal themes: preparation for a voyage into the unknown, and arrival of an "outsider" who sets things right. And Verne arranges his events so they gradually widen his characters' scope. The story rises steadily from their struggle with narrowly technical questions to their involvement in humanistic problems to their many-sided, scientific-and-human, triumph.

Verne deliberately introduces his Gun Clubbers as mere stick figures, mere blueprints of what men can be, before the "outsider" arrives. Ardan's main mission is to bring flesh-and-blood into the picture, to humanize the Club and their project, to "pacify" American duelists and artillerists.

Before Ardan, Barbicane is the best personality the Gun Club can produce: a chronometer on scissors-legs, a narrow technical genius, the utilitarian, the living proof of the efficacy of the work ethic, the enemy of fun and other trifles. True, in Maston he seems to have a comic sidekick, but Maston provides fun not so much for the Club as for the reader. Nicholl is the sinister enemy of "progress" and hence the villain. All these farcical figures are transformed through meeting Ardan. Maston, an all-out chauvinist who can't bear to hear of accomplishments by any nationality except his own, suddenly becomes an outright hero-worshiper of a foreigner. The straightahead rational Barbicane also cracks under the sweet influence of the Frenchman: first Barbicane zigzags, contradicts himself, then softens, slows down, actually learns how to chat casually, and becomes fond of someone who wants most of all to enjoy life. Even the villain yields to Ardan, who has correctly sensed that the captain's hate is really love and proves it.

In relying on archetypal characters and situations, Verne explores basic dream and sexual symbolism. He names Barbicane after a commanding tower, he makes Nicholl feel impotent and jealous when Barbicane erects his 900-foot tube. Verne uses the dreams of these rivals to show that their military ecstasy is really displaced sexual energy and anxiety: Barbicane always penetrating, Nicholl striving mightily to remain unviolated. At several points, just as he did in *Twenty Thousand Leagues,* Verne resorts to withdrawal into the womb. The Gun Clubbers stage a stag banquet deep in the Earth, fed by a 900-foot umbilical cord. Maston withdraws for a week of sealed-in solitude in the capsule. At the end, the puritanical president, the ex-villain, and the humanizing hero all return to the womb for their longed-for rebirth.

Verne's talent for orchestrated symbolism is nowhere clearer than in the forest scene. He first creates the overall vista of the Kentucky duel. Then he zooms in on the spider-and-bird conflict.

The spider's web becomes a microcosm of the woods as arena for the duel, the spider's snare a symbol for the ambush that Nicholl wants to stage for Barbicane. The very language needed to describe the primitive animal conflict meanwhile advances the "human" drama: contrapuntally.

That he was in touch with his own Unconscious when he explored such phallic, womb, and snare symbolism is evident in Verne's failures as well as his successes. We have noted how he falters over the length of certain telescopes, unable to grant Herschel's and Rosse's tubes their full, stupendous length. His fidelity to his unconscious resources—which leads him into such baffling personal discomfort—makes him a pioneer of surrealist and psychoanalytic techniques in fiction.

For today's reader, Verne's worst stumbling, in the literary dimension, occurs when he violates his point-of-view. In Chapters V and VI he loses sight of his characters as he switches from drama to essay. And in Chapter XVIII he starts to describe Ardan as the Frenchman first impresses a stranger, but then Verne gets so carried away he tells us things Barbicane could never perceive as first impressions. Such shifts are more annoying to us post-Henry-Jamesians than they were to Verne's original readers. Raised on Scott and Cooper, they accepted a blurring of a character's perceptions with the author's views.

In this novel Verne continues to develop the science-fiction techniques we have (in the Foreword) seen him as inventing in *Five Weeks in a Balloon*. He continually reminds his readers of the ongoing successes of real scientists of their own day—Deville, Reiset, Ménard, Maynard. Thus he encourages his readers to believe in the success of his fictitious scientists and their futuristic projects. He invokes present scientific wonders to "prove" future ones. When he's up against a problem he can't really solve, like gees acceleration, at least he fusses with it until we become so familiar with it we relax about it. Meanwhile he has honestly solved so many other problems we accept success in all of them, again, "success by association."

All these triumphs—scientific, socio-political, literary—were muffled by the "standard" translators who were most responsible for shaping the Verne known to the English-speaking world. Readers interested in retracing the career of *From the Earth to the Moon* in translation may mull over the detailed evidence we give in Appendix B. But all of us, by simply comparing Verne revisited with the Verne myth we knew, can rest content at this point, having come to appreciate the rehabilitated Verne: the Verne of broad social as well as scientific vision.

WALTER JAMES MILLER

New York University

APPENDIX A
How Barbicane Calculated His Initial Velocity

Barbicane has arrived at his "initial velocity of 12,000 yards per second" (p. 13) by using an "energy-balance" equation with values derived from some standard text. His audience knows the basic assumptions on which his calculations are based. Any object suspended above the Earth's center has, as a consequence of the Earth's gravity, a certain energy known as *potential energy*. For a simple illustration, we need only release the object and observe that when it strikes the ground, it gives off energy in the form of sound, dust clouds, heat. Now, according to the law of conservation of energy, in order to raise that object in the first place, we need to expend another kind of energy, *kinetic energy,* or energy of motion.

As every Gun Clubber knows, for Barbicane's projectile the kinetic energy is to be provided by the initial, or muzzle, velocity. As the projectile rises, its speed diminishes because its energy of motion is being gradually converted into its energy as suspended object. When it reaches its highest point—and for Barbicane, that's the moon—all its kinetic energy will be in the form of potential energy.

Putting it mathematically, Barbicane sees the potential energy required as:

$$\frac{GmM}{r_1} - \frac{GmM}{r_2}$$

where G is the universal gravitational constant; M is the Earth's mass; m is the projectile's mass; r_1 is the Earth's radius; and r_2 is the radius of the moon's orbit or distance from the Earth when it is in its perigee position (closest to the Earth). He knows that the kinetic energy is $\frac{1}{2}mv^2$, where v is the projectile's speed. This gives Barbicane his equation for balancing the potential and kinetic energy involved:

$$\frac{GmM}{r_1} - \frac{GmM}{r_2} = \frac{1}{2}mv^2$$

Through simple algebra, Barbicane cancels m out of the equation. In other words, a projectile of any weight would require the same initial velocity; it's irrelevant that he does not yet know the mass of his projectile. And for G times M, he can substitute μ, a measure of the Earth's gravitational attraction, which is calculated from the moon's period and distance. And so he now has:

$$\frac{\mu}{r_1} - \frac{\mu}{r_2} = \frac{1}{2}v^2$$

He transposes:

$$v = \sqrt{2\left(\frac{\mu}{r_1} - \frac{\mu}{r_2}\right)}$$

Now he substitutes values for μ, r_1, and r_2. These he takes from any one of many standard astronomical works which, we must remember, varied in details because astonomers were continually refining their measurement techniques. Consulting at random some textbooks of the time, we find, for example, that values for the Earth's radius varied from 3,920 to 3,960 miles; for the moon's perigee from 219,000 to 222,000 miles; for the moon's period from 27.32 to 27.3217 days; for μ from 88,900 to 93,700. But simply to illustrate how Barbicane worked, let us use here the higher values, with no assurance at all that these are the same ones he employed. Thus

$$\frac{\mu}{r_1} = 23.66 \qquad \frac{\mu}{r_2} = .42$$
$$v = \sqrt{2(23.66 - .42)}$$

or $v = \sqrt{46.48}$ or 6.82 miles per second.

Multiplying by 5,280 for the number of feet per mile, Barbicane arrives at 36,0009.6 feet, or 12,003.2 yards per second, and rounds off his figure to 12,000 yards per second.

DAVID WOODRUFF
WALTER JAMES MILLER

APPENDIX B
Some Notes for Purists on Verne's Translators

As a guide for readers who might want to retrace, in greater detail, Verne's career in America, here's a rating of five earlier versions of *From the Earth to the Moon*. Let's start with the Mercier-King team:

They weakened the scientific integrity of the novel by cutting out: how all America enjoyed Barbicane's speech via telegraphy (Chapter III); one-third of Chapter V, including ancient hypotheses about the moon; descriptions of eclipses and the way the moon's rotation and revolution are accomplished in the same period (VI); references to Deville's successes with aluminum, to the original shape of the projectile and the possibility of using it to send messages (VII); 300 words on the shape of the Columbiad (VIII); Verne's history-of-science joke about Ménard-Maynard (IX); his satire on American railroads, his background material on earlier successes with deep wells (XIV); his background information on the cooling of Rodman's giant gun (XVI); many of Ardan's references to astronomic phenomena and to a future "train of projectiles," although this last explains the most famous illustration in the book! (XIX); discussion of the need to change the projectile's shape, of the Reiset-Regnault experiments, of many details about the structure and interior of the capsule (XXIII); eight paragraphs of adult education on the different types of telescopes and the advantages of each (XXIV); many of the effects of the blastoff, including the distress of Mercier's countryman Fitzroy (XXVII); and a passage that sums up the overall effects of the enterprise! (XXVIII).

The Reverend Mercier, a Protestant, showed his annoyance over Verne's remarks of a religious nature by cutting, for example, his references to the Club's enshrinement of Matson's gun-bits as holy relics (II), to the Catholic Saint Barbara, to the Clubbers as "Exterminating Angels," to their translation of Newton's law into its "moral equivalent" (I).

Englishpersons Mercier and King further weakened Verne's social satire and prophecy by cutting: his review of the murderous effects of artillery (I), Maston's first effort to find new grounds for war (II), the passage on the brutal tactics of imperialist nations (III), Maston's curse at the English, Verne's remark about the Bastille and Charenton (VII), 300 words on Maston's second effort to find new grounds for war (XI), 400 words on the miraculous growth of Florida as the space base (XVI), and many colorful details about the people who flock there (XXV).

They repeatedly weakened Verne's characterization of the supporting cast by cutting, for example, witty paragraphs about Blomsberry (I) *and of the main characters by cutting,* for example: the description of Maston's ideal cannon (without which the illustration makes no sense!) and Maston's clever joke about why an artilleryman is like a cannonball (VIII); Verne's naughty sexual symbolism (X); the paragraph about Barbicane's virtuosity and ubiquity (XIV); one-half the full-length portrait of Ardan (XVIII); and 500 words of dialogue which contrasts Barbicane's utilitarianism with Ardan's estheticism and reveals Barbicane as learning to relax (XVIII).

We have listed here only the major omissions. Needless to say, translators working with such bias and such haste tended to chop away anything they didn't like, anything technical that would have taken time to understand and to phrase well, any nicety the reader unfamiliar with the original would never miss. *They cut about one-quarter of Verne's novel.*

Schoolteacher Edward Roth, as we indicated in the Foreword, simply used Verne as an outline for Roth, as a rubric for his own free associations. He defused Verne's message by making it diffuse. All of the characters sound alike, that is, like Roth himself. For example, in Chapter II, Verne's cool, dignified Barbicane becomes a raving maniac: "he roared till he was black in the face. His arms played around his head like the sails of a windmill. . . ."

Philadelphian Roth uses Verne as a garbage can for Roth's grievances against Women's Rights, Congressmen, the Philadelphia High School, and the Orion Debating Society of Catharine Street, Philadelphia. He gives us the impression that Verne wrote the story in the first person. So thoroughly does he confuse himself with Verne we think the French author once composed verses for an address to the Polytechnic College of Philadelphia. And Roth quotes the verses. Further to suit his local pride and promote the Philadelphia Centennial Exposition (1876), he updates all the action by a decade, so that Barbicane can step right out of the moon novels to render "the great CENTENNIAL of his country a still greater and more wonderful success than his . . . JOURNEY through the boundless fields of ether. . . ."

That this travesty could reappear, in our time, in England as well as in America, shows the depths of neglect Verne had fallen into.

Even three new versions published between 1967 and 1970 failed to displace the "standards" from schools, libraries, and gift shops. Each was, in its own way, unequipped for such a cyclopean task. The first, *almost* a complete translation, failed to capture the zest of Verne's work and, besides, appeared only in paperback in a day when that meant reviewers would ignore it. The second, a plodding, cautious work, was aimed at juvenile audiences, and it also failed to attract serious critical attention. The third, based on the Mercier-King text with conscientious restorations, was issued in a limited high-priced bibliophile edition.

Worst of all, none of these new editions took the pains to explain how it differed from the "standard" versions or even to indicate that there was a Verne problem. Such gestures, in other words, did little to threaten the hegemony of the Reverend Lewis Page Mercier, who—translating under the bylines of Louis Mercier or Mercier Lewis—had all but doomed Verne's reputation in America.

WALTER JAMES MILLER

New York University

SELECTED BIBLIOGRAPHY

Listed here are selected writings—biographical, critical, historical, scientific, technical—likely to prove interesting to readers of *The Annotated Jules Verne*. Works from Verne's own period (1828–1905) show the state of knowledge in his day, the kinds of raw material out of which he fashioned his science fiction. Background works from our own day are helpful to us in judging the validity of Verne's predictions and in gaining new perspective on problems he tackled. Some writings listed are out of print and must be hunted down in libraries, antique shops, and rare-book stores. A few are not yet translated into English. Every one of these writings has figured in the shaping of *The Annotated Jules Verne*.

AGRICOLA, GEORGIUS. *De Re Metallica*. Translated, with introduction, notes, and appendixes, by Herbert Clark Hoover and Lou Henry Hoover. Second edition. New York: Dover Publications, 1950. Also see Chapter 2, "Agricola's Classic Treatise," in Walter James Miller, *Engineers as Writers* (cited below).

ALDISS, BRIAN W. *Billion Year Spree: The True History of Science Fiction*. Garden City, New York: Doubleday & Company, Inc., 1973.

ALLOTT, KENNETH. *Jules Verne*. New York: The Macmillan Company, 1941.

ALLOTTE DE LA FUŸE, MARGUERITE. *Jules Verne*. Translated by Erik de Mauny. New York: Coward-McCann, Inc., 1956.

ALTER, DINSMORE. *Pictorial Guide to the Moon*. Revised by Joseph H. Jackson. Third Revised Edition. New York: Thomas Y. Crowell Company, 1973.

ASIMOV, ISAAC. "An Introduction to this Edition." Jules Verne, *A Journey to the Center of the Earth*. New York: The Heritage Press, 1966.

BAILEY, SOLON I. *History and Work of the Harvard Observatory*. New York: McGraw-Hill Book Co., Inc., 1931.

BARING-GOULD, SABINE. *The Book of Were-Wolves: Being an Account of a Terrible Superstition*. London: 1865.—New York: Causeway Books, 1973.

BARTRAM, WILLIAM. *Travels through North & South Carolina, Georgia, East & West Florida*. Philadelphia: James & Johnson, 1791.—Edited by Mark Van Doren. New York: Dover Publications, 1955.—Edited, with commentary and annotated index, by Francis Harper. Naturalists edition. New Haven: Yale University Press, 1958.

BEIRNE, FRANCIS F. *The Amiable Baltimoreans*. Hatboro, Pennsylvania: Tradition Press, 1968.

BERRY, ARTHUR. *A Short History of Astronomy*. London: John Murray, 1898.—New York: Dover Publications, 1961.

BRAUN, WERNHER VON, and FREDERICK I. ORDWAY III. *History of Rocketry and Space Travel*. Third Revised Edition. New York: Thomas Y. Crowell Company, 1975.

BREVARD, CAROLINE MAYS. *A History of Florida*. Deland: The Florida State Historical Society, 1925.

BRINTON, CRANE, JOHN B. CHRISTOPHER, and ROBERT LEE WOLFF. *A History of Civilization: 1815 to the Present*. Fifth edition. Englewood Cliffs, New Jersey: Prentice-Hall, Inc., 1976.

BROWNE, MALCOLM W. "Scientists Expect New Clues to Origin of Universe." *The New York Times,* March 12, 1978.

CADE, MAXWELL C. *Other Worlds Than Ours.* New York: Taplinger Publishing Company, 1967.

CHESNEAUX, JEAN. *The Political and Social Ideas of Jules Verne.* Translated by Thomas Wikeley. London: Thames and Hudson, 1972.

CLARKE, ARTHUR C. "Introduction." Jules Verne, *From the Earth to the Moon* and *Round the Moon.* New York: Dodd, Mead & Company, 1962.

COCHRAN, HAMILTON. *Noted American Duels and Hostile Encounters.* Philadelphia: Chilton Books, 1963.

COGGINS, JACK. *Arms and Equipment of the Civil War.* Garden City, New York: Doubleday & Company, Inc., 1962.

COMPARATO, FRANK E. *Age of Great Guns.* Harrisburg, Pennsylvania: The Stackpole Company, 1965.

CYRANO DE BERGERAC, SAVINIEN. *Histoire comique des Estats et Empires de la Lune.* Paris, 1656.—*Histoire comique des Estats et Empires du Soleil.* Paris, 1662.—*Voyages to the Moon and the Sun.* Richard Aldington, translator. Philadelphia: Richard West, 1962.

DEPUY, W. H., editor. *The World-Wide Encyclopedia and Gazetteer.* Twelve volumes. New York: The Christian Herald, 1899.

DRUYAN, ANNE. "Earth's Greatest Hits." *The New York Times Magazine,* September 4, 1977.

DUFAY, JEAN. *Introduction to Astrophysics: The Stars.* Translated by Owen Gingerich. New York: Dover Publications, Inc., 1964.

DUNN, HAMPTON. *Yesterday's Tampa.* Miami, Florida: E. A. Seeman Publishing, Inc., 1972.

Encyclopaedia Britannica, The. Ninth edition. Twenty-four volumes. New York: The Henry G. Allen Company, 1890.

FONTENELLE, BERNARD LE BOVIER DE. *Entretiens sur la Pluralité des Mondes.* Paris, 1686.—*Conversations on the Plurality of Worlds.* W. Gardiner, translator. London: A. Bettesworth, 1715.

FOOTE, SHELBY. *The Civil War: A Narrative.* Three volumes. New York: Random House, 1958–1974.

FORBES, R. J., and E. J. DIJKSTERHUIS. *A History of Science and Technology.* Two volumes. Baltimore, Maryland: Penguin Books, 1963.

GELMAN, DAVID, et al. "Seeking Other Worlds." *Newsweek,* August 15, 1977.

[GODWIN, FRANCIS.] *The Man in the Moone: or a Discourse of a Voyage thither. By Domingo Gonsales The speedy Messenger.* London, 1638.—Reprinted in *Smith College Studies in Modern Languages* XIX, 1937.

HAMMOND, J. L. and BARBARA. *The Rise of Modern Industry.* London: Methuen, 1925.—New York: Harcourt, Brace, 1926.

HARTMANN, WILLIAM K. "Cratering in the Solar System." *Scientific American,* January 1977.

HAYES, JOHN R., editor. *The Genius of Arab Civilization: Source of Renaissance.* New York: New York University Press, 1975.

HEIDMANN, J. Letter. *Sky and Telescope.* July 1977.

HOGG, BRIGADIER O. F. G. *Artillery: Its Origin, Heyday and Decline.* Hamden, Connecticut: Archon Books, 1970.

JASTROW, ROBERT, and MALCOLM M. THOMPSON. *Astronomy: Fundamentals and Frontiers.* Second edition. New York: John Wiley & Sons, Inc., 1974.

JONES, BESSIE ZABAN, and LYLE GIFFORD BOYD. *The Harvard College Observatory: The First Four Directorships, 1839–1919.* Cambridge, Massachusetts: The Belknap Press of Harvard University Press, 1971.

JULES-VERNE, JEAN. *Jules Verne.* Translated and adapted by Roger Greaves. New York: Taplinger Publishing Company, 1976.

———. "Introduction." Jules Verne, *From the Earth to the Moon* and *Around the Moon.* New York: The Heritage Press, 1970.

KANE, HARNETT T. *Gentlemen, Swords, and Pistols.* New York: William Morrow and Company, 1951.

KENNEDY, STETSON. *Palmetto Country.* New York: Duell, Sloan & Pearce, 1942.

LANIER, SIDNEY. *Florida: Its Scenery, Climate, and History.* Philadelphia: J. B. Lippincott & Co., 1875.—Gainesville: University of Florida Press, 1973.

LEY, WILLY. *Watchers of the Skies*. New York: The Viking Press, 1963.

Lou Ana. A History of Lou Ana Foods, Inc. Opelousas, Louisiana, no date.

MARX, ADRIEN. "Introduction. Jules Verne." *The Tour of the World in Eighty Days*. Translated by George M. Towle. Boston: James R. Osgood and Company, 1873.

MAURY, MATTHEW FONTAINE. *The Physical Geography of the Sea and its Meteorology*. New York: Harper and Brothers, 1855.—Edited by John Leighly. Cambridge, Massachusetts: The Belknap Press of Harvard University Press, 1963.

MEYER, M. WILHELM. *Das Weltgebaüde. Eine gemeinverständliche Himmelskunde*. Leipzig und Wien: Bibliographisches Institut, 1898.

MILLER, NATHAN. *The Founding Finaglers*. New York: David McKay Company, Inc., 1976.

MILLER, WALTER JAMES. *The Annotated Jules Verne: Twenty Thousand Leagues under the Sea*. New York: Thomas Y. Crowell Company, 1976.—New York: New American Library, 1977.

———. "Jules Verne in America: A Translator's Preface." Jules Verne, *Twenty Thousand Leagues under the Sea*. New York: Washington Square Press, 1965.

———. *Engineers as Writers: Growth of a Literature*. New York: D. Van Nostrand, 1953.—New York: Arno Press, Inc., A *New York Times* Company, 1971.

———. "Introduction." Homer, *The Odyssey*. New York: Pocket Books, 1969.

———. *Making an Angel: Poems*. New York: Pylon Press, Inc., 1977.

MITCHELL, S. AUGUSTUS. *Mitchell's School Geography*. Revised edition. Philadelphia: Thomas, Cowperthwaite & Co., 1863.

MORÉ, MARCEL. *Nouvelles explorations de Jules Verne*. Paris: Gallimard, 1963.

———. *Le très curieux Jules Verne*. Paris: Gallimard, 1960.

NEEDHAM, JOSEPH. *Clerks and Craftsmen in China and the West*. London: Cambridge University Press, 1970.

———. *Science and Civilization in China*. Five volumes. London: Cambridge University Press, 1954–1974.

NICOLSON, MARJORIE HOPE. *Voyages to the Moon*. New York: The Macmillan Company, 1948, 1960.

NORTON, A. P. *Norton's Star Atlas*. Cambridge, Massachusetts: Sky Publishing Corporation, 1973.

O'DONNELL, ELLIOTT. *Werwolves*. New York: Longvue Press, 1965.

OLMSTED, DENISON. *An Introduction to Astronomy; Designed as a Text Book for the Students of Yale College*. New York: Collins, Keese & Co., 1843.

OWENS, HAMILTON. *Baltimore on the Chesapeake*. Garden City, New York: Doubleday, Doran & Company, Inc., 1941.

PATRICK, REMBERT W. *Florida under Five Flags*. Gainesville: University of Florida Press, 1960.

POE, EDGAR ALLAN. *The Works of Edgar Allan Poe*. Introduction by Hervey Allen. New York: P. G. Collier & Son Company, 1927.

POPE, ALEXANDER. *An Essay on Man*. Edited by Maynard Mack. New Haven: Yale University Press, 1950.

PROCTOR, RICHARD A. *Other Worlds Than Ours*. New York: Hurst & Company, 1870.

RIDPATH, IAN, editor. *The Illustrated Encyclopedia of Astronomy and Space*. New York: Thomas Y. Crowell Company, 1976.

RIPLEY, GEORGE, and CHARLES A. DANA, editors. *The American Cyclopaedia: A Popular Dictionary of General Knowledge*. Sixteen volumes. New York: D. Appleton and Company, 1873–1876.

RIPLEY, WARREN. *Artillery and Ammunition of the Civil War*. New York: Van Nostrand Reinhold Company, 1970.

ROMANS, BERNARD A. *A Concise and Natural History of East and West Florida. 1775*. Edited by Rembert W. Patrick. Floridiana Facsimile and Reprint Series. Gainesville: University of Florida Press, 1962.

ROTH, EDWARD, translator. "Preface." Jules Verne, *The Baltimore Gun Club*. Philadelphia: King & Baird, 1874.

———. "Preface." Jules Verne, *All Around the Moon*. New York: Catholic Publication Society, 1876.

ST. HILL, THOMAS NAST, editor. *Thomas Nast: Cartoons and Illustrations*. New York: Dover Publications, Inc., 1974.

SEITZ, DON C. *Famous American Duels*. Freeport, New York: Books for Libraries Press, Inc., 1966.

SERRES, MICHEL. *Jouvences sur Jules Verne*. Paris: Les Éditions de Minuit, 1974.

SHKLOVSKII, I. S., and CARL SAGAN. *Intelligent Life in the Universe*. New York: Dell Publishing Co., Inc., 1966.

Sky and Telescope. "Long-Term Stability of the Earth-Moon System." July 1977.

SMILEY, NIXON. *Yesterday's Florida*. Miami, Florida: E. A. Seeman Publishing, Inc., 1974.

STRAHLER, ARTHUR N. *Physical Geography*. Third edition. New York: John Wiley and Sons, Inc., 1969.

SULLIVAN, WALTER. "Uranus Is Encircled by 5 Rings, Scientists Report in Key Finding." *New York Times*, March 31, 1977.

———. "Age of Universe Now Estimated as 20 Billion Years." *New York Times*, March 29, 1977.

SZEBEHELY, V., and R. MCKENZIE. "Stability of the Sun, Earth, Moon." *Astronomical Journal*, April 1977.

TEBEAU, CHARLTON W. *A History of Florida*. Coral Gables: University of Miami Press, 1971.

TOULMIN, STEPHEN, and JUNE GOODFIELD. *The Fabric of the Heavens*. New York: Harper & Row, Publishers, 1961.

UNITED STATES WAR DEPARTMENT. *Instruction for Field Artillery*. Philadelphia: J. B. Lippincott & Co., 1861.—New York: Greenwood Press, 1968.

WELLINGTON, ARTHUR MELLEN. *The Economic Theory of the Location of Railways*. Sixth edition. New York: John Wiley and Sons, 1900. Also see Chapter 8, "Wellington's Memorable Sentences," in Walter James Miller, *Engineers as Writers* (cited above).

WHITTAKER, SIR EDMUND. *A History of the Theories of Aether and Electricity*. London: Thomas Nelson and Sons Ltd., 1910—revised and enlarged, 1951—Harper & Brothers, 1960.

WILLIAMS, JOHN LEE. *A View of West Florida*. Philadelphia: Printed for H. S. Tanner, 1827.

———. *Territory of Florida. 1837*. Edited by Herbert J. Doherty, Jr. Floridiana Facsimile and Reprint Series. Gainesville: University of Florida Press, 1962.